CLEVELAND

DOUGLAS TRATTNER

May 2019

CONTENTS

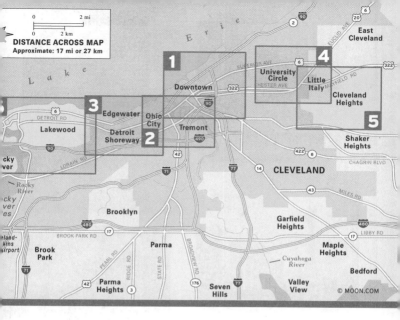

MAPS

DISCOVER
CLEVELAND

There's a level of enthusiasm, optimism, and momentum in Cleveland that hasn't been felt in decades. Population in the city center has more than doubled in the past 10 years, introducing an abundance of fresh energy to downtown streets. Many of those new residents are young professionals, who bring with them all the positive trappings of a modern generation. Look around today and you'll see more bikes, breweries, coffee shops, pocket parks, urban gardens, and creative start-ups—not to mention a slower pace to the day.

6

Those outside the region are taking notice, too. Major film studios have discovered that Cleveland's grand 20th-century architecture makes a fine backdrop to just about any story. The dining scene continues to attract more than its fair share of attention, creating a boom in food-related tourism. Visitors are increasingly beating a path to Cleveland's world-class museums, stages, and attractions.

But more than anything, there is a genuine sense of civic pride. After decades of serving as the nation's favorite punch line, Cleveland has shaken off the rust, put its house in order, and emerged as a contemporary city with an authentic Midwestern vibe. Rather than wait for others to label and define their town, locals are simply embracing the affordability, accessibility, and beauty of this city on a Great Lake and a crooked river.

These days, it seems you can't pick up a magazine or newspaper without reading another story about Cleveland's "Rust Belt Revival." Around here, folks just call that Tuesday.

5 TOP
EXPERIENCES

1 **Be a Part of Rock and Roll History:** Immerse yourself in the city's storied musical history by checking out the **Rock and Roll Hall of Fame and Museum** (page 18).

∨
∨
∨

2 **Go to Foodie Heaven:** Cleveland has every type of cuisine you could ever want. To sample for yourself, head to **Asiatown** (page 48), the **West Side Market** (page 57), or explore the innumerable diverse **ethnic restaurants** (page 66) around town.

3 **Get Out on the Water:** There's no better way to experience the city in the summer than by exploring its main waterways, Lake Erie and the Cuyahoga River. Relax on a pleasure cruise or get your heart rate up on a kayak or stand-up paddleboard (page 130).

>>>

4 Root for the Home Team: Attend a **Cavs** (page 125), **Indians** (page 125), or **Browns** (page 127) game and join the locals who champion their teams regardless of score or standings.

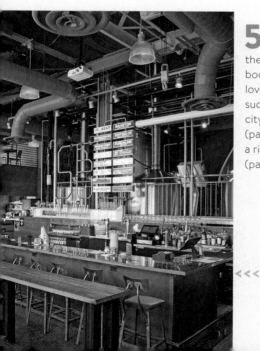

5 Sip Some Suds: Cleveland is in the midst of a beer boom. Craft beer lovers can sample the suds at one of the city's many **breweries** (page 79) or hitch a ride on the **Brew Bus** (page 87).

EXPLORE
CLEVELAND

THE THREE-DAY BEST OF CLEVELAND

DAY 1

Visit the **West Side Market**, a bustling public market that is a treat not just for foodies, but also for people-watchers and architecture buffs. Grab a cup of coffee from City Roast Coffee and peruse the 100 or so stalls, which sell everything from goat meat to goat cheese. For brunch, eat like a local by ordering a sausage sandwich from **Frank's Bratwurst.** Get it with kraut, horseradish, and brown mustard on a hard roll. Don't leave without checking out the attached produce annex.

Craft beer lovers should sign up for a behind-the-scenes tour of the **Market Garden Brewery** production facility, located a few hundred yards from the West Side Market. Tours are offered throughout the weekend. When done, visit the nearby breweries of **Great Lakes Brewing Co.** and **Platform Beer** to sample some of Cleveland's freshest suds. If ice cream is more your speed, head down to **Mitchell's Homemade Ice Cream** for a scoop of strawberry rhubarb crisp from one the city's best makers.

Artsy types can stop into **Glass Bubble Project,** a garage glassblowing studio that has an open-door

West Side Market

BEST FOR FAMILY FUN

WHEN IT'S SUNNY:

- Take in a **Cleveland Indians** baseball game at Progressive Field. To snag player autographs, arrive up to 45 minutes before the first pitch and head to sections 125-134 or 169-175.

- Hop aboard the *Goodtime III* for a narrated cruise on Lake Erie and the Cuyahoga River. Bring a camera to capture the amazing skyline and bridges.

- Go bananas at the **Cleveland Metroparks Zoo,** with its gorillas, chimps, lemurs, and baboons.

WHEN IT'S RAINY:

a vintage steam engine on the Cuyahoga Valley Scenic Railroad

- Loaded with 42 tanks filled with one million gallons of water and thousands of fish, the **Greater Cleveland Aquarium** is a great place to kill an hour or so in inclement weather.

- The **Cleveland Museum of Natural History** is loaded with cool stuff: a Foucault pendulum, tyrannosaur and stegosaur skeletons, and a planetarium, to name a few.

- Take the **Cuyahoga Valley Scenic Railroad** through the scenic forests, wetlands, and prairies of the lush Cuyahoga Valley National Park.

- Classic movie buffs should ring the bell at *A Christmas Story* **House,** the fully restored Parker house from the cult classic movie.

policy and often hosts impromptu demonstrations. If it happens to be the first or third Saturday of the month between mid-May and mid-October, wander into Ohio City's Market Square for **Open Air in Market Square,** a weekly bazaar.

When hunger sets in, hit **Bar Cento** for Neapolitan-style pizza or **Black Pig** for farm-to-table French-inspired fare starring heritage-breed pork. Stop by **The Plum** for progressive American fare with an edge.

For a post-meal nightcap, go directly to **Porco Lounge and Tiki Room** for delicious Polynesian-style cocktails like Mai Tais, Zombies, and Pain Killers served up in a wild tiki bar setting.

DAY 2

Start your day with a little Parisian flair by grabbing breakfast at **Le Petit Triangle Café,** a quaint and quiet café that serves sweet and savory crepes, fluffy omelets, and a heavenly café au lait.

Make your way over to the Nautica entertainment complex on the West Bank of the Flats and hop aboard Lolly the Trolley with **Trolley Tours of Cleveland,** which offers fun and informative sightseeing tours of the city and surrounding neighborhoods.

When the trolley ride is over, make your way to the North Coast Harbor and into the **Rock and Roll Hall of Fame and Museum.** Though the museum looks small from the outside, it can gobble up an entire afternoon. If the kids are in tow, swap the Rock Hall for a visit to the adjacent Great Lakes Science Center.

If the Cleveland Indians are in town, check the box office at Progressive Field for last-minute bleacher seats, where you'll enjoy cold beer, hot dogs, and great baseball. Otherwise, go play some shuffleboard at Forest City Shuffleboard, a roomy entertainment venue with indoor courts and a full bar. If filling shopping bags sounds like more fun, wander into the 5th Street Arcades, a historic downtown mall with an eclectic mix of shops, boutiques, and cafés.

Grab a pre-dinner aperitif at Spotted Owl in Tremont before hitting any of the amazing chef-driven bistros in the area. For eclectic Mediterranean dished up in a converted colonial, visit Fat Cats. For stellar sushi in a hip, grotto-like setting go to Dante Boccuzzi's Ginko.

After dinner peruse the wonderful collection of art, film, and music books at Visible Voice Books while sipping a glass of wine or cup of coffee.

DAY 3

If it's Sunday, join the locals for a long, leisurely dim sum brunch at Li Wah in Cleveland's Asiatown neighborhood. Home cooks in search of hard-to-find recipe ingredients should visit Park to Shop or Tink Holl market for a bewildering selection of items.

For proof that there's more to do in Cleveland than eat and drink, head to University Circle for a day filled with art, architecture, and history. The Cleveland Museum of Art has never

looked better thanks to a seven-year, $350 million overhaul. Science and history nerds will be thrilled to spend some time exploring the Cleveland Museum of Natural History, while the horticulturally minded might prefer the Cleveland Botanical Garden. Contemporary art lovers should check out the latest exhibits at the Museum of Contemporary Art.

Down in the Flats, a long-dormant entertainment district along the banks of the Cuyahoga River, a $750 million waterfront redevelopment project ushered in new restaurants, bars, and entertainment venues, all of which are connected by a meandering boardwalk. Collision Bend Brewing Company is a lively restaurant and brewery set inside a 150-year-old brick building on the river's edge. Roll a few games of bocce at Backyard Bocce before hopping aboard the free water taxi to the other side of the river. That's where you'll find the Harbor Inn, the oldest continuously operating bar in Cleveland.

Cleveland Botanical Garden

BEST RECREATION

Ray's MTB Indoor Park

Thanks to its diverse geography, Cleveland has no shortage of recreation options.

WATER SPORTS

- Rent a kayak from **Great Lakes Watersports** and take a sunset trip along the Cuyahoga River.
- Learn the basics of rowing by taking a class from **Western Reserve Rowing Association.**
- For some of the best steelhead trout fly-fishing in the country, charter a trip with **Chagrin River Outfitters,** who know the top spots.

WINTER SPORTS

- Fly down the toboggan chutes at **Mill Stream Run Reservation.** Hike 110 steps up and then zip 70 feet down and 1,000 feet out on this exhilarating thrill ride.
- **Alpine Valley Ski Resort** gets around 120 inches of snowfall a year, making it the region's best place to downhill ski, snowboard, or snow tube.

BIKING AND SKATEBOARDING

- Encompassing more than 100,000 square feet of indoor mountain bike paradise, **Ray's MTB Indoor Park** is the only attraction of its kind in the country. Race around steeped embankments, over uneven bridges, and into the air off vertical jumps.
- The outdoor steel and wood bicycle racing track at the **Cleveland Velodrome** is the only one of its kind in the region.
- Drop in for some fun at **Crooked River Skatepark,** a 15,000-square-foot snake-style run in Rivergate Park.
- Ride along the 87-mile **Ohio & Erie Canal Towpath Trail.** The best scenery is in the portions that pass through Cuyahoga Valley National Park.

NEIGHBORHOODS

DOWNTOWN

Downtown serves as the financial, legal, and governmental nucleus of the entire county, but an influx of hotels and residential buildings have instilled a fresh sense of vitality. After dark, areas like East 4th Street and the revitalized Flats East Bank teem with restaurants, cocktail lounges, and live-music venues like the House of Blues.

Downtown also is the place to enjoy live theater, cheer on professional sports teams, and explore the ephemera at the Rock and Roll Hall of Fame and Museum. Clean, compact, and walkable, downtown rewards urban hikers with an abundance of glorious classical architecture.

Rock and Roll Hall of Fame and Museum

OHIO CITY AND TREMONT

Known to locals as OHC, Ohio City is a neighborhood that's long been anchored by the West Side Market. In addition to breweries like Great Lakes Brewing Co., Market Garden Brewery, and Platform Beer, this hip 'hood is home to the edgy art gallery Transformer Station. Celebrated eateries like Flying Fig and Momocho Mod Mex make OHC ground zero for adventurous foodies.

Great Lakes Brewing Co. in Ohio City

The adjacent neighborhood of Tremont has a high concentration of chef-owned bistros, like Dante and Fat Cats, but is equally known for the creative energy on display in its numerous galleries. Architecture fans enjoy the historic churches in this former university neighborhood, and shoppers come for the upscale boutiques.

DETROIT SHOREWAY AND EDGEWATER

Detroit Shoreway and adjacent Edgewater are some of the most dynamic and developing parts of town. Anchored by the decades-old Cleveland Public Theatre, the trendy Gordon Square Arts District is home to art galleries, architecture studios, and thriving neighborhood theater. Lively taverns like the Parkview Nite Club and Happy Dog join fine eateries such as Luxe Kitchen & Lounge and Spice Kitchen & Bar. Antiques hunters prowl the secondhand shops of Lorain Avenue in hopes of scoring a treasure, while beachgoers enjoy Edgewater Park.

UNIVERSITY CIRCLE AND LITTLE ITALY

Often referred to as "One Perfect Mile," University Circle is home to an unmatched concentration of educational, medical, and cultural institutions, including the Cleveland Museum of Art and Museum of Contemporary Art. The Old World is alive and well in neighboring Little Italy, a lively borough featuring red-brick lanes, authentic Italian eateries, and eclectic art galleries.

Cleveland Museum of Art in University Circle

CLEVELAND HEIGHTS AND SHAKER HEIGHTS

Incorporated in the early 1900s, the neighboring communities of Cleveland Heights and Shaker Heights developed as leafy streetcar suburbs on the fringes of town. Today, these popular inner-ring cities boast all the amenities of a self-sufficient town. The Main Street-like districts of Shaker Square, Cedar-Lee, and Coventry Village keep visitors and residents alike entertained with restaurants, jazz clubs, and movie theaters. It's also possible to explore the impressive mansions built by Cleveland's wealthy industrialists.

LAKEWOOD

The bulk of the commercial activity in this West Side neighborhood is found on the thoroughfares of Detroit, Madison, and Clifton, which are dotted with indie shops, restaurants, and bars. But one of the biggest draws here is the Rocky River Reservation, part of the Cleveland Metroparks system. Boasting a dog park, a web of trails, and a scenic strip of rushing river, this picturesque retreat attracts joggers, bicyclists, anglers, and picnickers. Lakewood is also home to the Beck Center for the Arts, a long-standing community arts beacon.

GREATER CLEVELAND

The Greater Cleveland area stretches for miles in every direction save for north, where it is bounded by Lake Erie. The majestic Cuyahoga Valley National Park is just south of town, while the equally verdant Holden Arboretum can be found out east. In the wintertime, mountain bike enthusiasts travel from throughout the Midwest to hit Ray's MTB Indoor Park. Meanwhile, shoppers flock to upscale boutiques in Beachwood, Rocky River, and Chagrin Falls, and live music fans venture to the Beachland Ballroom and Blossom Music Center.

SIGHTS

In 1920, Cleveland was the fifth most populous city in the United States. Its position on a lake, a river, and a grand canal helped it develop into an industrial powerhouse. As the city expanded, so too did its need for new local, county, and federal buildings. Fortuitously, that need happened to coincide with the City Beautiful movement, a progressive philosophy that believes a well-planned, visually appealing downtown goes a long way toward boosting the spirit of its inhabitants. Those heady times left behind a legacy in the form of stunning architecture, world-class cultural institutions, and idyllic residential suburbs on the fringes of town.

Free Stamp

It would take Cleveland another 75 years to match its building boom of the early 20th century. But in the mid-1990s, shaking off its Rust Belt reputation, the city pulled off a slew of public projects that included new sports venues, a state-of-the-art science and technology museum, and a glass-and-steel temple to rock and roll. Following that, the city added attractive new hotels and completely redeveloped the Flats neighborhood.

At the same time, downtown population began to soar, climbing roughly 80 percent over the past two decades. Attracted by the city's increasing amenities, millennials, empty nesters, and scores of other urban pioneers gravitate to the city center, where they have easy access to the arts, professional sports, food, drink, and that Great Lake and twisty river.

HIGHLIGHTS

✪ **BEST-SOUNDING HISTORY LESSON:** If all school was as entertaining as this "school of rock," there would be no more truancy. The **Rock and Roll Hall of Fame and Museum** boasts a dizzying kaleidoscope of rock memorabilia, both familiar and obscure (page 18).

✪ **MOST CONTROVERSIAL POP ART:** Love it or loathe it, the *Free Stamp* never fails to incite an opinion. Sure, artist Claes Oldenburg's 30-foot-tall faux rubber stamp is silly—bordering on ridiculous. But the fact that we're still discussing it after all these years has to count for something (page 19).

✪ **MOST GLORIOUS OLD MALL:** Built in 1890, **The Arcade** is an absolutely stunning Victorian-style atrium that flaunts a 300-foot-long, 100-foot-high skylight comprising 1,800 panes of glass (page 23).

✪ **MOST ICONIC BRIDGE ART:** The art deco statues carved into the 43-foot sandstone pylons of the **Hope Memorial Bridge** are fondly referred to as the "guardians of traffic." Eight separate figures stand sentry at either end of the mile-long bridge, making even the worst commute a little easier to stomach (page 25).

✪ **BEST OLD-WORLD GROCERY STORE:** Other cities have grand old public markets; but many have replaced the actual food stalls with shops selling T-shirts and incense. At Ohio City's **West Side Market,** people actually shop—for pork, halibut, cheese, pierogies, tomatoes, and everything in between. Look up at the barrel-vaulted ceiling and you'll forget everything on your shopping list (page 26).

✪ **MOST FILM-FAMOUS CHURCH:** Featured in the Academy Award-winning film *The Deer Hunter*, the 13 onion-shaped domes atop **St. Theodosius Russian Orthodox Cathedral** hover like a battalion of faded copper weather balloons (page 29).

✪ **MOST EXTREME MAKEOVER:** Art fans endured an eight-year, $350 million renovation and expansion, but in 2013, the **Cleveland Museum of Art** officially said goodbye to the scaffolding. Now, the breathtaking galleries manage to make the impressive art collection look even better (page 31).

✪ **FINEST FINAL RESTING PLACE:** Lake View Cemetery, a 290-acre oasis on the border of Cleveland Heights, is equal parts botanical garden, history lesson, and alfresco art gallery. Approximately 400,000 people visit the grounds each year, many to gander at Wade Chapel's Tiffany interior (page 34).

✪ **BEST WAY TO GET TO KNOW CLEVELAND:** The clang, clang, clang of the open-air Lolly the Trolley resounds as guides for **Trolley Tours of Cleveland** weave historical, architectural, and cultural tidbits into memorable city tours (page 39).

✪ Rock and Roll Hall of Fame and Museum

They say you can't cage an animal like rock and roll, but this iconic shrine does a laudable job of telling the story of rock's gritty past, present, and future. Some 150,000 square feet of space is crammed with permanent and temporary exhibits, interactive displays, and live-performance spaces. An incredible array of memorable costumes, instruments, personal effects, and ephemera provide visitors with a unique perspective on rock's roots and culture. The museum features experiences like the Power of Rock and a new Hall of Fame that honors inductees. Sure, the entry fee is a bit steep, but where else are you going to see a Janis Joplin blotter acid sheet drawn by comic book artist Robert Crumb and the hand-written lyrics of "Lucy in the Sky with Diamonds" in one afternoon?

To take a little bit of rock home with you, stop by the well-stocked museum store, which is loaded with music-themed books, CDs, and genuine memorabilia. The plaza out front is home to summer concerts, a beer garden, and a massive "LONG LIVE ROCK" sign for can't-miss photo ops. **MAP 1:** 1100 Rock and Roll Blvd., 216/781-7625, www.rockhall.com; 10am-5:30pm Sun.-Tues. and Thurs.-Fri., 10am-9pm Wed. and Sat.; $26 adults, $24 seniors, $16 children, free for children 8 and under, discounted rates for advance online purchase

Rock and Roll Hall of Fame and Museum

Great Lakes Science Center

This modern steel-and-glass structure boasts some 400 hands-on science-centric activities on three floors of exhibits. One of the largest of its type in the country, the 165,000-square-foot museum makes science, technology, and the local environment fun and accessible for children and adults alike. Favorite exhibitss include the indoor twister, static generator, and photoluminescence shadow wall. The *Great Lakes Story* explores the physical characteristics, geography, and geology that make this region unique. The complex is also home to a six-story dome theater and the Science Store, a great source for science-related books, games, and kits.

The museum's NASA Glenn Visitor Center is a hands-on space that lets visitors explore the 1973 Skylab 3 Apollo Command Module, see a real moon rock from the *Apollo 15* mission, and check out space suits worn by astronauts like Buzz Aldrin. The Glenn center's *Discover Gallery* highlights the science and engineering behind space travel and even lets visitors experiment with a pressurized bottle rocket.

Out front, a 150-foot wind turbine generates enough juice to satisfy 7 percent of the center's electrical needs. Open May through October, the adjacent steamship, the *William G. Mather,* is a retired Great Lakes freighter that offers a glimpse of life aboard a commercial vessel.

MAP 1: 601 Erieside Ave., 216/694-2000, www.greatscience.com; 10am-5pm Mon.-Sat., noon-5pm Sun. summer, 10am-5pm Tues.-Sat., noon-5pm Sun. winter; $17 adults, $14 children

USS *Cod* Submarine

Launched in 1943, this 312-foot fleet submarine made seven war patrols in the South Pacific during World War II. It is credited with sinking a Japanese destroyer, minesweeper, several cargo ships, and troop transports with its steam-powered torpedoes. The *Cod* also performed the only international sub-to-sub rescue in history, saving 56 Dutch sailors before destroying their grounded ship.

A popular tourist attraction since 1976, the *Cod* is unique among restored display submarines in that visitors use the very same ladders and hatches employed by the crew (making it challenging for travelers with mobility issues). On shore is a Mark 14 steam-driven torpedo, a five-bladed 2,080-pound bronze sub propeller, and a plaque honoring submariners who have lost their lives throughout the history of the United States. Service members in uniform and spouses and family of active-duty submariners are admitted free.

MAP 1: E. 9th St. and N. Marginal Rd., 216/566-8770, www.usscod.org; 10am-5pm daily May-Sept.; $12 adults, $10 seniors and veterans, $7 children, free for service members in uniform

✪ Free Stamp

The *Free Stamp* placed Cleveland squarely on the pop art map. Located on an expanse of green just east of City Hall, the comically large aluminum-and-steel sculpture of a rubber office stamp was created by artist Claes Oldenburg for Standard Oil of Ohio (SOHIO). When Standard Oil was purchased by BP, new management wanted nothing to do with the modern sculpture, so it was relegated to storage out of state. Tired of paying storage fees for years, BP

HOW CLEVELAND LANDED THE ROCK HALL

Since opening its doors in 1995, the **Rock and Roll Hall of Fame and Museum** has become such a symbol of Cleveland that the notion of it being located anywhere else seems absurd. Yet, despite the fact that "Cleveland Rocks"—thank you very much, Ian Hunter—this city had to pull off nothing short of a miracle to land the big prize.

When the Rock and Roll Hall of Fame Foundation was established in New York in 1985, with the aim of creating a museum to honor the legends of rock and roll, Cleveland wasn't even considered as a potential site. It took heroic efforts by Cleveland-based rock historian Norm N. Nite to convince the board to humor a contingent of city boosters. Those in attendance, including Ahmet Ertegun of Atlantic Records and Jann Wenner of *Rolling Stone*, were impressed enough by the presentation to schedule a fact-finding mission to C-Town.

Cleveland certainly had the rock chops to warrant a visit. This is where celebrated DJ Alan Freed and Record Rendezvous owner Leo Mintz first popularized the phrase "rock and roll." The Moondog Coronation Ball, considered the world's first rock concert (and subsequent rock concert fracas), took place in the Cleveland Arena in 1952. Groundbreaking DJs like Bill Randle, Pete "Mad Daddy" Myers, Casey Kasem, and Kid Leo all worked the turntable and microphone here. The region has a proven track record for delivering stars, from Joe Walsh and Chrissie Hynde to Eric Carmen and Nine Inch Nails. All the biggest names in rock made certain to stop and say "Hello, Cleveland" when touring, including Elvis, the Beatles, the Rolling Stones, David Bowie, Led Zeppelin, and the Who. Those big names performed, and their successors continue to do so, in some of the best live-music venues in the land, like Public Music Hall, Cleveland Agora, Peabody's, Beachland Ballroom, Grog Shop, and House of Blues. Ahead of its time, the album-oriented WMMS—Home of the Buzzard—was one of the most important rock-and-roll radio stations in the country. Jane Scott, one of the greatest, and most unlikely, rock reporters of anybody's generation made her living at the Cleveland *Plain Dealer*.

But ultimately it was the good people of Cleveland who tipped the scales in their own favor. When a *USA Today* telephone poll asked its readers to cast a vote for their choice of home for the Rock Hall, Cleveland trounced the competition, garnering 15 times the votes of second-place Memphis. When the foundation did eventually make that fact-finding mission to Cleveland, it was an impromptu pit stop at the original (now gone) Record Rendezvous that sealed the deal for some decision makers.

Cleveland officially won the Hall in 1986, but it would take an additional nine years and $90 million to see it through to completion. Today, the iconic I. M. Pei-designed glass-and-steel pyramid is a globally recognized affirmation of this city's rock-and-roll clout. And the museum has been a smash hit: Drawing more than six million guests since its opening, the Rock Hall is the most-visited hall of fame in the world.

Despite all the success, Cleveland was far from content. The Rock and Roll Hall of Fame Foundation's most prominent event, the annual induction ceremony, maintained a permanent residence at New York's Waldorf-Astoria hotel. Lobbying once again paid off: Starting in 2009, Cleveland began hosting the Hall of Fame induction gala every three years, and in 2018, that stretch was whittled down to two years, a fitting tribute to a city that has proven that the Rock Hall belongs on the shores of Lake Erie.

ultimately offered the work to the City of Cleveland—for free. A new site was selected, the artist modified the design to better suit the locale, and the *Free Stamp* was officially dedicated in 1991. To this day many abhor its design—but just count the number of folks scrambling for a picture.

MAP 1: Williard Park, E. 9th St. and Lakeside Ave.

Cuyahoga County Courthouse

A county courthouse must possess a certain amount of charm for it to become popular with brides as a wedding site. Photographers love this historic building because the beaux arts interior serves as the most dramatic backdrop a shutterbug could hope for: sweeping marble staircases, soaring three-story vaulted ceilings, jaw-dropping stained glass, and art deco light fixtures. Along with city hall, the building serves as the northern terminus of the 1903 Group Plan, which arranged local and federal buildings around a public mall.

MAP 1: 1 Lakeside Ave., 216/443-8800

Old Stone Church

This church is formally called **First Presbyterian Society,** but because it is the oldest surviving structure on Public Square, and because it was constructed of hand-hammered native sandstone, the church has become known simply as the Old Stone Church. Twice ravaged by fire, the Romanesque Revival structure was thrice built—in 1855, 1858, and 1884. The awe-inspiring interior boasts a barrel-vaulted ceiling, handsome oak pews, and a 3,000-pipe Cleveland-built Holtkamp organ. Perhaps more impressive are the four Louis Comfort Tiffany stained-glass windows, all of which have undergone complete restoration. But this building is not relegated to museum status; it is a contemporary place of worship for its congregants, and families gather for weekly prayer, attend free concerts (row 77 center is the sweet spot), or practice yoga. Dwarfed by modern skyscrapers, this elegant old church also serves as a gentle reminder that sanctuary is never too far away.

MAP 1: 91 Public Sq., 216/241-6145, www.oldstonechurch.org; guided tours 11am-3pm Mon.-Fri., self-guided tours 9am-4pm Mon.-Fri.

War Memorial Fountain

Alternatively known as the *Fountain of Eternal Life, Peace Arising from the Flames of War,* or simply, the *Green Guy,* this regal statue enjoys prominent placement in a large open space called the Mall. The 35-foot granite-and-bronze sculpture depicts a stately male figure rising from the flames of war, his outstretched arm reaching toward the heavens. Illuminated fountains ring the base. Designed by a Cleveland Institute of Art graduate, the monument serves as a memorial to those who perished during World War II and the Korean War. During the planning stages, in the mid-1960s, conservative city officials insisted that the artist "cover up" his too-naked male form, which he did with strategically placed flames. Since its dedication, the names of local service members who have died or gone missing during the wars in Vietnam, Iraq, and Afghanistan have been added to the memorial.

MAP 1: Veterans Memorial Plaza, St. Clair Ave. NE and W. Mall Dr.

Public Square

Public Square sits on the very same 6.5-acre plot today as it did in 1796, when Moses Cleaveland set the land aside for the local townspeople to congregate. Thanks to a sweeping renovation that wrapped up in 2016, residents have once again begun congregating

Old Stone Church

Public Square

here. An elevated green space offers a nice place to sit and enjoy lunch; white granite seating lines a concert hill; a summertime splash pad brings sweet relief to gleeful kids; and it's all wrapped by a butterfly-shaped promenade that circumscribes the square. In addition to being home to the Soldiers and Sailors Monument and a statue of former mayor Tom L. Johnson, Public Square is the site of peaceful protests, classical music concerts, and wintertime ice skating.

MAP 1: Superior Ave. at Ontario St., www.clevelandpublicsquare.com

Soldiers and Sailors Monument

Since 1894, this stately bronze-and-granite statue has served to commemorate the men and women of Cuyahoga County who served their country during the Civil War. Situated on the southeast quadrant of Public Square, the monument features a 125-foot granite spire, four exterior sculptural groupings, and an interior Memorial Hall. A walk around the base reveals arresting scenes of the four principal branches of service—infantry, artillery, cavalry, and navy—in the throes of battle. Wander inside to see the carved names of 9,000 Civil War veterans, some stained-glass windows, and distinctive bronze panels of Abraham Lincoln proclaiming emancipation.

MAP 1: 3 Public Sq., 216/621-3710, www.soldiersandsailors.com; 10am-5:30pm Tues.-Sun.

Old Federal Building

Originally constructed as a U.S. post office, customs house, and courthouse, the so-called Old Federal Building was the first structure built under the 1903 Group Plan, setting the tone for the five buildings that followed. Today, the building is known as the Howard M. Metzenbaum U.S. Courthouse, housing district and bankruptcy courts as well as the Departments of Homeland Security and Agriculture. The inspiration for this classical beaux arts beauty is said to be the Place de la

Concorde in Paris. Clad in gray granite, and mirroring in size and scope the nearby public library, the majestic landmark occupies a full city block. Artist Daniel Chester French created two monumental sculptures for the exterior, *Jurisprudence* and *Commerce*, which flank the Superior Avenue entrance. Climb the stone steps and enter the magnificent marble lobby, taking in its grand vaulted ceiling, turn-of-the-20th-century chandeliers, and original postal windows.

MAP 1: 201 Superior Ave. NE, 216/615-1235; 7am-5pm Mon.-Fri.

Cleveland Public Library, Main Branch

The main branch of the Cleveland Public Library, one of the nation's most respected urban library systems, comprises two buildings linked by a subterranean passageway. Built in 1925 by the noted architecture firm Walker & Weeks (the talent behind Severance Hall), the main library is a neoclassical citadel.

This building sits in stark contrast to the Louis Stokes Wing, a striking postmodern tower added in the mid-1990s. Look closely, however, and a nexus can be found. With a nod to the original structure, the annex features a facade of the same height and stone. Rising from that six-story marble frame, the 10-story glass tower matches the height of the neighboring Federal Reserve Bank.

Inside the glorious old frame, a magnificent globe-shaped chandelier greets visitors, and grand marble stairs lead to upper floors. Vaulted ceilings, some 44 feet high, contain vivid geometric patterns and paintings of historical figures. Leaded-glass windows flood the hushed reading rooms with light. Decorative friezes, original paintings and sculpture, and New Deal-commissioned murals are sprinkled throughout.

MAP 1: 325 Superior Ave. NE, 216/623-2800, www.cpl.org; 10am-6pm Mon.-Sat.

Federal Reserve Bank

Headquarters of the Fourth Federal Reserve District, the Federal Reserve Bank of Cleveland is an opulent palace of prosperity, security, and wealth. Designed by the noted Cleveland firm Walker & Weeks, the 12-story granite and marble fortress resembles a Medici-style palazzo. The gilded interior features hand-painted vaulted ceilings, polished marble walls and pillars, and intricately detailed ironwork. Surprisingly, visitors are free to enter the bank's lobby, Learning Center, and **Money Museum.** Tours, offered Tuesday at 2pm and Thursday at 10am, fill up fast, so it is wise to reserve a spot well in advance.

MAP 1: 1455 E. 6th St., 216/579-3188, www.clevelandfed.org; 9:30am-2:30pm Mon.-Thurs.; free

✪ The Arcade

One of the most picturesque Cleveland interiors, this Victorian-style atrium flaunts a 300-foot-long, 100-foot-high skylight composed of 1,800 panes of glass. Fabricated in 1890 and modeled after a similar structure in Milan, Italy, the building holds the dubious distinction of being this country's first indoor shopping mall. The staggering-for-its-time price tag of $875,000 was covered by John D. Rockefeller and other wealthy Cleveland industrialists. Five years after it was built, the grand space hosted the National Republican Convention.

The Arcade's intricate brass-and-iron detail can stop visitors dead in their tracks. Especially appealing are the cast-iron griffins and gargoyles that ring the skylight. A well-executed renovation of the historic structure in 1999 repurposed the upper floors into hotel rooms for the **Hyatt Regency at the Arcade.** Shops, services, and restaurants occupy the lower levels of this five-story gem.

MAP 1: 401 Euclid Ave., 216/696-1408, www.theclevelandarcade.com; free

Terminal Tower

When it was completed in 1930, this graceful skyscraper was the second-tallest building in the world. Rising 710 feet above Public Square, the building was the crown jewel of the Terminal Tower Complex, a mixed-use development that included Cleveland Union Terminal rail station, hotels, department stores, and a post office. While it no longer competes for height records, Terminal Tower still serves as a beautiful reminder of this city's former status as the nation's fifth-largest city. Belying its neoclassical exterior, the building's interior spaces ooze with beaux arts and art deco details. Today, the complex houses hotels; a modern mall with restaurants, shops, and movie theaters; and a terminal for Cleveland's light-rail system, RTA. Tunnels and pathways connect to Progressive Field and Quicken Loans Arena.

The 42nd-floor **observation deck** (tickets required, www.eventbrite.com; $5) is open to visitors on select weekends. Bird-watchers should keep an eye out for peregrine falcons, which nest high on the tower and occasionally swoop down for a meal of fresh pigeon.

MAP 1: 50 Public Sq., 216/623-4750, www.towercitycenter.com; 24 hours daily

The Arcade

CITY BEAUTIFUL

In the late 1800s, as city populations continued to rise, so too did levels of crime, poverty, and disease. In response, the City Beautiful movement began to creep across the land. Advocates behind this civic-minded movement believed that a beautiful city could improve the spirit of its inhabitants. In cities like Chicago, Washington DC, and Cleveland, the initiative took the form of architectural "group plans"—cohesive arrangements of similar structures positioned around a great public mall.

The movement reached the shores of Lake Erie at an opportune time, as federal, county, and municipal governments all were planning to erect sizable new structures. Cleveland's Group Plan of 1903, executed by New York and Chicago architects Daniel Burnham, John Carrere, and Arnold Brunner, advocated a monumental grouping of civic buildings around a mall. Built in the beaux arts style, which emphasizes symmetry, uniformity, and harmony, the structures all share similar scale and design. Six of the classically designed buildings were completed: the **Old Federal Building, Cleveland Public Library,** City Hall, **Cuyahoga County Courthouse,** Public Auditorium, and Board of Education building (now the **Drury Plaza Hotel**). A rail station, proposed for the northern boundary of the plan, was abandoned in favor of the **Terminal Tower.**

Sitting like near-identical twins to the south are the Old Federal Building and Cleveland Public Library. To the north, the Cuyahoga County Courthouse and City Hall are similar, but not identical. Classic design, comparable scale, and the use of granite and marble created a unified look.

But these reserved exteriors belie the grandeur of the interiors within, most featuring soaring vaulted ceilings, polished marble staircases, intricate ironwork, and original commissioned artwork. Linking all the buildings is an expanse of green space known as the Mall, which forms a corridor from Public Square to Lake Erie.

Eventually, height limitations and "grand plans" gave way to modern skyscrapers. But the Group Plan, an ambitious schematic hatched more than a century ago, still serves as the backbone of this city.

✪ Hope Memorial Bridge

Bridges typically are utilitarian affairs, elevated roadways designed to move commuters from here to there. But the Hope Memorial Bridge, also known as the Lorain-Carnegie, incorporates elements of beauty. Built in 1932, the gently arched span over the Cuyahoga River connects the East and West Sides of town. For many commuters, the highlight of each crossing is not safe arrival on the other side, but the epic sculptures that sit sentry on either end. Carved into the bridge's 43-foot sandstone pylons, the art deco figures are known fondly as the "Guardians of Traffic." Like bookends, the monuments stand back-to-back, for a total of eight unique designs. Cradled in the hands of each is a mode of transportation, from covered wagon and stagecoach to automobile and truck. The mile-long bridge features generous walkways on either side, offering easy passage from downtown to Ohio City, as well as fantastic vantage points for skyline photos.

MAP 1: Connects Carnegie Ave. and Lorain Ave. where they cross the Cuyahoga River

DOWNTOWN DEVELOPMENT BOOM

Not since the mid-1990s, when Cleveland unveiled the Rock Hall, Great Lakes Science Center, Gund Arena (now Quicken Loans), Browns Stadium (now FirstEnergy), and Jacob's Field (now Progressive) to great fanfare, has the city experienced such an explosive downtown development boom. In just a few short years, the city experienced a multibillion dollar face-lift that shows little sign of abating.

In 2017, **Public Square** debuted anew following a renovation that introduced new fountains, green space, and a health-focused café. On the square is the 2016 **JACK Cleveland Casino,** a Las Vegas-style casino in the heart of downtown. Built within the walls of the historic Higbee department store building, the casino is one of the most attractive to hit any strip. Inside, 1,500 slot machines, 100 table games, a World Series of Poker room, and tons of amenities service millions of visitors per year. A short walk away, the opening of the **Hilton Cleveland Downtown** in 2016 added a shiny 32-story tower to the city skyline.

Down in the Flats, a long-dormant entertainment district along the banks of the Cuyahoga, a waterfront redevelopment project began in 2013 and is ushering in new restaurants, entertainment venues, and office and residential space, along with the 150-room **Aloft Cleveland Downtown,** all of which are connected by a riverfront boardwalk.

Just across the river, on the West Bank of the Flats, the **Greater Cleveland Aquarium** saw more than 400,000 visitors during 2012, its first year. Designed by New Zealand-based Marinescape, the one-million-gallon aquarium features a walk-through SeaTube.

The **Children's Museum of Cleveland** reopened in 2017 in a new space, a stunning mansion on Cleveland's famed Millionaire's Row.

Playhouse Square, the second-largest performing arts center in the nation, continues to beautify its stock of glorious old theaters, while breaking ground on a glassy new 34-story apartment tower for folks clamoring to live downtown.

Ohio City and Tremont · Map 2

✪ West Side Market

Though it looks like a grand railway station, the building that houses this historic public market was purpose built to sell food. Built in 1912, and added to the National Register of Historic Places in the mid-1970s, the West Side Market attracts food fans, architecture buffs, and campaigning politicians. But mostly it functions as the city's most fantastic supermarket, where residents buy their weekly eggs, meat, produce, and bread. Unlike prominent public markets elsewhere that stock everything from incense to T-shirts, this market is almost exclusively focused on food. Some 100 individually operated stalls hawk everything from Polish pierogies and Hungarian sausage to fresh pasta and exotic herbs and grains. There are multiple butchers for poultry, pork, beef, lamb, and goat, various fishmongers, and a handful of artisan bakers. Notice the conspicuous absence of fresh produce? That's because it's all next door in the fruit and vegetable annex, situated on the north and east sides of the complex.

MAP 2: 1979 W. 25th St., 216/664-3387, www.westsidemarket.org; 7am-4pm Mon. and Wed., 7am-6pm Fri.-Sat., 10am-4pm Sun.

Jay Avenue Homes

Jay Avenue can be viewed as a microcosm of the whole of Ohio City. Not long ago, this leafy tree-lined block in

Cleveland's oldest neighborhood was a picture of despair, with once majestic Victorians inching ever closer to collapse and oblivion. Today, nearly every one of those homes has been thoughtfully restored, transforming each from eyesore to attraction. Stroll south on Jay from West 25th to its terminus at West 30th and explore the Archibald Willard House (2601 Jay), built in 1860 and once home to the famous painter of *The Spirit of '76,* and the Marquard Mansion (2920 Jay), built in 1903 by Philip Marquard, owner of the Marquard Sash and Door Co.

MAP 2: Jay Ave. between W. 25th St. and W. 30th St.

John Heisman's Birthsite

Sports fans know that the Heisman (officially the Heisman Memorial Trophy) is awarded annually to the best athlete in college football. Most, however, do not know that John W. Heisman was born in Ohio City and, according to many, in this very house. A commemorative plaque marks the site, but the house is not open to the public. Heisman was a wildly successful coach at Oberlin College, University of Akron, Auburn, Clemson, and Georgia Tech, where he guided his team to a mind-boggling 222-0 victory over the Cumberland College Bulldogs.

MAP 2: 2825 Bridge Ave.

St. Patrick's Church

The story of this church's construction in 1873 truly is an inspiring tale of commitment and allegiance. When parishioners outgrew their original place of worship, land at the present site was purchased, an architect was hired, and plans for a Gothic Revival structure were drawn up. And that was the easy part. Offered all the free blue limestone they could cut and carry, parishioners made weekly trips to a quarry 65 miles away, where they would cut stone for days on end before returning by wagon to Cleveland. The parishioners who remained on-site had the task of sizing and positioning the stone. This process continued for a full two years. These days, neighbors often gather and cheer as newlyweds make their way down the church steps.

MAP 2: 3602 Bridge Ave., 216/631-6872, www.stpatrickbridge.org

Carnegie West Library

Outside of philanthropist Andrew Carnegie's hometown of Pittsburgh, more Carnegie libraries were constructed in Cleveland than anywhere else. Of the 15 built here, all but three are still used as libraries. One of them is this graceful Renaissance Revival structure, a triangular-shaped edifice designed by Edward Tilton and completed in 1910. The interior of this Ohio City branch of the Cleveland Public Library boasts Corinthian columns, expansive windows, and room-illuminating skylights. Original Arts and Crafts touches can be found throughout the warm space, like the charming green-glazed Alice in Wonderland tiles, crafted by noted potter William Grueby, that frame the fireplace in the children's room. Set on a roomy and open green space, the library forms a graceful backdrop for impromptu strolls, neighborhood gatherings, and lazy Sunday mornings with coffee and the paper.

MAP 2: 1900 Fulton Rd., 216/623-6927, http://cpl.org; 10am-7pm Mon.-Tues. and Thurs., 10am-6pm Wed. and Fri.-Sat.

St. Ignatius High School

With 13 majestic buildings spread across a lush 16-acre campus, St.

KEEPING THE CHURCH LIGHTS ON

Cleveland neighborhoods are graced with scores of architecturally stunning churches, their steeples and bell towers visible from area highways. And thanks to a generous donation by a retired dentist, many are visible day or night.

Before he died, **Reinhold W. Erickson** saw to it that his life savings of $370,000 would be used to improve his city's image to outsiders. His plan was specific: By illuminating church steeples along Cleveland interstates, he could give folks arriving via Cleveland Hopkins International Airport something beautiful to look at during their ride into the city. His goal was to light 20 churches along the oft-traveled I-90 and I-71 corridors. To date, 19 churches are participating in the ambitious **Steeple Lighting Program.** See how many you can spot along the way.

Today, the Reinhold W. Erickson Fund is managed by the Cleveland Foundation and the Cleveland Restoration Society.

Ignatius High School looks more like a tony liberal arts college than a Catholic prep school for boys. Founded in the late 1800s by a group of German Jesuits, the school is both a neighborhood icon and a Cleveland educational institution. Along with the West Side Market's clock tower, St. Ig's 160-foot redbrick spire is one of the most recognizable skyline landmarks in the area. Respected equally for its athletics and academic excellence, this school has graduated both Olympic gold medalists and Ohio Supreme Court justices. Ohio City is often filled with the youthfully exuberant sounds of lacrosse, football, and track-and-field athletes as they compete on the pro-style turf field.

MAP 2: 1911 W. 30th St., 216/651-6313, www.ignatius.edu

Franklin Castle

For decades, this 9,000-square-foot, carved-sandstone Gothic mansion has remained unoccupied, quietly haunting passersby. Built in the late 1800s by a wealthy banker, the mansion boasts 26 rooms, five marble fireplaces, and some 80 windows. It is also, according to lore, the site of a few grisly slayings, including that of a housekeeper who was murdered on her wedding day.

Neighbors often report seeing a ghost in the upstairs window, while others hear blood-curdling cries. Efforts to transform the iconic property over the years included plans for a swanky private club, but the latest shot at reincarnation will come courtesy of Norton Records of Brooklyn, New York, which plans to open an office within those haunted, er, hallowed halls.

MAP 2: 4308 Franklin Blvd.; not open to the public

St. John's Episcopal Church

Cleveland's oldest church, this Ohio City landmark was built by a Connecticut settler in 1836. Beloved for its Gothic Revival style and its facade of local sandstone, the building has survived both a devastating fire and a violent tornado. In the mid-1800s, Ohio offered safe passage for tens of thousands of slaves; St. John's was the last stop on the so-called Underground Railroad before arriving in Canada. The newest acquisition for this storied church is a fully restored 500-pipe organ, originally crafted in 1926, which has made its way through at least three separate places of worship.

MAP 2: 2600 Church Ave., 216/781-5546, www.stjohnsohiocity.org

✪ St. Theodosius Russian Orthodox Cathedral

Fans of *The Deer Hunter* will surely recognize the characteristic onion-shaped domes that dot the top of this magnificent cathedral, which served as the backdrop for that film's wedding scenes. The 13 copper-clad domes that rise above the structure represent Christ and the 12 apostles. Opened in 1911, St. Theodosius is the oldest Russian Orthodox cathedral in Ohio, and it is considered one of the finest examples of traditional orthodox architecture in the country. Nearly every inch of the interior is adorned with vivid religious murals, icons, and holy pictures, the highlight of which is a screen bearing images of Christ, the Virgin Mary, the 12 apostles, and St. Theodosius. A 2001 renovation has breathed fresh life into the historic church.

MAP 2: 733 Starkweather Ave., 216/741-1310, www.sttheodosius.org

A Christmas Story House

Lincoln Park

Once part of Cleveland University, a short-lived mid-1800s college, this leafy green expanse is Tremont's version of Public Square. Ringed by bars, restaurants, and lovingly restored century-old homes, this park sees activity all day long. It is the site of numerous neighborhood festivals, alfresco summer concerts, and weekly farmers markets in season. Throughout the summer, free dance and music concerts attract large picnicking crowds at night, while the park's municipal swimming pool attracts overheated locals during the day. A stroll around the park's perimeter will unearth such haunts as the neighborhood coffeehouse, neighborhood pub, and various churches. On the southern end of the park, modern townhomes occupy the Lincoln Park Bath building, which was constructed in 1921 as a public bathhouse for the many residents who still lacked modern plumbing.

MAP 2: Starkweather Ave. and W. 14th St.

A Christmas Story House

People thought Brian Jones, a West Coaster who had never stepped foot in Cleveland, was out of his mind when he purchased the house that served as the visual backdrop for the classic film *A Christmas Story*. A lifelong fan of the flick, Jones bought the 1895 Tremont structure sight unseen, with plans of restoring the "Parker house" to its original movie splendor. Every effort was made to recapture the authentic look and feel of the times, including exchanging vinyl siding with real wood, ditching the replacement windows, and converting the building from a duplex back to a single-family home. Jones took pains to match the interior layout of the movie home, scouting out identical furnishings. Fans of the movie will recognize the familiar yellow-and-green of the building's exterior. Super fans can even spend the night in a private third-floor loft while having free rein of the house. Directly across the street from the house is a gift shop and museum, where film buffs can view original props, costumes, and memorabilia.

THE CITY'S BEST SELFIE SPOTS

These days, one of the most important aspects of traveling is capturing that perfect selfie to post on social media. To help with this quest, the local tourism bureau has installed six signs that spell out "Cleveland" in script, in tourist-friendly spots around the city that offer spectacular backdrops for those memorable snaps. The beefy white sculptures are sturdy enough to support nimble photo subjects, but the signs also make wonderful photo ops without a single human face. Each location offers views of the Cleveland skyline from a different vantage point.

Five of the six signs are located within city limits. They can be found at these spots:

- North Coast Harbor by the **Rock and Roll Hall of Fame and Museum** (page 18)

- **Edgewater Park** (page 30)

- Abbey Avenue and West 14th Street, near **Sokolowski's University Inn** (page 54)

- **The Foundry** near Rivergate Park (page 133)

- **Cleveland Hopkins International Airport** (page 234)

Feel deserving of a "major award?" Pick up a full-size replica of the notorious leg lamp to take home and proudly display in the front window.

MAP 2: 3159 W. 11th St., 216/298-4919, www.achristmasstoryhouse.com; 10am-5pm daily; $11 adults, $9.50 seniors, $8 children

Detroit Shoreway and Edgewater

Map 3

Edgewater Park

Since taking over management of Edgewater Park from the Ohio Department of Natural Resources in 2013, Cleveland Metroparks has continued to drastically improve its every aspect. Comprising the 2,400-foot Edgewater Beach and a sprawling elevated greenspace that offers dramatic views of downtown Cleveland, this urban playground is enjoying more visitors now than ever. The Edgewater Beach House boasts stellar lake vistas from its open-air balconies, while offering food and drink options to the park, including alcoholic beverages. Walkers, joggers, and bicyclists crisscross the park on paved pathways.

Anglers drop lines off nearby fishing piers. And kayakers and paddleboarders launch from various spots. Every Thursday evening from late May through early August, **Edgewater Live** draws thousands to the sandy shores for live music, food trucks, and picture-perfect sunsets. Sailors can book a guest docking spot at nearby Edgewater Yacht Club, a private club.

MAP 3: 6500 Memorial Shoreway, 216/635-3200, www.clevelandmetroparks. com; 6am-11pm daily; free

Gordon Square Arts District

Thanks to a multi-year, multimillion-dollar revitalization project, this arts-focused district has become the nucleus not only of the Detroit Shoreway neighborhood, but likely the entire near-West Side of Cleveland. Two miles west of downtown, with easy access to Lake Erie, the district is the site of ambitious new residential, commercial, and cultural development. Anchored by the Cleveland Public Theatre, the walkable area boasts a restored 1921 art-house movie theater, a pedestrian-friendly streetscape, and the new homes of Near West Theatre and Talespinner Children's Theatre. Already, the vibrant area is picking up steam. Shoppers are beginning to discover funky new boutiques, design studios and art galleries, and book and record shops. Sharp new cafés, restaurants, and bars keep the diverse streets peopled day and night.

MAP 3: Centered around Detroit Ave. and W. 65th St., www.gordonsquare.org; hours vary

St. Stephen Catholic Church

This stunning Gothic-style church was built in 1881 to serve the West Side's large contingent of German-speaking Catholics—by 1900 there were nearly 40,000. Many of the original parishioners agreed to mortgage their homes to ensure that construction was completed. What distinguishes a German Catholic church from, say, a Roman Catholic one? For starters, the interior features a blond Virgin Mary, the hand-carved altars and statuary were imported from Munich, and the image of the Lord is a bearded one. Mass is still held in German on the first Sunday of each month. The freestanding hand-carved oak pulpit, a 25-foot tower of ornamental figurines, was initially exhibited at the Chicago World's Fair. Basket-weave marble tiles cover the sanctuary floor. St. Stephen's imported stained-glass windows were shattered by a tornado in 1999 and have since been replaced. Sunday socials are held on the first Sunday of each month following the 9:30am and 11am Masses.

MAP 3: 1930 W. 54th St., 216/631-5633, www.ststephencleveland.org

University Circle and Little Italy
Map 4

✪ Cleveland Museum of Art

The Cleveland Museum of Art has always been regarded as one of the nation's finest repositories of art and antiquities. The multiple wings of the original 1916 building are united by a jaw-dropping central atrium that is the site of numerous events. The classical marble-clad main building gives the art a wide berth and visitors an easy path to navigate. Skylights create optimal lighting conditions for viewing the work, while state-of-the-art mechanicals provide a comfortable environment.

Thanks to 40,000 square feet of gallery space, there's plenty of room to exhibit the museum's vast permanent collection of 43,000 works of art. Among the permanent exhibits on display are 17th-century to early-19th-century European art; 18th-century and 19th-century American art; 19th-century European sculpture, painting, and decorative arts; and Islamic, Medieval, and Renaissance art, textiles, and manuscripts. Long a favorite, the Armor Court contains one of the largest and finest compilations of medieval and Renaissance arms and armor. Set on a picturesque bluff in University Circle, the museum presides over a sweeping landscape designed by Frederick Law Olmsted Jr., whose father created New York's Central Park.

MAP 4: 11150 East Blvd., 216/421-7350, www.clevelandart.org; 10am-5pm Tues., Thurs., and Sat.-Sun., 10am-9pm Wed. and Fri.; free

Wade Park

No ordinary park, Wade is the epicenter of arts, culture, and education in Cleveland, surrounded by the city's top museums, performing-arts venues, and universities. It is also the site of Wade Oval and Wade Lagoon. Whether one is off to a museum, concert, or lunch date—or none of the above—time should be set aside for a leisurely stroll through this urban oasis. The grounds are dotted with moving public art, architecturally stunning buildings, and meticulously tended gardens. On sunny spring, summer, and fall days, it isn't uncommon to see numerous newlywed couples roaming the green space with photographer in tow. During a random stroll, a visitor might encounter Rodin's *The Thinker,* a garden designed by Frederick Law Olmsted Jr., or a colorful neighborhood parade. Wade Oval is the site of WOW! (Wade Oval Wednesdays), weekly free outdoor concerts held on Wednesday June through August. In winter, the Rink at Wade Oval offers outdoor ice skating for a nominal fee.

MAP 4: Bordered by East Blvd. and Martin Luther King Jr. Blvd.

Cleveland Botanical Garden

With origins in a converted boathouse on nearby Wade Park Lagoon, the botanical garden moved to its current site in 1966. The facility's most conspicuous asset is the 18,000-square-foot Glasshouse, which contains faithful re-creations of two fragile ecosystems, a Costa Rican cloud forest and the desert of Madagascar. Inside, visitors glide from biome to biome, immersed in environments rich with magical fauna and flora. Some 400 varieties of plants and animals take up residence in the conservatory, including 20 species of butterfly, the world's most diminutive orchids, and an army of hungry leaf-cutter ants.

Perhaps even more spectacular are the 10 acres of award-winning outdoor gardens. Among them are a traditional Japanese dry garden, a show-stopping rose garden, perennial and woodland gardens, and an herb garden with 4,000 distinct plants. The Hershey Children's Garden caters specifically to the littlest green thumbs in the bunch with mini forests, caves, worm bins, and a wheelchair-accessible tree house. An on-site library houses one of the largest repositories of gardening information in the country, with more than 17,000 garden-related books and periodicals. All gardens are open year-round except the children's garden, which closes during winter.

MAP 4: 12055 East Blvd., 216/721-1600, www.cbgarden.org; 10am-5pm Tues. and Thurs.-Sat., 10am-9pm Wed., noon-5pm Sun.; $12 adults, $8 children

Peter B. Lewis Building

Set amid the tranquil tree-lined streets that make up the campus of Case Western Reserve University, the Peter B. Lewis Building doesn't just stand out, it explodes onto the landscape. Home to the Weatherhead School of Management, the Frank Gehry-designed building is precisely what one would expect from the acclaimed avant-garde architect. Seemingly lacking a single right angle, the twisting brick structure corkscrews out of the ground. There is no roof, per se, but rather a riot of stainless steel ribbons that festoon the top, reflecting whatever the sky happens to be doing at any given moment. Like the coiling tail of a wrangling fish, the scaly steel tiles provide a flurry of movement and whimsy. Visible for blocks and blocks, the architectural landmark has become an attraction all to itself. Group tours can be arranged by calling ahead two weeks in advance.

MAP 4: Bellflower Rd. and Ford Dr., 216/368-4771, www.weatherhead.case.edu

Severance Hall

The saga of Severance Hall is a love story. One month after tycoon and Cleveland Orchestra president John Long Severance committed to building the concert hall, his wife, Elisabeth, died suddenly of a stroke. Vowing to dedicate the venue to the memory of his beloved partner, Severance went on to build a performance hall that rivals in beauty and sound of any found in Vienna, Boston, or New York. Severance Hall was designed by leading architecture firm Walker & Weeks to mimic a Greek temple. The majestic building's neoclassical facade, with its Ionic column-supported pediment,

harmonizes with the nearby Cleveland Museum of Art. Tributes to Mrs. Severance can be found throughout the hall. Silvery shapes high above the main concert floor are reported to be modeled after the lace from her bridal veil. Lotus blossoms, Elisabeth's favorite flower, appear in the grand foyer's terrazzo floor and elsewhere.

Entering the Grand Foyer, visitors are immersed in an opulent environment of two-story red marble columns, art deco chandeliers, decorative metalwork, and dazzling floors. Cleveland Orchestra concerts are held year-round except during the summer, when performances occur at Blossom Music Center.

MAP 4: 11001 Euclid Ave., 216/231-1111, www.clevelandorchestra.com

Hessler Road and Hessler Court

It may not look like much at first blush, but these two tiny lanes in University Circle have been the site of many battles, protests, and celebrations. The buildings here date back to the early 1900s, so it's understandable that folks didn't take too kindly to the notion of their neighborhood being demolished to make room for parking lots. A vigilant street association formed in 1969 and managed to fight off the proposed development. Before long, the neighborhood was declared a historic district and was placed on the National Register of Historic Places. Hessler Court is just 300 feet long and is the only street in Cleveland that is paved with wood blocks. Held each May, the Hessler Street Fair is a spirited block party that unites friends and neighbors through art, music, food, and dance.

MAP 4: Ford Dr. and Hessler Rd.

✪ Lake View Cemetery

This 290-acre plot of land is much more than just a final resting place; it is an outdoor museum visited by approximately 400,000 people each year. Botanical garden, history lesson, and art gallery all in one, Lake View is a tranquil oasis in the middle of a congested urban environment. Best known as the burial site for many of this city's movers and shakers, the cemetery is "home" to John D. Rockefeller, Eliot Ness, 22 Cleveland mayors, and Alan Freed, whose site is marked by a giant jukebox headstone. The most notable resident, perhaps, is President James A. Garfield, whose stately memorial provides views clear to Lake Erie. Hidden behind the simple, classical lines of the Jeptha Wade Memorial Chapel is a fairy-tale interior designed by Louis Comfort Tiffany. Four-ton bronze doors protect a deliriously beautiful stained-glass window, worthy of a cross-town visit itself. A few hours spent wandering the grounds and viewing the architecturally appealing markers and headstones is time well spent. Numerous walking tours are offered during spring and summer. The Garfield Memorial and Wade Chapel are open 9am-4pm daily April to mid-November, though weddings might be taking place in the chapel. MAP 5: 12316 Euclid Ave., 216/421-2665, www.lakeviewcemetery.com; 7:30am-7:30pm daily Apr.-Oct., 7:30am-5:30pm daily Nov.-Mar.; free

Cain Park

The crown jewel of this 22-acre urban park is Evans Amphitheater, a 1,200-seat covered venue with accompanying open-air lawn for outdoor seating. Despite its meager size, the stage attracts top-talent touring acts who appreciate the intimacy of the setting. Pick a show, pack a picnic, and spend a glorious summer night under the stars. Varied performances on either of the two stages include dance, cabaret, singer-songwriters, and Broadway musicals. In addition to some modest biking and hiking trails, the wooded parkland contains basketball and tennis courts, a toboggan hill, and a skate park. Every July, Cain Park hosts one of the most impressive arts festivals in the region, the Cain Park Arts Festival. For three full days, thousands gather to shop the wares of some 150 artists, covering a broad swath of disciplines. MAP 5: Superior Ave. at Lee Rd., 216/371-3000, www.cainpark.com

the park-like setting at Lake View Cemetery

THE COMMERCIAL DISTRICTS OF CLEVELAND HEIGHTS

Cleveland Heights is a progressive and diverse inner-ring suburb of about 45,000 residents. The area's unique physical layout and history as a "streetcar city" caused the creation of various commercial districts within its borders, each boasting its own look, feel, and flair.

Cedar-Lee, so named for the major intersection in its midst, acts as "Main Street" for Cleveland Heights. This walkable mile-long strip of shops, services, restaurants, and bars serves the students, young professionals, and families who call the neighborhood home. Running south from Cain Park to the public library, the street includes the **Cedar Lee Theatre**, local bakeries, a yoga studio, numerous galleries and boutiques, and various bars, breweries, and restaurants. There is rarely a time of day or night that finds the street totally deserted.

Coventry Village is perhaps best known for its counterculture past, a time when underground cartoonists R. Crumb and Harvey Pekar made the street their living room. Over the years, the strip has succumbed to more than a few national chains, causing a mild erosion of its infamous indie spirit. But all is not lost; Coventry still deserves attention thanks to a quirky amalgam of shops, restaurants, bars, and clubs.

Cedar-Fairmount should be forgiven its Starbucks, mainly because this picturesque gathering of Tudor-style buildings looks today much as it did in 1920. Known as the "Gateway to the Heights," the district sits at the pinnacle of Cedar Hill. That aforementioned coffeehouse teems with activity all day long, while world-renowned jazz club **Nighttown** bops all night. A spirited mix of independent shops includes a bookstore, wood-fired pizza shop, bakery, and cocktail bar. The nearby professional buildings are filled with architects, lawyers, psychiatrists, and doctors.

Fairmount Boulevard District

In the early 1900s, industry tycoons began migrating from the city core to the eastern suburbs. At the time, Cleveland Heights still was considered "the country" despite being a mere nine miles from Public Square. Serviced by the Cleveland Electric Railway, which traveled from downtown and up Cedar Hill, the area quickly became home to the city's wealthiest residents. Employing the architect hotshots of the day, those moguls and tycoons built some of the finest homes of the 1910s and 1920s. Today, Fairmount Boulevard in Cleveland Heights is dotted with stately Georgian mansions, terracotta-clad Italian villas, and wildly asymmetrical Tudor Revivals. Park your car on any of the side streets and make the trek on foot in order to enjoy architectural details like original copper gutters, leaded-glass windows, steeply pitched slate roofs, and wrought-iron balconies. The annual Heights Heritage Home and Garden Tour, held in September, offers participants intimate access to some of these homes and their magnificent gardens. **MAP 5:** Fairmount Blvd. from Cedar Rd. to Wellington Rd.

Shaker Square

More an octagon than a square, Shaker Square is the heart of a spirited and diverse neighborhood six miles east of downtown. Built in the late 1920s, and connected to downtown via the Rapid Transit line, the square is considered the second-oldest outdoor shopping district in the nation. But more than just a collection of shops, the square is a public space, where neighbors meet over coffee, take in a summer concert, or simply wander the circumference with a baby stroller. On warm nights, the roomy front patios of the numerous restaurants fill with diners. A movie theater shows both the latest releases as well as more offbeat indie flicks. Coffee, ice cream, and popcorn, all available on the square, provide the perfect post-movie nosh. A smattering of galleries, boutiques, and shops make for entertaining window-shopping. Held every Saturday morning mid-April through fall, the North Union Farmers Market attracts a massive sampling of small growers and producers, making it the largest fresh-food bazaar in the region.

MAP 5: Bordered by Shaker Blvd., N. Moreland Blvd., and S. Moreland Blvd., www.shakersquare.net

Lakewood   Map 6

Oldest Stone House

In the 1830s, Lakewood was a densely forested hamlet populated by a handful of rugged pioneer types. Back then, now-busy Detroit Road was a dusty trail dotted with log-cabin homes. In 1838, John Honam built this small stone house out of locally quarried sandstone, pretty much signaling the end for log-cabin construction. The building, which served at various times as a residence, post office, and barbershop, remained at its original location for 117 years. In the mid-1950s, at a cost of around $10,000, the solidly built stone house was moved to its current location and established as the home of the Lakewood Historical Society and Museum. Though tiny, the museum boasts a rich tapestry of pioneer relics, including a preserved pioneer kitchen, four-harness loom, furnished parlor with horsehair sofa, and bedrooms with roped beds and homespun sheets. The museum also displays samplers, quilts, and folk art. An on-site herb garden is representative of those pioneer families would maintain as a source of scents, dyes, and food seasonings.

MAP 6: 14710 Lake Ave., 216/221-7343, www.lakewoodhistory.org; open by guided tour only, 1pm-4pm Wed., 2pm-5pm Sun. Feb.-Nov.; free

Beck Center for the Arts

The Beck is the largest nonprofit performing-arts and arts-education organization on the West Side of Cleveland. In addition to professional theatrical productions, which take place on two stages, the center offers comprehensive arts-education programming in dance, music, theater, and visual arts. Lead by artistic director Scott Spence, Beck's productions of musicals, dramas, and comedies consistently draw rave reviews from area critics and fans. The center's ambitious schedule of offerings attracts 100,000 people per year. Folks looking to try something new scramble for spots in classes that range from hip-hop to life drawing from the nude. Two on-site art galleries regularly feature the works of local, regional, and nationally recognized artists.

MAP 6: 17801 Detroit Ave., 216/521-2540, www.beckcenter.org; cost varies by performance, art exhibits free

Museum of Divine Statues

Within the walls of a former church is a remarkable display of more than 200 pieces of ecclesiastical art. As Catholic churches were being shuttered all around him, makeup artist Lou McClung worked to collect, restore, and preserve that history in a professional, respectful manner, opening this museum in 2011. The moving museum is filled with statues, sacred relics, and stunning stained-glass windows. By scanning the artifacts with a smartphone, visitors can see pictures of the churches that they came from as well as their original, unrestored condition.

MAP 6: 12905 Madison Ave., 216/228-9950, www. museumofdivinestatues.com; noon-4pm Sat.-Sun.; $10

Greater Cleveland Map 7

Cleveland Metroparks Zoo

With more than a million visitors each year, the zoo continues to be one of the region's top draws. Spread across 170 acres, the park contains 3,000 animals representing 600 different species. The most popular attraction is the RainForest, a two-acre, two-story steam bath overflowing with a cornucopia of plants and animals, including birds, monkeys, and curious beasts. A simulated tropical rainstorm washes over the room every few minutes. 'Roo fans will hop over to Australian Adventure, home to parrots, koalas, and kangaroos. Like an African safari in Ohio, the Savannah teems with lions, rhinos, giraffes, zebras, and gazelles. Black bears and grizzlies take up residence in the Northern Trek, while tortoises and cheetahs race behind the Primate Building. In 2011, African Elephant Crossing was unveiled, the zoo's largest exhibit to date. That spectacular addition was joined, in 2018, by Asian Highlands, a dynamic three-dimensional environment home to Amur and snow leopards, red pandas, and a goat-antelope species called a takin.

There are numerous fast and casual food options at the park, but guests are free to bring in a packed lunch to save money.

MAP 7: 3900 Wildlife Way, Cleveland, 216/661-6500, www.clemetzoo.com; 10am-5pm Mon.-Fri., 10am-6pm Sat.-Sun. and holidays Memorial Day-Labor Day, 10am-5pm daily Labor Day-Memorial Day; $15 adults, $13 seniors, $11 children

Maltz Museum of Jewish Heritage

Jewish or not, visitors to this East Side museum typically leave moved beyond words: This museum tells the story of 200 years of Jewish-American history, but it could just as easily be recounting the experience of many American immigrants. Opened in 2005, the Maltz Museum is modern, well-planned, and thoughtfully executed. It was created by the folks behind the International Spy Museum in Washington DC, and like that highly immersive facility, it relies on cutting-edge interactive exhibits to tell its tales. Through oral histories, artifacts, and films, visitors experience what it might be like to leave everything behind to start life anew in a foreign place. Yes, there is reference to the dark days of the Holocaust, but there are also humorous examinations into the contribution of Jews to the world of entertainment. The museum's Temple-Tifereth Israel Gallery is a treasure trove of significant Judaica, including scrolls and documents of antiquity, European silverwork, and 18th-century tapestries.

MAP 7: 2929 Richmond Rd., Beachwood, 216/593-0575, www.maltzmuseum.org; 11am-9pm Wed., 11am-5pm Thurs.-Tues., closed Rosh Hashanah, Yom Kippur, and Thanksgiving; $10 adults, $5 children, free for children under 5

Cuyahoga Valley National Park

The National Park Service ranked Cuyahoga Valley National Park the 11th most visited park in the country since 2013, but that doesn't surprise nature lovers from this area. This resplendent 33,000-acre park follows the twists and turns of the Cuyahoga River for 22 miles. Thanks to a wide range of habitats, from deep ravines and wetlands to open prairie and grasslands, the park is home to a great diversity of wildlife. Bird-watchers routinely spot great blue herons, short-eared owls, bobolinks, even bald eagles. Anglers pluck from the rushing waters steelhead trout, bullhead, bluegill, and bass. White-tailed deer seem to be everywhere, coyotes prowl the hillsides, and spring peepers provide the evening soundtrack.

Bicycling is the most popular activity in the park, taking place along four major trails, including the perennially popular Ohio & Erie Canal Towpath Trail, which follows the path of the historic Ohio & Erie Canal for 20 miles. Over 125 miles of hiking trails wend and weave their way through the park, offering treks of varying degrees of difficulty. In wintertime, folks don snowshoes, cross-country skis, and ice skates for some blustery fun. The Cuyahoga Valley Scenic Railroad provides a more passive, albeit no less scenic, park experience, giving riders an eagle's-eye view of the landscape from the comfort of a vintage railcar.

Cleveland Metroparks Zoo

Cyclists hop on the train with bicycle in tow to get to or from favorite paths. A new visitors center opened in Boston Township in 2019.

MAP 7: 7104 Canal Rd., Valley View, 216/524-1497, www.nps.gov/cuva; free

Holden Arboretum

This nature preserve east of Cleveland began as a modest 100-acre parcel of land. Today it encompasses 3,500 acres and includes more than 120,000 diverse plants, making it one of the largest arboretums and botanical gardens in the country. The lush and rambling landscape features a vast array of natural habitats, including bogs, gulches, ponds, lakes, rivers, meadows, and forests, combining to create a wildlife lover's paradise. Various display and specimen gardens specialize in trees, shrubs, and herbaceous perennials, colorful butterfly-attracting plants, even nut-bearing trees.

The Murch Canopy Walk is an elevated walkway that takes visitors through the tree canopy, while the Kalberer Family Emergent Tower rises to a height of 120 feet, offering spectacular views of the surrounding forest and even Lake Erie. Both are open daily April through October.

Winter is no time to shun the arboretum; it evolves into an absolute wonderland punctuated by bounding deer, frozen-in-time waterfalls, and a downy blanket of snow.

Numerous guided tours (held largely from spring through fall) focus on various regions of the park, while 20 miles of pathways offer visitors a host of self-guided treks through easy, moderate, and rugged terrain.

MAP 7: 9500 Sperry Rd., Kirtland, 440/946-4400, www.holdenarb.org; 9am-5pm daily; $10 adults, $4 children, Canopy Walk $14 adults, $6 children (includes admission to park)

Sightseeing Tours

TROLLEY AND TRAIN TOURS

✪ Trolley Tours of Cleveland

The *clang, clang, clang* of Lolly the Trolley is a familiar sound for locals, who for years have observed these bright red open-air carriages shuttle the curious about town. Despite the hokeyness factor, these trolleys provide a wonderful perspective on a city that often obscures its assets, with seasoned guides weaving historical, architectural, cultural, and political tidbits into memorable excursions.

General tours (1-2.5 hours) hit the major sights of North Coast Harbor,

Warehouse District, Ohio City, Playhouse Square, Millionaire's Row, and University Circle, while numerous specialty tours focus on Little Italy and Lake View Cemetery, ethnic markets of Cleveland, unique churches about town, and the trail of Eliot Ness. Tours, which leave from the Powerhouse at Nautica entertainment complex in the Flats, take place year-round, but occur more frequently from Memorial Day to Labor Day. All customers are required to reserve a spot by calling in advance. Also, children under five are not permitted on the longer tour.

Downtown: 2000 Sycamore St., 216/771-4484, www.lollytrolley.com; 1-hour tour $15 adults, $13 seniors, $10 children, 2.5-hour tour $23 adults, $21 seniors, $15 children

Cuyahoga Valley Scenic Railroad

One of the longest scenic railroads in the nation, the CVSR stretches a full 51 miles, from just south of Cleveland all the way down to Canton. And "scenic" is the operative word. For much of the journey, the tracks bisect the majestic Cuyahoga Valley National Park while hugging the Cuyahoga River and paralleling the popular Towpath Trail. Passengers ride in authentic climate-controlled coaches built in the 1950s.

More than just a tour train, the railroad is a key resource for visitors to the valley. Many hop aboard just to travel to their favorite park spot, while bicyclists take advantage of the popular bike-and-ride program, which offers them and their rig a $5 (cash) lift back home.

But you don't need to bike, hike, or climb to enjoy this train. Sign up for a lengthy scenic expedition through the park and watch as nature unfolds outside your window. The lush forests, wetlands, and prairies of the park teem with flora and fauna. White-tailed deer and wildflowers, songbirds and snapping turtles, cattails and coyotes—it's all on display in the valley. The trains operate all year long and offer dozens of different excursions, from midwinter charmers to evening wine-tasting trips. Without question, this railroad is one of the brightest gems in Northeast Ohio. Check the website for more information.

Greater Cleveland: 13512 Station Rd., Brecksville, 800/468-4070, www.cvsr.com; tickets from $15 adults, $10 children, free for children under 3

WALKING TOURS
Electric Transit

For inquisitive groups large and small, longtime guide Karl C. Johnson answers a simple question: What's in Cleveland? Once this curious, gregarious host is through with them, participants will know plenty about Cleveland's rich history, architecture, politics, even sports. Johnson offers tours on foot, by car or van, and even aboard two-wheeled Segways. Two separate three-mile, two-hour walking tours are available: one of downtown, the other through Ohio City. The downtown tour covers notable spots like the Arcade, Cuyahoga County Courthouse, Terminal Tower, and Old Stone Church in deeply intimate fashion. In Ohio City, Johnson not only guides folks past grand Victorian homes, he tells tales about occupants past and present. The tour works its way through the West Side Market, past old brewers' mansions, and along church-dotted lanes. Narrated and escorted Segway tours last one hour and require a brief instructional introduction.

Downtown: 230 Huron Rd., Ste. 100.31, 216/309-1615, www.clevelandsegwaytours.com; by appointment only; $60 up to four people, $15 each additional person

Take a Hike

Each Saturday from the middle of May through the middle of September, the Gateway District organization offers free 1.5-hour tours of distinct and distinctive downtown neighborhoods. Tours cover the history and architecture of areas such as Gateway District, Warehouse District, Civic Center, Playhouse Square, and University Circle. Tours often feature

LOLLY THE TROLLEY

Lolly the Trolley on Public Square

Since 1985, Sherrill Paul Witt has been leading narrated sightseeing tours through Cleveland on bright red vehicles called Lolly the Trolley. In that time, the company has grown from one trolley and one guide to several trolleys and numerous guides. The clientele has shifted from mostly locals to mostly out-of-towners, including visitors from every U.S. state and most countries. I asked Witt some questions about the city she loves to show off.

How did the trolley tours start? I began giving tours of Playhouse Square theaters and loved it. Soon, I was leading walking and bus tours of Cleveland. When I went to Boston for a wedding and saw a trolley tour, I decided Cleveland needed one.

What opinions do first-time visitors often have of Cleveland? Some think we are provincial and have a Rust Belt city mentality. They don't know that Cleveland is a sophisticated multicultural city with all the big-city pluses and few of the minuses. There is a tremendous amount of quiet wealth in the area, and people are generous to a fault.

What are some of your favorite places to take visitors? I love the Arcade. It is a Victorian delight that opened in 1890, and its huge glass ceiling and fabulous wrought-iron railings just stun people. Also, Lake View Cemetery has the Garfield Memorial, John D. Rockefeller's gravesite, and Wade Chapel, the only Tiffany-designed interior in the United States.

What do kids get a kick out of? They love the lake, USS *Cod* Submarine, and the jets on display at Burke Lakefront Airport. They also love all of our professional sports venues and bridges.

What impression of Cleveland do your customers leave with? People always say what a beautiful city we have. They love the classical downtown architecture and how clean our streets and Lake Erie are. Also, they like how affordable Cleveland is both for visitors and residents. You can go to Broadway shows for a fraction of the cost of the East Coast.

What's the best excursion from town? Pedaling along the Ohio & Erie Canal Towpath in Cuyahoga Valley National Park.

actors portraying historic figures from Cleveland's past. Check the website to see where the starting point is for each particular tour.

Downtown: 216/771-1994, www. clevelandgatewaydistrict.com; free

BIKE TOURS
Cleveland Bike Tours

One of the best ways to experience a new city is on two wheels, and Cleveland Bike Tours offers just that.

Two separate tours take riders of all skill levels on scenic and informative routes through downtown or nearby Ohio City. Each is approximately four miles and two hours long. The downtown option takes riders past sights like Public Square, the Rock Hall, and Playhouse Square. Tickets must be purchased at least two hours prior to start time. There's a $10 discount for bringing your own bike. Tours depart from the north end of the East 9th Street Pier.

Downtown: 1000 E. 9th St., 330/532-8687, www.clevelandbiketours.com; 10:30am and 2pm daily Apr.-Oct., weather permitting; $40

SELF-GUIDED TOURS

CityProwl

The website CityProwl.com offers free downloadable audio tours for use in any MP3 player. Each covers about a mile in distance and takes around 40 minutes to complete. Loaded with historical, architectural, and anecdotal information, the tours are an easy, cheap, and entertaining way to squeeze more into a leisurely stroll. At least five different downtown tours, or prowls, are available, including ones covering Public Square, the Warehouse District, and the old arcades. Simply visit the site, download the file, print out a map, and make your way to the starting point.

Downtown: www.cityprowl.com; free

RESTAURANTS

Many people visit Cleveland strictly for the food scene, and who can blame them? Save for Chicago, no Midwestern city has garnered as much national buzz for its rich tapestry of independent eateries as The Land. Certainly, celebrity chef and hometown booster Michael Symon gets and deserves a lot of that attention, but he's just the appetizer. Scores of other talented chefs call this livable city home, and the eclectic cafés, bistros, taverns, and brasseries they operate are as unique and creative as the cooks themselves. Around here, progressive chefs have easy access to some of the freshest local, seasonal, and sustainable ingredients around thanks to a network of farmers markets overflowing with bounty from the fertile Cuyahoga Valley.

inside Urban Farmer

Many of Cleveland's most popular eateries are clustered in hip urban neighborhoods like Tremont, Ohio City, and Detroit Shoreway, but downtown's East Fourth Street might just be the epicenter of good taste. It's not just the chef-driven places that entice locals and visitors alike, but also the diversity of ethnic offerings. Within a few short blocks, hungry diners can enjoy Polish pierogies, Lebanese falafel, Salvadorian *pupusas,* and South Indian *idli* with *sambar.* A few blocks east of downtown, the Asiatown district is flush with Chinese, Korean, and Vietnamese restaurants and markets.

When it comes to eating in Cleveland, the hardest part is deciding where to go.

HIGHLIGHTS

✪ **BEST SLAB OF RIBS:** Cleveland is fortunate to have some great barbecue places, but it's hard to beat **Mabel's BBQ,** the exceptional smoke shack from celebrity chef Michael Symon, when it comes to the meats (page 46).

✪ **DIG IN TO A STEAMER OF SOUP DUMPLINGS: LJ Shanghai,** a relative newcomer in Cleveland's Asiatown neighborhood, has been besieged by diners who recognize quality *xiao long bao* (soup dumplings) when they see and slurp them (page 47).

✪ **SLURP THE BEST BOWL OF PHO:** Long before pho became a fixture on the Cleveland culinary landscape there was **Superior Pho.** Find the odd little Golden Plaza, park in back, and take a seat in this simple eatery to enjoy the city's best bowl of beef noodle soup (page 47).

✪ **WORLD'S BEST CORNED-BEEF SANDWICH:** Visit the always-popular **Slyman's Deli** to see what mile-high corned-beef perfection tastes like (page 50).

✪ **BEST CAFETERIA MEAL:** Locals can't seem to get enough of **Sokolowski's University Inn.** This 100-year-old institution dishes up old-school Eastern European classics like stuffed cabbage, potato pierogies, and chicken paprikash in a tchotchke-filled cafeteria setting (page 54).

✪ **BEST LATE-NIGHT CHOW: Bar Cento** serves food until 2am every single day of the year. The hardworking chefs here turn out approachable Mediterranean fare like charcuterie, warm herbed olives, Neapolitan-style pizza, and grilled Ohio meats (page 54).

✪ **TASTIEST HANGOVER CURE:** Head to **Brewnuts** and you can combine the healing powers of hair of the dog with a fresh, delectable donut. At this funky "donut bar," not only are the confections made with beer, but also they're served with draft beer (page 60).

✪ **BEST HOPE FOR A VEGETARIAN: Tommy's** began in the 1970s as a hippie-run soda fountain. Today, it is the most popular eatery on Coventry Road. While not solely a vegetarian restaurant, Tommy's has a wildly eclectic menu with loads of delicious meat-free options (page 64).

PRICE KEY

$	Entrées less than $15
$ $	Entrées $15-25
$ $ $	Entrées more than $25

NEW AMERICAN

Greenhouse Tavern $$$

James Beard Award-winning chef Jonathon Sawyer has a knack for bridging the gap between every day and special occasion. This isn't a somber tasting-menu temple, but rather a lively downtown tavern that serves a creative, satisfying mix of updated classics and mind-blowing originals. If you're able to pull yourself away from crowd favorites like hand-ground Ohio beef tartare, chicken wings fried in duck fat, clams simmered in a foie gras-enriched broth, and the best lamb burger you'll ever eat, take a chance on any of the specials. For a special experience, call ahead and reserve seats at the chef's table.

MAP 1: 2038 E. 4th St., 216/393-4302, www.thegreenhousetavern.com; 11am-11pm Sun.-Thurs., 11am-12:30am Fri.-Sat.

Lola $$$

This cosmopolitan downtown bistro is the flagship of food celeb Michael Symon's ever-growing empire. Come here to sample creative Midwestern fare constructed from local, seasonal, and artisanal ingredients. Pierogies are stuffed with slow-braised beef cheeks; strip steak is gilded with melting blue cheese; and Dover sole is deboned tableside. Sweets fans will doubtless swoon over this restaurant's house-made selections. If you can't score a dinner reservation, grab a stool at the glowing alabaster bar for a glass of bubbly and some oysters on the half shell.

MAP 1: 2058 E. 4th St., 216/621-5652, www.lolabistro.com; 5pm-10pm Sun.-Thurs., 5pm-11pm Fri.-Sat.

Butcher and the Brewer $$

Butcher and the Brewer is a gymnasium-size bar, restaurant, and brewery set inside a renovated 100-year-old warehouse in the heart of downtown. At the far end of the room is the shiny brewery, which produces a wide range of stellar suds. As for the food, it's head and shoulders above typical pub grub thanks to skilled in-house butchers, who turn out a broad menu of meaty fare like charcuterie, steak tartare, roasted bone marrow, and house-smoked corn dogs. There are enough vegetable and seafood entrées to please the meat-averse in the group as well. When the Tribe or Cavs are in town, this place gets loud, crowded, and a wee bit crazy.

MAP 1: 2043 E. 4th St., 216/331-0805, www.butcherandthebrewer.com; 4pm-midnight Mon.-Thurs., 4pm-2am Fri., noon-2am Sat., 3pm-9pm Sun.

Collision Bend Brewing Company $$

Mega-restaurateur Zack Bruell has a bushel of restaurants around the city, but few rival the riverside setting of Collision Bend. The 1860s brick building in the Flats features subtle nautical touches, but little detracts from the views of passing freighters and zippy kayaks. The sprawling menu is hard to pin down, but there's something for all tastes. Can't-miss items include wood-fired pizzas, fish tacos, Moroccan-spice lamb ribs, and burgers. Tack on a flight of the house-brewed beer.

FOOD TRUCK FIESTA

Every Wednesday (11am-1:30pm) from early May through late September, a large caravan of food trucks descend upon Perk Plaza at Chester Commons (Superior Ave. at E. 12th St.) downtown. **Walnut Wednesdays,** as the long-running event is called, attract approximately 20 popular trucks, which sell everything from burgers and tacos to Philly steak and pierogies. On nice days, thousands of downtown workers come for lunch, which can be enjoyed in the park while listening to live music.

MAP 1: 1250 Old River Rd., 216/273-7879, www.collisionbendbrewery.com; 3pm-10pm Mon.-Thurs., 3pm-11pm Fri., noon-11pm Sat., noon-8pm Sun.

✪ Mabel's BBQ $$

Yes, Michael Symon is a big-time celebrity chef who rarely tends the pit at this buzzy downtown spot, but nobody cares. They come for the slow-cooked goodness that exits the real wood-fired smokers. Items like pork ribs, beef brisket, turkey breast, and kielbasa are cooked low and slow until they are tender, smoky, and delicious. Starters like crispy pork rinds, pig ears and tails, and crunchy fried potatoes round out the roster. This full-service eatery is often packed to the rafters, but service is speedy, efficient, and friendly. A full bar loaded with whiskey keeps bourbon fans smiling.

MAP 1: 2050 E. 4th St., 216/417-8823, www.mabelsbbq.com; 11:30am-close daily

STEAK AND SEAFOOD
Blue Point Grille $$$

In the business of fish since 1998, this Warehouse District mainstay serves up some of the most consistent seafood in the city. The drop-dead gorgeous warehouse space boasts soaring ceilings, castle-thick brick walls, and modest nautical accents. Blue Point is famous for its crab cakes, chowders, surf and turf, and grouper with lobster mashed potatoes. Meat lovers are in good hands, too, since this small restaurant group also operates a wonderful steak house. For a more affordable way to savor the atmosphere, grab seats at the bar and enjoy the best oyster selection around.

MAP 1: 700 W. St. Clair Ave., 216/875-7827, www.bluepointgrille.com; 11:30am-3pm and 5pm-10pm Mon.-Fri., 5pm-11pm Sat., 4pm-10pm Sun.

Marble Room $$$

It's impossible to understate the opulence of Marble Room. Designed by the dream team behind Severance Hall, the former beaux arts-style bank lobby turned dining room is ringed by columns, embellished with gilded chandeliers, and bedecked with cool marble staircases. High-rollers can bank on fresh oysters, great steaks, and sumptuous seafood entrées. Even if a full steak dinner isn't in the plans, do pop into this stunner for happy hour drinks at the quartz bar.

Mabel's BBQ

MAP 1: 623 Euclid Ave., 216/523-7000, www.marbleroomcle.com; 11:30am-10pm Mon.-Thurs., 11:30am-11pm Fri., 5pm-11pm Sat.

Red, the Steakhouse $$$

When the object is to secure the best steak in town regardless of price, head to this swanky downtown chophouse. The Brat Pack-style decor offers a touch of Old Vegas, with red, white, and black splashes throughout. Here, high rollers win big with the city's finest steaks, freshest seafood, and chef-driven specials. Start with crab cakes, move on to the wedge salad, and dig into a fat USDA Prime rib-eye. There's a reason why *Playboy, USA Today,* and *Esquire* have all proclaimed their love for Red.

MAP 1: 417 Prospect Ave., 216/664-0141, www.redthesteakhouse.com; 11:30am-2:30pm and 5pm-10pm Mon.-Wed., 11:30am-2:30pm and 5pm-11pm Thurs.-Fri., 5pm-midnight Sat.

Urban Farmer $$$

Located in the Westin Downtown hotel, this farm-to-table steakhouse bucks the old-school chophouse vibe in favor of one that evokes Portland on the Cuyahoga. Cowhide-swaddled banquettes sit beneath chicken-wire chandeliers and alongside yards of reclaimed timber. When it comes to the goods, few menus offer such variety in terms of cuts, sizes, origin, and aging as Urban Farmer, where steak pedigrees are listed like wine varietals. But the restaurant also excels at charcuterie, salads, sides, and seafood.

MAP 1: 777 St. Clair Ave., 216/771-7707, www.urbanfarmercleveland.com; 6:30am-close Mon.-Fri., 8am-close Sat.-Sun.

ASIAN

✪ LJ Shanghai $

LJ Shanghai, a relative newcomer in Cleveland's Asiatown neighborhood, has been besieged by diners who recognize quality *xiao long bao*—soup dumplings—when they see them. Those amazing dumplings are joined by equally satisfying soup, noodle, and meat dishes like plump shrimp wonton soup, spicy beef noodle soup, Shanghai-style scallion noodles, and soy-braised duck. An interior window offers views into the kitchen, where the cooking staff prepares everything from scratch. The food is reasonably priced, the service is speedy, and the double dining room space is just comfortable enough.

MAP 1: 3142 Superior Ave., 216/400-6936; 11:30am-9pm Tues.-Sun.

Otani Noodle $

There's nothing better than a steamy bowl of ramen on a chilly winter day, and this quick-serve noodle shop more than fills that niche. The straightforward menu consists of about a dozen predesigned bowls built with pork-, shrimp- and miso-based broths. Each bowl is fortified with bouncy noodles and topped with sliced *char-siu* (roast pork), simmered pork belly, or crispy tempura-fried shrimp. Most also contain a soy-marinated soft-boiled egg, scallions, seaweed, and mushrooms.

MAP 1: 234 Euclid Ave., 216/762-1815, www.otaninoodle.com; 11am-10pm Mon.-Fri., noon-10pm Sat.-Sun.

✪ Superior Pho $

Long before pho became a fixture on the Cleveland culinary landscape, there was Superior Pho. This low-profile restaurant is tucked away in Golden Plaza, a small Asiatown mall. Park in back and take a seat in

DIM SUM AND THEN SOME:
A GUIDE TO ASIATOWN

Korean barbecue

Some 46,000 Cuyahoga County residents identify themselves as Asian American, making them one of the larger ethnic populations. Many reside or do business in **Asiatown** (www.asiatowncleveland.com), an area just east of downtown that is loosely bordered by East 30th and 40th Streets, and St. Clair and Payne Avenues. This vibrant, diverse neighborhood is teeming with Asian-owned shops, restaurants, and markets. A visit here is a must for ethnic food fans, adventurous home cooks, and lovers of all things exotic.

The Chinese are Cleveland's oldest Asian immigrant group, dating all the way back to the 1860s, but the area that used to be called Chinatown is now referred to as Asiatown to better reflect the residents who call the area home. Recent decades have welcomed arrivals from Korea, Vietnam, and Thailand, and immigrants from each of these countries have established restaurants and markets in this area.

Pho has become an absolute food craze in Cleveland, with at least a dozen shops devoted to the popular Vietnamese beef noodle soup.

this clean but spare eatery to enjoy the city's best bowl of pho, bar none. There are a dozen different iterations from which to choose. To round out the meal order a dish of cool, crisp chicken cabbage salad, an amazing *banh mi* sandwich, or any of the vermicelli noodle dishes.

MAP 1: 3030 Superior Ave., 216/781-7462, www.superiorpho.com; 10:30am-8pm Tues.-Sat., 10:30am-7pm Sun.

Szechuan Gourmet $

Located inside Tink Holl, a wonderful Asian foods market, this eatery quickly rose to the top of the list thanks to its authentic Szechuan cuisine. Fire-engine-red dishes look more dangerous than they are thanks to a delicate balance of spice and flavor. Comforting *ma po* tofu features soft, silky cubes of tofu set off by finely ground and sautéed pork. Fried fish dry pot is a wok-size bowl filled with tender fish and tongue-tingling

Cleveland's best bowl can be found at **Superior Pho,** a hard-to-find but worth-the-effort gem. This place also happens to sell Cleveland's best banh mi sandwich. Another Asiatown restaurant that is drawing steady crowds is **LJ Shanghai.** The specialty here are *xiao long bao,* or soup dumplings. Tucked inside a delicate house-made wrapper is a dollop of meat swimming in intensely flavored broth.

Dim sum is a popular weekend brunch in Cleveland—the practice of selecting food as it rolls by on carts is pretty much a universal delight. Two local dim sum institutions are **Bo Loong** (3922 St. Clair Ave., 216/391-3113) and **Li Wah** (2999 Payne Ave., Asia Plaza, 216/696-6556, www.liwahrestaurant.com). Both have wonderful selections, efficient service, and reasonable prices. Try the barbecue pork buns, turnip cakes, shrimp dumplings, crisp-skinned duck, and, if you're brave, chicken feet. A notable destination on the dim sum circuit is **Emperor's Palace** (2136 Rockwell Ave., 216/861-9999, www. emperorspalacecleveland.com).

There are few greater culinary joys than a platter of freshly grilled garlicky beef bulgogi, served alongside a wide array of *banchan,* those pungent condiments like kimchi that accompany every Korean meal. That's precisely why in-the-know folks flock to **Rising Grill** (3709 Payne Ave., 216/465-3561, www. risinggrill.com), one of the few places in town with large tables that feature built-in gas grills.

Thai food fans are not overlooked in Asiatown. One of the city's most reliable providers of this delicious, vibrant cuisine is **Map of Thailand** (3710 Payne Ave., 216/361-2220, www.mapofthailandrestaurant.net), where the menu is filled with pitch-perfect renditions of duck noodle soup, country-style pad Thai, and mouthwatering curries of every stripe.

Asiatown is blessed with great ethnic food markets that transform an everyday grocery trip into a culinary expedition. These bustling groceries stock live seafood items like crabs, frogs, and eels, hard-to-find herbs and spices, and even cookware. One of Cleveland's oldest and best is **Tink Holl** (1735 E. 36th St., 216/881-6996), a large, bright space crammed with everything from baby bok choy to freshly made soy milk. For a treat, purchase half a roasted duck to go. **Park to Shop** (1580 E. 30th St., 216/781-3388, www. parktoshopmarket.com) is a supermarket-size grocery that stocks more than 15,000 items, from China, Korea, Japan, Vietnam, and Thailand. It has a produce section, butcher shop, and large frozen foods aisle. Also worthy of a visit is **Koko Bakery** (3710 Payne Ave., 216/881-7600, www.kokosbakery.com), a colorful shop that sells an amazing selection of Asian baked goods. Come here for sweet and savory buns, Chinese cakes, egg custards, and bubble tea.

peppers. Bright sautéed greens with garlic are sweet and savory.

MAP 1: Tink Holl, 1735 E. 36th St., 216/881-9688; 11am-10pm daily

MEXICAN
Barrio Tacos $

Barrio is neither typical Tex-Mex nor authentic regional Mexican. Instead, it's a fun, festive, and affordable design-your-own-taco bar. Diners employ a stubby No. 2 pencil to select various shell, filling, and topping combos. They are all priced the same regardless of the formula (hint: cheap). Start with chips and *queso* (cheese), toss in some fruity margaritas, and pretty soon you've got a fiesta on your hands. This local chain began in 2012 and has since spread like *fuego* across the landscape, with at least half a dozen spots.

MAP 1: 503 Prospect Ave., 216/862-4652, www.barrio-tacos.com; 4pm-2am Mon.-Thurs., 11am-2am Fri.-Sun.

RESTAURANT WEEKS

Two different organizations host separate events that offer diners great deals when eating out. Held in late February, **Downtown Cleveland Restaurant Week** (www.downtowncleveland.com) encourages guests to dine downtown with specially priced multicourse lunches and dinners. Special parking deals also help budgets. Held the first two weeks in March, **Cleveland Independents Restaurant Week** (www.clevelandindependents.com) is broader in both geography and participation, with upward of 60 independent restaurants getting in on the action. Those restaurants typically offer special three-course menus for around $33 per guest. Many offer lunch deals as well.

Puente Viejo $

Puente Viejo takes the traditional Tex-Mex concept and updates it for the downtown crowd. In place of dark hand-carved booths, chipped tableware, and blowup Corona bottles, this warehouse-style space features exposed brick, industrial lighting, a marble-topped bar, and tastefully understated murals. While the menu of staples will look familiar, diners can expect fresher ingredients, tighter execution, and more attractive plating. Meals might include crisp chips and salsa, creamy queso, crispy shredded beef flautas, enchiladas, chiles rellenos, and fajitas. An order of tacos includes a trip to the well-stocked taco bar.

MAP 1: 1220 Huron Rd., 216/713-2689, www.puenteviejocle.com; 11am-9:30pm Mon.-Fri., 1:30pm-10pm Sat., noon-9pm Sun.

BREAKFAST AND BRUNCH

Mike & Dee's Diner $

This modest little café, tucked inside the Holiday Inn Express on Euclid Avenue, sports the classic diner chassis. There's a lengthy counter with stools and a handful of tables. In the morning, the griddle fills up with breakfast items like French toast, pancakes, three-egg omelets, and corned beef hash. Come lunchtime, folks are filling up on matzo ball soup, patty melts, and mile-high corned beef sandwiches.

MAP 1: 629 Euclid Ave., 216/621-1505, www.mddiner.com; 6:30am-2pm Mon.-Fri., 8am-1pm Sat.

Yours Truly $

Since its inception in 1981, Yours Truly has been a growing local chain of suburban diners serving approachable American food. This downtown spot—the group's eighth location—brings that winning formula downtown. From breakfast items like buttermilk pancakes, omelets, and eggs Benedict with hash browns to great salads, burgers, and desserts, this broad menu covers pretty much every base. Don't overlook the Notso Fries, cottage fries capped with melted cheese, bacon, and sour cream.

MAP 1: 1228 Euclid Ave., 216/621-2700, www.ytr.com; 6:30am-10pm Mon.-Thurs., 6:30am-11pm Fri.-Sat., 7:30am-10pm Sun.

DELIS

✪ Slyman's Deli $

A lot of places claim it, but Slyman's really does have the best corned-beef sandwich in America. Just before noon on weekdays, a line begins forming at the deli counter. Soon, that line is snaking down the sidewalk. But don't worry, it moves quickly, and waiting at the other end is a mile-high, butter-soft, gut-busting beauty that puts all others to shame. In addition to those famous

sandwiches, this bustling sit-down diner also prepares breakfast items, tuna melts, Reubens, and fries with gravy.
MAP 1: 3106 St. Clair Ave., 216/621-3760, www.slymans.com; 6am-2pm Mon.-Fri.

COFFEE
Erie Island Coffee $
Modeled after a Pacific Northwest coffeehouse, Erie blends a rustic, wood-paneled vibe with top-notch java drinks like coffee, espresso, and cappuccino. From bean to barista, every step is taken to ensure a consistently delicious cup. While caffeine is the company's stock in trade, customers also can fuel up from the light menu of salads, breakfast and lunch sandwiches, and real-fruit smoothies. The prime location on East Fourth Street makes this shop especially convenient.

MAP 1: 2057 E. 4th St., 216/394-0093, www.erieislandcoffee.com; 6:30am-8pm Mon.-Thurs., 6:30am-10pm Fri., 9am-10pm Sat., 9am-4pm Sun.

Pour Cleveland $
People who are serious about their coffee know to come to this sleek coffee bar downtown, where only the best beans from the best roasters (including Pour's own roastery) end up in their mug. Don't expect a laundry list of complicated beverages, just pour-overs and espressos done right every single time. This spare, sharp shop also offers fresh pastries, retail beans, and brewing equipment.

MAP 1: 530 Euclid Ave., 216/479-0395, www.pourcleveland.com; 7am-6pm Mon.-Fri., 8am-6pm Sat.-Sun.

Ohio City and Tremont   Map 2

NEW AMERICAN
Black Pig $$$
At this approachable Ohio City bistro, chef-owner Mike Nowak sources high-quality heritage breed pork from local farmers to craft some of this city's most agreeable French-inspired fare. The farm-to-table menu indeed is a paean to pork, with the menu featuring house-made charcuterie, supple slow-braised belly, fat grilled chops, and tasting menus built around the same. But the kitchen always provides delicious options, from steak and seafood to pasta and vegetarian specials, that will appeal to the rest of the gang. Bourbon fans will be in barrel heaven here.

MAP 2: 2801 Bridge Ave., 216/862-7551, www.theblackpigcleveland.com; 4pm-close Tues.-Fri., 11am-2pm and 5pm-close Sat., 11am-3pm Sun.

Black Pig

Dante $$$
Native Clevelander and Michelin-starred chef Dante Boccuzzi has worked his way around the globe,

51

with stints in London, Milan, Hong Kong, San Francisco, and New York. At this contemporary Tremont bistro, the chef showcases his knack for Italian, American, and Asian cuisines. He has a deft hand when it comes to sushi and seafood; his house-made pastas, polentas, and risottos are otherworldly; and there are enough meat dishes to satisfy the carnivore at the table. Die-hard (and deep-pocketed) epicureans book a spot at the kitchen table for an epic 21-course tasting menu.

MAP 2: 2247 Professor Ave., 216/274-1200, http://dantetremont.com; 4:30pm-10pm Mon.-Thurs., 4:30pm-1am Fri.-Sat.

Fat Cats $$

Thanks to pioneering eateries such as this one, Tremont has blossomed into an epicurean's playground. For decades, Fat Cats has been tucked into an old colonial on the end of a residential block, and this cozy bistro never fails to delight first-time visitors. Guests might come for the charm, but they invariably return for the delicious, eclectic food. The Mediterranean, Asian, and Latin American menu often features grilled octopus, Korean steamed buns, seafood stew, and grilled skirt steak. Copious portions, genial service, and modest prices make this restaurant a popular destination for both lunch and dinner.

MAP 2: 2061 W. 10th St., 216/579-0200, www.coolplacestoeat.com; 11am-10pm Mon.-Thurs., 11am-midnight Fri.-Sat., 11am-4pm Sun.

Flying Fig $$

Located on a brick-paved lane in Ohio City, this bistro is frequented by fawning locals and well-heeled travelers. Chef-owner Karen Small works closely with local farmers, farmers markets, and artisanal producers to craft a menu that changes nearly as frequently as the calendar. Guests can always look forward to delightful small plates with big flavors, plenty of seasonal vegetarian options, and a concise roster of meat, fish, and pasta choices. Hit this restaurant's wonderful happy hour for discounted drinks, nibbles, and house-made chips, all dished up in a hip bistro setting.

MAP 2: 2523 Market Ave., 216/241-4243, www.theflyingfig.com; 3pm-9pm Mon., 11am-10pm Wed.-Thurs., 11am-11pm Fri.-Sat., 11am-9pm Sun.

The Plum $$

Some of the most ambitious, creative American cooking is taking place at this Ohio City bistro. Regulars keep returning to see what clever creations will turn up on the menu, while newbies continue to discover the restaurant's unique joys. Playful snacks like fried chicken skin butt up against daring but delicious (and safe) pork tartare. Crowd-pleasing dishes like fried chicken sandwiches and lamb burgers compete for attention with brash shareable platters like whole fried General Tso's chicken. Killer drinks, a sleek interior, and relaxed service all come together for a great experience.

MAP 2: 4133 Lorain Ave., 216/938-8711, www.theplumcafeandkitchen.com; 4pm-11pm Tues.-Thurs., 4pm-1am Fri.-Sat, 11am-2pm Sun.

ASIAN
Ginko $$$

Most folks wrongly assume that the Midwest can't have nice things when it comes to sushi. Chef Dante Boccuzzi's stellar Tremont hot spot Ginko will quickly upend those misconceptions. Most of the seats in this grotto-style den are at a large horseshoe-shaped

THE POLISH BOY: A CLEVELAND ORIGINAL

Google the Polish Boy and you'll likely spot blurbs crowning it Cleveland's signature sandwich. Not to be confused with the Southern po' boy, this culturally significant food is a unique and delicious creation that has local roots stretching back to the 1940s. It was then that a man named Virgil Whitmore opened the first of what would become a small chain of barbecue spots around town. Like all enterprising small business operators, Whitmore tried to stretch and sell his inventory any way he could. He looked around the shop at what he had on hand and came up with the now-famous sandwich.

Polish Boy

To the uninitiated, a Polish Boy is a Polish kielbasa tucked into a large hot dog bun, topped with coleslaw and French fries, and then smothered in barbecue sauce. Messy, tasty, filling, and affordable, this brainchild spread like wildfire to other barbecue shacks, shops, and storefronts.

Folks growing up in Cleveland over the past 60 years largely got their fill of Polish Boys from neighborhood smoke shops like **Mt. Pleasant BBQ** (12725 Kinsman Rd., 216/561-8722, www.whitmoresbbq.com), a Whitmore's spinoff that opened in the Mt. Pleasant neighborhood in 1942. But in recent years, the sandwich has been making quite the revival. One of the best versions around is handed through the window of **Seti's Polish Boys** (216/240-0745, @setispolishboys), a roving food truck that is frequented by Michael Symon and was featured on the Food Network. Folks typically track its movements via Twitter.

Symon has such love for the sandwich that he put a version of it on the menu at **Mabel's BBQ.** Order the Polish Girl at his popular downtown barbecue restaurant and you'll get a mouthwatering sandwich starring local kielbasa from the nearby West Side Market. Over at **Banter**, a fun poutine, sausage, and bottle shop concept in Detroit Shoreway, the Polish Boy stars juicy house-made kielbasa tucked into a split-top bun and crowned with slaw, perfect fries, and sauce. In downtown Cleveland, **Gillespie's Map Room** prepares a sandwich called the Drew Carey. It's a Polish Boy that swaps the kielbasa for an all-beef hot dog topped with slaw, fries, and barbecue sauce.

Wherever you go, make sure to ask for extra napkins.

---

sushi bar, where diners can watch skilled sushi chefs craft edible art. Brilliant sashimi, sushi, and rolls are the main order of the day, as are fish-focused starters and salads. Diners seated at one of the two booths can also enjoy shabu-shabu.

MAP 2: 2247 Professor Ave., 216/274-1202, http://restaurantginko.com; 4:30pm-10pm Tues.-Thurs., 4:30pm-midnight Fri.-Sat.

Ushabu $$$

Ushabu is Cleveland's first purpose-built shabu-shabu restaurant, and they hit it out of the park. Just 25 seats fill

this peaceful Tremont dining room, and each comes with its own built-in induction burner. In those pots of simmering broth go seasonal vegetables, heritage-breed pork, Wagyu beef, and ocean-fresh fish. Asian-themed small plates and high-concept Japanese tasting menus are also on the menu. Do make reservations, and note that small parties might share large booths with new friends.

MAP 2: 2173 Professor Ave., 216/713-1741, www.ushabu.com; 5pm-10:30pm Tues.-Thurs., 5pm-11:30pm Fri.-Sat., 5pm-9:30pm Sun.

Xinji Noodle Bar $

This chef-driven noodle bar starts with excellent broths, made by slowly simmering meat bones. Those rich pork and chicken broths (along with veggie) are the foundation for a handful of excellent ramen bowls, which are further supplemented with meats, mushrooms, eggs, seaweed, and other tasty additions. Also available at this buzzy but informal neighborhood haunt are dumplings, steamed buns, and crispy Korean fried chicken. To drink, there's beer and sake.

MAP 2: 4211 Lorain Ave., 216/465-2439, www.xinjinoodle.com; 5pm-10pm Tues.-Thurs., noon-11pm Fri.-Sat.

EASTERN EUROPEAN
✪ Sokolowski's University Inn $$

There may be no more authentically Cleveland restaurant than Sokolowski's, which opened in 1923. What makes this restaurant unique is the cafeteria-style dining comprising a smorgasbord of Eastern European delicacies. All manner of folks work their way down the chow line, loading up trays with heaping portions of stuffed cabbage, potato pancakes, pierogies, chicken paprikash, and rice pudding. The homey lodge-like dining room features a fireplace, live piano music, and the curious collection of ephemera that nearly 100 years in business inevitably generates. In 2014, the restaurant garnered the prestigious James Beard "American Classics" Award.

MAP 2: 1201 University Rd., 216/771-9236, www.sokolowskis.com; 11am-3pm Mon.-Thurs., 11am-3pm and 5pm-9pm Fri., 4pm-9pm Sat.

Sokolowski's University Inn

MEDITERRANEAN
✪ Bar Cento $$

Connected to the lively Belgian beer hall Bier Market, this wine bar attracts diners for a number of reasons, not the least of which is the pizza. The crisp Neapolitan-style pies fly out of the brick ovens topped with clams, pancetta, or seasonal items like locally foraged ramps. In addition to those stellar pies, the chef-driven European-inspired menu offers platters of house-cured meats and cheeses, fresh pastas, creative seafood dishes, and hearty entrées like steak frites. Serving food until 2am every day, Bar Cento is the preferred late-night hangout of post-work industry types and night owls.

MAP 2: 1948 W. 25th St., 216/274-1010, www.barcento.com; 4:30pm-2am Mon.-Fri., 11am-2am Sat.-Sun.

MEXICAN
Bakersfield Tacos $

This Ohio City taqueria goes the extra mile by making fresh corn tortillas every day. From the chips and guac to the tacos and tostadas, quality shines through. Options include crispy fried mahi-mahi fish tacos and braised short rib tostadas. The salads are big, bright, fresh, and visually appealing, and the patio of this sleek, chill spot is a great place to enjoy a pitcher of margaritas with friends and dogs in tow.

MAP 2: 2058 W. 25th St., 216/443-0460, www.bakersfieldtacos.com; 11am-midnight Mon.-Thurs., 11am-2am Fri.-Sat., 11am-10pm Sun.

Momocho Mod Mex $$

Not your typical chips-and-salsa Mexican joint, this dark, clubby eatery elevates south-of-the-border cuisine to a delicious art form. Set in a two-story colonial, Momocho features a colorful first-floor bar and lounge and a more serene upstairs dining room. Locals stop in for a festive meal of appetizers and margaritas, starring smoked-trout guacamole, creative taquitos, and the rightly famous pumpkin-seed-and-pecan-crusted trout. Wash it all down with a fruity margarita or ice-cold Mexican beer. Momocho has one of the longest tequila and mezcal lists around.

MAP 2: 1835 Fulton Rd., 216/694-2122, www.momocho.com; 5pm-close Tues.-Fri., 4pm-close Sat.-Sun.

BREAKFAST AND BRUNCH

The Cleveland Bagel Co. $

This indie bagel bakery does everything right, from slowly leavening and hand-rolling the dough to dropping the bagels into an old-fashioned water bath to baking them fresh every single day. Pop into this bright, modern café to pick up a dozen plain, everything, or salt bagels, or a single bagel with a schmear of cream cheese. Breakfast sandwiches, like the bacon, egg, and cheese or the house-cured lox, cream cheese, and onion, are a great way to start the day. Hot coffee is served as well.

MAP 2: 4201 Detroit Ave., 216/600-5652, http://clebagelco.com; 6:30am-1pm daily

Le Petit Triangle Café $

As the name suggests, this café is a wee wedge of a place (with an addition). On warm days, that capacity jumps thanks to a grouping of bright-red bistro furniture that tumbles out onto the sidewalk. Inside or out, this charming neighborhood spot captures the carefree spirit of a Parisian café, complete with sweet and savory crepes, fluffy omelets, and an ethereal café au lait. Get here early on weekend mornings to enjoy an authentic slice of Ohio City life along with your fluffy smoked-salmon omelet.

MAP 2: 1881 Fulton Rd., 216/281-1881, www.lepetittrianglecafe.com; 10am-10pm Mon.-Thurs., 10am-11pm Fri.-Sat., 10am-9pm Sun.

Lucky's Café $

In addition to being the de facto java stop for many Tremont residents, Lucky's features one of the most popular weekend brunches in town. Chef-owner Heather Haviland scours the countryside in search of local eggs, sustainable produce, and ecofriendly meats. Breakfast means big plates of Ohio sweet-corn waffles with strawberry-rhubarb compote, freshly baked cheddar-scallion scones topped with scrambled eggs and sausage gravy, and a delicious disaster dubbed the Shipwreck, featuring scrambled eggs, bacon, white cheddar, and fried

The Cleveland Bagel Co.

OHIO CITY GALLEY

Ohio City Galley (www.ohiocitygalley.org) is an innovative food hall concept from the Galley Group. The large, animated space is in the historic Forest City Bank Building (Detroit Ave. at W. 25th St.), a turn-of-the-20th-century structure on the National Register of Historic Places. Four separate food operators stay for a year or longer, selling foods like authentic regional Mexican, classic American diner fare, Asian-fusion rice bowls, Nashville hot chicken, and other options. Look for new food concepts to cycle in and out over time. In addition to the food component, Ohio City Galley is anchored by an impressive four-sided bar serving local and regional craft beer and top-notch cocktails.

potatoes. Haviland is also a fine pastry chef, so you can count on phenomenal sweets, tortes, brownies, and cakes.

MAP 2: 777 Starkweather Ave., 216/622-7773, www.luckyscafe.com; 7am-3pm Mon.-Sat., 9am-3pm Sun.

West Side Market Café $

On Saturday, the busiest shopping day at the West Side Market, this café is absolutely buzzing with activity as folks fuel up on eggs Benedict, corned-beef hash, and righteous blueberry pancakes. Weekday mornings and lunches are decidedly calmer affairs, but the café is still worth a visit thanks to quality ingredients and consistent attention to detail. Fans of stick-to-your-ribs diner fare will dig this café for not only its food but also its decor, which features original fixtures and historical photos of the market's earliest days.

MAP 2: 1995 W. 25th St., 216/579-6800, www.westsidemarketcafe.com; 7am-5pm Mon. and Wed., 7am-2pm Tues. and Thurs., 7am-6pm Fri.-Sat., 8am-4pm Sun.

PUB GRUB
South Side $$

Besides having the largest patio in Tremont, South Side has a great bar scene. Appealing comfort food, a rambunctious atmosphere, and friendly bartenders keep this joint jumping most hours of the day. The menu features fresh salads, tasty burgers and sandwiches, quality pastas, and some of the tastiest fried chicken and

waffles in town. The South Side can get crowded during important televised sporting events, so get to the bar early to secure a spot. The weekend brunch is always a hit.

MAP 2: 2207 W. 11th St., 216/937-2288, www.southsidecleveland.com; 11am-2am Mon.-Fri., 11:30am-2am Sat., 10:30am-2am Sun.

Tremont Taphouse $$

As one of Cleveland's first true gastropubs, the Taphouse has been dispensing high-caliber pub grub and killer craft beer since 2007. Though others have followed, this off-the-beaten-path tavern still shows how it's done thanks to flavorful small plates, killer burgers, great pizza, and chef-driven entrées. But it's the exceptional beer list that keeps hopheads and neighborhood residents frequent flyers. Check out the great patio on warm days.

MAP 2: 2572 Scranton Rd., 216/298-4451, www.tremonttaphouse.com; 4pm-close Mon.-Fri., 11am-close Sat., 10am-close Sun.

DELIS
Larder Delicatessen $

At its heart, Larder is a Jewish deli, with matzo ball soup, thick pastrami sandwiches, and flaky fruit-filled rugelach. But there's a lot more going on here than that. Chef-owner Jeremy Umansky utilizes techniques like *koji* (a Japanese mold) curing, foraging for wild edibles, cold and hot smoking, and fermentation and pickling

FOODIE HEAVEN: BEST OF THE WEST SIDE MARKET

The West Side Market is a big, bustling bazaar, with more than 80 indoor food stands and dozens more next door in the produce annex. Here's a taste of what's inside.

- Many shoppers begin or end their visit with a quick and tasty meal. The best options include **Maha's Falafel** for freshly fried falafel sandwiches, **Kim Se** for prepared Thai and Cambodian dishes, **Crepes DeLuxe** for amazing savory crepes filled with fresh ingredients, or **Frank's Bratwurst** for, you guessed it, bratwurst sandwiches (ask for horseradish).

- Diet-shattering baked goods are around every turn. For artisan-style European bread, hit **Mediterra Bakehouse.** If your tooth leans more sweet than savory, wander over to **Cake Royale,** where the luscious pastries are made from scratch. Over at **Campbell's Popcorn,** the offerings include cotton candy, chocolate-covered pretzels, and amazing cheesy popcorn.

- **Ohio City Pasta** supplies dozens of upscale restaurants with fresh pasta, ravioli, and gnocchi. At the ever-popular **Pierogi Palace,** dozens of varieties of stuffed Polish dumplings are sold frozen to go. Hit **Orale! Mexican Cuisine** for empanadas, corn husk-wrapped tamales, freshly fried chips, and the best salsas in town.

- Adventurous home cooks shop at **Urban Herbs** and **Narrin's Spice** to track down hard-to-find herbs, spices, grains, and chiles. Narrin's also stocks a wide assortment of hot sauces. And if **Mediterranean Imported Foods** doesn't carry the ingredient you're looking for, it probably doesn't exist. Tucked into the corner of the market, this jam-packed Italian grocery offers a dizzying array of high-quality cheeses, olives, salamis, dried fruit, and nuts.

- To purchase old-world Hungarian-style meats, like double-smoked bacon, rice sausage, and cottage ham, stroll over to **Dohar Meats. Old Country Sausage** sells authentic German favorites like liverwurst and Black Forest salamis. And if you're in the market for sparkling fresh seafood, seafood salads, and smoked fish, head to **Kate's Fish.**

to produce an ever-shifting roster of seasonal plates. On special might be a house-smoked whitefish salad sandwich, wild-cherry blintzes, or a mushroom "pastrami" sandwich. The in-house pastry chef loads up the counter with chocolate-swirled babka, dark and chewy chocolate chip cookies, and flaky potato knishes. Half the fun is in the setting, a historic firehouse in Ohio City.

MAP 2: 1455 W. 29th St., 216/912-8203, http://larderdb.com; 10am-7pm Tues.-Sat., 10am-2pm Sun.

Nate's Deli $

A local institution, Nate's is reflective of Cleveland's rich ethnic diversity and the city's love for all things delicious. Possessing a sort of split personality, this modest café serves traditional deli-style breakfast and lunch items alongside Middle Eastern specialties. This means that while diners at one table are enjoying pastrami on rye and char-grilled burgers, their neighbors are cooing over a platter of hummus, tabbouleh, and stuffed grape leaves. On Saturdays this deli buzzes with shoppers fueling up for their trip to the nearby West Side Market.

MAP 2: 1923 W. 25th St., 216/696-7529, www.natesohiocity.com; 10am-5pm Mon.-Fri., 10am-4pm Sat.

COFFEE
Civilization $

This European-style coffeehouse is right on Lincoln Park and features a generous sidewalk patio for enjoying a post-dinner espresso. The beans are locally roasted by the owner, who also runs the City Roast Coffee stand at the West Side Market. The rustic 1881 storefront feels like a general store from days gone by. The fare is light and simple, such as pastries, soups, and sandwiches.

MAP 2: 2366 W. 11th St., 216/621-3838, www.cafecivilization.com; 7am-7pm Mon.-Thurs., 7am-11pm Fri.-Sat., 8am-6pm Sun.

Duck-Rabbit Coffee $

Located in a patch of town between Ohio City and Tremont known as Duck Island, this exceptional craft roastery draws coffee purists from near and far. The owner directly sources his beans from farmers in Sumatra, Rwanda, Ethiopia, and Colombia, paying above Fair Trade minimums. Thanks to skilled baristas, those expertly roasted beans become some of Cleveland's finest cups of java.

MAP 2: 2135 Columbus Rd., no phone, www.duckrabbitcoffee.com; 7am-5pm daily

Rising Star Coffee Roasters $

Since setting up shop in a former Ohio City firehouse, Rising Star Coffee has quickly become the bean of choice at numerous coffee shops, restaurants, and bakeries. It's also stop number one for coffee geeks thanks to quality beans, obsessive technique, and proper equipment. Pour-over, AeroPress, and vacuum pot brewers turn out the city's best espressos, cappuccinos, lattes, and macchiatos. House-roasted beans are sold by the pound.

MAP 2: 1455 W. 29th St., 216/273-3573, www.risingstarcoffee.com; 6am-6pm Mon.-Thurs., 6am-8pm Fri.-Sat., 8am-6pm Sun.

DESSERT
Mason's Creamery $

Set inside a former walk-up ice cream stand, this delicious local upstart has developed a huge following thanks to expertly conceived creations that produce big smiles. The small-batch creamery uses great, often local, ingredients when crafting classic and seasonal flavors like sea salt caramel, Rising Star coffee, sweet potato pie, and vegan lemon ginger. On warm summer nights, this off-the-beaten-path sweets shop can feel like the center of town.

MAP 2: 4401 Bridge Ave., 216/762-1095, www.masonscreamery.com; 2pm-10pm Sun. and Wed.-Thurs., 2pm-11pm Fri.-Sat.

Mitchell's Homemade Ice Cream $

The granddaddy of local ice cream producers, Mitchell's has scoop shops all over town. But this Ohio City location is more than just another retail outlet (which it is): It's the company headquarters, production facility, and year-round neighborhood destination for sweets lovers. Made using grass-fed milk and cream, along with seasonal fruits, blends like chocolate peanut butter cup, Geauga maple walnut, and strawberry rhubarb crisp have hungry folks lined up out the front door. Sign up online for a **tasting tour** ($3.75) that winds customers through a gallery space with views of the kitchen where ice cream is being made. Tours include free samples and a Free Scoop Certificate to use anytime.

MAP 2: 867 W. 25th St., 216/861-2799, www.mitchellshomemade.com; 11am-11pm daily

Detroit Shoreway and Edgewater

Map 3

NEW AMERICAN
Spice Kitchen & Bar $$$

Chef-owner Ben Bebenroth is widely regarded as one of the leading farm-to-table chefs in the region, going so far as to operate his own working farm just south of town. This elegant, unpretentious bistro prepares expertly crafted food that evolves with the seasons but always manages to hit the spot. While the dishes change with the calendar, diners can count on options built around local produce, pork, chicken, and beef and sustainable fish and seafood. The cheery, flower-trimmed space makes a lovely spot for weekend brunch.

MAP 3: 5800 Detroit Ave., 216/961-9637, www.spicekitchenandbar.com; 5pm-11pm Tues.-Sat.

MEDITERRANEAN
Astoria Market and Café $$

Astoria is one of those places that is active morning, noon, and night. A retail market sells gourmet Mediterranean foods like imported cheeses, Italian cured meats, and olives by the pound. The large bar is an ideal place to meet up with a friend over cocktails, glasses of wine, and a fully loaded meat and cheese platter. The animated dining room is where folks land for full meals of tender wine-poached octopus, veal and ricotta meatballs, pizzas, and grilled lamb chops. On the weekend, the brunches draw reliably enthusiastic crowds.

MAP 3: 5417 Detroit Ave., 216/266-0834, www.astoriacafemarket.com; 9am-9pm Tues.-Thurs., 9am-10pm Fri.-Sat., 10am-3pm Sun.

Luxe Kitchen & Lounge $$

With a wide range of small plates, shareable platters, and entrées, this super-cool Mediterranean restaurant satisfies just about every taste, mood, and budget. Starters include steamed mussels, spicy shrimp with grilled bread, and crispy crab cakes. For the main event there's pizza, fettuccine carbonara, seafood stew, or a burger and fries. The stylish lounge-like space is outfitted with a salvaged art deco bar, shabby-chic chandeliers, and a wine cellar built into an old bank vault. On nice evenings, everybody is likely out back on the patio.

MAP 3: 6605 Detroit Ave., 216/916-8732, www.luxecleveland.com; 5pm-10pm Mon.-Thurs., 5pm-midnight Fri., 10am-midnight Sat., 10am-9pm Sun.

Il Rione Pizzeria $

Il Rione might be "just a neighborhood pizza parlor," but it elevates the genre thanks to warm lighting, a stylishly weathered interior, and a killer playlist from the golden age of rock. While the menu is spare, the New York/New Jersey-style pizza exiting the open kitchen is something to behold, with the clam pie taking the cake. Diners can choose from a half dozen predesigned pies or can build their own from the crust up. Beer, wine, and cocktails round out the fun.

MAP 3: 1303 W. 65th St., 216/282-1451, www.ilrionepizzeria.com; 4pm-10pm Tues.-Thurs., 4pm-midnight Fri.-Sat.

PUB GRUB
Banter $

Banter introduced many a Clevelander to authentic and delicious poutine, that north-of-the-border treat of gravy-topped French fries dotted with cheese curds. This spare, contemporary bar offers a dozen different varieties, some straightforward, others topped with chicken paprikash or braised rabbit. The other half of the menu is devoted to handcrafted sausages that wind up in currywurst sandwiches, Polish Boys, or on sticks as dreamy corn dogs. This laidback neighborhood spot has a great draft beer and wine-by-the-glass selection and stocks many more for sale to go at retail.

MAP 3: 7320 Detroit Ave., 216/801-0305, www.bantercleveland.com; 11am-midnight Mon.-Thurs., 11am-1am Fri.-Sat., noon-8pm Sun.

Happy Dog $

The legendary Cleveland tavern's most impressive physical feature is its august wooden bar, a 45-stool behemoth that commands a full third of the room. Original wood-fronted coolers chill the beverages; walls are wrapped in genuine wood paneling; weathered linoleum blankets the floor. The menu

here is simple, yet wild. Hot dogs come with your choice of 50 toppings, which are checked off on a paper chit. Select an unlimited number of fresh veggies, spicy pickles, savory sauces, creamy cheeses, and wild cards like Fruit Loops and SpaghettiOs. Frequent events like trivia night, live music, and serious discussions on current global affairs keep this place active.

MAP 3: 5801 Detroit Ave., 216/651-9474, www.happydogcleveland.com; 4pm-close Mon.-Wed., 11am-close Thurs.-Sun.

BREAKFAST AND BRUNCH
✪ Brewnuts $

Brewnuts is not your average corner donut shop. It's more like a donut bar, where mornings see busy commuters grabbing coffee and a donut before rushing off to work. Later in the day, those donuts are enjoyed on-site at the bar or communal tables alongside a frosty draft beer. Did I mention that the donuts are made with beer? Adoring fans gobble up creations like maple-bacon bourbon ale, coffee porter with toffee, and the classic glazed made with Great Lakes Dortmunder. On a busy day, the shop flies through thousands of donuts, each and every one rolled, cut, fried, and glazed by a human.

MAP 3: 6501 Detroit Ave., 216/600-9579, www.brewnutscleveland.com; from 6:30am until sold out Tues.-Thurs., 6:30am-10pm Fri., 8am-11pm Sat., 8am-3pm Sun.

Frank's Falafel $

Don't expect a fancy meal at Frank's. But do expect wholesome, affordable breakfasts that cross cultural boundaries. Like the name suggests, this is a Middle Eastern deli, so diners can look forward to hearty gyro skillets loaded with eggs, hash browns, and veggies.

But the mile-long menu also has spots for classic American diner fare, like omelets, French toast, pancakes, and biscuits and gravy. For lunch, there are salads, gyros, burgers, and Mediterranean platters of hummus, shawarma, falafel, and grape leaves. Frank's has a parking lot, a rarity in this neighborhood.

MAP 3: 1823 W. 65th St., 216/631-3300; 7am-9pm Mon.-Sat., 8am-3pm Sun.

BAKERIES AND CAFÉS
Gypsy Beans & Bakery $

Situated in the heart of the Gordon Square Arts District, and serving as its unofficial community center, Gypsy Beans has earned its reputation as a bona fide "third place." Open from early morning until late in the evening, the attractive double storefront serves coffee drinks, freshly baked muffins and croissants, pasta salads, thick-crust pizza by the slice, and sandwiches. This is a great place to meet up before or after a show at Cleveland Public Theatre.

MAP 3: 6425 Detroit Ave., 216/939-9009, www.gypsybeans.com; 7am-9pm Mon.-Thurs., 7am-10pm Fri.-Sat., 8am-9pm Sun.

DESSERT
Sweet Moses Soda Fountain $

Grab a stool at the antique soda fountain and watch soda jerks create classic sundaes, floats, and malts using the shop's own homemade ice cream. Savor the aroma as the kitchen churns out batches of hot fudge, caramel sauce, baked goods, chocolates, and caramel corn. Then step over to the candy counter and take home more sweet memories with a box of handmade confections and treats. If this throwback sounds like a candy-covered dream, that's because it is.

MAP 3: 6800 Detroit Ave., 216/651-2202, www.sweetmosestreats.com; noon-11pm Sun.-Thurs., noon-midnight Fri.-Sat.

University Circle and Little Italy

Map 4

MEDITERRANEAN
L'Albatros $$$

Situated in a tastefully modernized 19th-century carriage house, L'Albatros is a contemporary French brasserie with style to spare. Set against this sleek backdrop is a menu brimming with bistro classics like onion soup gratinée, garlicky escargot, pork terrine, and cassoulet. For those who prefer less far-flung fare, there are pasta, fish, and poultry dishes that satisfy just as heartily. Popular with the pre-theater and post-orchestra set, the charming restaurant features items specifically selected for rapid enjoyment. In warm weather, in-the-know folks flock to this restaurant's idyllic tree-shaded patio for food and drink.

MAP 4: 11401 Bellflower Rd., 216/791-7880, www.albatrosbrasserie. com; 11:30am-11pm Mon.-Wed., 11:30am-midnight Thurs.-Sat., 3pm-8pm Sun.

La Dolce Vita $$

On pleasant days and nights, the prime sidewalk space surrounding this popular Little Italy restaurant overflows with diners. The attitude is festive and easygoing; the food is flavorful and unfussy. Consistently satisfying salads, pizzas, pastas, and Italian classics are dished up in large portions. Try the clams Tarantino, a pasta dish with clams and fresh zucchini, or the veal Pavarotti, made with portobello mushrooms and marsala. Visit on a Monday night and you'll enjoy live opera with your pizza.

MAP 4: 12112 Mayfield Rd., 216/721-8156, www.ladolcevitamurrayhill.com; 5pm-10pm Mon.-Thurs., noon-11pm Fri.-Sat., 1pm-10pm Sun.

Nora $$

Nora upends the Little Italy stereotype of the spag-and-ball joint by applying classic French technique to Italian ingredients to come up with dishes that are in sync with the season, if not the surrounding restaurants. While you won't be dabbing red sauce off your shirt, you will be awash in the old-world charm that the neighborhood is known for. Beneath a pressed-tin ceiling, behind a wall of windows, and tucked into an intimate dining room, guests dig into creamy burrata cheese, wild-mushroom-stuffed agnolotti, and fettuccine carbonara topped with crispy matchstick potatoes and a buttery poached egg.

MAP 4: 2181 Murray Hill Rd., 216/231-5977, www.noracleveland.com; 5pm-close Tues.-Sat.

BAKERIES AND CAFÉS
Corbo's Bakery $

This long-standing Little Italy bakery is known far and wide as the source for delectable Italian sweets, treats, and classic desserts. If there is an Italian wedding happening within 100 miles

of the shop, chances are good the bride and groom will be slicing into a Corbo's *cassata* cake. Likewise, if you arrive at any Italian-American household bearing a box filled with this bakery's famous cannoli, you will forever be in their good graces.

MAP 4: 12210 Mayfield Rd., 216/421-8181, www.corbosbakery.net; 8am-9pm Tues.-Thurs. and Sun., 8am-11pm Fri.-Sat., 8am-8pm Sun.

Presti's Bakery & Café $

This airy corner café in Little Italy is busy morning, noon, and night thanks to a full range of necessities, delicacies, and delights. Espresso and cappuccino attract the early-morning set, who on nice days take their mugs outside to enjoy alongside the newspaper. At lunch, students from nearby college campuses pop in for rectangular slices of Sicilian pizza, sandwiches, and scoops of gelato. After work, folks drop by to pick up tidy white boxes laden with buttery cookies, flaky pastries, and killer cannoli.

MAP 4: 12101 Mayfield Rd., 216/421-3060, www.prestisbakery.com; 6am-7pm Mon., 6am-9pm Tues.-Thurs., 6am-10pm Fri.-Sat., 6am-4pm Sun.

TEA
Algebra Tea House $

As much an art-filled gallery as it is a teahouse, Algebra is a welcoming bohemian hangout in Little Italy. This quirky den is outfitted with original furniture, wall hangings, and paintings. The floor is a one-of-a-kind mosaic; the ceiling is hand-painted; the cups and saucers are the handiwork of artist-owner Ayman. Tea fans will find dozens of superior-quality flavors, including house blends. Light eats run mainly to salads, sandwiches,

Lebanese dishes, and desserts. Try the hummus and pita platter or the toasted pita sandwich with cheese and veggies. On weekends, the affordable breakfast items are popular with nearby students.

MAP 4: 2136 Murray Hill Rd., 216/421-9007, www.algebrateahouse.com; 9am-11pm daily

Cleveland Heights and Shaker Heights

Map 5

NEW AMERICAN

Fire Food & Drink $$$

Relying almost exclusively on local, seasonal, and sustainable ingredients, popular chef Doug Katz is ahead of the curve when it comes to "slow food." Located at Shaker Square, just steps from the largest farmers market in the region, this snazzy bistro serves simply prepared and boldly flavored American fare. Sit at the poured-concrete bar and enjoy a glass of wine and a clay-oven pizza. Or sit in the industrial-chic dining room and tuck into crispy chicken livers, tandoor-roasted pork chops, or diver scallops with Ohio sweet corn. Fire has an incredible Sunday brunch and boasts an expansive sidewalk patio overlooking the square.

MAP 5: 13220 Shaker Sq., 216/921-3473, www.firefoodanddrink.com; 5pm-10pm Tues.-Thurs., 5pm-11pm Fri., 9:30am-2:30pm and 5pm-11pm Sat., 9:30am-2:30pm and 5pm-10pm Sun.

Felice Urban Café $$

When it comes to curb appeal, Felice pretty much has a lock on the competition. Set in a renovated Craftsman-style home, this charming eatery is as cozy as they come. Arriving here for dinner feels more like dropping in on a friend than entering a public restaurant. Inside, diners discover original leaded-glass windows, warm wooden fixtures, and a historical hearth. The eclectic menu features Mediterranean-inspired treats like grilled baby octopus, chorizo-spiked mussels, lamb sliders, and skirt steak with chimichurri. An intimate bar and dining room can be found on the second level. Out back, you'll find a beautiful patio, carriage-house bar, and fire pit.

MAP 5: 12502 Larchmere Blvd., 216/791-0918, www.feliceurbancafe.com; 5pm-10pm Tues.-Thurs., 5pm-midnight Fri.-Sat., 10:30am-2:30pm Sun.

MEDITERRANEAN

Edwins $$

Edwins is a restaurant with a purpose loftier than simply feeding guests. Employees at this French-themed bistro are formerly incarcerated citizens, who are accepted into a six-month program during which they learn the ins and outs of working in a fine-dining restaurant. For their part, guests enjoy exceptional fare like frog legs in garlic butter, snails in fennel cream sauce, and horseradish-crusted salmon, all dished up in an elegant but relaxed environment. The best cheese cart in town is parked in this dining room.

MAP 5: 13101 Shaker Sq., 216/921-3333, www.edwinsrestaurant.org; 4pm-10pm Mon.-Wed., 4pm-11:30pm Thurs.-Sat.

Vero Bistro $$

Boasting one of the few wood-burning ovens in this part of town, Vero turns out the most authentic Neapolitan-style pizza in Cleveland. Owner Marc-Aurele Buholzer is obsessive when it comes to his dough—and there's only so much of it to go around at this modestly proportioned pizza bistro. An airy, chewy outer crust blistered with char gives way to a thin, crisp inner crust supporting a few seasonal ingredients. Don't try ordering any pies to go; these are meant to be enjoyed fresh from the oven on-site. Those pies are paired with a few starters, sides, beer, and wine.

MAP 5: 12421 Cedar Rd., 216/229-8383, www.verocleveland.com; from 5pm until dough runs out Tues.-Sat.

BAKERIES AND CAFÉS

Luna Bakery & Cafe $

This bustling bakery and café in the Cedar-Fairmount District is crisp, cosmopolitan, and user-friendly. Equal parts bakery and café, the shop specializes in sweets of every size, color, and seductiveness. Cupcakes, scones, sugar cookies, cakes, brownies, croissants, and pastel-hued macarons are just some of the offerings. On the savory side of things are made-to-order crepes, salads, breakfast sandwiches, and crispy panini. Seating is available inside and out.

MAP 5: 2482 Fairmount Blvd., 216/231-8585, www.lunabakerycafe.com; 7am-7pm Mon.-Fri., 8am-5pm Sat.-Sun.

On the Rise $

Artisan baker Adam Gidlow and his team craft everything by hand the old-fashioned European way, and many restaurants choose him as their supplier. Neighbors come for coffee, buttery scones, gooey brownies, flaky croissants, dense and chewy focaccia, and the best French baguette in Cleveland. At lunch, a line forms out the door for made-to-order sandwiches like grass-fed roast beef, smoked brisket, and Vietnamese *banh mi* sandwiches, all built atop that great bread. There is limited seating inside, which extends outdoors on nice days.

MAP 5: 3471 Fairmount Blvd., 216/320-9923, www.ontheriseartisanbreads.com; 7am-6pm Tues.-Fri., 8am-5pm Sat., 8am-2pm Sun.

Stone Oven $

This fine Cleveland Heights bake-shop is one of the most popular spots on Lee Road for a quick, casual lunch or early dinner. This bright, contemporary café specializes in soups made daily, fresh salads, pizza by the slice, and gourmet sandwiches. Built atop wonderful house-baked bread, the sandwiches include dreamy egg salad and chive, chicken curry salad, and roast beef and Swiss with horseradish mayo. Pastries, cookies, and cakes are on hand for dessert. Outdoor dining is available behind the restaurant.

MAP 5: 2267 Lee Rd., 216/932-3003, www.stone-oven.com; 7am-8pm Mon.-Fri., 8am-8pm Sat., 8:30am-7pm Sun.

✪ Tommy's $

What started in the 1970s as a hippie-run soda fountain has become the anchor of Coventry Village. A few moves and iterations later, this bustling family-friendly café now commands a large and sunny space in the middle of the action. A lengthy menu features an amazing range of vegan, vegetarian, and meaty options, many of which are named after the owner's friends and longtime customers. Soups are made from scratch, an entire page is devoted to fresh and inventive salads, meat and spinach pies are a house specialty, falafel sandwiches come with fillings too numerous to list, and the hand-dipped milk shakes are the best in the city.

MAP 5: 1824 Coventry Rd., 216/321-7757, www.tommyscoventry.com; 9am-9pm Sun.-Thurs., 9am-10pm Fri., 7:30am-10pm Sat.

BREAKFAST AND BRUNCH
Big Al's Diner $

Greasy spoon? Neighborhood diner? Working-class lunch spot? Whatever you call it, Al's is a well-trafficked East Side institution. Get here before church lets out on weekends and you'll score one of the coveted booths, which offer room enough for both a newspaper and a plate of corned-beef hash.

On the border of Cleveland and Shaker Heights, this popular diner is popular with progressive politicians, hungover hipsters, and oil-stained auto mechanics. The draws are monster portions of hearty home-style grub, like biscuits and gravy, blueberry pancakes, three-egg omelets, and the aforementioned corned-beef hash. Pay at the counter when you're done.

MAP 5: 12600 Larchmere Blvd., 216/791-8550; 6:30am-2:30pm Mon.-Sat., 7am-2:30pm Sun.

Inn on Coventry $

This homey café is *the* place to go on Coventry Road for hearty home-cooked breakfast fare. Ricotta pancakes, overstuffed omelets, and delish French toast are just a few of the reasons this place gets slammed most weekend mornings. The intimate place fills up fast, and there is often a wait for a table, so once served and sated,

On the Rise

CLEVELAND'S GLOBAL SMORGASBORD

Cleveland's melting pot past and present means that fans of ethnic food have their pick of delicious, adventurous delights. There are dozens of mom-and-pop shops dishing up authentic foods from the homeland, just waiting to be discovered. Cleveland has restaurants devoted to Italian, Greek, German, Irish, Lebanese, Turkish, Hungarian, Slovenian, Ethiopian, Indian, Mexican, Central American, and Jewish foods, not to mention Chinese, Vietnamese, Thai, Korean and Japanese. Some neighborhoods, like Little Italy and Asiatown, are densely populated with restaurants serving a specific cuisine.

Consider beginning with something you might never have tried before, like Ethiopian food at **Empress Taytu** (6125 St. Clair Ave., 216/391-9400, www.empresstayturestaurantcleveland.com). Meals are served family-style at traditional basket tables, and silverware is replaced with *injera*, a spongy flatbread.

Ever tried Turkish food? Visit **Anatolia Café** (2270 Lee Rd., 216/321-4400, www.anatoliacafe.com) in Cleveland Heights to see how good *döner* and *iskender* kebabs are. For amazing Middle Eastern food, pencil in a trip to **Nate's Deli** (1923 W. 25th St., 216/696-7529, www.natesohiocity.com) in Ohio City or the fast-casual **Zaytoon Lebanese Kitchen** (1150 Huron Rd., 216/795-5000, www.websitezaytoonlebanesekitchen.com) downtown.

There might be no more comforting comfort food than Polish stuffed cabbage, and there may be no finer version than the one served at **Sokolowski's University Inn** (1201 University Rd., 216/771-9236, www.sokolowskis.com). Folks come here not just for the rib-sticking fare but also for the old-school cafeteria setup and the cozy lodge-like setting. The Hungarian food at **Balaton Restaurant** (13133 Shaker Sq., 216/921-9691, www.balaton-restaurant.com) includes paprikash, goulash, and roast duck, but one out of four diners orders the Wiener schnitzel. These platter-size cutlets are pounded thin,

a diner might feel rushed to move on. But take your time and enjoy creative wholesome and fresh breakfast fare before exploring the shops of Coventry.

MAP 5: 2785 Euclid Heights Blvd., 216/371-1811, www.innoncoventry.com; 7am-1:30pm Mon.-Thurs., 7am-8:30pm Fri., 8am-1:30pm Sat.-Sun.

Lakewood   Map 6

NEW AMERICAN
Pier W $$$

Despite being situated on the shores of a Great Lake, Cleveland is woefully underserved when it comes to lakeside restaurants. But this sparkling Lakewood gem helps alleviate that deficiency. Perched high above the waterline, the restaurant offers stunning views of the lake and Cleveland skyline—and a tiered dining room means that every diner enjoys the vista. Unlike most restaurants with a view, this one delivers stellar food in the form of contemporary seafood dishes built around fin fish, mussels, clams, scallops, shrimp, and lobster. Winners include a showy breaded, and fried, and served with spaetzle and applesauce. For delectable Hungarian pastries, visit the Ohio City-based **Farkas Pastry Shoppe** (2700 Lorain Ave., 216/281-6200, www.farkaspastries.com) for world-famous Dobos torte, buttery hazelnut Linzer torte, and layered chocolate napoleons.

If you've never tried a Salvadorian *pupusa* head straight to **Pupuseria La Bendicion** (3685 W. 105th St., 216/688-0338). At this casual eatery, thick corn tortillas are filled with ingredients like spicy Mexican-style chorizo and cheese and griddled until hot and crisp. For Guatemalan food, go directly to **El Rinconcito Chapin** (3330 Broadview Rd., 216/795-5776) for cheesy *pupusas,* crispy *dobladitas* (stuffed bread), and *garnachas* (corn cakes topped with savory shredded beef, crisp raw onion, mellow salsa, and salty cheese). For some savory Puerto Rican food, hit **Rincón Criollo** (6504 Detroit Ave., 216/939-0992, www.rinconcriollocle.com) in Detroit Shoreway for crisp *empanadillas* (fried dough stuffed with meat), hot pressed Cubano sandwiches, and savory beef stew with *mofongo* (mashed fried plantains).

Lakewood is where you'll find the fantastic Latin grocery called **La Plaza Supermarket** (13609 Lakewood Heights Blvd., 216/476-8000, www.laplazataqueria.com). In addition to the great selection of produce, meats, cheeses, chiles, tortillas, and crunchy chicharróns, this unassuming place prepares the best tacos in the city. Meats like chorizo, al pastor, carne asada, and tongue are ladled onto a pair of warm corn tortillas. Diners dress them up with salsa and other fresh garnishes.

Indian-food lovers come in one of two categories: vegetarian or omnivore. **Tandul** (2505 Professor Ave., 216/860-4530, www.tandulintremont.com) in Tremont takes care of both thanks to a sprawling menu of northern and southern favorites dished up in a comfortable setting. For some of the most authentic, spicy, and delicious southern Indian food, make the trip east to Woodmere, where **Taste of Kerala** (3429 W. Brainard Rd., 216/450-1711, www.tasteofkeralam.com) prepares puffy *idli* (rice cakes) with *sambar* (stew), chickpea curry, and a goat biryani that is absolutely electric with spice.

Seafood Tower, oysters Rockefeller, and the rightly famous lobster bisque and bouillabaisse.

MAP 6: 12700 Lake Ave., 216/228-2250, www.pierw.com; 11:30am-2:30pm and 5pm-10pm Mon.-Fri., 5pm-11pm Sat., 9:30am-2:30pm and 5pm-9pm Sun.

Salt $$

Since the dawn of time, the conventional wisdom in these parts has been that meat-and-potato diners would never go for small plates. At this whip-smart Lakewood tapas restaurant, chef Jill Vedaa continues to upend that old saw by composing exceptional dishes that focus on a single theme. In place of a meat-and-three, diners zero in on carrots three ways, or earthy beets blasted with sparkle, or a savory lamb ragu over a few supple gnocchi. Mix

and match your way to the perfect meal, while pairing course after course with the perfect wine or cocktail.

MAP 6: 17625 Detroit Ave., 216/221-4866, www.saltcleveland.com; 5pm-10pm Mon. and Wed.-Thurs., 5pm-11:30pm Fri.-Sat., 4pm-9pm Sun.

ASIAN
Thai Thai $

It can be a challenge to stand out in the crowded Thai restaurant market. But this small, perennially busy family-run eatery does just that by stripping the genre down to its bare essentials. In place of a pages-long menu filled with dozens of dishes, this spot works from a tidy single sheet of addictive street foods and greatest hits. On the lineup are chubby grilled sausages, shredded green papaya salad, duck noodle soup, coconut-scented curries, and incendiary *pad krapow* (basil chicken). There are just 15 seats in the diminutive space, and a handful of those are simply stools at a wall-facing counter.

MAP 6: 13735 Madison Ave., 216/961-9655; 11:30am-9pm Mon. and Wed., 11:30am-10pm Thurs.-Sat., 4:30pm-9pm Sun.

LATIN
Barroco Grill $$

This father-and-son Colombian restaurant grew from a 12-seat café dispensing little more than arepas to a multi-unit chain offering a full menu of pan-Latin dishes. This original location now seats about 80 (150 when you add the patio), but the crowd is often dancing to live music, so it's difficult to count. In the colossal appetizer platter *tostadas con todo,* thin, crisp plantains are paired with guacamole, shredded beef, chili beans, and chicharrones. Latin classics like *ropa vieja* (braised beef with white rice, black beans, and plantains), carne asada, and *bandeja paisa* (braised beef, chorizo, red beans, chicharróns, plantains, and a fried egg) are delicious appetite slayers. Barroco still offers those amazing arepa sandwiches—thick corn tortillas filled with chorizo, steak, or pork—but now also boasts a full bar to go with them.

MAP 6: 12906 Madison Ave., 216/221-8127, www.barrocogrill.com; 11am-close daily

PUB GRUB
Buckeye Beer Engine $$

When you serve some of the best burgers and craft beer in the county, people will beat a path to your door. That's been the case since 2007 at this beloved neighborhood pub. Hopheads will find dozens of spectacular and hard-to-find drafts, including cask-conditioned real ales. While those beers come and go, the menu of hearty American pub grub does not. The menu is filled with 20 different half-pound burgers topped with everything from pulled pork or smoked bacon to fried eggs. Start with an order of smoky wings or deep-fried jalapeño slices.

MAP 6: 15315 Madison Ave., 216/226-2337, www.buckeyebeerengine.com; 11am-2:30am daily

Deagan's Kitchen & Bar $$

This lively establishment is rightly billed as a gastropub, where a menu of approachable chef-driven comfort foods is matched with a top-notch craft beer list. The hip tavern setting, with exposed brick and reclaimed woods, is an agreeable place to meet up with friends over platters of gravy-topped tots, buttermilk fried chicken skin, fried oysters, and deviled eggs. Move on to meaty mains like fried chicken and waffles, tender baby back ribs, and creamy mac-and-cheese. If it's happy hour and you happen to be close by, get there.

MAP 6: 14810 Detroit Ave., 216/767-5775, www.deagans.com; 11am-10pm Tues.-Fri., 10am-10pm Sat., 10am-9pm Sun.

CASUAL AMERICAN
Melt Bar & Grilled $$

In the relatively brief period since this restaurant opened in 2006, the concept has exploded into a regional chain of more than a dozen locations. Even this original spot has grown, from a small corner bar to a multi-storefront destination. What's all the fuss about? Overstuffed grilled cheese sandwiches, with nearly three dozen creative versions on the menu. The Wake

& Bacon is loaded with bacon, egg, and cheese; the Parmageddon is an intimidating stack of potato pierogies, kraut, onions, and cheese; and the Lake Erie Monster nets a diner deep-fried walleye, jalapeño tartar sauce, and—you guessed it—*cheese!*

MAP 6: 14718 Detroit Ave., 216/226-3699, www.meltbarandgrilled.com; 11am-10pm Sun.-Thurs., 11am-11pm Fri.-Sat.

Proper Pig Smokehouse $$

With a name like Proper Pig Smokehouse, you might expect a place to dish up some proper barbecue. No surprises here, just a steady smoke-scented stream of Texas-style barbecue served up in a colorful, casual eatery. Here, the meat is the star of the show, with beef brisket, St. Louis pork ribs, pulled pork, and Texas hot links drawing consistent and enthusiastic crowds. You can buy those delectable meats by the pound or as the filling to a handful of jaw-dropping sandwiches. There are a handful of cold beers available to wash it all down with.

MAP 6: 17100 Detroit Ave., 440/665-3768, www.properpigsmokehouse.com; 4pm-9pm Mon.-Wed., 11:30am-9pm Thurs.-Sat., 11:30am-7pm Sun.

BAKERIES AND CAFÉS

Blackbird Baking Company $

Nothing lifts a neighborhood like a great bakery. And for the residents of Lakewood, Blackbird does just that. Every effort was made to convert a shabby building into a sleek metropolitan bakery. The open design gives customers views of the bakeshop, including its flour-dusted work tables and massive deck ovens. Everything is made from scratch daily and displayed on counters and baker's racks. Bread fans will crow about Blackbird's baguettes, batards, focaccia, and ciabatta. Sweets fans will head straight for

Melt Bar & Grilled

the pecan sticky buns, cherry scones, apricot croissants, and dreamy chocolate chip cookies. Blackbird offers coffee, espresso, and tea as well.

MAP 6: 1391 Sloane Ave., 216/712-6599, www.blackbirdbaking.com; 6am-6pm Mon.-Fri., 7am-5pm Sat.-Sun.

Borderline Café $

You know those small, slightly cramped, always busy neighborhood diners with a line out the door? That's Borderline. What motivates those groggy folks to stand in line is pitch-perfect breakfast and brunch fare delivered by friendly, efficient staffers. The grub here has a Southern and Tex-Mex edge, with killer huevos rancheros, chorizo-stuffed breakfast burritos, and Southwestern-style omelets. American standards like pancakes, French toast, and scrambled eggs are also on the roster. This joint is cash-only.

MAP 6: 18510 Detroit Ave., 216/529-1949, www.borderlinelakewood.com; 7am-1pm Wed.-Sun.

The Root Cafe $

This warm and woodsy corner café has blossomed over the past decade or so from standard-issue coffeehouse to essential neighborhood asset. They still serve superbly brewed teas and locally roasted coffees, but also prepare a lengthy roster of healthy foods that appeal to a broad swatch of eaters. Those in search of raw, vegan, vegetarian, and gluten-free foods have their pick from a selection of delicious soups and salads, veggie-filled wraps and sandwiches, pizzas and calzones, and even house-baked pastries. Get there any day before 11am to enjoy an entire menu devoted to egg sandwiches.

MAP 6: 15118 Detroit Ave., 216/226-4401, www.theroot-cafe.com; 6:30am-9pm Mon.-Fri., 7am-9pm Sat., 8am-9pm Sun.

DESSERT
Malley's Chocolates $

The Malley family has been making and selling fine chocolates in and around Cleveland since 1935. At this old-fashioned ice-cream parlor, guests can sit at a real soda fountain and splurge on amazing cones, shakes, and sundaes. This being a chocolate company, anything with hot fudge pretty much rules the roost. Kids just love the decor, a Pepto-pink playground reminiscent of Grandma's kitchen. The candy counter is stocked with unique bars, holiday sweets, chocolate-covered cookies, dark chocolate-covered marshmallow, pecan-and-caramel clusters called Billy Bobs, and many others. Mr. Malley has Willy Wonka beat.

MAP 6: 14822 Madison Ave., 216/529-6262, www.malleys.com; 10am-11pm Mon.-Sat., noon-10pm Sun.

Rosso Gelato $

You don't have to explain the virtues of gelato to its countless fans, who prefer the brighter flavors and silkier textures over its dairy sibling, ice cream. At this crisply tailored, Ferrari red-trimmed sweets shop, house-made gelato stars Italian ingredients like chocolate, almonds, pistachios, and hazelnut. Fruity and refreshing *sorbettos* burst with the essence of just-picked strawberry or summery lemon.

MAP 6: 19056 Old Detroit Rd., 216/712-7764, www.rossogelato.com; noon-9pm Mon.-Thurs., noon-10pm Fri.-Sat., 2pm-9pm Sun.

NIGHTLIFE

Cleveland hasn't earned a reputation as one of the coolest places to visit by being a snooze. The city has more than its share of bars, cocktail lounges, breweries, and live-music venues.

Since 1952, when Cleveland hosted the Moondog Coronation Ball, considered the world's first rock concert, this city has been an important stop for emerging artists. Bands like Pere Ubu, Devo, the Dead Boys, Nine Inch Nails, Machine Gun Kelly, and Cloud Nothings all got their start here, while many who originated elsewhere rose to fame thanks to airtime and sold-out performances here. Countless venues throughout town beckon fans with an endless calendar of live jazz, rock, punk, folk, blues, metal, and alt-country lineups.

Noble Beast Brewing Co.

Cleveland is in the midst of a brewery boom, with no fewer than 35 new, old, and middle-aged producers located within 25 miles of downtown. Craft beer lovers can sample the suds at a garage-style nano brewery on up to a 100,000-square-foot mega-maker, with no shortage of options in between.

"Fun" means different things to different people, which has given rise to the so-called "anti-bar." A wave of action-packed entertainment spots offer good, clean fun in the form of classic arcade games, board games, bocce, shuffleboard, duckpin bowling, or singing the night away in a karaoke parlor.

Whatever sort of fun you're after, it's likely right around the bend waiting for you.

HIGHLIGHTS

✪ **BEST SMALL BREWERY:** When it comes to craft breweries, there is no shortage of great options, but **Noble Beast Brewing Co.** seems to best represent the latest batch. This garage-style brewery on the edge of downtown scores major points for setting, suds, and snacks (page 74).

✪ **DRINK A COLD ONE IN CLEVELAND'S OLDEST BAR:** Since 1895, the **Harbor Inn** has been a refuge for all sorts of interesting characters, from dockworkers and innkeepers to judges and scribes. These days, it's a delightfully anachronistic watering hole in an increasingly gentrified landscape (page 74).

✪ **BEST PLACE TO SING IN STYLE:** Most karaoke nights come courtesy the corner bar, but **Galaxy KTV** is the Rolls Royce of the genre thanks to glitzy private rooms, high-tech consoles, and push-button service (page 75).

✪ **BEST COMEDY CLUB:** Nick Kostis is a brilliant judge of up-and-coming comedic talent, and his club, **Hilarities 4th Street Theater,** is the place to catch it. This upscale 425-seat comedy club attracts the very best touring comics, and the theater is as nice as they come (page 76).

✪ **BEST OLD-SCHOOL ENTERTAINMENT:** Sure, shuffleboard is what cruisers do when it's raining on the lido deck, but **Forest City Shuffleboard** is a blast thanks to top-notch indoor courts, a full bar, and a retro-themed space that conjures memories of the high school gym (page 80).

✪ **WHERE TO TIKI THE NIGHT AWAY:** The aloha-shirted pros at **Porco Lounge and Tiki Room** will forever change your opinion of Polynesian cocktails. The Mai Tais, Zombies, and Pain Killers poured here are smile-inducing mugs of heaven served up in a magical setting (page 81).

✪ **WHERE CLOSE SHAVE MEETS COCKTAIL:** After rising from the barber chair, customers headed for **Quintana's Speakeasy** climb a few stairs, press a magic button, and watch as a wood-trimmed lounge reveals itself. Inside, exquisite Prohibition-era cocktails await (page 86).

✪ **MOST FUN WHILE STANDING:** There might be no better place for those of us who grew up on classic arcade games than **16-Bit Bar + Arcade.** This lively "barcade" is home to some 40 video games. Play Galaga, Asteroids, and Defender while sipping a Molly Ringwald cocktail (page 88).

✪ **BEST LIVE MUSIC VENUE:** Acts big and small play the **Beachland Ballroom,** a former Croatian social hall with both an intimate tavern and a larger ballroom. Both are used for concerts starring the best touring acts of the day (page 89).

LIVE MUSIC

Music Box Supper Club

This newer venue on the West Bank of the Flats tastefully fills the niche between small live-music bar and large auditorium. A contemporary take on the old-fashioned supper club, this complex has two separate concert halls, both of which offer seating and a full menu of food and drinks (available before and during shows). The upstairs hall has a capacity of about 350, while the lower level club accommodates 250, ideal fits for singer-songwriters, folk bands, and touring acts that prefer cozier environs.

MAP 1: 1148 Main Ave., 216/242-1250, www.musicboxcle.com; hours and cover vary depending on show

Hofbräuhaus Cleveland

Wilbert's Food & Music

Another club with deep Cleveland roots, Wilbert's has seen its share of superstars. Jeff Buckley, Ryan Adams, Buckwheat Zydeco, and Buddy Guy have all played either here or at the club's previous site. Performing in the modern, spacious, and comfortable club are mainly local and regional blues, jazz, reggae, and roots-rock acts. The venue's site right by Progressive Field makes it a convenient postgame stop for live music. Wilbert's serves food with a Mexican and Southern slant, with items such as quesadillas, burritos, and barbecue ribs.

MAP 1: 812 Huron Rd. E., 216/902-4663, www.wilbertsmusic.com; hours and cover vary depending on show

BREWERIES

Hofbräuhaus Cleveland

When it comes to capturing the spirit and flavor of the Munich original, Cleveland's own Hofbräuhaus does a more than commendable job. Liters of freshly brewed beer in hand, guests easily get swept up in the fun, standing on benches and singing along to the sounds of an oom-pah band. In addition to the gymnasium-size main hall, there's a historic back room called the Hermit Club, an upstairs event space, and a sprawling gravel-covered biergarten. To eat, there's paprikash, Wiener schnitzel, and sauerbraten.

MAP 1: 1550 Chester Ave., 216/621-2337, www.hofbrauhauscleveland.com; 11am-close daily

Masthead Brewing

Since opening in early 2017, Masthead has brought a bit of nightlife to an otherwise sleepy corner of downtown. sSet inside a 1920s-era warehouse that began life as a car dealership, this airy and active brewery can and does accommodate big crowds. A beefy 20-barrel brewhouse keeps the taps flowing, while a fire engine-red wood-burning oven turns out pitch-perfect Neapolitan-style pizzas. On warm days, 120 linear feet of garage doors lift and melt away the divide between inside and out.

MAP 1: 1261 Superior Ave., 216/206-6176, www.mastheadbrewingco.com; 11am-close Tues.-Sat., 1pm-8pm Sun.

✪ Noble Beast Brewing Co.

Despite its out-of-the-way locale, Noble Beast continues to attract craft beer fans thanks to clean, stellar, and delicious brews. Largely grounded in European classics, the ever-changing roster of taps cycles through grisettes, altbiers, kölsches, and saisons, but also trots out "beastly" concoctions like Imperial IPAs as well. The warehouse-style brewery feels a bit like a throwback from the dawn of American craft brewing, where everything is done right out in the open. A full menu of upscale pub grub keeps hungry guests from leaving before they've tried all the beer.

MAP 1: 1470 Lakeside Ave. E., 216/417-8588, www.noblebeastbeer.com; 11am-close Tues.-Sun.

BARS AND PUBS

Flannery's Pub

For more than 20 years, this convivial Irish pub has been pouring perfect pints of Guinness and Harp in a prime location just steps from Progressive Field and Quicken Loans Arena. Ground zero on St. Patrick's Day, the warm and roomy saloon can accommodate massive crowds, yet it still feels cozy enough for an Irish boxty supper for two during the week. Recent improvements to all aspects of the operation signal more good years to come.

MAP 1: 323 Prospect Ave., 216/781-7782, www.flannerys.com; 11:30am-close daily

Gillespie's Map Room

It's rare to find a true neighborhood pub in the heart of downtown Cleveland, but that's precisely what this pub is. Loved by locals who shy away from fancier, pricier, stodgier clubs, the Map Room is a reliable sanctuary. A solid draft and bottled beer list, surprisingly good pizza, and more than enough seating to go around have kept this low-key hangout around longer than most of its competition.

MAP 1: 1281 W. 9th St., 216/621-7747, www.maproomcleveland.com; 11:30am-close Mon.-Sat., 11am-close Sun.

✪ Harbor Inn

As Cleveland's oldest continuously operating bar, the Harbor Inn is dripping with history. Dark, cool, and largely quiet, the shot-and-a-beer joint has long been the refuge of reporters, politicians, lawyers, and judges, who lose track of time discussing the pressing issues of the day. Some call it a dive, but this is just an everyday joint where folks gather to throw a game of darts, roll of few frames at the old-school bowling machine, and knock back cheap beer and booze. The nautical theme harkens back to a time when the Flats was the epicenter of the Great Lakes maritime industry and dockworkers filled every stool.

MAP 1: 1219 Main Ave., 216/241-3232; 11am-close Tues.-Sat.

Harbor Inn

Ontario Street Café

The last of a dying breed, Ontario Street is a classic Cleveland watering hole, where ridiculously cheap beer and cocktails are served up in a dimly lit lounge by necktie-clad staffers. A gruff exterior gives way to an old-school vibe with red vinyl booths, wood paneling, and a wildly diverse clientele that includes casino workers, bus drivers, and anybody else who knows a good deal when they see it. There are no tabs at Ontario Street: Drinks are paid for in cash, round by blessed round. When hunger strikes, order a corned beef or pastrami sandwich, some of the best in town.

MAP 1: 2053 Ontario St., 216/861-6446; 10am-close daily

Shooter's

During the summer, there are few better places to unwind with a cocktail and watch the commercial and pleasure boat traffic cruise up and down the Cuyahoga River. An outdoor bar and stage for live music keep this place hopping most nights, but especially on weekends. To go with the nautical theme, a seafood-centric menu, with items like shrimp cocktails, crab legs, and lobster rolls, is available all year long. During the off-season, the place slows down considerably, and the patio is all but put to bed.

MAP 1: 1148 Main Ave., 216/861-6900, www.shootersflats.com; 11:30am-close daily

LOUNGES
Bar 32

Cocktails at this cosmopolitan bar in the glassy Hilton Cleveland Downtown come with one of the best views in the city. Perched on the 32nd floor, the aptly named Bar 32 is roughly 400 feet above terra firma,

and the open-air veranda offers unobstructed views of Burke Lakefront Airport to the east, the setting sun to the west, and FirstEnergy Stadium and the Rock Hall in between. While priced a buck or three more than at other bars, drinks (like the Proper Daiquiri) are expertly crafted, balanced, and delicious.

MAP 1: 100 Lakeside Ave., 216/413-5000, www3.hilton.com; 5pm-close daily

Society Lounge

Situated below ground, this speakeasy delivers to the downtown crowds an authentic cocktail lounge experience. The vibe is decidedly Rat Pack, with low lighting, high-backed banquettes, and red velvet sectionals. Walls are gilded with Venetian plasterwork, faux bricks, and rich tapestry. Some 32 feet of hand-painted murals depicting high-society life envelop entire walls. Catering to a more mature demographic, Society offers live jazz, classic and contemporary cocktails, and small plates and desserts.

MAP 1: 2063 E. 4th St., lower level, 216/781-9050, www.societycleveland.com; 5pm-close daily

KARAOKE
✪ Galaxy KTV

Hidden inside a squat brick shell in Asiatown is a showstopper of a karaoke bar. There's a large main lounge outfitted with a small stage, banquettes, and a Jumbotron-size monitor so everyone can follow along with the lyrics. An additional nine private rooms can accommodate groups from small to large. Each is equipped with a touch-screen system that plays songs in various languages, controls the sound, lighting, and video, and even features call buttons to summon the

Galaxy KTV

wait staff for another round of fear-reducing drinks.

MAP 1: 1593 E. 30th St., 216/203-2222, www.galaxyktv88.com; 5pm-close Wed.-Mon.

COMEDY CLUBS
✪ Hilarities 4th Street Theater

This is the premier comedy club in Cleveland, featuring the best talent in the best setting. Located inside Pickwick & Frolic, a $5 million entertainment complex on East 4th Street, Hilarities attracts every big name in the biz. Owner Nick Kostis has been running comedy clubs in this town since the 1980s, and he has earned a reputation as a brilliant judge of up-and-coming talent. Shows take place in a sharp 425-seat theater, the backdrop of which is a brick wall left over from the old Euclid Opera House. Before the show, hit the rustic American restaurant upstairs. After, visit Kevin's Martini Bar for cocktails.

MAP 1: 2035 E. 4th St., 216/736-4242, www.pickwickandfrolic.com; showtimes and cost vary

The Improv

With venues in about 20 U.S. cities, The Improv is a well-known comedy club and restaurant. Top touring comedians, rising-star talent, and local favorites confront audiences most nights of the week. Those who want to secure the best spots in the 350-seat house must make dinner reservations, but the wiser choice may be to dine elsewhere and take your chances on seating. Like every other comedy club in the world, The Improv charges a little more than it probably should for drinks.

MAP 1: 1148 Main Ave., 216/696-4677, www.clevelandimprov.com; showtimes and cost vary

CASINOS
JACK Cleveland Casino

The JACK Cleveland Casino is unlike most casinos. For starters, it's in the center of town rather than on some patch of repurposed farmland miles away. Second, it's built into the historic Higbee building, a once-famous department store that boasts stunning architectural details throughout the 300,000-square-foot complex. The attractive urban casino offers 1,600 slot and video poker machines, 100 table games, and a 30-table poker room.

During busy times, there can be short waits to grab a stool at table games like blackjack and roulette. In addition to a handful of bars, the property has a 400-seat buffet restaurant and a small food court with deli, Italian, and sandwich options.

MAP 1: 100 Public Sq., 216/297-4777, www.jackentertainment.com/cleveland; 24 hours daily

Ohio City and Tremont   Map 2

LIVE MUSIC
Bop Stop
This purpose-built space is all about the music. The curved, tiered, and intimate room offers ideal sight and sound lines to the stage, where an eclectic calendar of jazz, hip-hop, and soul acts light up the room. As part of the nonprofit Music Settlement, this unique venue offers music education by day and performances after dark. Enjoy up-and-coming talent as well as rightly celebrated stars, all with amazing views of Lake Erie through the glass.

MAP 2: 2920 Detroit Ave., 216/421-5806, www.themusicsettlement.org; hours and cover vary depending on show

BREWERIES AND CRAFT BEER
Great Lakes Brewing Co.
Housed in the former home of a seed and feed company, this saloon-style pub is equally famous for its world-class beer and for the bullet hole in the vintage bar, rumored to have come from Eliot Ness's pistol. To go with those wonderful suds is a menu of hearty pub classics like sausage samplers, burgers, fish-and-chips, and pot roast. Start with an order of the barley pretzels, which are made from spent grains left over from the brewing process. Beer fans will want to visit on Friday or Saturday afternoon, when brewery tours ($5) are offered. Great Lakes operates a biodiesel bus (dubbed the Fatty Wagon) that shuttles diners to Indians games for $1 round-trip. If you're looking for a nice outdoor roost, this place has a great (doggie-friendly) sidewalk patio. A gift shop sells apparel, barware, and beer.

MAP 2: 2516 Market Ave., 216/771-4404, www.greatlakesbrewing.com; 11:30am-close Mon.-Fri., 11am-close Sat.

Market Garden Brewery
Located shoulder-to-shoulder with the West Side Market, this generously sized brewpub seats well over 300 guests in multiple dining rooms, at various bars, and in an attractive beer garden. Upscale pub grub joins an ever-evolving list of world-class suds, cooked up by an award-winning brewmaster. Thanks to a massive stone hearth, the outdoor beer garden is an all-seasons affair.

THE FLATS: A BRIEF HISTORY

The **Flats,** the low-lying part of the city that surrounds either side of the Cuyahoga River, was once part of Cleveland's burgeoning rock scene. The area's history, however, goes back much further than its glory days of the 1990s.

In the early 1800s, thanks to the Ohio & Erie Canal, this river basin was a major shipping port filled with docks and dockworkers, shipyards and sailors, and saloons and boarding houses. Heavy industry followed in subsequent decades, and the valley soon filled with railyards, steel mills, and oil refineries.

But in the 1970s, a few scrappy club owners began moving into the district. In the beginning, only the bravest of music fans would venture down to spots like Pirate's Cove, home to ground-breaking Cleveland acts like Pere Ubu, Dead Boys, and the Pagans. By the early 1990s, clubs like D'Poos, Fagan's Rumrunners, Peabody's Down Under, and the Basement had transformed the area into one of the country's first true "entertainment districts." In fact, the Flats had become so widely renowned that mainstream brands like Dick's Last Resort, Hooters, and Fado Irish Pub soon followed.

Thanks to rowdy crowds, underage drinking, frequent brawls, and bar owners who offered 50-cent beers in hopes of undercutting the competition, the Flats quickly descended into chaos. A handful of drowning deaths and the birth of a new entertainment zone just up the hill in the Warehouse District were the final straws. As quickly as it all came together it seemed to disintegrate.

By the fall of 2015, however, the East Bank of the Flats had been completely reshaped, reborn, and repopulated thanks to a $750 million waterfront redevelopment project. This multifaceted neighborhood now features high-end residential buildings, an 18-story office tower, and the trendy **Aloft Cleveland Downtown** hotel. There are bars like Beerhead, FWD Day + Nightclub, and Big Bang dueling piano bar. When it comes time to eat, there are local spots like Alley Cat Oyster Bar and **Collision Bend Brewing Company,** along with national chains like Margaritaville and Punch Bowl Social. There's even a free water taxi to shuttle fun-seekers from the East Bank to the West Bank and back again.

For a taste of the "Old Flats," make a pilgrimage to the **Harbor Inn,** the oldest continuously operating bar in Cleveland thanks to an established date of 1895. Not far away is the Flat Iron Café, which has been chugging merrily along since 1910.

MAP 2: 1947 W. 25th St., 216/621-4000, www.marketgardenbrewery.com; 11am-2:30am Mon.-Sat., 10am-2:30am Sun.

MAP 2: 1859 W. 25th St., 216/621-4000, www.nanobrewcleveland.com; 4:30pm-2am Mon.-Fri., noon-2am Sat.-Sun.

Nano Brew

Little sister to Market Garden Brewery, this lively bar features a teensy one-barrel brewhouse that is prominently displayed in the main room. But the real draw is the epic craft beer selection, which flows from breweries down the street, the next town over, and out of state. A full-service restaurant offers an approachable, delicious pub-style menu loaded with creative burgers and snacks. Nano's dog-friendly backyard beer garden is one of the sweetest around, with a second bar and tons of seating on two levels.

Platform Beer

What began life as a modest microbrewery in 2014 has exploded into one of the fastest-growing craft brands in the country. In addition to this flagship taproom in Ohio City, Platform has added a 120,000-square-foot production facility down the road and taprooms in Columbus and Cincinnati. This buzzy brew-focused pub boasts a great selection of house and guest beers, plus a roomy side patio that connects to the main space.

MAP 2: 4125 Lorain Ave., 216/202-1386, www.platformbeerco.com; 3pm-close Mon.-Fri., 10am-close Sat.-Sun.

THE MANY BREWERIES OF CLEVELAND

Cleveland, like the rest of the country, has been in the throes of a brewery boom. But this thirsty town appears to be blowing past the competition thanks to the rise of no less than two dozen new or relatively new producers. While hitting them all is a commendable, even noble, pursuit, it might be wise to bite off a few at a time.

When it opened in 1986, **Great Lakes Brewing Co.** became the first modern-day microbrewery in the state of Ohio. Thanks to consistent growth and expansion, it is now one of the largest craft breweries in the nation, with its beer flowing into numerous states around the country. Its flagship brewpub in Ohio City should be stop #1 for craft beer lovers visiting the city. Head downstairs into the basement cellar for special pours and a rathskeller-like vibe.

Market Garden Brewery started with a lone brewpub but has since expanded its output considerably thanks to a massive new production facility behind the West Side Market. (Just look for the 10-foot-tall illuminated "BEER!" sign.) Both are worth visiting for different reasons. The brewpub is a great place to sit, eat, and enjoy a few pints, while the brewery offers sweet tours, a shop filled with great swag, and a retail beer selection.

Like Market Garden, **Platform Beer** is outpacing most of the local competition in terms of inventory thanks to a sizable new production brewery and aggressive distribution strategy. But its Ohio City taproom, where it all began a few short years ago, is a stellar place to hang out and sample the portfolio. The chill West Coast vibe, great patio, and hip location keep this joint jumping.

Noble Beast Brewing Co. is a bit off the beaten path, but it should be on every craft beer lover's itinerary. From his 5,000-square-foot garage-style brewery, Shaun Yasaki is making some of the cleanest beers in town. Pop in for a crisp, refreshing pilsner, kölsch, altbier, or witbier, and then wash it down with some stellar pub grub.

While it's more a full-blown restaurant than a brewery, **Collision Bend Brewing Company** is producing some stellar beers thanks to a very deep talent pool in the brewhouse. Perched along the Cuyahoga River in the Flats, this brewery also happens to be one of the most scenic spots in town to savor a flight of crisp German-style lagers.

Others great taprooms worth visiting include, in no particular order, **Bookhouse Brewing** (1526 W. 25th St., no phone, www.bookhouse.beer), **Goldhorn Brewery** (1361 E. 55th St., 216/465-1352, www.goldhornbrewery. com), **Terrestrial Brewing** (7524 Father Frascati Blvd., 216/465-9999), **Hansa Brewery** (2717 Lorain Ave., 216/631-6585, www.hansabrewery.com), **Masthead Brewing,** and **Brick and Barrel** (1844 Columbus Rd., 216/331-3308, www.brickandbarrelbrewing.com).

Saucy Brew Works

Another great example of adaptive reuse, this wildly popular brewery and pizza concept set up shop in a former machine warehouse. The 14,000-square-foot space has been completely reshaped into a glassy, loft-like brewery that retains industrial elements like boom cranes and rigging. Brewer/owner Eric Anderson pumps out a line filled with classic styles, sours, and experimental beers. To eat, there's thin-crust New Haven-style pizza.

MAP 2: 2885 Detroit Ave., 216/666-2568, www.saucybrewworks.com; 11am-close daily

BARS AND PUBS
ABC the Tavern
This decades-old bar in Ohio City went from largely ignored to hard to ignore thanks to new ownership, who improved the craft beer list, upped the food, and vastly boosted attendance. Don't expect much in the way of scenery—just a ruggedly handsome tavern built to stand the test of time. Great pub grub like diner-style burgers and bacon-wrapped hot dogs is served late, making this joint hugely popular with service industry peeps punching out from area restaurants. An old-school bowling machine and an upstairs pool table add to the authentic saloon-style fun.

MAP 2: 1872 W. 25th St., 216/861-3857, www.abcthetavern.com; 4pm-2:30am Mon.-Fri., noon-2:30am Sat.-Sun.

Edison's Pub
Over the decades, Tremont has evolved from blue-collar residential neighborhood to trendy enclave of art galleries, high-end townhomes, and chef-driven bistros. Throughout it all, Edison's has sat quietly on the sidelines of progress, serving as a no-frills watering hole for the folks who call this area home. There's a needlessly lengthy bottled beer list, and the pizza is the stuff of legends (especially when you're tipsy), but it's the come-as-you-are vibe that turns first-timers into regulars. Don't overlook the secluded back patio on warm nights.

MAP 2: 2373 Professor Ave., 216/781-8862, www.edisonspub.com; 4pm-close Mon.-Fri., 1pm-close Sat.-Sun.

✪ Forest City Shuffleboard
Good, clean fun abounds at this indoor/outdoor shuffleboard social club. The well-designed and spacious destination sets aside plenty of room for the five regulation courts, as well as an attractive bar with two lengthy tabletop versions. A vintage varsity theme, with high school gymnasium scoreboard, sports banners, and baseball stadium seats, adds to the timeless, nostalgic vibe of the place. Owing to league play, special events, and general popularity, reservations are advisable.

MAP 2: 4506 Lorain Ave., 216/417-5838, www.forestcityshuffle.com; 4pm-11pm Mon.-Thurs., 4pm-1am Fri.-Sat., noon-10pm Sun.

Jukebox
As the name suggests, Jukebox is a music-focused bar, at the heart of which is a jukebox with an ever-shifting inventory that pays tribute to Cleveland's rock-and-roll roots. In addition to the steady stream of Rock Hall inductees and homegrown acts, the tunes run the gamut from new to old. With a chill neighborhood feel, killer local beer selection, and simple menu built around pierogies, this tavern quickly settled into a groove as the go-to pub in Hingetown.

MAP 2: 1404 W. 29th St., 216/206-7699, www.jukeboxcle.com; 5pm-close Mon.-Fri., noon-close Sat.-Sun.

Prosperity Social Club
If you're looking for a laid-back neighborhood bar with century-old authenticity, head straight to Prosperity. They don't build taverns like this anymore, which is precisely why owner Bonnie Flinner bought a historic bar, dusted it off, and introduced it anew to an appreciative city. There are no hokey themes here, just real folks meeting up for solid food and drink in a ruggedly handsome setting. A freestanding woodstove adds wintertime charm, while a rec room with pool table, antique bowling machine, and classic

board games adds a bit of wholesome fun. A garden-style patio has a fun and funky decor.

MAP 2: 1109 Starkweather Ave., 216/937-1938, www.prosperitysocialclub.com; 4pm-close Mon.-Fri., 10:30am-close Sat.-Sun.

LOUNGES

Lava Lounge

When this low-key lounge opened in 1999, it was a well-kept secret. These days, it's on most people's radar, but in no way has it lost its edge. More of an anti-club, Lava is for folks who enjoy great tunes without the sweaty gyrations and personal advances. Dark, clubby, and candlelit, the small lounge features martinis, a great beer and wine selection, and vinyl-spinning DJs. It has a second-floor bar and lounge, a small back patio, and a surprisingly good menu that is available right up until last call.

MAP 2: 1307 Auburn Ave., 216/589-9112, www.coolplacestoeat.com; 4pm-2:30am Mon.-Sat., 5pm-2:30am Sun.

Porco Lounge and Tiki Room

✪ Porco Lounge and Tiki Room

Porco Lounge is routinely hailed as one of the best tiki bars in the country by its cocktail colleagues, with fans of the genre making long-distance trips just to check it out in person. The interior is a wonderland of period-appropriate memorabilia, much of it collected over the years from long-shuttered pioneers in the industry. In place of cloyingly sweet knock-offs built from mixes, the Mai Tais, Zombies, and Pain Killers prepared by the aloha-shirted bartenders are crafted only with the best booze, freshly squeezed fruit juices, and house-made syrups. A small kitchen turns out creative snacks and specials.

MAP 2: 2527 W. 25th St., 216/802-9222, www.porcolounge.com; 5pm-close Mon.-Thurs., 4pm-close Fri.-Sat.

Spotted Owl

The best bars in the world are run by the best bartenders in the world, folks who honestly believe that bars are very special and necessary places. Owl owner Will Hollingsworth is one of those bartenders. For years he's been on a single-minded mission to build the perfect bar, and this half-buried Tremont spot is the result of those labors. With a masculine "Massachusetts customs house" feel, this is the kind of cave where you can start your night, end your night, and make the kind of memories with friends that last a lifetime. Truly original cocktails push the art and craft of boozing to its apogee.

MAP 2: 710 Jefferson Ave., no phone, www.spottedowlbar.com; 5pm-close daily

Velvet Tango Room

Long considered Cleveland's most exclusive speakeasy, Velvet Tango Room has long shed its cloak-and-dagger guise in favor of delightfully democratic service for all. Tucked inside a plain brick wrapper is an anachronistic world of courteous customers, professional staffers, and upscale furnishings. Labor-intensive classic cocktails are constructed gram by gram on a scale to ensure consistency. Ingredients are top-flight, with house-made mixers, freshly squeezed fruit juices, and cut-to-order garnishes coming together in perfect form.

MAP 2: 2095 Columbus Rd., 216/241-8869, www.velvettangoroom.com; 4:30pm-1am Mon.-Fri., 6pm-1am Sat.

Detroit Shoreway and Edgewater

Map 3

LIVE MUSIC

Brothers Lounge

A multimillion-dollar renovation of this historic blues club has transformed it into a sleek entertainment complex with neighborhood pub, wine bar, and concert hall. Amish oak flooring, mahogany bars, and a high-tech sound system conspire to create an upscale musical experience not found at most clubs. There is a nightly lineup of local, regional, and national acts, and a great house band plays every Sunday. Open-mic nights and jam sessions allow others to get in on the action. Don't bother eating elsewhere before or after the show—this place also dishes up some mighty fine grub.

MAP 3: 11609 Detroit Ave., 216/226-2767, www.brotherslounge.com; 11:30am-close Mon.-Thurs., 11am-close Fri., 3pm-close Sat., noon-close Sun.; cover varies depending on show

BARS AND PUBS

Judd's City Tavern

From the outside, Judd's looks like every other blue-collar dive, a lackluster brick exterior offering few clues as to what lies behind those cloudy glass-block windows. But step inside and find yourself in what appears to be a perfectly preserved relic from another era. Every surface of the 40-seat tavern is a canvas for beer, sports, toy, automotive, postal and first-responder collectibles, all of it in top nick. As a bonus, the joint sells some of cheapest drinks in town.

MAP 3: 10323 Madison Ave., 216/675-4316; 4pm-close Tues.-Sat.

Judd's City Tavern

Parkview Nite Club

You'd be hard pressed to find a joint in Cleveland with more history than the Parkview Nite Club. The saloon officially opened up in 1934, when the ink was barely dry on the 21st Amendment, but this place has likely been serving hooch since the early 1900s. These days, as the neighborhood changes all around it, the old-school saloon serves as a steady reminder of the city's blue-collar roots. Setting the bar apart from other dives, in addition to the timeworn interior, is the food, which has always punched well above its weight.

MAP 3: 1261 W. 58th St., 216/961-1341, www.parkviewniteclub.com; 11am-close daily

Stone Mad Irish Pub

A stickler for quality craftsmanship, owner Pete Leneghan made sure that every element in this Irish pub was constructed with the finest materials and labor around. From the hand-laid cobblestone parking lot and oil-rubbed walnut bars to the stained-glass windows and intricately carved ironwork, this stunningly attractive space is loaded with eye candy (even the restrooms). The sizable pub boasts two separate barrooms, a casual dining room with sunken bocce court, and an outdoor courtyard featuring stone-slab tables and a towering four-sided fireplace.

MAP 3: 1306 W. 65th St., 216/281-6500, www.stonemadpub.com; 11am-2am daily

Tina's Nite Club

One of the busiest bars in town also happens to be one of its most isolated and bedraggled. People don't come to Tina's for the decor; they come for the cheap drinks, rowdy atmosphere, and hilarious karaoke. Warming up the grim mason-block interior is often a full house of slightly inebriated customers singing along to whatever song is being belted out (often terribly) over the sound system. Come with a group, tip a few cold ones, and join in on the fun.

MAP 3: 5400 Herman Ave., 216/961-1341; 6pm-close daily

Tributary

Tributary is a bit of a hybrid, equal parts casual corner bar and upmarket cocktail lounge. Located smack dab between Ohio City and Detroit Shoreway, the place also serves to bridge the gap between neighborhoods. Locals like the dimly lit saloon because it puts on no airs—the sort of place that happily pours cheap domestic beer with one hand while simultaneously stirring a Sazerac or old-fashioned with the other. The industrial-tinged interior features beefy metal furnishings softened by reclaimed timber and original photography.

MAP 3: 5304 Detroit Ave., 216/713-2946, www.tributarycle.com; 4pm-close Mon.-Sat.

DANCE CLUBS

Twist Social Club

Located at the epicenter of Cleveland's gay-friendly district, Twist is more laid-back than many other LBGTQ bars. A large main room features a central bar, some soft-seating areas, and loft balconies. A sleek subterranean lounge offers a quiet hideaway for guests hoping to escape the upstairs action. On warm nights, two overhead garage doors are raised high, spreading the party out onto the sidewalk. Affordable martinis, upbeat tunes, and welcoming employees have kept Twist popular for more than 25 years.

MAP 3: 11633 Clifton Blvd., 216/221-2333, www.twistsocialclub.com; 4pm-close Mon.-Fri., noon-close Sat.-Sun.; no cover

University Circle and Little Italy

Map 4

LIVE MUSIC

Happy Dog at the Euclid Tavern

For more than 100 years, the Euclid Tavern was an anchor of the Cleveland live-music scene. After falling into disrepair and closing, the historic venue was saved by current management, who also run the popular West Side spot Happy Dog. While the club retains its weathered, authentic vibe, it boasts an updated interior, stage, and sound system. The 200-guest main room hosts rock, country, folk, and polka bands, as well as poetry slams, open mic nights, and scholarly talks. As for the fare, Happy Dog offers the same lineup of tasty hot dogs, veggie dogs, tater tots, and fries as its sibling.

MAP 4: 11625 Euclid Ave., 216/231-5400, www.happydogcleveland.com; 4pm-close Mon.-Tues., 11am-close Wed.-Sun.; cover varies depending on show

BARS AND PUBS

ABC the Tavern

This sister establishment to the Ohio City bar of the same name is one of the few dive bars in the area. While it's relatively new construction, the owners took pains to make it every bit as approachable and casual as the original. Enjoyed equally for its bar program as it is for the menu of pub grub, this lively oasis attracts a pleasantly diverse clientele.

MAP 4: 11434 Uptown Ave., 216/721-1511, www.abcthetavern.com; 11:30am-close Mon.-Fri., noon-close Sat.

Tavern of Little Italy

When this tavern debuted in 2015, it was obvious that it was going in a direction very different from its kin. While there is no shortage of charming Italian restaurants in the area, there was a dearth of casual American pubs where folks could meet up to watch sports, enjoy a craft beer, and order some gastro-style grub. That's where TOLI comes in, as an approachable neighborhood pub that serves flatbreads, meatballs, tacos, and more.

MAP 4: 12117 Mayfield Rd., 216/331-1069, www.tolicleveland.com; 11am-close Tues.-Sun.

LIVE MUSIC
Grog Shop

Since 1992, this edgy club has been a nonstop riot of live music, bringing in the very best of well-known and soon-to-be-famous acts. This standing-room-only club for 400 has played host to acts like pre-Grammy Bruno Mars, Oasis, and Kid Rock. Most nights are filled with an eclectic mix of local, regional, and national touring acts. Genres run the gamut from indie rock and reggae to hip-hop and jam bands.

MAP 5: 2785 Euclid Heights Blvd., 216/321-5588, www.grogshop.gs; hours and cover vary depending on show

Nighttown

Reminiscent of the great old-school jazz supper clubs, Nighttown is a one-stop shop for killer music, great grub, and sparkling conversation. Named by *Downbeat* magazine as one of the 100 Great Jazz Clubs in the world, this joint snags the biggest names in music as they travel between Chicago and New York. Cleveland Heights is known for its diverse and progressive populace, and this club acts as the neighborhood's living room. An eclectic crowd gathers for dinner shows, cocktails at the bar, or to enjoy a warm night on the various patios. Seating for shows is on a first-come, first-served basis, and it's always wise to reserve your ticket in advance.

MAP 5: 12387 Cedar Rd., 216/795-0550, www.nighttowncleveland.com; hours and cover vary depending on show

BREWERIES
Boss Dog Brewing

Situated in the heart of the Cedar-Lee district, this family-friendly brewpub is contemporary and open, with a pleasing industrial bent. The various seating options cater equally to a pair of buddies watching a game at the bar, a couple grabbing a quick weekend lunch, and a full-on dinner for the family. A shiny 10-barrel brewhouse, prominently positioned behind glass, cranks out a wide range of classic and creative brews, while a sprawling patio spreads the fun to the great outdoors. A full-service kitchen turns out gastropub fare that appeals to broad tastes and budgets.

MAP 5: 2179 Lee Rd., 216/321-2337, www.bossdogbrewing.com; 4pm-close Mon.-Fri., noon-close Sat.-Sun.

Bottlehouse Brewery

This small-batch brewery in Cleveland Heights has developed into a beloved neighborhood gathering place. The backyard-barbecue vibe is fueled by communal seating and fun events like trivia, open mic night, and live music. Over the years, the owners have developed a real following for their exceptional barrel-aged beers, approachable meads, complex ciders, and unique sours and wild ales. A wide sidewalk patio is a great place to watch the world go by.

MAP 5: 2050 Lee Rd., 216/214-2120, www.thebottlehousebrewingcompany.com; 4pm-close Mon.-Fri., 2pm-close Sat.-Sun.

BARS AND PUBS
Parnell's Pub
You can't pen a St. Patrick's Day story in Cleveland without including this perennially popular Irish pub. As if the perfect pints of Guinness, dyed-in-the-wool Irish ownership, and a real bristle dartboard weren't enough, this is also the place to go to watch World Cup soccer, regardless of the hour when games are televised. Located next to one of the most popular wood-fired pizza parlors around, this bar is also a great place to meet up before or after the pie.

MAP 5: 12425 Cedar Rd., 216/321-3469; 4pm-close daily

LOUNGES
B Side Liquor Lounge
This basement lounge lives beneath the live-music club Grog Shop, offering a nice alternative to that scene and others on Coventry Road. Here, introverts belly up to the vintage arcade games and pinball machines, while B movies endlessly roll on the screens. A great drink selection, friendly bartenders, and a jam-packed calendar of fun, oddball, and wild events like Silent Disco and deliberately awful karaoke keep this cellar hopping.

MAP 5: 2785 Euclid Heights Blvd., 216/932-1966, www.bsideliquorlounge.com; 6pm-close Tues.-Sat., 7pm-close Sun.-Mon.

The Fairmount
Cleveland Heights is a tight-knit community that supports its own, especially when those people return the favor. Since opening this upscale lounge, owner Jake Orosz has rolled every penny back into the business. There's a new kitchen, greatly expanded dining room, and oasis-like back patio that's packed all summer long. Sure the setting is a bit fancier than the average neighborhood pub, but the folks who frequent this bar, restaurant, and lounge are the very same people.

MAP 5: 2448 Fairmount Blvd., 216/229-9463, www.thefairmount.net; 4pm-close Mon.-Fri., 5pm-close Sat.-Sun.

✪ Quintana's Speakeasy
Where better to hide one of the city's sweetest little speakeasies than above the local barbershop. After rising from their chair, customers at Quintana's Barbershop climb a short flight of stairs, crack the spine of an old book on a shelf, and press the magic button. When the shelf swivels open, a gorgeous wood-trimmed speakeasy is revealed, an elegant escape of hushed voices and exquisite cocktails. Both original and Prohibition-era creations are on the menu. The entrance is in the rear.

MAP 5: 2200 S. Taylor Rd., 216/421-8380, www.qbds.net/speakeasy; 3pm-close Mon.-Thurs., noon-close Fri.-Sat.

WINE BARS
CLE Urban Winery
If Cleveland is a craft-beer town, don't tell that to the people at CLE Urban Winery. As the name suggests, this is a bona fide wine-making operation in the heart of busy Cleveland Heights. While the production part is serious, with wines like cabernet sauvignon, syrah, and merlot earning industry buzz, the rest of the operation is not. There's no room for pretentiousness here, where peach chardonnay and ice-cold wine slushies are just as popular as the barrel-aged reds. It's located in a casual garage-style space with an open plan, so guests can watch most of the action.

TAKE A RIDE ON THE BREW BUS

There might be no better way to dip one's toe into the Cleveland craft beer scene than by hopping aboard the **Cleveland Brew Bus** (216/773-2567, www.clevelandbrewbus.com). Led by knowledgeable and passionate guides (in fact, owner Leslie Basalla-McCafferty co-authored the book *Cleveland Beer: History and Revival in the Rust Belt*), this is no party bus, but rather an informative and immersive dive into beer, beer tasting, and local beer lore. Various tours explore different neighborhoods and themes, such "small breweries," "Cleveland classics," or "ambitious breweries" and last approximately 4.5 hours. In that time, guests will visit three separate breweries, sample four beers at each, and enjoy at least one brewhouse tour, often led by a principal brewer. The $65 ticket price covers everything but food if you choose to order any along the way.

MAP 5: 2180B Lee Rd., 216/417-8313, www.cleurbanwinery.com; 5pm-9pm Mon., 3pm-10pm Tues.-Thurs., 3pm-11pm Fri.-Sat.

The Wine Spot

What began life largely as a retail wine shop, set up in a former hardware store, has developed into something a little less straightforward. Sure, you can still shop the well-curated selection of bottles to go, but many customers never end up going anywhere.

Thanks to a full bar, concise but ever-shifting craft beer list, and variety of seating options, this welcoming place has become the de facto gathering spot in the neighborhood for people who typically avoid bars. To eat, there are a few wine bar-style nibbles or pizza brought in from next door.

MAP 5: 2271 Lee Rd., 216/342-3623, www.thewinespotonline.com; 1pm-8pm Mon., 11am-10pm Tues.-Thurs., 11am-11pm Fri.-Sat., noon-9pm Sun.

Lakewood

Map 6

LIVE MUSIC
Mahall's 20 Lanes

Mahall's spent most of its life as a smoke-filled bowling alley whose business dried up over time. These days, it's a multifaceted entertainment complex that houses a bar, café, live-music venue, and, yes, those very same lanes, albeit these days with more bowlers and zero smoke. This long-established neighborhood asset was saved by industrious young owners who dialed up the food, booze, and setting, while transferring the former pool room into a stage that hosts an eclectic lineup of regular shows.

MAP 6: 13200 Madison Ave., 216/521-3280, www.mahalls20lanes.com; 5pm-close Mon.-Fri., noon-close Sat.-Sun.; cover varies depending on show

Winchester Tavern and Concert Club

The Winchester is a Lakewood institution. Formerly a bowling alley, the neighborhood tavern and ballroom has seen its fair share of ups and downs, owners and managers. These days it plays host to a wide range of live acts that include cover bands, singer-songwriters, punk acts, and hard-charging rock-and-roll bands. A full bar and food menu mean that you'll have enough fuel to see you through until the encore.

MAP 6: 12112 Madison Ave., 216/226-5681, www.thewinchestermusictavern.com; hours and cover vary depending on show

BARS AND PUBS
Around the Corner Saloon

As the crowds at this meet-and-greet tavern continued to grow, so too did the bar's footprint. What started out as a one-room corner saloon has ballooned into a multidimensional hot spot with the largest and best drinking patio in Lakewood, graced with a full bar, flat-screen TVs, and amusing Midwestern yard games, so there's rarely a good reason to head inside (snow included, thanks to protection and heating). Come on Monday for two-for-one hamburgers or 3pm-7pm any weekday for $5.50 pitchers. A profusion of single guys and girls makes this place hookup central.

MAP 6: 18616 Detroit Ave., 216/521-4413, www.atccafe.com; 3pm-2am Mon.-Thurs., 11am-2am Fri.-Sat., 9:30am-2am Sun.

Five O'Clock Lounge

Like any great neighborhood dive, the Five offers cheap beer, uncomfortable seats, and well-spun rock and roll. Come around happy hour and the crowd is strictly gin-blossomed regulars, noses firmly ensconced in beer mugs. But like the hands on an analog timepiece, the atmosphere here is always shifting. On weekend nights, the better-dressed set scuttles into large round booths, the padding flattened by 70 years of abuse, to while away the night gripping and sipping PBR tallboys. DJs spin a tasty mix of rock, punk, and new wave, and the

occasional live band hits the small stage.

MAP 6: 11904 Detroit Ave., 216/521-4906; 2pm-2:30am Mon.-Sat., 8pm-2:30am Sun.

LBM

People weren't sure of what to make of LBM when it debuted as "a friendly neighborhood Viking bar." This Lakewood spot with the cryptic moniker might not be for everyone, but it has earned a huge following thanks to its kitschy, high-spirited setting. While that might seem at odds with a serious cocktail program, that's the point: This dimly lit lair offers an intimidation-free environment in which to dip one's toe into the world of excellent, affordable drinks. Don't miss the generous happy hour deals or the menu of hearty gastro-fare.

MAP 6: 12301 Madison Ave., 216/712-4692, www.lbmbar.com; 4pm-close Mon.-Sat.

Lizardville

Run by the same fine folks as Winking Lizard, a local chain of casual eateries, Lizardville is a combination beer store and whiskey bar. More than 600 beers from around the world are sold at retail to go, or they can be enjoyed on-site in the clubby, pub-like setting. Whiskey lovers go crazy over what is very likely the largest selection of brown booze in Ohio, all of which can be enjoyed neat, in cocktails, or as part of themed flights.

MAP 6: 14018 Detroit Ave., 216/226-4396, http://www.lizardville.net; 4pm-close Tues.-Sat.

✪ 16-Bit Bar + Arcade

For those of us who grew up riding our bikes to the corner arcade, where a week's worth of quarters disappeared into games like Galaga, Asteroids, Defender, and Tron, 16-Bit Bar is a nostalgic joyride. This lively, contemporary bar is home to some 40 classic video games set on free play. Those cabinets are joined by pinball machines and a full bar dispensing craft beer and cocktails bearing names like Winnie Cooper, Molly Ringwald, and Patrick Swayze. This arcade is adults-only but for one Sunday a month when it's "Bring Your Shorty Day."

MAP 6: 15012 Detroit Ave., 216/563-1115, www.16-bitbar.com; 4pm-close Mon.-Fri., noon-close Sat.-Sun.

WINE BARS
Humble Wine Bar

Run by the same great folks as Deagan's Kitchen & Bar, this Lakewood wine bar puts guests at ease thanks to its easy, breezy contemporary vibe. Gleaming white subway tile is set against warm woods and distressed tin ceilings. On warm days, the entire front of the bar opens up to create a seamless inside/outside space. Select from dozens of wines by the glass, including always-fresh wine on tap, as well as 100 more by the bottle. A small but excellent craft beer list is also available. In addition to a phenomenal cheese and cured meat selection, Humble turns out thin, crisp Neapolitan-style pizzas from its prominently displayed wood stone pizza oven.

MAP 6: 15400 Detroit Ave., 216/767-5977, www.humblewinebar.com; 4pm-close daily

COMEDY CLUBS
Something Dada

This fast-paced improvisational comedy troupe formed in 1994, making it the longest-running improv show in town. These days, the team operates out of Lakewood's Beck Center for the Arts. Fueled by audience suggestions, however silly they might be, Dada manages to manufacture a roller-coaster ride of laughs. Shows are never the same experience twice. Shows take place at 8pm on Saturday in Beck Center's Studio Theater when a production is not taking place.

MAP 6: Beck Center for the Arts, 17801 Detroit Ave., 216/696-4242, www.beckcenter.org; 8pm Sat.; $12

Greater Cleveland   Map 7

LIVE MUSIC
✪ Beachland Ballroom

What once served as a Croatian social hall is now one of the premier live-music venues in the Midwest. The popular concert venue comprises an intimate tavern and a larger ballroom, both original to the 1950 structure. Attracted by an eclectic roster of local, regional, and national acts, not to mention the unique setting, live music fans travel here from as far away as Columbus, Pittsburgh, and Detroit. Grab a bite to eat before shows in the tavern, or come back for the amazing weekend brunch. While you're in there, check out the vintage 80-record Rock-Ola jukebox that *Blender* magazine labeled in 2008 as the best in the country.

MAP 7: 15711 Waterloo Rd., Cleveland, 216/383-1124, www.beachlandballroom.com; hours and cover vary depending on show

GAME ON

There has never been a better time to be a game player in Cleveland. It used to be that if you wanted a beer, you went out, and if you wanted to play games, you stayed in (and drank beer). But thanks to a landslide of eclectic nightlife destinations that combine the two pastimes, there is no shortage of nightlife built around good, clean fun.

There might be no better place for those of us who grew up on classic arcade games than **16-Bit Bar + Arcade** in Lakewood. This lively, contemporary bar is home to some 40 video games set on free play. Galaga, Asteroids, Joust, Defender, NBA Jam, and Tron are joined by pinball machines and a full bar dispensing craft beer and cocktails bearing the names of Winnie Cooper, Molly Ringwald, and Patrick Swayze.

Shuffleboard might sound like a snooze, but **Forest City Shuffleboard** is anything but. FCS has given the passé pastime new life at this spacious social club boasting spotless indoor and outdoor courts. A vintage varsity theme comes through in details like baseball stadium seats, tables fabricated from basketball court hardwood, and a functional high school scoreboard. There's a full bar and a kitchen for visiting chefs.

You can't get more old-school than **Superelectric Pinball Parlor** (6500 Detroit Ave., 440/822-1011, www.superelectric.tv), a Technicolor dream filled with vintage arcade games that span more than seven decades. Try your luck on the Love Tester, play a few games of flipper hockey, bounce the bumpers on a 1970s-era pinball machine, and plug the retro jukebox. This place runs off tokens, drips with nostalgia, and dings like mad.

If you thought board games belonged at home, you haven't been to a place like **Tabletop** (1810 W. 25th St., 216/512-3053, www.tabletopcleve.com) or **Side Quest** (17900 Detroit Ave., Lakewood, 216/228-1212, www.thesidequestbar.com). For a small fee, these welcoming social clubs open up their libraries of hundreds (thousands in the case of Tabletop) of board games to nerds, geeks, and pop culture fans. Both offer beer, wine, and snacks and host regular cosplay and trivia nights.

Duckpin bowling might be a big thing along the East Coast, but it was new to locals when **Hi and Dry Bowling and Beer** (2221 Professor Ave., 216/566-9463, www.hianddrycleveland.com) opened up in Tremont. For the uninitiated, duckpin features short, squat pins, softball-sized balls, and a system of string-based pinsetters. Pinball, arcade games, and a full bar and food menu flesh out the fun.

Bocce never seems to go out of style, but it does appear to be making a bit of a resurgence in area bars, backyards, and social clubs. **Backyard Bocce** (1059 Old River Rd., 216/523-1504, www.backyardbocceflats.com), right on the river in the Flats, offers both indoor and outdoor courts for year-round enjoyment. And because you can't play bocce without a beer or bourbon in your other hand for counterbalance, there's a full bar.

BREWERIES
Fat Head's Brewery

Award-winning brewer Matt Cole simply ran out of room at his old brewery, so he built an even larger one right off the interstate south of town. This 100,000-square-foot facility is home not only to a massive 75-barrel system that cranks out Head Hunter IPA (and Bumble Berry and Sunshine Daydream), but also to a 250-seat restaurant, 30-handle taproom, sprawling beer garden, and gift shop. The unique and open layout of the brewhouse offers visitors a firsthand glimpse into the process.

MAP 7: 17450 Engle Lake Dr., Middleburg Heights, 216/898-0242, www.fatheads.com; 11am-11pm Mon.-Thurs., 11am-midnight Fri.-Sat., 11am-10pm Sun.

CASINOS
Hard Rock Rocksino Northfield Park

For more than 50 years there has been live harness racing at this track about a half hour south of downtown, where "trotters" pulled two-wheeled "sulkies" around a half-mile course. In late 2013, following a massive renovation, Northfield Park reopened as Hard Rock Rocksino Northfield Park. In addition to a Hard Rock Cafe, 2,000-seat live music club, and 350-seat comedy club, the complex features 2,300 video lottery terminals. Similar to slot machines and video poker terminals, the games of chance attract gamers of all levels. Because of the way the new gambling legislation was written, only JACK Cleveland Casino downtown has real table games, slot machines, and poker rooms.

MAP 7: 10777 Northfield Rd., Northfield, 330/908-7625, www.hrrocksinonorthfieldpark.com; 24 hours daily

JACK Thistledown Racino

This mile-long track about 20 minutes southeast of Cleveland has been home to thoroughbred racing since 1925. In 2013, following an $88 million renovation that saw the arrival of 1,100 video lottery terminals (VLTs), this racetrack officially became a "racino." While you won't find craps, blackjack, or Texas Hold 'Em, you will find a whole host of slot machine-like games that pay out real money. Updated bars and eateries make the entire experience nicer for those betting on the ponies or the machines. There is live racing Friday through Monday from May to October, with simulcasted races every day of the week.

MAP 7: 21501 Emery Rd., North Randall, 216/662-8600, www.jackentertainment.com; 24 hours daily; admission and parking free

ARTS AND CULTURE

Cleveland has long been an arts-rich city. From the incomparable Cleveland Museum of Art on down to the countless studios and galleries that helped re-

Capitol Theatre

animate old neighborhoods into relevant, desirable communities, there is no shortage of creative energy. Up near the top of the arts pyramid are gifted rainmakers like the Cleveland Orchestra, Cleveland Institute of Art, Cleveland Institute of Music, Museum of Contemporary Art, and the aforementioned Cleveland Museum of Art, consistently ranked as one of the best in the world.

Playhouse Square is billed as the second-largest performing-arts center in the country, boasting five grand and gorgeously renovated vaudeville-era theaters plus scores of more intimate performance stages. Smaller but no less professional productions fill the calendars at area institutions such as Cleveland Public Theatre, Dobama Theatre, Cleveland Play House, Karamu House, and others.

The Cleveland International Film Fest has blossomed into an epic 12-day whirlwind with 500 screenings and more than 100,000 viewers, while the Cleveland Institute of Art Cinematheque was described by *The New York Times* as "one of the country's best repertory movie theaters."

In historical neighborhoods like Tremont, Little Italy, Detroit Shoreway, and Ohio City, arts-loving residents flock to regularly scheduled art walks and gallery hops, while the rest of the social calendar fills up with seasonal block parties, global culture festivals, and alfresco summer concerts.

HIGHLIGHTS

✪ **SHAKESPEARE, WITH A TWIST:** The historic Hanna Theatre, home to **Great Lakes Theater,** offers a diversity of seating options that range from traditional theater chairs to bar stools (page 99).

✪ **BEST REUSE OF A TROLLEY POWER STATION:** In 2013, nationally known art collectors Fred and Laura Bidwell opened the 8,000-square-foot **Transformer Station,** a jewel box of a museum in Ohio City, adding a world-class contemporary art outlet on the west side of town (page 102).

✪ **FINEST EXPERIMENTAL THEATER:** Since the early 1980s, **Cleveland Public Theatre** has produced innovative and adventurous original theater. In fact, the success of this very outfit has in large part triggered the revival of the entire Detroit Shoreway neighborhood (page 104).

✪ **WHERE ART AND ARCHITECTURE MEET:** Designed by London-based architect Farshid Moussavi, the new **Museum of Contemporary Art** in University Circle has forever changed the look of its neighborhood. Brawny, angular, and reflective, the structure is already a local icon (page 107).

✪ **BEST DAMN BAND IN THE LAND:** It isn't just locals who fawn all over the **Cleveland Orchestra;** critics in London, Salzburg, and Vienna have hailed the symphony as one of the very best in the world. Check them out at either Severance Hall or Blossom Music Center to hear what the world is talking about (page 108).

Museum of Contemporary Art

CONCERT VENUES
Agora Theatre & Ballroom

The Cleveland Agora has a rich history that dates all the way back to the 1960s. The live-music club has been an important force not only in the Cleveland music scene, but also the national one, breaking bands too numerous to list. All the great performers have graced its stages, from Bruce Springsteen and Bob Marley to the Clash and U2. The music hall comprises one large and one small room, with space for 2,000 and 500 fans respectively. In 2018, following a seven-month, $3-million top-to-bottom renovation, the club debuted anew. In addition to new lobbies, restrooms, lighting, and sound, the building has air conditioning for the first time in more than a century. Seating is general admission for many shows, so get there early if you want to secure a specific spot. Tickets for shows can be obtained through the club's website or at the box office on show nights.

MAP 1: 5000 Euclid Ave., 216/881-2221, www.agoracleveland.com; showtimes and cost vary

Cleveland Masonic Temple

For the first decade of its existence, the Cleveland Masonic Temple was the home of the Cleveland Orchestra, which tells you a little something about its stellar acoustics. The orchestra, of course, long ago moved to its present residence at Severance Hall. These days, the 2,000-seat auditorium space is the sweet spot for touring acts that prefer modest halls over tiny clubs or vast arenas. Bands like the Shins, Band of Horses, Pixies, and Wilco all are recent hosts. The auditorium is part of the Live Nation family of venues, which includes House of Blues, Jacobs Pavilion, and Blossom Music Center.

MAP 1: 3615 Euclid Ave., 216/881-6350, www.livenation.com; showtimes and cost vary

House of Blues

One of a dozen or so HOBs sprinkled across the United States, the Cleveland venue was built in 2004. With its considerable might, the company snags most of the biggest acts that sweep through town. The large main hall accommodates approximately 1,200 guests, while the more intimate Cambridge Room, with its modest 120-seat capacity (350 reception capacity), is better suited to smaller attractions. The compound boasts numerous bars, a full-service restaurant, gift shop, and the exclusive members-only Foundation Room. Sundays at the House are all about the popular Gospel Brunch, which features a mile-long buffet and rousing live gospel performance. Tickets for shows can be obtained by phone, online through Ticketmaster (www.ticketmaster.com), or at the box office (10am-6pm Mon.-Sat., hours vary Sun.).

MAP 1: 308 Euclid Ave., 216/523-2583, www.hob.com; showtimes and cost vary

Jacobs Pavilion at Nautica

Pretty as a picture, this sharp urban amphitheater is on the West Bank of the Flats, adjacent to the Nautica entertainment complex, and boasts great views of the river, bridges, and passing watercraft. Largely covered, the roughly 5,000 seats are spread among general-admission floor seats, bleachers, and standing-room areas. Approximately 12 shows per summer come here, ranging from megastars like Dylan to folk rockers like the Avett Brothers. This snug venue also is ideal for local legends like First Light and Michael Stanley.

MAP 1: 2014 Sycamore St., 216/ 622-6557, www.livenation.com; showtimes and cost vary

Quicken Loans Arena

Quicken Loans Arena

Known simply as the "Q," Quicken Loans Arena is the permanent home of the Cleveland Cavaliers and Cleveland Monsters and the temporary home of touring musicians, professional wrestlers, and Olympic gymnasts. Located in the Gateway District, the 20,000-seat arena sits on the southwestern edge of downtown, directly adjacent to Progressive Field. In advance of potentially hosting an NBA All-Star Game, the arena underwent a multimillion dollar renovation and transformation project that was completed in the fall of 2018. In case of nasty weather it's good to know that both the Q and Progressive Field can be reached from Tower City and the RTA via protected walkways.

MAP 1: 1 Center Court, 216/420-2000, www.theqarena.com; showtimes and cost vary

Wolstein Center

Cleveland's other main arena is actually part of the Cleveland State University campus. This 14,000-seat venue is home to the CSU Vikings, men's and women's Division I basketball teams. It is also used year-round for major performers like Carrie Underwood and touring spectacles like the Wiggles. Tickets are available through Ticketmaster (www.ticketmaster.com) or at the box office (Prospect Ave. entrance, 10am-6pm Mon.-Fri.).

MAP 1: 2000 Prospect Ave., 216/687-9292, www.wolsteincenter.com; showtimes and cost vary

GALLERIES
Bonfoey Gallery

The Bonfoey has rightfully earned a reputation as one of Cleveland's largest and finest art galleries. Established in 1893, it is certainly the most venerable. Located in Playhouse Square, the large space is filled with original 19th-century paintings, signed lithographs, photographs, pastels, glass, and sculpture. Rotating exhibits throughout the year bring in fresh merchandise. The shop also maintains a great selection of original art priced under $500, making it a must-stop on any home-design outing. Come here, too, for appraisals, art restoration, framing, packing, shipping, and installation.

MAP 1: 1710 Euclid Ave., 216/621-0178, www.bonfoey.com; 8:30am-5pm Mon.-Fri., 9am-noon Sat.; free

Cleveland Print Room

Dismayed by the demise of darkrooms at schools and universities, not to mention the disappearance of iconic films like Polaroid and Kodachrome, the founders of this photography co-operative endeavor to advance the art and appreciation of the printed photo. Part community darkroom, part exhibition space, the Print Room offers a full calendar of programming that includes darkroom orientation sessions, pinhole camera workshops, and shows that feature the works of international and emerging photographers.

MAP 1: ArtCraft Bldg., 2550 Superior Ave., 216/802-9441, www.clevelandprintroom. com; noon-6pm Tues. and Thurs.-Fri., 3pm-6pm Wed., noon-5pm Sat.; free

The Galleries at Cleveland State University

Though this great exhibition space is located on the ground floor of the CSU Art Building, the exhibits are not limited to student shows. In addition to the annual juried student art show, these three galleries present five or six shows per year that explore contemporary political and social themes. The thematically curated exhibits cover a broad range of media and styles from local, national, and international artists. They are recognized by critics as some of the most visually stimulating in town.

MAP 1: 1307 Euclid Ave., 216/687-2103, www.csuohio.edu; 9am-5pm Tues. and Thurs., noon-7pm Fri.-Sat., or by appt.; free

Morgan Conservatory

Long an industrial machine shop, the Morgan is the largest arts center in the United States dedicated to papermaking, book arts, and letterpress printing. Within its walls exist a working studio, gallery, and supplier of fine handmade papers. Exhibits in the gallery can range from three-dimensional multimedia works to handmade paper installations. An annual national juried exhibition examines the boundaries of paper and papermaking as an artistic medium. Workshops are offered in papermaking, book arts, and letterpress.

MAP 1: 1754 E. 47th St., 216/361-9255, www.morganconservatory.org; 10am-4pm Tues.-Sat.; free

Wooltex Gallery

One of the newer and better visual art galleries in the city, Wooltex is roomy, contemporary, and easy to find. Set in an old warehouse that has been converted to live/work space for artists, the gallery need not search far for talent. The large space serves as a backdrop for high-quality painting, sculpture, video, and installations from largely local artists. Exhibits come and go every six weeks or so. Like many other galleries in town, this one is used for private events, so it is always smart to call before visiting.

MAP 1: Tower Press Bldg., 1900 Superior Ave., 216/241-4069, www. thewooltexgallery.com; 11am-3pm Mon.-Sat.; free

Zygote Press

In its formative stage, this gallery was merely a small printmaking studio for its owners. In little more than a decade, it has developed into the most important nonprofit fine-art printmaking collaborative in the region. Located in an old warehouse in the artistically blossoming St. Clair Superior neighborhood, Zygote Press exhibits a monthly exhibition schedule of printed works of art, including letterpress, waterless lithography, etchings, relief, screen printing, and photo-crossover. Their exhibits feature the work of local, national, and international artists and printmakers.

MAP 1: 1410 E. 30th St., 216/621-2900, www.zygotepress.org; noon-4pm Wed. and Sat. and by appt.; free

MUSEUMS

Children's Museum of Cleveland

My, how fortunes have shifted for this longstanding Cleveland institution. Long housed in a former Howard Johnson restaurant that was later razed for development, the Children's Museum found new life in a new (old) home. In 2018, the museum debuted in the former Stager-Beckwith mansion, one of the few remaining homes along Cleveland's famed Millionaire's Row. Following a $10 million renovation, the 1860s-era structure opened with more space and all-new exhibits. The Making Miniatures exhibit features a top-floor display of handcrafted dollhouses. Adventure City boasts an 18-foot wall that children can ascend. And a wall of clear vacuum tubes sucks up fabric scarves and discharges them into the air high above.

MAP 1: 3813 Euclid Ave., 216/791-7114, www.cmcleveland.org; 9am-4pm Mon.-Wed. and Fri., 10am-5pm Sat., noon-5pm Sun.; adults and children over 11 months $12

Cleveland Police Museum

Cleveland was gripped by fear in the mid-1930s as a result of the Kingsbury Run Murders, better known as the Torso Murders. Over the course of four years, 13 people were brutally murdered. Because most of the victims were unidentified transients, plaster casts, or "death masks," were made of their faces for public viewing in hopes of identifying the deceased. Four of these chilling masks are on display at this law enforcement museum, which chronicles the history of the Cleveland Division of Police from its inception in 1866. Roughly 4,000 square feet of space contains thousands of photos, scrapbooks, old police blotters, and artifacts. Learn about Safety Director Eliot Ness and the achievements of the Cleveland Police Department during a guided tour, available by appointment. Stop by the Cop Shop to snag your very own CPD T-shirt or a book about the Torso Murders.

MAP 1: 1300 Ontario Ave., 216/623-5055, www.clevelandpolicemuseum.org; 10am-4pm Mon.-Fri.; free

Greater Cleveland Aquarium

In January of 2012, Cleveland added another top regional attraction with the opening of this splashy new aquarium, the first of its kind in the state. Built into the bones of the historic Powerhouse building on the West Bank of the Flats, the 70,000-square-foot structure boasts 42 tanks filled with one million gallons of water. The Ohio Lakes and Rivers exhibit educates visitors on local freshwater species that are native to Ohio, including tortoises, catfish, and other local residents. The shark exhibit teems with toothy sharks, eels, and other saltwater sea life. A lengthy 145-foot underwater "Sea Tube" offers an impressive experience, with visitors passing through a tank with more than 5,000 fish. Roughly 300,000 visitors check out the aquarium per year, and designs are already in the works to expand the facility. Plan to spend about 90 minutes here.

MAP 1: 2000 Sycamore St., 216/862-8803, www.greaterclevelandaquarium.com; 10am-5pm daily; $20 adults, $18 seniors, $14 children

Money Museum at Federal Reserve Bank

How did we buy things before we had money? Who makes money? Why is a dollar worth a dollar? Answers to these and other cash conundrums are answered most days of the week at this fortress of funds. Designed to teach students and, perhaps, spend-thrift adults about what money is, where it comes from, and how to manage it, this museum doesn't exactly sound like a thrill ride, but interactive exhibits help deliver the message in a fun way. For instance, a display on ancient currency shows that stones, shells, and even cows were once traded as cash (imagine sticking a cow in your purse!). One of a dozen Federal Reserve Banks, the Cleveland office is worth a visit solely to gander at the 12-story Medici-style palazzo designed by the noted firm of Walker & Weeks.

MAP 1: 1455 E. 6th St., 216/579-2000, www.clevelandfed.org; 10am-2pm Mon.-Thurs.; free

Rock and Roll Hall of Fame Library and Archives

In 2012, the Rock and Roll Hall of Fame and Museum opened a separate library and archives, the most comprehensive repository of materials relating to the history of rock and roll. On the campus of Cuyahoga Community College, two miles from the museum, the library gives music scholars access to more than 200 archival collections, including the personal papers of performers, disc jockeys, photographers, journalists, critics, historians, poster artists, collectors, and fans. The collections contain books, sound recordings, video recordings, and individual items like personal letters penned by Aretha Franklin and Madonna, handwritten lyrics by Jimi Hendrix, and rare concert recordings from CBGB in the 1970s. A Rock Hall library card is free (with a valid photo ID) at the library. Call 24 hours before you'd like to visit to reserve a spot.

MAP 1: 2809 Woodland Ave., 216/515-1956, http://library.rockhall.com; 9am-5pm Mon.-Thurs., 10am-5pm Fri.; free

PERFORMING ARTS
Cleveland Ballet

As a resident dance company of Playhouse Square, Cleveland Ballet is the highly professional group that stages annual productions of the *Nutcracker* at the Hanna Theatre. The rest of the calendar is an exquisite mix of classical and neoclassical works produced under the expert leadership of Gladisa Guadalupe, an award-winning dancer, artistic director, and choreographer. The company also operates the School of Cleveland Ballet, which provides high quality instruction to toddlers, teens, and adults.

MAP 1: Playhouse Square, 216/320-9000, www.clevelandballet.org; showtimes vary; tickets from $25

Cleveland Opera Theater

Cleveland Opera Theater's motto is "Opera for All," with the guiding mission of making live opera accessible, affordable, and fun. Performing in venues around town, the company presents full-scale productions like *Madama Butterfly* and *Threepenny Opera*, new opera works by up-and-coming composers, and free family-friendly shows under the open skies.

MAP 1: Various locations, 216/512-0268, www.clevelandoperatheater.org; showtimes vary; tickets $25-100

Cleveland Play House

If you're looking for big names and bright lights, this is the theater company

ARTS RENAISSANCE ON THE CUYAHOGA

Thanks to progressive-minded industrialists of the last century, Cleveland boasts a rich arts landscape dotted with the likes of the **Cleveland Museum of Art**, the theaters of Playhouse Square, and the **Cleveland Orchestra.** But recent changes have boosted to new heights both the stature and reach of the Cleveland arts scene.

The Cleveland Museum of Art has always enjoyed a reputation as one of the premier repositories of fine art, but the museum has gotten bigger, better, and more user-friendly. A multiyear, $350 million renovation and expansion of the museum has left it in the best shape of its life. Begun in 2005, the project celebrated its official grand opening in late 2013.

Both the original 1916 beaux arts building and Marcel Breuer's 1971 addition underwent complete renovations. Two marble and granite wings have been added on. And a massive 39,000-square-foot atrium with a soaring glass ceiling now connects all the spaces. Today's footprint gives the museum 30 percent more gallery space to show off its permanent collection.

To better plan your visit, the museum introduced Gallery One, the largest multi-touch screen in the United States. This 40-foot interactive wall allows visitors to view 3,500 objects from the museum's collection and learn more about their literal and figurative place in the museum. Add to that new fine and casual dining and you see why the museum is operating at a whole new level.

The same can be said for the **Museum of Contemporary Art,** which, given its humble beginnings, has had an even more dramatic rise. For too long, the museum lived in a plain and odd-fitting space far removed from the epicenter of Cleveland culture, University Circle. That all changed in 2012, when the museum unveiled to the world its stunning new home. Designed by London-based architect Farshid Moussavi, the $27 million, 34,000-square-foot jaw-dropper is garnering serious buzz in the art and architecture world. The museum also serves as the cornerstone for the new and growing Uptown neighborhood just steps from the campus of Case Western Reserve University.

In Ohio City, Fred and Laura Ruth Bidwell have restored and expanded an old brick power substation into one of the newest and most talked about contemporary art spaces on the West Side. For half the year, the **Transformer Station,** as it's called, serves as home for the Bidwells' own impressive collection, while the other half of the year it features contemporary art programming from the Cleveland Museum of Art.

These are in addition to a $63.5 million renovation of the **Cleveland Institute of Art,** including a new 300-seat home for the **Cinematheque,** and an ever-growing collection of smaller yet important galleries, like **SPACES Gallery, Screw Factory Artists,** and **78th Street Studios,** which are breathing new life into old neighborhoods.

for you. Established in 1915, the Play House is one of America's longest-running professional theater companies. Producing a full lineup of popular and dramatic plays from well-established playwrights, the company routinely enjoys packed houses. A recent move to the renovated Allen Theatre complex in Playhouse Square has managed to boost already great attendance and sales figures while improving quality and creativity. The popular production of *A Christmas Story*, based on the motion picture set in Cleveland, is an annual tradition that runs from late November through late December.

MAP 1: 1407 Euclid Ave., 216/241-6000, www.clevelandplayhouse.com; showtimes vary; tickets from $25

✪ Great Lakes Theater

The Great Lakes Theater has been around since the early 1960s and has seen talent the likes of Tom Hanks, Piper Laurie, Hal Holbrook, and Olympia Dukakis. A high-tech overhaul of the historic Hanna Theatre has given this company a striking new home. The reconfigured theater is now an intimate 550-seat space featuring a flexible thrust stage that brings the action right into the laps of audience members. The futuristic stage is appropriate for a company renowned for reimagining classic productions. Unique, too, is the diversity of seating options, ranging from traditional theater chairs and private boxes to more casual lounge and bar seating. Plays are performed in rotating repertory, with shows alternating every few nights. Scheduled performances run from September through June and feature works by Shakespeare, Chekhov, and Sondheim, to name but a few. The Charles Dickens holiday classic *A Christmas Carol* is performed from late November through Christmas.

MAP 1: Hanna Theatre, 2067 E. 14th St., 216/241-6000, www.greatlakestheater.org; showtimes vary; adult tickets $15-90

Playhouse Square

Comprising five 1920s-era theaters—the Palace, State, Ohio, Allen, and Hanna—plus numerous smaller performing spaces, Playhouse Square is the nation's largest performing-arts center outside of New York City. More than 1,000 shows take place every year, including the best of Broadway, musical acts, opera, literary presentations, and comedy shows. Playhouse Square is also the creative backbone of a district that includes hotels, bars, restaurants, offices, and the home of Cleveland's public radio and television stations. Tickets are available by phone, online, or at the State Theatre box office (11am-6pm daily). A nearby parking garage is at the corner of East 15th Street and Chester Avenue. Free 90-minute tours are typically offered the first Saturday of the month, leaving the State Theatre lobby every 15 minutes 10am-11:30am.

MAP 1: Euclid Ave., 216/241-6000, www.playhousesquare.org; showtimes and cost vary

Playhouse Square

CINEMA
Dome Theater
That big brown sphere on Lake Erie's shore is not a large egg waiting to hatch; it's the exterior of the Great Lakes Science Center's Dome Theater. While IMAX films are praised for their scale and richness, Dome takes the experience to another plane. A six-story wraparound screen surrounds the viewer, creating an extraordinarily immersive experience. The movies shown are largely the science-museum type, focusing more on education than sheer enjoyment. Still, taking a virtual ride in an F-15 or through the Amazon jungle is pretty sweet, especially tilted back at a comfortable 30 degrees.

MAP 1: 601 Erieside Ave., 216/694-2000, www.glsc.org; showtimes vary; $11 adults, $9 children

Tower City Cinemas
Downtown's only multiplex, this 11-screen theater shows popular first-run fare. While you won't likely catch the latest Guillermo del Toro drama here, you will find slapstick, horror, and superhero megahits. Every March, Tower City Cinemas plays host to the impressive Cleveland International Film Fest, a 12-day, 500-screening extravaganza. Like Cedar Lee Theatre and Shaker Square Cinemas, this theater hosts Bargain Mondays, with $5 tickets and discounts on certain concession items. Free parking (up to four hours) is available at Tower City Center's parking garage on Huron Road. Present your parking voucher to the box office for validation when you purchase your movie tickets.

MAP 1: Tower City Center, 230 W. Huron Rd., 216/621-1374, www.clevelandcinemas.com; showtimes vary; $9.75 adults, $7 seniors, $6.75 children

Ohio City and Tremont   Map 2

GALLERIES
Paul Duda Gallery
As your fondness for the city grows, stop into Paul Duda for a memento. This sleek Tremont gallery sells remarkable art photographs of ruggedly handsome Cleveland. Printed in dreamy giclée, an archival ink-jet printing process, images of the Guardians of Transportation, Lake Erie shoreline, and Terminal Tower are mantel-worthy mementos of a fine visit. Vibrant and full-color shots of the skyline, Playhouse Square, and Progressive Field will serve as permanent reminders of fun days and nights gone by.

MAP 2: 2342 Professor Ave., 216/589-5788, www.pauldudagallery.com; 7pm-9pm Fri., 6pm-11pm second Fri. of the month, noon-9pm Sat.; free

Rob Hartshorn Studios
Robert Hartshorn is a master portrait artist; his expressive paintings conjure the work of Old Masters. His brother Peter paints moody, colorful landscapes from his travels around the world. At this Tremont gallery and studio, visitors can experience works from both, as well as those from other talented painters, sculptors, graphic designers, and even lighting designers.

MAP 2: 2342 Professor Ave., 216/403-2734, www.hartshornstudios.com; 10:30am-9pm Mon.-Thurs., 11am-5pm Sat. or by appt.; free

SPACES Gallery

It's been around since 1978, but a 2017 move to Ohio City has upped the visibility and vitality of this experimental art gallery considerably. Through approximately four major shows a year, and spanning every conceivable medium, this leader in contemporary art showcases the talent of emerging and mid-career artists. Much of the art attempts to tackle the most important issues of the day, including political, social, and cultural themes. All events are free and open to the public, and the gallery's lively opening-night parties are some of the best in town. The gallery's home in Ohio City's Van Rooy building puts it within walking distance of the sharp Transformer Station.

MAP 2: 2900 Detroit Ave., 216/621-2314, www.spacesgallery.org; noon-5pm Tues.-Sun., noon-8pm Thurs.; free

✪ Transformer Station

In 2013, nationally known art collectors Fred and Laura Bidwell opened this 8,000-square-foot jewel box of a museum in a building that once housed a trolley car power station—hence the name. The angular, contemporary space features soaring ceilings, clerestory windows, and a beefy and original metal hoist in the center of the room. The exhibits are programmed jointly by the Bidwells and the Cleveland Museum of Art, which long sought a West Side space to show contemporary art. Much of the work—local, regional, national, and international—comes from the Bidwells' own stunning collection of photography.

MAP 2: 1460 W. 29th St., 216/938-5429, www.transformerstation.org; 11am-5pm Wed. and Fri.-Sun., 11am-8pm Thurs.; free

PERFORMING ARTS

Convergence-Continuum

Shattering the theater's fourth wall since 2002, this oddball company is anything but traditional. But with success comes a little more convention—a good thing considering that until recently, the company rarely announced its roster of plays ahead of time. Its stage, called the Liminis, is set in a former garage on the fringes of trendy Tremont and seats only 50 in a very immersive experience. Its six-show season runs March through December and zeroes in on contemporary, cutting-edge plays that examine our culture.

MAP 2: 2438 Scranton Rd., 216/687-0074, www.convergence-continuum.org; showtimes vary; tickets from $20

Transformer Station

WALKING IN TREMONT

Tremont exemplifies the transformative power that art, artists, and galleries can have on a neighborhood. In the 1990s, this south-side community was in a state of decline and decay, which translated into affordable rents for artist studios, naturally. Soon came the chefs and bistros, followed by young new residents, higher rents, and exclusive new townhomes.

On the second Friday of every month, the city streets fill up with art lovers, street performers, pop-up art exhibits, and crafts vendors during **Walkabout Tremont** (5pm-10pm, www.walkabouttremont.com). The neighborhood's many artist studios, galleries, and boutiques unlock their doors early and stay open late. In addition to the dozen or so galleries shoehorned into the district, most bars, bistros, and coffee shops in the area exhibit local art, extending the virtual canvas.

Walkabout Tremont also happens to dovetail nicely with happy hour at the numerous restaurants in the area, so pop into one early on for a bite to fuel you through an evening of shopping.

Detroit Shoreway and Edgewater

Map 3

GALLERIES

1point618 Gallery

This architecturally appealing storefront in the Gordon Square Arts District contains a first-floor art gallery and the offices of an award-winning architect. The gallery, 1point618, holds approximately six to eight shows per year, focusing on contemporary art from regional, national, and international talents. The symbiosis between art and space serves to somehow elevate both, creating an atmosphere teeming with artistic tension.

MAP 3: 6421 Detroit Ave., 216/281-1618, www.1point618gallery.com; 11am-4pm Tues.-Fri., during shows and by appt.; free

78th Street Studios

This out-of-the-way complex of red-brick buildings has attracted artistic types for years. It's long been home to *Alternative Press* music magazine, as well as a busy recording studio and Internet radio station. It has been developing into the largest art

and design complex in Northeast Ohio, home to dozens of art galleries, artist studios, and art-services businesses. **Eileen Dorsey Studio** (www.eileendorsey.com) is home to lively, colorful landscape paintings; **E11even 2** (440/724-9261, www.e11even2.com) is a fun-spirited contemporary art space; **Kenneth Paul Lesko Gallery** (216/631-6719, www.kennethpaullesko.com) is a sharp contemporary space that shows fine art, sculpture, and photography. **Hedge Gallery** (216/650-4201, www.hedgeartgallery.com) shows contemporary art in all media with a focus on local, emerging talent. **Tregoning & Co.** (216/281-8626, www.tregoningandco.com) displays important works of art from notable and established artists. The popular Third Friday events, which run 5pm-9pm, attract thousands of art-curious visitors. Many galleries and studios are by appointment only at other dates and times.

MAP 3: 1305 W. 78th St.,
http://78thstreetstudios.com; hours vary;
free

PERFORMING ARTS
Blank Canvas Theatre
Established in 2011, Blank Canvas Theatre bills itself as a "Theatre for the People." In the artsy 78th Street Studios, the explosive upstart's inaugural season included a sold-out run of the Ohio premiere of *The Texas Chainsaw Musical* and a sold-out run of the Cleveland premiere of *Debbie Does Dallas, The Musical*. The diverse schedule includes dramas, musicals, even sketch comedy shows, and other wildcards geared to make theater fans out of even the most theater-averse guests in the house. Seating is general admission.

MAP 3: 1305 W. 80th St., Ste. 211,
440/941-0458, www.blankcanvastheatre.
com; 8pm Thurs.-Sat., 7pm Sun.; tickets
from $12

✪ Cleveland Public Theatre
There may be no more important stage in Ohio for experiencing innovative and adventurous original theater. Anchoring the bustling Gordon Square Arts District, this public theater opened in 1981 and offers so much more than just modern drama. CPT's groundbreaking performances entertain and inspire an entire community, and, in the process, propel it to a better place. From fall through early summer, the calendar is loaded with theatrical gems, many of which are Ohio and regional premieres. On top of the regular roster, special events might include a festival of 10-minute plays, readings of new works by emerging playwrights, and the popular Big Box series of new resident-produced work.

In September, CPT's annual fundraising extravaganza, Pandemonium, is the place to be.

MAP 3: 6415 Detroit Ave., 216/631-2727,
www.cptonline.org; showtimes vary; tickets
from $15

Maelstrom Collaborative Arts
After more than a decade as a nomadic theater group that performed pop-up plays in atypical spaces, Theater Ninjas landed a storefront home in the Gordon Square Arts District in 2017. Now, under the moniker Maelstrom Collaborative Arts, this rare brand of interactive theater takes place in the Courtland Building. With the stated goal of presenting theater as an event, the troupe presents a broad mix of original productions that include devised plays, classical reinventions, and participatory game-based art experiences.

MAP 3: Courtland Building, 5403
Detroit Ave., 440/941-1482, www.
maelstromcollaborativearts.org; showtimes
vary; tickets from $10

Near West Theatre
It's amazing what a few footlights can do for a person. Since 1978, this community-based theater has changed the lives of more than 15,000 children, teens, and adults, many from poverty-stricken families and neighborhoods. By committing to a schedule that is intense, difficult, and ultimately rewarding, participants come out on the other end more confident and with a stronger sense of self. But don't let the grassroots cause delude you; the productions are as good as any amateur youth theater around. A 300-seat theater in the Gordon Square Arts District that opened in 2015 signals many good years to come.

SPARED FROM THE WRECKING BALL: CLEVELAND'S GREAT THEATERS

Like all cities, Cleveland has blown it by demolishing buildings with great architectural merit. Only in hindsight do civic leaders and city residents typically grasp the value of what's been lost in the name of progress. If not for the work of a few visionary preservationists in the 1970s, Cleveland's Playhouse Square would have vanished like so many other architectural gems.

Playhouse Square's five opulent theaters opened between 1921 and 1922. Built in the classical style, the Ohio, State, Palace, Allen, and Hanna theaters boasted expanses of marble, lush hardwoods, hand-painted murals, and extravagant lobbies. For decades these houses entertained pleasure seekers with a variety of vaudeville acts, cinema, and dramatic performances.

In the late 1960s, downtown suffered from a disastrous cocktail of economic distress, suburban flight, and racial disquiet. Shops closed, people fled, and the theaters went dark. Vandals, thieves, and inattention so damaged the shuttered theaters that demolition was all but ensured.

Led by Ray Shepardson, a nonprofit called Playhouse Square Association campaigned to save the theaters. Thanks to public and private partnerships, money was raised not only to save the buildings from destruction, but also to begin repairing and restoring them. By the late 1990s, four of the five theaters had been restored to their former glory. In 2008, the last of the five, the **Hanna Theatre,** reopened as the stunning new home of the **Great Lakes Theater.** These days, every year more than a million visitors see performances at these venues and scores of smaller performance spaces concentrated in the two-block zone, and the economic overflow can be observed at area restaurants, shops, and hotels.

Walk through Playhouse Square on a brisk fall night and it's easy to see what Shepardson worked so hard to preserve. After all, without the arts, where is the beauty of life?

MAP 3: 6702 Detroit Ave., 216/961-9750, www.nearwesttheatre.org; showtimes vary; tickets $10 adults, $8 children

Talespinner Children's Theatre

Talespinner is a community theater company that presents original works by professional actors aimed specifically for youthful audiences. Often adapted from fairy tales or mythology, the highly imaginative productions might include dance, music, and/or puppetry, typically with elaborate costumes. While the stated goal is child development, the results are always sheer delight.

MAP 3: Reinberger Auditorium, 5209 Detroit Ave., 216/ 264-9680, www. talespinnerchildrenstheatre.org; showtimes vary; tickets $15 adults, $10 children

CINEMA
Capitol Theatre

In 2009, the Capitol Theatre showed its first film in 24 years, following a $7.5 million renovation. The restoration of the 1920s-era vaudeville and silent-movie house was just one aspect of a larger redevelopment of the Gordon Square Arts District, which is home to arts anchor Cleveland Public Theatre and the Near West Theatre. Now featuring three smaller screens, and run by Cleveland Cinemas, the popular venue shows a mix of popular new releases and indie-minded film fest fodder.

MAP 3: 1390 W. 65th St., 216/651-7295, www.clevelandcinemas.com; showtimes vary; $9.75 adults, $7 seniors, $6.75 children

University Circle and Little Italy

Map 4

GALLERIES
Murray Hill Galleries

Once a neighborhood schoolhouse, this warren of redbrick buildings now houses upscale apartments, condos, offices, and galleries. The numerous and ever-evolving roster of shops ranges from tiny incubator-sized studios to full-on retail and exhibition spaces. Art at the School House (216/721-1507, www.artattheschoolhouse.com) exhibits four artists per year, each of whom works in varied media, such as painting and photography. Beautiful and stirring figurative paintings are available at Tricia Kaman Studio and Gallery (216/559-6478, www.triciakaman.com). Murray Hill Bolt & Spool (216/229-2220, www.boltandspool.com) is a charming fabric boutique.

MAP 4: 2026 Murray Hill Rd., www.murrayhillcondos.net/galleries; hours vary; free

Reinberger Gallery

The Reinberger Gallery is housed in the 80,000-square-foot George Gund Building on the campus of the Cleveland Institute of Art. Billed as the largest college art gallery in Ohio, this exhibition space often features the work of established artist graduates. In addition to displays of the graduate theses of BFA students and the popular CIA Faculty Exhibition, the gallery presents thousands of art and design objects, plus film, video, animation, and art installations. Visitors can look forward to approximately eight shows per year, including the often whimsical and always brash Student Independent Exhibition.

MAP 4: 11610 Euclid Ave., 216/421-7407, www.cia.edu; 10am-5pm Mon.-Thurs., 10am-3pm Fri., noon-5pm select Sat. summer; 10am-5pm Mon.-Thurs., 10am-9pm Fri., noon-5pm Sat.-Sun. fall-spring; free

Verne Collection

Established in 1953, the Verne Collection of Japanese Art includes work from respected Japanese artists and printmakers from the 17th, 18th and 19th centuries, as well as contemporary Western artists living and working in Japan. This Little Italy gallery boasts some of the highest-quality Japanese prints in America, and it consistently exhibits in top shows throughout the country and beyond.

MAP 4: 2207 Murray Hill Rd., 216/231-8866, www.vernegallery.com, 11am-5pm Tues.-Sat.; free

MUSEUMS
Cleveland Museum of Natural History

History is on display at this fine institute of scientific education. From the moment folks cross the threshold, they are immersed in a world of past, present, and future wonder. Exhibits shed light on the mysteries and truths at work in our universe. A Foucault pendulum demonstrates in dramatic, albeit slow, fashion the Earth's rotation on its axis. As one might expect of a natural history museum, there are bones, and lots of them. A cast of the original skeleton of *Australopithecus afarensis,* also known as "Lucy," is on display. Dino fans will delight at a tyrannosaur, stegosaur, and "Happy," one of the most complete mounted sauropods on display in the world. A domed planetarium features the Sky-Skan projector, which shows the positions of more than 5,000 stars, nebulae, and galaxies. Outside, explore a two-acre wildlife center that highlights native Ohio flora and fauna, including bobcats and bald eagles, river otters, and owls, while traversing a treetop trail. The on-site café serves delicious lunches.

MAP 4: 1 Wade Oval Dr., 800/317-9155, www.cmnh.org; 10am-5pm Mon.-Tues. and Thurs.-Sat., 10am-10pm Wed., noon-5pm Sun.; $15 adults, $12 seniors, children, and students; planetarium tickets $5 with general admission

MOCA

✪ Museum of Contemporary Art

In 2013, MOCA completed a monumental move to a new home in University Circle, the epicenter of art in Cleveland. Designed by London-based architect Farshid Moussavi, and built at a cost of $27 million, the gem-like structure has forever changed the look of its new neighborhood. Now the noncollecting museum has more room than ever to showcase risk-taking and provocative visual art from emerging and established artists. Stunning installations, sculptures, paintings, photography, and video are just some of the works that routinely make layovers here. Lectures, readings, films, and performances round out the arts-education programming.

MAP 4: 11400 Euclid Ave., 216/421-8671, www.mocacleveland.org; 11am-5pm Tues.-Sun.; $9.50 adults, $6 seniors, $5 students

Western Reserve Historical Society

Chronicling the history of the Western Reserve, this University Circle institution is composed of a cultural history museum, an auto and aviation museum, and a research library. In addition to high-profile touring exhibits, the museum holds a bounty of local artifacts, treasuries, and tales from the area once known as the Western Reserve. The Chisholm Halle Costume Collection is one of the top-ranked costume collections in the nation, with some 30,000 garments on rotating display. The Crawford Auto-Aviation Museum displays historically significant automobiles, aircraft, bicycles, motorcycles, and spacecraft, paying special attention to the significant contribution of Northeast Ohio companies. Approximately 150 unique vintage models are on hand. As the principal repository for documents relating to Western Reserve history, the library at WRHS is a popular and important research facility.

MAP 4: 10825 East Blvd., 216/721-5722, www.wrhs.org; 10am-5pm Tues.-Sat., noon-5pm Sun.; $10 adults, $9 seniors, $5 children

PERFORMING ARTS
Cleveland Institute of Music

Gifted classical musicians from all over the globe come to Cleveland to study at this world-class conservatory. Those of us who can only dream about such talent flock to this school's matchless concert series. Students, faculty (including many Cleveland Orchestra members), and visiting luminaries perform year-round on the stages of this University Circle institution. Concerts range from solo guitar recitals to full-on string quartets. These days, concertgoers have it better than ever thanks to the stunning Mixon Hall, a 235-seat rectangular glass recital hall. Most concerts are free, and seating for free concerts is generally on a first-come, first-served basis, though some passes may be reserved one week ahead of time by phone. Cameras and recording devices are prohibited.

MAP 4: 11021 East Blvd., 216/791-5000, www.cim.edu; showtimes vary; free unless otherwise noted

✪ Cleveland Orchestra

There is little contention that the Cleveland Orchestra, under the leadership of music director Franz Welser-Möst, is one of the finest orchestras playing today. Audiences and critics from New York to Vienna routinely praise the band, which celebrated its centennial in 2018, as sheer musical triumph. From late September through May, the orchestra performs at breathtaking Severance Hall. From early July through Labor Day, the orchestra performs weekend concerts at its summer home, Blossom Music Center, in Cuyahoga. On a fine summer night, there is nothing better than spreading out a blanket on the lawn at Blossom to enjoy some classical music. For decades, the Cleveland Orchestra has performed a free concert in downtown's Public Square in honor of Independence Day. The annual event takes place the week of July 4, attracts 40,000 people or more, and is capped off with a rousing performance of Tchaikovsky's *1812 Overture* followed by a fireworks display. Get there early, bring a picnic dinner, and enjoy one of Cleveland's finest moments.

MAP 4: 11001 Euclid Ave., 216/231-1111, www.clevelandorchestra.com; showtimes vary; tickets from $31

CINEMA
Cleveland Institute of Art Cinematheque

If it weren't for the nonprofit Cinematheque, obsessive Cleveland film fans would never lay eyes upon some of the finest foreign, classic, and independent movies of our time—or any other, for that matter. As the name suggests, this paean to alternative film is on the campus of the Cleveland Institute of Art, in the George Gund Building to be exact. Films are shown in 16mm, 35mm, and digital format 50 weekends per year. Visit the all-new 300-seat theater and see why *The New York Times* called Cinematheque "one of the country's best repertory movie theaters."

MAP 4: 11610 Euclid Ave., 216/421-7450, www.cia.edu/cinematheque; showtimes vary; most films general admission $10, ages 25 and under $7

CONCERT VENUES

Evans Amphitheater

This gem of an urban amphitheater is nestled in a wooded Cleveland Heights park. Wholly invisible to drivers and passersby, the concert venue always delights first-timers. While small—1,200 seats under cover, 1,200 on the lawn—Evans Amphitheater draws top-talent artists who crave more intimate settings. The venue is a favorite of singer-songwriters like Lyle Lovett, Bruce Hornsby, and others. Concerts run from about the middle of June through August. Specials include $2 Tuesdays and free jazz in the afternoon. The smaller 300-seat Alma Theater is the site of musicals, cabarets, and local acts. Pack a blanket and a picnic, or buy snacks at the concession stand. Though you can't bring in alcohol, you can buy beer and wine inside. Tickets are available through Ticketmaster (www.ticketmaster.com), but to save on fees, hit the Cain Park box office.

MAP 5: Cain Park, Superior Rd. at Lee Rd., 216/371-3000, www.cainpark.com; showtimes and cost vary

GALLERIES

Heights Arts Gallery

Small but mighty describes this East Side gallery. Run by Heights Arts, a nonprofit community arts organization, the exhibition space focuses largely on the work of local artists. And when it comes to creative talent, residents of Cleveland Heights tend to be unfairly gifted. The gallery puts on five exhibitions a year plus a popular seasonal event: "A Holiday Store" features affordable art gifts by local artists only. Next to the Cedar Lee Theatre, the gallery is a popular pre- and post-film stopover.

MAP 5: 2175 Lee Rd., 216/371-3457, www.heightsarts.org; noon-9:30pm Mon. and Fri.-Sat., noon-6pm Thurs., noon-5pm Sun.; free

Still Point Gallery

A recent move to the Cedar Fairmount Historic District has provided a more visible gallery space for the owners to display the fine works of various painters, photographers, jewelers, sculptors, glassmakers, and ceramicists. Highlights include the drama-filled landscape photography of C. Geoffrey Baker, one-of-a-kind jewelry, and hard-to-find specialty products.

MAP 5: 12427 Cedar Rd., 216/721-4992, www.stillpoint-gallery.com, 10am-6pm Tues.-Wed. and Sat., 10am-7:30pm Thurs.-Fri.; free

Wolfs Gallery

Wolfs began life as an upscale auction house dealing in a wide range of periods and styles, a practice that they continue as a gallery of fine art and antiques. Its current spacious, multi-level building has given them more room to store, display, and sell art. While diverse, the inventory generally covers European and American paintings ranging from the 18th century to today, with a nice emphasis on local works from the late 19th century through the 1950s. Openings, temporary exhibits, and special events flesh out the calendar.

MAP 5: 13010 Larchmere Blvd.,
216/721-6945, www.wolfsgallery.com;
11am-5pm Wed.-Sat.; free

PERFORMING ARTS
Dobama Theatre

For more roughly 60 years, Dobama Theatre has been a Cleveland Heights performing arts institution, attracting people to its various stages. In 2009, the off-Broadway theater company finally landed a more permanent space at the renovated and expanded Cleveland Heights Public Library. Dobama's mission is to highlight contemporary plays by established and emerging playwrights. Each season, Dobama produces five or six plays, the bulk of which are Cleveland, U.S., or world premieres. For a half century, the company has cultivated a reputation for being professional, innovative, and progressive.

MAP 5: 2340 Lee Rd., 216/932-3396, www.dobama.org; showtimes vary; tickets $12-18

Ensemble Theatre

Ensemble is a small professional theater company dedicated to the performance of classic American plays that are socially relevant and that celebrate the human spirit. Many are state, national, and even world premieres, like *Alabama Story*, which depicts the story of an Alabama state librarian who was persecuted for protecting a children's book depicting the marriage of a white and a black rabbit. Also on a recent calendar was a world premiere adaptation of Jules Verne's *Around the World in Eighty Days*. Ensemble conducts a weekly StageWrights Workshop for writers and playwrights.

MAP 5: 2843 Washington Blvd., 216/321-2930, www.ensembletheatrecle.org; showtimes vary; tickets $12-29

CINEMA
Cedar Lee Theatre

The Cedar Lee shows the very best in first-run independent film. If it played well at Sundance, chances are good you'll see it on the marquee of this Cleveland Heights landmark. But it isn't only esoteric head-scratchers on the schedule; Oscar-worthy Hollywood fare is also screened here. Cult-movie fans have been coming in to catch the midnight showing of *The Rocky Horror Picture Show* since 1998, when the theater began screening it. At the better-than-average concession stands, you'll find fresh pastries, wraps, coffee drinks, herbal tea, imported beers, and wine—and popcorn, of course. Some of the six theaters are roomier than others. Like Tower City Cinemas and Shaker Square Cinemas, this theater hosts Bargain Mondays, with $5 tickets and discounted concession items.

MAP 5: 2163 Lee Rd., 216/321-5411, www.clevelandcinemas.com; showtimes vary; $9.75 adults, $7 seniors, $6.75 children

Shaker Square Cinemas

This renovated art deco movie house now features six state-of-the-art theaters that screen major Hollywood releases plus some independent and foreign fare. Located on Shaker Square, the theater is near numerous bars and restaurants, making a dinner-date a breeze. In addition to the typical sugary and crunchy provisions, the concession stand also sells pastries, beer, and wine. Like Tower City Cinemas and Cedar Lee Theatre, this theater hosts Bargain Mondays, with $5 tickets and discounted concession items.

MAP 5: 13116 Shaker Sq., 216/921-9342, www.clevelandcinemas.com; showtimes vary; $9.75 adults, $7 seniors, $6.75 children

Lakewood

GALLERIES
Screw Factory Artists

This rambling brick warehouse, commonly referred to as the Screw Factory, houses dozens of live/work studios and teaching spaces. The building houses more than 30 artist studios and businesses, including those of ceramicists, enamel artists, painters, glassworkers, painters, and mixed-media artists. Hours are kept individually by artist and studio, but exploration is encouraged. Official events are held the first Saturday in May and November, and the popular Last Minute Market, which attracts thousands, is held on the third Saturday of December.

MAP 6: 13000 Athens Ave., 216/521-0088, www.screwfactoryartists.com; hours vary; free

PERFORMING ARTS
Beck Center for the Arts

In addition to its impressive arts-education programming, the Beck produces a full season of professional theater, including comedies, musicals, and contemporary drama. Roughly eight performances per year are presented from fall through late spring on one of two stages. Recent productions include ambitious takes on *She Loves Me* and *33 Variations*. An equally impressive roster of youth theater is performed by Beck drama students. Make sure you leave a little extra time to wander through the Beck's art gallery, which often is filled with compelling exhibits.

MAP 6: 17801 Detroit Ave., 216/521-2540, www.beckcenter.org; showtimes vary; tickets from $12

Greater Cleveland

CONCERT VENUES
Blossom Music Center

Built in the late 1960s as the summer home of the Cleveland Orchestra, this amphitheater sees a full range of live-music action from spring until fall. Tucked into Cuyahoga Valley National Park, its setting is one of dense forests, leafy hillsides, and wide-open skies. On a warm summer evening, there is no greater joy than tossing down a blanket and enjoying a picnic under the stars while the orchestra or your favorite band performs. Then again, that night can sour quickly if the clouds darken and the rain falls.

Be prepared with tarps, rain gear, and an extra set of dry clothes for the long drive home. Or do what many regulars do: Spring for seats in the covered pavilion as insurance. Traffic in and out of the park can be brutal, so leave plenty of extra travel time.

MAP 7: 1145 W. Steels Corners Rd., Cuyahoga Falls, 888/225-6776, www.clevelandorchestra.com; showtimes and cost vary

MUSEUMS
Polka Hall of Fame Museum

Fans of the "happiest sound around" will want to make the short journey to Euclid to visit this museum dedicated to the preservation of polka. Cleveland-style polka has its roots in Slovenian folk music, which was popularized by local musicians such as Frankie Yankovic and Johnny Vadnal. Inside, you'll find memorabilia and artifacts from past and present polka stars, including accordions, stage outfits, and photographs. Learn about not just the Cleveland style, but also Chicago, Czech, Slovak, and German. Prominent placement is also devoted to the winners of the annual Polka Hall of Fame awards.

MAP 7: 605 E. 222nd St., Euclid, 216/261-3263, www.clevelandstyle.com; 11am-4pm Tues.-Wed. and Fri.-Sat.; free

PERFORMING ARTS
Karamu House

Karamu is the nation's oldest African-American cultural arts institution. The famous interracial theater company was the site of many Langston Hughes premieres. Under new direction, Karamu once again is electrifying and edifying new generations of theatergoers. While there is no shortage of knee-slapping comedies and musicals, many of the works are serious and thought-provoking examinations of race and culture. A recent improvement grant has paved the way for upgrades to the entire facility. The regular schedule runs fall through early summer.

MAP 7: 2355 E. 89th St., Cleveland, 216/795-7077, www.karamuhouse.org; showtimes vary; tickets from $20

Various Locations

PERFORMING ARTS
Apollo's Fire

The *Boston Globe* called Apollo's Fire one of America's leading baroque orchestras. When they are not touring the nation or recording, this professional ensemble moves listeners at home through its calendar of performances. Concerts are held fall through spring at various locations in and around Cleveland and Akron, primarily in large churches. For a bite-size portion of baroque, check the schedule for one of the popular matinee concerts, 45-minute programs geared toward young children and antsy adults. Tickets for these and other programs can be purchased by phone or online.

Various locations: 216/320-0012, www.apollosfire.org; showtimes vary; tickets from $22

DANCECleveland

Dedicated to bringing the very best of modern and contemporary dance to town, DANCECleveland presents the works of nationally and internationally recognized troupes. Performances are held in Playhouse Square, Cain Park, and the University of Akron's E. J Thomas Hall and feature the best touring companies out there, including those of BalletX, Paul Taylor Dance Company, and Cedar Lake Contemporary Ballet. Approximately four to six bookings take place each season, which runs from fall through spring.

SMART SEATS

Looking for an affordable way to catch a show in Playhouse Square? Many performances set aside a number of discount tickets that can be purchased ahead of time. These Smart Seats run just $10 apiece, roughly the cost of going to a movie. Simply surf over to www. playhousesquare.org and search for a show that interests you. If the play, concert, or dance listing has the Smart Seats logo under the ticket information, that means there are cheap seats available. You likely will be seated in the rear of the balcony, but at a savings of up to 80 percent off the primo seats, there is little to complain about.

Various locations: 216/241-6000, www. dancecleveland.org; showtimes vary; tickets from $25

GroundWorks Dance Theater

GroundWorks breaks ground by taking risk. The small but professional company's repertory of contemporary dance includes pieces choreographed by artistic director David Shimotakahara as well as works created by various guest choreographers. Performances are scattered about town throughout the year, with appearances at E. J. Thomas Hall in Akron, Cain Park in Cleveland Heights, Lincoln Park in Tremont, and others.

Various locations: 216/751-0088, www. groundworksdance.org; showtimes vary; tickets free-$50

Verb Ballets

This contemporary dance company maintains a deep repertory of pieces, many choreographed by former artistic director Hernando Cortez. A self-described curator of expressive movement, Verb "discovers, collects, interprets, and stages choreography that matters." Performances are scattered about town throughout the year, from Playhouse Square and Cain Park to Tremont's Lincoln Park and points south in Akron.

Various locations: 216/397-3757, www. verbballets.org; showtimes and cost vary

Festivals and Events

WINTER

Cleveland WinterFest

Thousands choose to get into the holiday spirit by attending Cleveland WinterFest, an annual downtown celebration that serves as the unofficial start of the joyous season. Festivities take place in Public Square on the first Saturday after Thanksgiving. A number of family-friendly events occur throughout the day in and around the square, but the real party kicks off with the holiday tree lighting at dusk. Depending on the weather, the parade of vintage horse-drawn carriages that follows can look like a scene ripped from a Currier and Ives print. Fire trucks, fife and drum corps, and marching bands also boisterously work their way around the square. The night is capped off by a spectacular fireworks display.

Downtown: Public Sq., www. downtowncleveland.com; Sat. after Thanksgiving; free

Cleveland Kurentovanje

Kurentovanje (koo-rahn-toh-VAHN-yay) is the most popular carnival event in Slovenia, and given Cleveland's large Slovenian contingent, it only made sense to import the unique and lively heritage festival. The event is named after costumed characters called *kurents*, fuzzy, sheepskin-clad beasts with belts of bells that are said to help chase away winter. The main event takes place on the Saturday nearest Fat Tuesday in February and includes a parade, polka music, bocce tournament, and plenty of food and drink.

Downtown: Slovenian National Home, 6417 Saint Clair Ave., www.clevelandkurentovanje.com; Feb.; free

Brite Winter Fest

Launched in 2010 by a few friends who thought Cleveland needed an outdoor festival in the dead of winter, Brite Winter Fest has grown like the proverbial snowball rolling downhill. After 800 crazy people showed up to an out-of-the-way urban park the first couple years, the event has been held in Ohio City and then the West Bank of the Flats, where the festival has grown to a staggering 20,000 attendees. Held in late February, the event features dozens of bands and live performances scattered across multiple stages, art-filled heated tents, food trucks, fire pits, and fun-spirited games like the 24-foot giant wooden Skee-Ball. Of course, the neighborhood bars and restaurants make ideal places to warm up over a hot cup of bourbon.

Downtown: www.britewinter.com; late Feb.; free

Cleveland International Film Fest

With more than 100,000 people attending some 500 screenings over a 12-day period, the Cleveland International Film Fest is a whirl of creative activity. Simultaneous screenings occur all day in multiple theaters at Tower City Cinemas. The March event always kicks off with an opening-night film and gala, followed by approximately 200 feature films, 200 short subjects from around the globe, and numerous interactive media projects. Filmmakers lead post-flick Q-and-A sessions. Attending the festival for the first time can be a little overwhelming. The best strategy is to look over the program guide, select the movies you want to see, and buy tickets in advance. Get to the cinema early to avoid being shut out. Tickets can be purchased in the lobby of Tower City Cinemas, online, or by phone. Discounts are offered for 10-packs and members of the Cleveland Film Society.

Downtown: Tower City Cinemas, 877/304-3456, www.clevelandfilm.org; Mar.; cost varies

St. Patrick's Day Parade

The Cleveland Irish community is large and proud. How else do you explain an outdoor parade in the middle of March attracting upward of 375,000 people? With roots stretching clear back to 1867, Cleveland's St. Patrick's Day Parade is one of the largest and oldest of its kind in the nation. The parade steps off at 1pm on March 17; if the holiday falls on a Sunday, start time is 2pm. More than 10,000 participants take part in the march, which works its way down Superior Avenue from East 18th to Public Square. Get to the parade route early to secure a good vantage point to watch the seemingly never-ending line of marching bands, Irish dancers, drill teams, military units, civic clubs, waving politicians, and local celebrities. Because this event is held in March, the weather can be wildly unpredictable. As the Boy Scouts say, "be prepared."

Downtown: Superior Ave., www. stpatricksdaycleveland.com; Mar. 17; free

SPRING

Dyngus Day Cleveland

After attending the Dyngus Day festivities in Buffalo, which attract upward of 60,000 people each year, Justin Gorski decided that Cleveland needed its very own. Often described as the Polish version of Mardi Gras, Dyngus Day always takes place on the Monday after Easter, known as Śmigus-Dingus to the Polish diaspora. The event is a traditional pagan holiday that began as a celebration of the rites of spring but has evolved into just another reason to skip work, drink beer, rock out to polka, and have silly fun. Since 2011, the event has grown from 1,500 people to more than 10,000. The bash includes an Accordion March, the traditional crowning of Miss Dyngus, live polka music and dancing at neighborhood bars, and a parade.

Detroit Shoreway: Gordon Square Arts District, www.clevelanddyngus.com; Mon. after Easter; free

Cleveland Asian Festival

Since 2010, Cleveland Asian Festival has grown from a quirky ethnic gathering to one of the most widely attended cultural events of the year, attracting close to 50,000 over a weekend. Intended to celebrate Asian Pacific Heritage Month, and spread over two days in May, the festival features outdoor stages hosting local musicians, martial arts demonstrations, Taiko drummers, and a traditional Asian fashion runway show. Also on the annual billing are

the crowd favorite Lion and Dragon dances, foods from multiple Asian and Pacific Island cultures, the ever-popular egg roll eating contest, and a pop-up marketplace offering diverse wares from handmade clothing to household goods.

Downtown: Payne Ave. at E. 30th, www. clevelandasianfestival.org; May; free

Rite Aid Cleveland Marathon

Started in 1978, the Rite Aid Cleveland Marathon is one of the oldest continuously held footraces in the nation. More than $20,000 in prize money is awarded to the winners of the men's and women's marathon, half-marathon, and 10K races. Of course, the 20,000 or so athletes who compete each year do so for bragging rights, not cash. The relatively flat 26.3-mile course takes runners past such notable landmarks as the Rock Hall, Great Lakes Science Center, Cleveland Browns Stadium, and through neighborhoods such as Tremont, Ohio City, Detroit Shoreway, and Lakewood. Even if you've never donned a pair of sneakers in your life, consider coming down for the party. In good weather, massive and enthusiastic crowds gather along the course and at the finish line to cheer on the runners.

Various locations: 800/467-3826, www. clevelandmarathon.com; May; free

Hessler Street Fair

Apart from a 10-year hiatus, the Hessler Street Fair has been going strong since 1969, when a group of residents banded together to save their artsy neighborhood from development. These days, it's a glorious two-day, late-spring, family friendly festival filled with live music, poetry, food and community. Hessler Court, where much of the action takes

food trucks lined up for Edgewater Live

place, is the last wood-paved street in Cleveland. Parking is a bear, so walk, ride or carpool.

Shaker Heights: Hessler Ct. at Hessler Rd., www.hesslerstreetfair.org; late May or early June; free

Pride in the CLE

In 2018, Cleveland's long-running Cleveland Pride event joined forces with Pride in the CLE, a newer tradition hosted by the LGBT Cleveland Community Center, to become one unified celebration of the local LGBTQ community. Held over the course of a weekend, typically in late May or early June, the festivities include a march followed by a festival, along with ancillary events around town.

Citywide: http://lgbtcleveland.org/pride-in-the-cle; late May or early June

SUMMER
Edgewater Live

Since taking over stewardship of Edgewater Park from the State, Cleveland Metroparks has found a million and one ways to improve every aspect of the experience. In 2014, the local parks organization launched this weekly happy hour concert series, a beachy bash that attracts nearly 100,000 revelers per season. Every Thursday evening from late May through early August, live bands take to the stage, food trucks line the pathways, and beverage vendors dispense cold beer and wine. Traffic getting in and out can be a bear on most nights, so ride a bike or park in nearby Detroit Shoreway and walk through pedestrian tunnels at West 65th and West 76th Streets.

Detroit Shoreway: 6500 Memorial Shoreway, 216/635-3200, www.clevelandmetroparks.com; 4:30pm-9pm Thurs. late May-early Aug.; free

Larchmere Porchfest

A little over a decade ago, this tiny grassroots festival started with a good idea and grew from there. Over the course of a day, bands of all genres (from classical to Americana) perform on the front porches and patios of great old homes in the Larchmere neighborhood. At last count, some 30 performances were presented at 30 locations, some of which take place simultaneously. Neighbors and music lovers walk or ride bikes from spot to spot, joining an impromptu dance party before moving on.

Shaker Heights: Larchmere Blvd., www. larchmereporchfest.org; June; free

Larchmere Porchfest

Wade Oval Wednesdays

On Wednesday evenings from mid-June through late August, folks gather on beautiful Wade Oval for free outdoor concerts, movies, and entertainment. This family-friendly event—simply referred to as WOW!—features local bands that play reggae, jazz, blues, and rock. Food, beer, and wine are sold on-site, and local artisans set up booths to sell their crafts. Many of University Circle's major cultural attractions offer extended evening hours that coincide with WOW! events, making it easy to plan a civilized night on the town. Concerts usually run 6pm-9pm.

University Circle: 216/707-5033, www. universitycircle.org; Wed. June-Aug.; free

Cleveland Shakespeare Festival

The only thing better than live Shakespeare is live Shakespeare performed in the great outdoors. That's precisely the M.O. of Cleveland Shakespeare Festival, a traveling troupe of actors that brings classic dramas, tragedies, and comedies to life in various alfresco locations throughout Greater Cleveland. Shows typically run weekends from mid-June through early August. Bring a low-slung chair or a blanket. Curtain is at 7pm.

Various locations: 440/794-1273, www.cleveshakes.com; 7pm Fri.-Sun. mid-June-early Aug.; free

Parade the Circle

University Circle's signature summer event Parade the Circle is not focused around a specific holiday, but on artistic expression, creativity, and the rich diversity of the neighborhood. The centerpiece of the event is the parade, which begins at noon and features a psychedelic pageant of whimsical costumed marchers. Approximately 2,000 people take part, some dressed as giant puppets, some towering over the crowd on stilts, and others taking spots on imaginative floats. Entertainment before and after the parade ranges from African dance and classical music to storytelling and puppet shows. The Circle Village area on Wade Oval is loaded with family-appropriate arts and crafts, food, and festivities. Typically held the second Saturday in June, the parade and subsequent activities can attract 60,000 people in nice weather. Grab your spot along East Boulevard or Wade Oval Drive by noon to enjoy the show.

University Circle: 216/707-5033, www.
clevelandart.org; 2nd Sat. in June; free

Clifton Arts & Musicfest

What started as a small neighborhood block party 30-plus years ago
has blossomed into a full-fledged arts
and music festival attracting close to
40,000 revelers per year. Only slightly
smaller than the renowned Cain Park
Arts Festival, Clifton Arts & Musicfest
features the works of about 120 different artists in every conceivable genre.
Long regarded as one of the more free-
spirited neighborhoods, Clifton knows
how to throw a bash. A full lineup of
live music covers most tastes, from
rock and blues to reggae and funk.
Scores of restaurants dish up local
specialties, and community and civic
organizations offer craft activities for
the little artists in the group. Look for
this event around the third Saturday
in June.

Lakewood: Clifton Blvd. at W. 117th St.,
216/228-4383, www.cudell.com; 3rd Sat. in
June; free

City Stages

When the Cleveland Museum of Art
launched City Stages, a global music
series that pops up every summer,
nobody could predict how quickly
it would flourish—especially given
the relative obscurity of the acts.
Well, those bands—an Afro-pop duo
from Mali, a Balkan brass band from
Romania, a bachata dance troupe from
the Dominican Republic—might not
be well known by the local masses,
but they are adored the world over for
their matchless talent. Typically held
Wednesdays in July, these free outdoor
concerts spark dancing in the streets,
community, and urban renewal.

Various locations: www.clevelandart.
org; July; free

City Stages

Rooms to Let: CLE

The Slavic Village neighborhood of
Cleveland was one of the hardest hit
during the 2008 foreclosure crisis. In
2014, this immersive art exhibition
was launched in an attempt to call attention to the issue by transforming
vacant houses, some slated for demolition, with temporary art installations. Additionally, vacant lots became
homes to edgy art installations and
the sites of hands-on activities. Slavic
Village Development selects a group of
curators, who assemble a team of artists to totally rework the interior and
exterior of the structures. Check the
website for dates.

Greater Cleveland: 216/429-1182, www.
slavicvillage.org; July; free

Cain Park Arts Festival

Held annually the second full weekend
in July, the Cain Park Arts Festival is
a top-rated juried arts event that runs
Friday through Sunday and features
the visual art of some 150 artists. Over
the course of a weekend, more than
60,000 visitors will stroll the wooded
grounds of Cain Park exploring original works of art, including paintings,
watercolors, photography, sculpture,
ceramics, and jewelry. Accompanying
the art show is a full complement of
adult and family entertainment at
nearby Evans Amphitheater and Alma

Theater. Local restaurants also set up shop and provide the fuel for an afternoon of delicious spending.

Cleveland Heights: Superior Rd. at Lee Rd., 216/371-3000, www.cainpark.com; 2nd weekend of July; $5

Taste of Tremont

Of all the summer neighborhood festivals, Taste of Tremont pretty much has a lock on the "best food" category, as the district is home to many of Cleveland's best restaurants and chefs, most of whom are on duty at this boisterous block party. Cordoned off from Literary Road to Jefferson Avenue, Professor Avenue turns into a blockslong street party, capped off with a celebratory open-air beer garden. Sample the specialties of more than 20 local restaurants, most of which are dished up personally by the chefs. Live bands perform throughout the day, as do various and sundry roaming entertainers. Many of the super-cool galleries and boutiques extend their hours to coincide with the festival. The Taste of Tremont usually runs noon-8pm around the third Sunday in July.

Tremont: Professor Ave., 216/575-0920, www.tasteoftremont.com; 3rd Sun. in July; free

Night Market Cleveland

Few seasonal events have taken off as quickly as Night Market Cleveland. Since 2014, this ever-expanding affair has become the can't-miss thing to do on the last Friday in July, August, and September. As darkness falls on Cleveland's former Chinatown, the strip transforms into a bustling Pan-Asian night market lined with more than 100 food hawkers selling everything from grilled squid on a stick and spicy lamb kebabs to Korean shave ice. Throughout the evening, cultural performances take the stage, a lion wends its way through the thick crowds, and the line for the bar continues to grow.

Downtown: Rockwell Ave. at E. 21st St., www.nightmarketcle.com; last Sat. July-Sept.; free

Burning River Fest

Stewarded by the eco-minded folks at Great Lakes Brewing Co., the Burning River Fest is more than just another occasion to party. Held for two nights in August at the historic Coast Guard Station on Whiskey Island, the fest is all about living responsibly. Important issues such as ecological conservation, environmental protection, historical preservation, and sustainable use of waterways are tackled through numerous exhibits, discussions, and demonstrations. Despite the lofty message, some 11,000 folks find plenty of reasons to smile at this bio-minded block party. Bands play on three separate stages, there's a diverse mix of food vendors, and Great Lakes Brewing will be pouring plenty of cold beer—served in 100 percent compostable corn cups, of course. Carpooling and bike riding are strongly encouraged.

Downtown: Coast Guard Station on Whiskey Island, www.burningriverfest.org; Aug.; $15

Sparx City Hop

Billed as Ohio's largest art walk, Sparx City Hop unites the efforts of more than 50 independent galleries into a weekend-long celebration of art and culture. Typically held in August, Sparx organizes a network of trolleys to link the major art districts in Ohio City, Playhouse Square, and St. Clair Superior. The goal not only is to spark interest in local art, but also is to stimulate excitement about these urban neighborhoods on a smaller, more intimate level. Over the day-long event, galleries and nearby retail shops extend their hours of operation. Satellite art exhibits, mini-festivals, and musical performances also take place at various locations over the course of the weekend. Brightly marked bike paths were recently added to the proceedings, making it easier to pedal one's way from gallery to gallery. Various locations: 216/736-7799, www.downtowncleveland.com; Aug.; free

Feast of the Assumption

Technically, the Feast of the Assumption celebrates the ascension of the Virgin Mary. Practically, it's an occasion to party and celebrate Italian-American heritage. This annual four-day blowout begins solemnly enough, with Mass followed by a procession of the Blessed Virgin through Little Italy. The real party hits the streets at night, when literally thousands descend upon the narrow lanes of this old-world neighborhood. Main attractions, apart from the booze, include authentic Italian treats like sausage-and-pepper sandwiches, creamy gelato, and delicious cannoli. Back-alley charity casino games tucked into smoky tents have a delightfully illicit feel to them. The festivities end with a bang thanks to a rousing fireworks display. Look for the event in mid-August.

Little Italy: Mayfield Rd. at Murray Hill Rd., 216/421-2995, www.clevelandlittleitaly.com; mid-Aug.; free

FALL
Cleveland National Air Show

If it's Labor Day weekend in Cleveland, you can be sure to hear the roar of the U.S. Navy Blue Angels' F/A-18s during Cleveland air show. The Angels perform a one-hour choreographed flight presentation each day. Other major tactical demonstrations include those of the Air Force's F-15 Eagle, F-16 Fighting Falcon, Navy's F/A-18F Super Hornet, and the Ohio Air National Guard's C-130 Hercules support aircraft. Look skyward, too, for amazing airborne acts like Cold War dogfights, biplane barnstorming, and the Army's Golden Knights precision parachute team. Attractions on the ground include an F/A-18 flight simulator, planes for viewing and cockpit picture-taking, and educational displays from NASA Glenn Research Center. Shows run 10am-5pm Saturday through Monday. Parking is expensive, so consider carpooling or taking RTA's Waterfront Line to East 9th Street, which leaves a relatively short walk. Or simply do as thousands of others do: Find a spot along the shoreline and watch the action for free. General admission and reserved box seating tickets are available at the gates the day of the show, by phone, or online.

Downtown: Burke Lakefront Airport, 216/781-0747, www.clevelandairshow.com; Labor Day weekend; from $23 adults, from $14 children

Oktoberfest

Fans of German food, beer, music, and even dogs will want to set aside time over Labor Day weekend for Oktoberfest, a four-day celebration of all things Deutschland. From the ceremonial tapping of the keg to the very last "pah" of the oompah bands, this popular seasonal attraction really does have something for everybody. Massive tents are erected to house the steady stream of performers, making this a rain-or-shine event. Music spans the generational divide, with polka, swing, disco, and rock. Food is provided by some of the most authentic German restaurants in the region. Beer is free-flowing and plentiful in the Bier Garten. One of the most eagerly anticipated events is the wiener-dog race, when vertically challenged dachshunds lumber their way down a 40-foot track in hopes of snagging the trophy. Parking is free all weekend.

Greater Cleveland: Cuyahoga County Fairgrounds, 19201 E. Bagley Rd., Middleburg Heights, 440/781-5246, www.clevelandoktoberfest.com; Labor Day weekend; $13

IngenuityFest

IngenuityFest is billed as the fusion of art and technology. That's as precise a definition as one is likely to get when it comes to this multi-day, free-flowing, high-concept, avant-garde celebration of interactive art. As far from a stodgy museum experience as one can get, Ingenuity historically has activated vacant or abandoned buildings, roving to a new spot every few years. Its newest home, Hamilton Collaborative, is a 350,000-square-foot industrial site in the St. Clair Superior area. With surprises at every turn, even in the strangest of places, Ingenuity is an interactive feast for a creativity-loving mind. Look for it in late September.

Downtown: Hamilton Collaborative, 5401 Hamilton Ave, 216/589-9444, www.ingenuitycleveland.com; late Sept.; $5

Ohio City Street Festival

In late September, the main drag through Ohio City is shut down to traffic and opened up to enthusiastic crowds who look forward to this popular street fest each fall. The strip is lined on both sides with dozens of local food, drink, and goods vendors; live musical performances take place throughout the day at nearby the Market Square Park; and family-friendly games and activities activate every pocket of the area. Large-scale versions of board games, temporary shuffleboard courts, and the usual assortment of face-painters and balloon-twisters will be on hand.

Ohio City: W. 25th St. at Lorain Ave., www.ohiocity.org; late Sept.; free

YEAR-ROUND

Open Air in Market Square

Ohio City's Market Square is the site of numerous social, cultural, and political events throughout the year. On select Saturdays from May through October (usually the first and third of each month), the urban park is home to Open Air in Market Square, a long-running neighborhood bazaar that attracts residents and visitors alike thanks to family-friendly offerings like live musical performances, arts and crafts vendors, secondhand goods dealers, and food offerings. Events run from 10am to 4pm.

Ohio City: Lorain Ave. at W. 25th St., 216/781-3222, www.ohiocity.org; select Sat. May-Oct.; free

Cleveland Flea

A few creative Clevelanders started the grassroots Cleveland Flea in 2013, and it has since blossomed into an event featuring 150 vendors that attracts upwards of 10,000 people on a great day. Taking place on the second Saturday of the month from June through October, the massive outdoor venue features stalls selling original crafts, industrial salvage, hand-built furniture, vintage items, used vinyl, fine jewelry, even home-baked foods. The all-day, rain-or-shine affair also boasts live music, a full bar, and a caravan of food trucks. An early winter Holiday Flea is an off-season one-off that makes easy work of gift shopping. **Downtown:** 3615 Superior Ave., www.theclevelandflea.com; 9am-4pm 2nd Sat. June-Oct.; $1

North Union Farmers Market

The North Union Farmers Market operates approximately eight seasonal markets throughout Greater Cleveland, mostly between July and October (see a complete listing of locations, dates, and times on the website). These are authentic producer-only markets; all food sold is grown, raised, or produced in the region by those who peddle it. Depending on the time of year, you'll find fresh produce,

grass-fed and free-range meats, along with homemade breads, cheeses, and honey. The oldest and best of the bunch is the **Shaker Square market** (Sat. mornings mid-Apr.-Dec.). A smaller indoor market even lasts through winter. In midsummer, the Shaker market teems with activity. Young couples sip coffee purchased from one of the nearby cafés and casually shop for dinner. The city's top chefs shop for the evening's specials. Other chefs give demonstrations on how to cook with local ingredients. To get the best selection, go early; many items sell out well before closing time. Bring cash, preferably small bills, and bags to cart your items home. Oh, and leave the dogs at home; they aren't welcome. **Various locations:** 216/751-7656, www.northunionfarmersmarket.org; July-Oct., but dates vary by market; free

RECREATION

Visitors are often bowled over by Cleveland's diversity and quality of outdoor recreational activities. A Great Lake and network of major waterways offer endless ways to play afloat, from kayaking the Cuyahoga River through the Flats to literally sailing off into the sunset on Lake Erie. For those who'd rather enjoy the water from terra firma, miles of beaches offer the perfect perch for sunbathing, enjoying live music, or just unwinding with a good book.

Progressive Field, home of the Cleveland Indians

Dubbed the "Emerald Necklace," Cleveland's matchless Metroparks system is a string of sparkling parks and reservations that cover more than 23,000 acres, meaning that nature lovers are never far from a trailhead, jogging path, or fishing stream. Close by, Cuyahoga Valley National Park is another 33,000-acre playground that beckons outdoor enthusiasts.

Cleveland has become a more bike-friendly community, adding hundreds of miles of new bike lanes, trails, and signage. Bike-share stations are popping up throughout the city.

Few cities can support more than one professional sports team, let alone three (five if you count Arena Football and the American Hockey League), but residents gleefully champion their local baseball, basketball, and football teams regardless of the score or standings.

Sure, it snows by the shovelful in the winter, but that means heading out to ski slopes, cross-country trails, toboggan runs, and sledding hills.

HIGHLIGHTS

✪ **BEST CLASSIC SUMMER ACTIVITY:** There's no better way to pass a glorious summer afternoon than at a **Cleveland Indians** game at Progressive Field with 35,000 of your closest friends (page 125).

✪ **BEST WAY TO GET ON THE WATER:** The amount of activity taking place on Cleveland's waterways has ballooned in recent years thanks to friendly outfitters like **Great Lakes Watersports,** a Flats-based outfit that rents kayaks, Jet Skis, and a party pontoon by the hour (page 129).

✪ **SWEETEST SPOT FOR QUICK SUMMER GETAWAY:** Seductive **Wendy Park at Whiskey Island** is adored for its lakeside locale, sand volleyball courts, and the casual Whiskey Island Still & Eatery. Live music just adds to the island vibe (page 132).

✪ **WORLD'S GREATEST OUTDOOR JOGGING TRACK:** The **Ohio & Erie Canal Towpath Trail** is an 87-mile gem that winds its way through the beautiful Cuyahoga Valley National Park. With a mostly smooth limestone surface, the path attracts millions of walkers, joggers, and cyclists each year (page 142).

✪ **WHERE TO RIDE WHEN THE SNOW FLIES:** Mountain bikers flock to **Ray's MTB Indoor Park** because it truly is one-of-a-kind. Inside a 100,000-square-foot warehouse, this remarkably wild indoor bike park is almost as good as the real thing (page 142).

Ohio & Erie Canal Towpath Trail

THE MASCOT CONTROVERSY

For years, the Cleveland Indians' home opener at Progressive Field was the annual site of Native Americans protesting the use of Chief Wahoo, the team's divisive mascot. There is little doubt that this caricature, with its red skin, toothy grin, and feathered headgear, is an offensive stereotype. The image stirs up a robust discussion about race, free speech, tradition, and the slippery issue of intent. Team history would have people believe that the character was meant to honor the first American Indian in pro baseball, not to disparage any particular group. Regardless, the time indeed has come for the chief to go. The logo will be removed from on-field uniforms by the start of the 2019 season, which coincidentally is the year that Cleveland will host the MLB All-Star Game.

Downtown

Map 1

SPECTATOR SPORTS
BASEBALL

TOP EXPERIENCE

⭐ Cleveland Indians

If there is anything better than spending a glorious summer afternoon or evening at the ballpark, don't tell the 35,000 or so happy souls catching a Cleveland Indians game at Progressive Field in the heart of downtown. Consistently selected as one of the best places in the major league to watch a game, this urban ballpark will make a baseball fan out of just about anybody. The stadium features a double-decker bar in right field called The Corner, which has large viewing patios; local food options; and great views of the bullpens, to better see the relief pitchers warming up. The seats are comfortable, with generous legroom. They're angled to provide unobstructed sight lines of the field. Park tours (May-early Sept.; adults $12, seniors and children $10) are offered throughout the season. Numerous Team Shops sell all manner of official gear. Heritage Park, located in center field, is home to the Indians Hall of Fame and other historical exhibits. Fans who want to try to get autographs of their favorite players may attempt to do so up to 45 minutes before game time in Sections 125-134 and 169-175.

About 80 home games are played April through September. Tickets can be purchased at the Progressive Field box office, through the Cleveland Indians website, apps like MLB Ballpark, or from unofficial scalpers who prowl the area before and during every game. For those who don't mind staying on their feet, a certain number of District Tickets are sold through the Indians' website. The price of $15 includes standing-room-only access and a free domestic beer or bottled water. Bring a hat and wear sunscreen; some seats are in full sun.

MAP 1: Corner of E. 9th St. and Carnegie Ave., 216/420-4487, www.mlb.com/indians; Apr.-Sept.; tickets $15-80

BASKETBALL

TOP EXPERIENCE

Cleveland Cavaliers

For their inaugural year in the NBA, 1970, the Cavs amassed the worst record in the league. Things wouldn't

Cavs game at Quicken Loans Arena

improve much until 1976, when the team made it to, but lost, the Eastern Conference Finals. Following a very sad period in Cavs history known as the "Ted Stepien Years," the team ultimately rebounded under new ownership, coaching, and talent. The late 1980s and early 1990s were good to Cleveland basketball fans, with a number of consecutive years of playoff appearances and a shot at the Eastern Conference Championship. This being Cleveland, you can guess how that one turned out.

The basketball gods smiled upon Cleveland in 2003, when the Cavs' first-pick choice in the NBA Draft netted a high school phenom by the name of LeBron James. Under the leadership of coach Mike Brown, "King James" and company would make it all the way to the Eastern Conference Finals in just three years. It would take four years, however, for the team to claim the title of Eastern Conference Champions. That year, 2007, the Cavaliers reached the NBA

Finals for the first time in their 37-year history—only to be swept by the San Antonio Spurs in four games. We all know what happened next, with LeBron taking his talents to South Beach. But fortunes began to shift in 2014, when LeBron James announced to the world that he would be "coming home" after four seasons with the Miami Heat. Under his lead, the team advanced to three consecutive Finals appearances and, in 2016, became the first team to overcome a 3-1 deficit to win the championship.

In Cleveland, the Cavaliers play about 40 games October-April at Quicken Loans Arena, a 20,000-seat venue downtown. Tickets are available through Ticketmaster (www.ticketmaster.com) or Flash Seats (www.cavs.flashseats.com), an online ticket exchange. In the summer of 2018, Quicken Loans Arena underwent a significant renovation project. MAP 1: 1 Center Court, 800/820-2287, www.nba.com/cavaliers; Oct.-Apr.; tickets $60-300

Cleveland State University Vikings

For those who prefer the unsullied action of college sports, the Cleveland State University Vikings play a full roster of men's and women's collegiate sports, including basketball, swimming, soccer, and softball. Men's basketball is without question the most closely followed. The Vikings, under the direction of coach Gary Waters and his successor, Dennis Felton, are fast becoming a team to watch in NCAA Division I ball, playing in the Horizon League. Meanwhile, in 2007 the women's basketball team made their first trip ever to the NCAA Tournament. Basketball games are played at the Wolstein Center, and tickets are available at the Wolstein Center box office or by calling 216/687-4848. For more information on all CSU sports action, visit the website.

MAP 1: Wolstein Center, 2000 Prospect Ave., 216/687-4848, www.csuvikings.com; Nov.-Mar.; tickets $120-250

FOOTBALL

Cleveland Browns

Cleveland is a football town. If you don't believe it, head over to the Municipal Parking Lot early in the morning on a brutally cold winter day. The scene one is likely to find will look as if an entire Jimmy Buffet concert was airlifted from Key West to the North Pole. Tailgaters get up early, brave traffic, and fight for spots just for the privilege of pre-partying with like-minded fans before games. Sure, alcohol plays a big part. But even the most sober Clevelanders can't help but get swept up in the passion of the pigskin. Einstein said that the definition of insanity is doing the same thing over and over again and expecting different results. Einstein obviously wasn't a Browns fan. Despite backing a team that has never even made it to the Super Bowl, Browns fans, game after game, year after year, merrily return to the scene of the crime.

Apart from three years in the late 1990s when team owner Art Modell (a name uttered only in the darkest of corners) moved the Browns to Baltimore, Cleveland has had a football team to support since 1946. And at many times, a very good one at that. The Browns have 15 former players in the Pro Football Hall of Fame, a number that is around the fifth-highest in the league. Names like Jim Brown, Otto Graham, Paul Warfield, and Ozzie Newsome will be instantly recognizable to even the most casual of fans. In the late 1980s quarterback Bernie Kosar led the team to the AFC Championship game, only to be defeated by John Elway and the Denver Broncos on a 98-yard march down the gridiron that will forever be known simply as "The Drive." As Cleveland fate would have it, the following year's AFC Championship game—*against the Broncos*—ended in a loss as the result of a fumble on the three-yard line. That play, by the way, is now called "The Fumble."

Regardless of who ultimately gets the start, come rain, shine, or lake effect snow, you can bet that 73,000 fervent fans will fill **FirstEnergy Stadium** every home game. Built in 1999, the modern stadium offers unobstructed views of the field and places fans closer to the action. Tickets are not cheap, and they are not easy to get. For the truly rabid Browns fans, a bleacher section known as the Dawg Pound, located at the east end zone, is home to hooting, hollering, and, yes, woofing. No matter where you end up sitting, it is imperative to dress for inclement weather. Open to the elements, the stadium can be insufferable for the ill-equipped. Again, alcohol helps.

Fans don't have to wait until the first game to inspect their team. Training camp normally opens in mid- to late July at a training facility in Berea, Ohio, not too far from downtown. All practices are open to the public and free of charge.

Eight regular-season home games are played September-December. Tickets for games can be purchased through the Cleveland Browns website, Ticketmaster (www.ticketmaster.com), or online ticket exchanges.

MAP 1: 100 Alfred Lerner Way, 440/891-5050, www.clevelandbrowns.com; Sept.-Dec.; tickets $75-300

Cleveland Gladiators

When former Browns quarterback and Cleveland sports legend Bernie Kosar relocated the Arena Football League's Gladiators from Las Vegas to Cleveland, he all but promised a postseason appearance in the first year. Considering that the team's record the prior year was a dismal 2-14, it was a bold statement. Kosar retooled the team and hired a new coach. In 2008, the team's first year in Cleveland, the Gladiators came up one win shy of the ArenaBowl. Under the leadership of coach Mike Wilpolt, and behind the arm of quarterback Ray Philyaw, the squad went 9-7 in the regular season, then beat Orlando in the wild-card round and Georgia in the division round. They lost the AFL National Conference title game to Philadelphia. In a fitting tribute, coach Wilpolt was selected Arena Football League coach

of the year. The 18-game season runs early March through late July, with nine home games played at Quicken Loans Arena. In 2017, the Cleveland Gladiators announced a two-year hiatus caused by renovations taking place at Quicken Loans Arena. The team is expected to resume play in the summer of 2020. Tickets are available at www.clevelandgladiators.com, www.ticketmaster.com, and the Quicken Loans Arena box office.

MAP 1: 1 Center Court, 216/420-2222, www.clevelandgladiators.com; Mar.-late July; tickets $20-150

HOCKEY
Cleveland Monsters

Pro hockey fans can enjoy the fast-paced puck action of the Cleveland Monsters, a team in the American Hockey League and affiliated with the NHL's Colorado Avalanche. Home games are played in Quicken Loans Arena, with roughly 40 dates between mid-October and mid-April. During the team's inaugural 2007-2008 season, it averaged a more-than-respectable 6,000 fans per game, but with each passing season the team's attendance figures climbed. By the 2017-2018 season, the team was drawing an average of 9,100 fans per game. Tickets can be purchased at the Quicken Loans Arena box office, at all Ticketmaster (www.ticketmaster.com) locations, or by calling 866/997-8257.

MAP 1: 1 Center Ice, 216/420-0000, www.clevelandmonsters.com; mid-Oct.-mid-Apr.; tickets $25-50

PARKS
Cleveland Public Library
Eastman Reading Garden

This semi-secluded urban park has the feeling of a secret garden. Wedged between the broad shoulders of the Main

Library and the Louis Stokes Wing, the space is buffered from wind, noise, and glaring sun. Yet open to the busy main streets on either end, the garden is still connected to the city around it. Beyond a pair of heavy bronze gates, the lovely open-air park unfolds gradually. Leafy trees and sturdy sculpture provide the bones, while a graceful fountain, designed by the Ohio-born artist behind Washington DC's Vietnam Veterans Memorial, cascades gently in the background. On warm summer days, the garden is a favorite lunch spot for office workers itching to escape their desks.

MAP 1: 325 Superior Ave. NE, 216/623-2800, www.cpl.org; 10am-6pm Mon.-Sat.

Downtown Dog Park

For visitors and residents with dogs in tow, this off-leash park is a blessing. While not massive, it is roomy enough for pooches to run around in a safe, fenced-in environment just steps from the Cuyahoga River. Located in Settler's Landing Park, on the East Bank of the Flats, the open area offers seating for humans, structures for dogs to hop atop, and doggie waste stations.

MAP 1: 1505 Merwin Ave., www. downtowncleveland.com; 8am-9pm daily

Voinovich Bicentennial Park

This 4.5-acre greenspace is a welcome oasis in a part of town with little to spare. Bicentennial Park sits at the north end of the East 9th Street Pier, near the Rock and Roll Hall of Fame and North Coast Harbor, and boasts a terraced lawn, fishing pier, outdoor stage, and bocce courts. The park is also home to one of four "Cleveland" signs installed by Destination Cleveland around town. The park offers a great vantage point for lake and skyline views.

MAP 1: E. 9th St. Pier, www. northcoastharbor.org; dawn-dusk daily

BOATING, ROWING, AND KAYAKING

✪ Great Lakes Watersports

The amount of activity taking place on Cleveland's waterways has ballooned in recent years thanks to new residents, fresh downtown development, improved access to the river and lake, and outfitters like Great Lakes Watersports. Located in the heart of the Flats, this well-staffed supplier stocks single and double kayaks, Jet Skis, and a handful of power boats for rental by the hour. In addition to a couple of speed boats (from $275 for 2 hours), Great Lakes rents a pontoon boat (from $275 for 2 hours) that accommodates up to 15 people, is easy to navigate, and offers great fun for group outings. Folks with their own kayak can launch from here for $5.

MAP 1: 1148 Main Ave., 216/771-4386, www.glwatersports.com; 11am-5pm Wed.-Mon. Memorial Day weekend-Labor Day; kayaks $25-30/hour, Jet Skis $110/hour

Rock & Dock at North Coast Harbor Marina

Rock & Dock is a 53-slip transient marina in the shadow of the Rock and Roll Hall of Fame and Museum. Those who already have a watercraft can dock here by the hour or by the day, while those who don't can rent a paddle boat, Jet Ski, kayak, or paddleboard. The location in the heart of downtown is ideal for skyline views and access to attractions like the Great Lakes Science Center.

GET OUT ON THE WATER

The amount of activity taking place on Cleveland's main waterways—Lake Erie and the Cuyahoga River—has ballooned in recent years thanks to active residents, improved access points, and well-stocked outfitters. Any summer day, you're likely to spot kayaks, stand-up paddleboards, Jet Skis, pontoon boats, and even water taxis all floating by. Here are the best ways to experience the city's plethora of water-based activities.

RIVER AND LAKE TOURS

- **Stay Dry While Sipping:** The *Goodtime III* offers narrated lake and river cruises, lunch and dinner-dance cruises, and the ever-popular rush-hour party cruise (page 130).

- **Feast with a View:** Aboard the *Nautica Queen,* you'll navigate down the Cuyahoga River and onto Lake Erie while enjoying skyline views and trips to the all-you-can-eat buffet (page 131).

KAYAKING AND STAND-UP PADDLEBOARDING

- **Float Through the Flats:** Located in the heart of the Flats, **Great Lakes Watersports** stocks single and double kayaks for rental by the hour. Paddle upstream to Jacobs Pavilion at Nautica for some free live tunes (page 129).

- **Onboard Balance:** At its locations in Edgewater Park and Wendy Park on Whiskey Island, **SUP Cleveland** spreads the love of stand-up paddleboarding through lessons, rentals, and SUP yoga classes (page 133).

MAP 1: 1020 E. 9th St., 216/804-1152, www. rockanddock.com; 9am-7pm daily; paddle boats, kayaks, and paddleboards $15/half hour or $25/hour, Jet Skis $60/half hour or $100/hour

RIVER AND LAKE TOURS

Goodtime III

If it weren't for the *Goodtime III*, countless locals and visitors would never get to view Cleveland from the water, which many assert is her best side. In the 50-plus years that the *Goodtime* has motored these waterways, that view has only improved. Passengers still journey up the Cuyahoga River, past the remnants of the city's mighty industrial past. But the landscape is cleaner, brighter, and more varied than ever before, with attractive new condos, promising development, and actual wildlife. Shutterbugs are afforded some of the best vantage points from which to capture Cleveland's skyline and its matchless assortment of bridges. The sheer romance of the setting inspires a number of couples to wed aboard this 1,000-passenger ferry each summer. Various tours are offered from Memorial Day through the end of September, including narrated lake and river cruises, lunch and dinner-dance cruises, and the ever-popular rush-hour party cruise. Prices range from $18 for a sightseeing tour up to $55 for the dinner and city lights cruise. Reservations are always recommended.

MAP 1: E. 9th St. Pier, 216/861-5110, www. goodtimeIII.com; $18-55

ROWING AND CANOEING

- **Row and Go:** Western Reserve Rowing Association teaches adults of all abilities and skill levels how to row at classes held throughout the spring, summer, and fall (page 133).

- **Canoe the Cuyahoga:** For more than 50 years, the family-run **Camp Hi Canoe & Kayak** has been putting folks in canoes on the Upper Cuyahoga, a scenic stretch of river about 45 minutes east of Cleveland (page 141).

LAKE AND RIVER FISHING

- **Angling for Dinner:** Sing up for a day on Lake Erie with Captain Bill of **Aabsolute Fishing Charters** and you'll likely walk away with walleye, perch, trout, and quite possibly a suntan (page 140).

- **Cast a Line:** The rivers of Northeast Ohio provide some of the best steelhead trout fishing in the country; the guides at **Chagrin River Outfitters** will happily lead you there (page 140).

GREAT FOR GROUPS

- **Pedal with Pals:** The **BrewBoat** is a pedal-powered paddle-wheel party boat that takes up to 14 guests on a leisurely voyage down the Cuyahoga River through the heart of town (page 133).

- **Switch Sides:** The East Bank of the Flats has bars, restaurants, and entertainment options. But the West Bank is no slouch either. Shuttle back and forth on the **free water taxi.**

Nautica Queen

You might not have the best food of your life aboard the *Nautica Queen,* but you will enjoy spectacular views. Like a floating restaurant patio, this beloved yacht offers a variety of cruises that combine dining and sightseeing. Passengers will navigate under historic bridges along the Cuyahoga River and out on Lake Erie, where they'll take in amazing skyline views, all while making trips to and from the all-you-can-eat buffet. The 330-seat ship offers lunch, dinner, sunset, and brunch themed cruises. Cruises depart rain or shine. **MAP 1:** 1153 Main Ave., 216/696-8888, www.nauticaqueen.com, $25-40 adults, $16-23 children

BOWLING
The Corner Alley

Knocking down pins in rented shoes hasn't looked this cool since Jeff "The Dude" Lebowski rolled in his pajamas. This gleaming hipster bowling emporium is downtown in the hopping East Fourth Street area. Combining 16 lanes, computerized scoring, oversize video screens, and comfy lounge areas, this popular nightlife spot is a far cry from the smoke-filled alleys of yesteryear. The lanes are within a

Nautica Queen

larger complex that features a restaurant, bar, and arcade, and bowlers are waited on lane-side. Weekend rates can seem steep, but divided by four or six bowlers, it becomes more palatable.

MAP 1: 402 Euclid Ave., 216/298-4070, www.thecorneralley. com; 11:30am-midnight Mon.-Thurs., 11:30am-2am Fri.-Sat., noon-midnight Sun.; $15-35/hour

Ohio City and Tremont   Map 2

PARKS

Clark Field Dog Park

For dog parents on the near-West Side, this Tremont dog park is just the place to socialize Fido while providing a safe, off-leash experience. The spacious, fenced-in area with gravel base even has a few benches and trees that provide shade. Water for both people and hounds, poop bags, waste stations, and hand sanitizer are also present at this pooch-friendly park.

MAP 2: W. 11th St. at Clark Ave.; dawn-dusk daily

Kentucky Gardens

Kentucky Gardens is the second-oldest community garden in Cleveland. This two-acre patch of organic earth is home to some 130 community garden plots, each no larger than 20 feet by 20 feet. For nearly seven decades, Ohio City residents have provided food for their families by working this urban patchwork. Neighbors pay as little as $10 a year for their plots but must work to maintain common spaces, which include mature fruit trees, working beehives, and aging compost piles. It's best to visit this park in summer and fall, when gardeners are busy tending to their pint-size farms, which are teeming with colorful life.

MAP 2: Fairview Park, Franklin Blvd. at W. 38th St., 216/288-3211, www. kentuckygardens.com; dawn-dusk daily

Rivergate Park

It's been 50 years since the Cuyahoga River famously caught fire, but head down to this three-acre plot in the Flats and it will seem like pure fiction. After decades of cleanup efforts, river water quality has improved to the point where kayakers and paddleboarders share the tree-framed waterways with massive freighters. Rivergate Park, managed by the Cleveland Metroparks, is a great place to park and launch watercraft, access the Lake Link Trail (and Towpath Trail), or enjoy a leisurely lunch at Merwin's Wharf restaurant (216/664-5696). Also here is Crooked River Skatepark.

MAP 2: 1785 Merwin Ave., 216/206-1000, www.clevelandmetroparks.com; dawn-dusk daily

✪ Wendy Park at Whiskey Island

Seductively elusive, 22-acre Wendy Park is so close you can practically touch it. Just across the mouth of the Cuyahoga River from downtown Cleveland, Whiskey Island—actually a peninsula, and named after the whiskey distilleries that dotted the land in the 1830s—is accessed from the west via the same entrance as Edgewater Park. At the peninsula's eastern end, Wendy Park has become one the gems gracing the North Coast. Permanent volleyball courts draw sports clubs, a marina brings in the boats, and the casual Whiskey

Island Still & Eatery (216/631-1800, www.whiskeyislandmarina.net) offers pub grub and live music to appreciative crowds. Bird-watchers come here for the amazing wildlife and shutterbugs for the matchless views of the Flats, city skyline, and setting sun over Lake Erie. Even architecture fans come here to gaze at the shell of a historic Coast Guard Station that is being repurposed for new recreational options.

MAP 2: 2800 Whiskey Island, www. wendypark.org; dawn-dusk daily

BOATING, ROWING, AND KAYAKING

BrewBoat

As Ohio's first and only pedal-powered paddlewheel party-boat, BrewBoat offers a fun-spirited way for groups of up to 14 guests to cruise up and down the Cuyahoga River through the heart of downtown. The 31-foot-long catamaran accommodates 10 riders at pedal stations that surround a mahogany bar and another four on benches. The excursions are BYOB, with each guest permitted to bring aboard three beers or one bottle of wine per couple. A sound system plays your tunes or theirs, and riders are free to carry on snacks. Individual tickets cost $35 per person, or the whole boat can be rented for $429.

MAP 2: Channel Park Marina, 5300 Whiskey Island, 440/941-6690, www. brewcle.com; late May-late Sept., weather permitting; $35 per person

The Foundry

This ambitious nonprofit is geared to getting young adults of all socioeconomic levels onto the water to row or sail. A state-of-the-art facility near Rivergate Park boasts indoor rowing tanks for year-round training and riverfront docks for launching watercraft. Both Learn to Row and Learn to Sail programs are offered to young athletes, the latter of which set sail from the historic Coast Guard Station at Whiskey Island. For exercise buffs with a tight schedule, the Foundry offers one-hour indoor Row for Fitness sessions ($15).

MAP 2: 1831 Columbus Rd., 440/596-7069, www.clevelandfoundry.org

SUP Cleveland

From its alternating home bases at Wendy Park on Whiskey Island and Edgewater Park, SUP Cleveland seeks to spread the love of stand-up paddleboarding through lessons and fun paddleboarding events like SUP yoga. Lessons take place on Lake Erie and are open to those who call ahead to reserve a board as well as people with their own equipment. See the website for a schedule.

MAP 2: Wendy Park and Edgewater Park, 440/212-5041, www.supcleveland.com; 90-minute lesson $69, $45 with your own board

Western Reserve Rowing Association

Western Reserve Rowing's sleek shells are a familiar sight on the Cuyahoga River. Adults of all ages, abilities, and skill levels come here to learn how to row from some of the best talent around. Classes range from basic fundamentals programs to pro-level competitive rowing. Fun and social summer and fall rowing leagues are very popular for both casual and serious scullers. The WRRA also fields teams at many regional and national regattas, offering truly competitive scullers an opportunity to test themselves against a larger field. Learn-to-row classes cost $48 and take place throughout spring,

BIKE SERVICES IN THE CITY

BIKE PARKING
The Bike Rack (2148 E. 4th St., 216/771-7120, www.clevelandbikerack.com; 6:30am-2:30pm Mon.-Fri.) is the city's first full-service bike parking and commuter center. Located downtown, the center offers secure bicycle parking, individual shower and changing facilities, lockers, bicycle rentals, and minor bicycle repairs. Air is always free, and flat tire repairs are just $5 per wheel plus the cost of the tube. It's free to park your bike outside (with your own lock), but use of the facilities is paid for on a daily ($8) or monthly ($30) basis. Also available are bicycle route maps, brochures discussing points of interest, and event information. Pass holders enjoy 24-hour access.

BIKE SHARING
Thanks to Cleveland winters, local bike-share programs have had a difficult time gaining traction. But **UH Bikes** (www.uhbikes.com), which is sponsored by University Hospitals, is expanding year over year. At last count, some 250 bikes were available from 30 or so stations scattered throughout University Circle and downtown Cleveland. Download the Social Bicycles app, set up an account, and off you go. Pay-as-you-go plans are $3.50 per half hour and $7 per hour. Student, monthly, and annual memberships also are available.

summer, and fall. Check the website for dates and information.

MAP 2: 1003 British St., 216/302-8399, www.westernreserverowing.com

BIKE RENTALS
Ohio City Bicycle Co-Op

For bike rentals close to downtown, you can't beat Ohio City Bicycle Co-Op. This great nonprofit organization awards free bikes to kids who spend a little time learning about bike repair and safe cycling. In addition to selling surplus bikes, the agency rents quality bikes, which helps fund their Earn-a-Bike program. Bikes for rent come in two classifications: normal and performance. For getting around town, the collection of older road and mountain bikes should fit the bill. Racers or off-roaders will want to go with a higher-end performance model. Rates are about $75 per week on up to $300 per month. OCBC does not offer hourly or daily rentals. To join in on a fun, casual ride, show up at the shop on the first Saturday of every month (except major holidays) by 10am. These rides are all-weather and all-year, so dress accordingly. You'll be back by noon.

MAP 2: 1840 Columbus Rd., 216/830-2667, www.ohiocitycycles.org; noon-6pm Tues., 3pm-9pm Wed., 10am-4pm Sat.

ROCK CLIMBING
Climb Cleveland

This urban rock-climbing gym is a bouldering facility, where in place of ropes and soaring cliffs there are color-coded holds and 8- to 12-foot-high walls. Numerous routes are laid out to achieve various levels of difficulty, and pads are in place to ensure a soft landing when the inevitable occurs. Serious climbers will doubtless appreciate the crack climbing area. Newbies can take a Bouldering Basics class for $30, shoes included.

MAP 2: 2190 Professor Ave., 216/906-4186, www.climb-cleveland.com; 3pm-10pm Mon.-Fri., 10am-10pm Sat., 10am-8pm Sun.

SKATEBOARDING
Crooked River Skatepark

Designed by Grindline Skateparks and completed in 2014, this free public skatepark is just one more amenity that is bringing people to a previously unpopulated part of the Flats. Located in Rivergate Park, the skate park covers 15,000 square feet and features an iconic snake-style run, street park elements, ledges, and smooth concrete. Bikes are allowed.

MAP 2: 1785 Merwin Ave., www. crookedriverskatepark.com; 7am-sundown daily; free

BOWLING
Dickey's Lanes

If only all bowling alleys were more like Dickey's, a no-frills eight-laner just south of Tremont. You won't find tipsy bachelorette parties, electronic scoring, or even pin setters that work 100 percent of the time. You will find passionate neighborhood bowlers, cheap games, cheaper beer, and sharp pencils. A dimly lit lounge dispenses cheap cocktails and a random selection of good and not-so-good beers, served up with a smile and story by the owners. When you're in that bar, ask one of the owners to flick the switch that illuminates the intricate scale model of the entire bowling alley, built entirely out of wooden matchsticks.

MAP 2: 3275 W. 25th St., 216/741-9774; noon-2am daily; $3 per game, $2 shoe rentals

Detroit Shoreway and Edgewater

Map 3

PARKS
Edgewater Park

Formerly known as Edgewater State Park, this lakefront park was taken over from state control by the Cleveland Metroparks. The turnaround has been swift and dramatic. Long suffering from insufficient amenities and management, the local parks organization has improved every aspect of the property. Comprising two main areas—an elevated bluff and a lake-level beach—the park is visited by walkers, joggers, bicyclists, kite-flyers, sunbathers, swimmers, and anglers, who drop lines off nearby piers and breakwalls. Amateur and professional shutterbugs flock to the bluff for unrivaled city, lake, and sunset views. The Edgewater Beach House (216/954-3408) offers great vistas from open-air balconies, while introducing a new food and drink option to the park, including alcoholic beverages. Every Thursday evening from late May through early August, Edgewater Live draws thousands to the sandy shores for live music, food trucks and picture-perfect sunsets.

If you can tolerate the near-freezing water temps, Lake Erie can actually provide a pretty decent winter surfing experience. Winter's steady winds whip across the lake, stirring up waves that routinely hit the 10-foot mark. Swells as large as 20 feet have been reported. Only a fool would hit these waters without a wetsuit, and it's wise to grab your longest, fattest board for increased buoyancy.

MAP 3: 6500 Memorial Shoreway, 216/635-3200, www.clevelandmetroparks. com; 6am-11pm daily; free

University Circle and Little Italy

Map 4

PARKS

Cleveland Cultural Gardens

Stretching approximately a mile and a half along Martin Luther King Jr. Drive between University Circle and Lake Erie, more than 30 attractive sculptural gardens are dedicated to, and maintained by, the various cultures and nationalities that call Cleveland home. With the mission of "peace through mutual understanding," these serene patches are often the sites of weddings, ethnic gatherings, and other cultural events. The earliest gardens were established by Italian, German, Polish, Hungarian, and Irish immigrants. Added since are those paying tribute to Albanian, Croatian, Armenian, and Syrian residents.

MAP 4: Martin Luther King Jr. Dr., from University Circle to Lake Erie, www. clevelandculturalgardens.org

Nord Family Greenway

This greenbelt peacefully connects pedestrians moving from Case Western Reserve University through the campus of the Cleveland Museum of Art and finally to the Maltz Performing Arts Center. The 2,200-foot-long by 300-foot-wide passageway incorporates the museum's picturesque Frederick Law Olmsted-designed Fine Arts Garden and Wade Lagoon, while adding new lawn and amphitheater space, bike and pedestrian bridges, and leafy walkways.

MAP 4: Case Western Reserve University to Maltz Performing Arts Center, http://case. edu/nordgreenway

Rockefeller Park

Rockefeller Park is a leafy 130-acre swath that links University Circle and Lake Erie. Mostly hugging Martin Luther King Jr. Boulevard, the park contains walking paths, tennis courts, picnic areas, playgrounds, and basketball courts. Gorgeous arched bridges move city traffic from one side to the other. The park is perhaps most widely recognized as the home of the Cultural Gardens, some 30 sculptural gardens dedicated to ethnicities that have made Cleveland their home. Here, too, is the Rockefeller Park Greenhouse (750 E. 88th St., 216/664-3103, www.rockefellergreenhouse. org), a year-round conservatory boasting lush tropical fruit plants, exotic orchids, and formal gardens. The greenhouse is a great place to park when visiting the Cultural Gardens, as it is free and close.

MAP 4: 690 E. 88th St., www.city. cleveland.oh.us

Cleveland Heights and Shaker Heights

Map 5

PARKS

Horseshoe Lake Park

Some of the many assets that attract residents to Shaker Heights are its green spaces. Deliberately laid out in the early 1900s as a garden community, the East Side suburb boasts numerous recreational gems, and Horseshoe Lake Park is one of them. Near the preservation-minded Nature Center at Shaker Lakes, this park shares a similar stance on the environment. Elevated boardwalks fashioned from recycled materials weave through wetlands, simultaneously protecting the natural habitats while providing visitors an immersive vantage point. Paved trails offer walkers, joggers, and bicyclists a safe route around the park, while nearby dirt paths wind their way through forests, ravines, and fields. Bird-watchers come here for the rich diversity of songbirds, waterfowl, and predators. Stone-clad shelters feature fireplaces and plenty of space to celebrate.

MAP 5: South Park Blvd. at Park Dr., www.shakeronline.com

Nature Center at Shaker Lakes

The Shaker Lakes, and the single-minded Nature Center that serves as their environmental steward, attract thousands of ecoconscious visitors each year thanks to an embarrassment of wildlife riches. The parklands encompass lakes, streams, marshes, fields, and dense forest, providing natural habitats for a host of native flora and fauna. Two trails—one wheelchair-accessible, the other more rugged—wind through this incredible landscape, providing the day-tripper an up-close and immersive experience. Die-hard bird-watchers flock here for regularly scheduled walks, ticking off warblers, thrushes, catbirds, juncos, red-tailed hawks, and barred owls from their checklists. Programming held throughout the year inspires visitors to live greener lives.

MAP 5: 2600 S. Park Blvd., 216/321-5935, www.shakerlakes.org; 10am-5pm Mon.-Sat., 1pm-5pm Sun., trails dawn-dusk daily; free

PARKS

Lakewood Off-Leash Dog Park

This great off-leash doggie park is off Valley Parkway, in the Rocky River Reservation of the Cleveland Metroparks. The fenced-in area takes up two-thirds of an acre and features mature trees, gravel surfaces, waste-bag dispensers, and water stations for both canines and humans. A double-gated entrance gives owners an opportunity to unleash the hounds safely. So they don't harass the big guys, dogs smaller than 25 pounds have their own fenced-in area. No aggressive dogs—or people—are welcome.

MAP 6: 1699 Valley Pkwy., www. lakewooddogpark.com; 8am-9pm daily; free

Lakewood Park

One of 15 city parks in neighboring Lakewood, Lakewood Park is a 31-acre lakefront recreational area with eight tennis courts, three sand volleyball courts, two softball fields, an outdoor swimming pool, picnic pavilions, a skateboard park, and a kid-friendly playground. The park's band shell offers free Friday night movies and Sunday night concerts throughout the summer. On or around the Fourth of July, thousands gather here for a celebration of games, food, music, and fireworks. The Oldest Stone House is also within the confines of this park. Thanks to the recent addition of the Solstice Steps, tiered seating sculpted into the bluff, this park has become one of the very best places to catch a sunset.

MAP 6: 14532 Lake Ave., 216/529- 5697, www.onelakewood.com

ROWING AND KAYAKING

41° North Kayak Adventures

Paddlers of all skill levels will find what they're looking for at this great local outfitter. For beginners, 41° North offers kayak and stand-up paddleboard courses taught by certified instructors. Those with even the littlest bit of paddling experience can sign up for an unforgettable sunset kayak tour, which takes participants into North Coast Harbor along Lake Erie's shore, right by the Rock and Roll Hall of Fame. More adventurous half-, full-, and multiday trips are available to those who make arrangements ahead of time. More advanced paddlers can rent their own rig and glide into Lake Erie alone or with friends. The rental center is at the Yak Shack in the Cleveland Metroparks Rocky River Reservation.

MAP 6: Rocky River Reservation, 1500 Scenic Park Dr., Lakewood, 866/529-2541, www.kayak41north.com; rentals Memorial Day weekend through October, $20 first hour, $5 each additional half hour

ROCK CLIMBING

Nosotros Rock Climbing Gym

Nosotros is a climbing gym established behind the mission of strengthening relationships just as much as bodies. The welcoming space provides a noncompetitive environment for singles, couples, and groups to bond, exercise, and have fun while bouldering at 14 feet and lower alongside trained staff and over soft floors. The lower-level church setting translates into the cheapest climbing rates in town.

MAP 6: Lakewood Baptist Church, 14321 Detroit Ave., www.gonosotros.com; noon-10pm Mon.-Fri., 9am-10pm Sat.; day pass $12 daily, $45 monthly membership, $3 shoe rentals

BOWLING

Mahall's 20 Lanes

A beloved Lakewood institution since 1924, this 20-lane bowling alley was given a second life in 2011 thanks to new owners with fresh ideas. For starters, the bar has a menu of craft beers and specialty cocktails. Food service features hip takes on burgers and tacos, while guest chefs and food trucks mix things up. Live music, often with multiple acts, attracts bowlers and non-bowlers alike. Bowlers had better know how to score a frame the old-fashioned way, because there are no machines to do it for you. Low-tech scoring translates into affordable bowling.

MAP 6: 13200 Madison Ave., 216/521-3280, www.mahalls20lanes.com; $4 per game, $20/hour Sat.-Sun., $2 shoe rentals

ICE-SKATING

Halloran Ice Skating Rink

What this rink lacks in luxury it makes up for in sheer curiosity. Run by the City of Cleveland's Department of Parks and Recreation, Halloran is one of the few outdoor refrigerated rinks in the region. In summer, the ice melts and the spot is opened up to roller skaters. Winter skating begins in October and runs until spring. If you don't mind weaving your way through exuberant youths, this rink can offer a nostalgic charm that borders on romantic. And because the fees are quite cheap, this trip will leave you with plenty of cash for that après-skate dinner-date.

MAP 6: 3350 W. 117th St., 216/664-4187, www.city.cleveland.oh.us; Mon.-Sat.; $1.25 including skate rental

Serpentini Winterhurst Arena

Formerly Winterhurst Ice Rink, this popular Lakewood city rink has been leased by a private operator and received about $1 million in improvements. With two ice rinks, the arena is busy most days of the week with open skating, drop-in freestyle, youth hockey, and speed skating. The arena is also home to four separate high school varsity ice hockey teams. The facility is open year-round and offers lessons, rentals, and concessions. Hours vary by day, week, and month, so check the website before dropping in.

MAP 6: 14740 Lakewood Heights Blvd., 216/529-4400, www.serpentiniarena.com; $8, less for Lakewood residents, skate rental $3

GONE FISHIN'

Cleveland offers both lake and river fishing options for anglers.

LAKE FISHING

As the warmest and most biologically productive of the Great Lakes, Lake Erie offers anglers some serious fishing opportunities, with championship walleye and tasty yellow perch coming in at the top of the list. In fact, more fish are caught each year in this Great Lake than in the other four combined. The easiest and cheapest is simply dropping a line in the water off a pier or breakwall. Edgewater Park is a popular site for shore-bound anglers, offering a generous fishing pier. **East 9th Street Pier,** just steps from the Rock Hall, has designated spots for pier fishing, as does the **East 55th Street Marina** (5555 N. Marginal Rd.) just east of downtown.

The next most economical alternative is to hop aboard a party boat, sometimes called a "head boat" because passengers are charged per head. Unlike pricey charter boats, head boats accept singles and couples for a modest fee. One of the few to depart from within the city, **Discovery Dive Charters** (16975 Wildwood Dr., 216/481-5771, www.discoverydive.com) operates out of Wildwood State Park Marina, just a few miles east of downtown. If you have a small group and a little extra cash, a private fishing charter like **Aabsolute Fishing Charters** (216/218-3788, www.aabsolutecharters.com) offers a full day of fishing for up to six people for between $550 and $750. For a totally unique fishing experience, consider signing up for an evening or nighttime walleye trip in the spring with **FishCrazy Charters** (216/408-0404, www.fishcrazycharters.com). The evening trip runs most days 5pm-11pm, while the weekend-only night trips run 11:30pm-5am. Rates are about $600 for up to five people.

Regardless of which option they choose, all anglers must possess a current Ohio Fishing License, available through the **Ohio Department of Natural Resources** (www.ohiodnr.com) or bait shops near the docks. Cost is $11 for a one-day license. When fishing, it is imperative to bring an ice-filled cooler to protect your catch. Many of the better charter companies will provide one for you. Also, be prepared for the weather.

RIVER FISHING

The well-stocked rivers and streams of Northeast Ohio provide some of the best steelhead trout fishing in the country. Fly fishers from throughout the Midwest make their way to Lake Erie tributaries from fall through spring hoping to catch and release one of the most beautiful sport fish of all. The rivers that offer the best fishing are the Rocky, Chagrin, and Grand, though gaining access isn't always easy due to private-property restrictions. The Rocky River and Mill Stream Run Reservations of the Cleveland Metroparks enjoy miles of access to the Rocky River, making those parks favorite destinations for anglers. On the other side of town, the North and South Chagrin Reservations provide access to the bountiful Chagrin River. When it comes to fly-fishing for steelhead, sometimes it's best to call in the pros. Professional guides know the rivers better than anybody, and they will take you to the fish. Plus, many offer lessons in casting before setting out. One exceptional guide is **Chagrin River Outfitters** (440/247-7110, www.chagrinriveroutfitters.com), which charges about $325 for a half day or $425 for a full day.

Greater Cleveland   Map 7

PARKS

Cleveland Lakefront Nature Preserve

While it has an inauspicious origin, seeing as it was the dumping site for sediment dredged from the Cuyahoga River, this peninsula just east of town has oddly blossomed into an 88-acre wildlife preserve as the result of almost zero human intervention. These days, it offers an out-of-the-way spot for nature lovers thanks to its status as an important stop for migratory birds. Observers have identified 280 different species of birds, 42 types of butterflies, 16 different mammals, a pair of reptiles, and a wide array of flower, grass, shrub, and tree species. The lakeside peninsula also boasts more than a mile of shoreline, some 2.5 miles of walking trails, and great skyline and sunset views.

MAP 7: 8701 Lakeshore Blvd., Cleveland, 216/241-8004; dawn-dusk daily; free

BEACHES
Headlands Beach State Park
Clear across town in Mentor, this beach is the largest in the entire state, boasting a mile-long stretch of natural sand perfect for sunbathing, people-watching, and navel-gazing. During summer, the beach attracts scores of folks from throughout the region, all eager for a little vacation close to home. Bird-watchers flock to adjacent Headlands Dunes State Nature Preserve, a native dune environment that sees a steady stream of migratory birds.

MAP 7: 9601 Headlands Rd., Mentor, 440/257-1331, http://parks.ohiodnr.gov

Huntington Beach
Tucked into the posh West Side communities of Bay Village and Rocky River, and within the Cleveland Metroparks Huntington Reservation, this small but well-maintained beach is one of the most active in the area. In addition to picnic shelters with charcoal grills, a concession stand sells hot dogs, nachos, and ice cream from May through September. Breakwalls give anglers a spot to fish in Lake Erie year-round.

MAP 7: Lake Rd. at Porter Creek, 216/635-3200, www.clevelandmetroparks. com

CANOEING AND KAYAKING
Camp Hi Canoe & Kayak
Northeast Ohio is blessed with waterways that weave throughout the Lake Erie Watershed, providing countless miles of scenic paddling fun. Some of the most enjoyable and relaxed floating can be found along the Upper Cuyahoga, a stretch of river that sits about 45 minutes east of Cleveland. For more than 50 years, the family-run Camp Hi has been doing all the heavy lifting for small groups of folks who seek to canoe, kayak, or standup paddleboard. Trips range from short one-hour jaunts to lengthy 10-mile, five-hour journeys, all of which are open to paddlers of all experience levels.

MAP 7: 12274 Abbott Rd., Hiram, 330/569-7621, www.camphicanoe.com; $23-36

BIKE RENTALS
Century Cycles
To experience as much of the scenic Ohio & Erie Canal Towpath Trail as possible, a bike is pretty much a necessity. Of course, most folks don't make a habit of traveling with their bikes in tow, and that's where Century Cycles comes in. In the heart of the Cuyahoga Valley National Forest, in the charming town of Peninsula, this great cycle

rowers on the Cuyahoga River

shop rents bikes of all shapes and sizes for use on the trail. Riders with little ones can also rent kiddie trailers that attach to the rear of the bike. Best of all, the shop is literally steps from the towpath. Credit cards are required for a security deposit.

MAP 7: 1621 Main St., Peninsula, 800/201-7433, www.centurycycles.com; 10am-8pm Mon.-Thurs., 10am-6pm Fri.-Sat., noon-5pm Sun., rentals $9/hour

BIKE TRAILS
✪ Ohio & Erie Canal Towpath Trail

When completed, this monumental path will stretch 101 miles from Lake Erie to New Philadelphia, following the path of the historic Ohio & Erie Canal. Already, some 87 miles of level crushed-limestone path attract millions of walkers, joggers, and bike riders per year. Pick up the trail at the southern end of Scranton Peninsula in the Flats and follow it all the way down to the beautiful Cuyahoga Valley National Park. The scenery along the path, which hugs and at times crisscrosses the Cuyahoga River, is simply amazing. Old canal locks and mile markers can be spotted, as can dense forests, fertile wetlands, and varied wildlife. Stop off at numerous visitors centers along the way to view historical and natural exhibits. Riders of all skill levels can enjoy this smooth trail. For those who have bit off a little too much and are now dreading the journey back, the Cuyahoga Valley Scenic Railroad (www.cvsr.com) Bike Aboard program is a lifesaver. Flag down the train at any boarding station, hop on with your bike, and ride as far as you want for $5 (cash only).

MAP 7: Cuyahoga Valley National Park, www.nps.gov/cuva

MOUNTAIN BIKING
Ohio & Erie Canal Reservation Mountain Bike Trail

Hats off to the Cleveland Area Mountain Bike Association, which built and maintains this single-track trail minutes from town at the Ohio & Erie Canal Reservation of the Cleveland Metroparks. Although it is just a two-mile loop, riders swear it feels longer thanks to a nice switchback pattern down the face of a wooded hillside. Given the terrain, which leaves little room for error, the trail is best for intermediate riders. A half-mile loop is available to beginners. This park connects with the Ohio & Erie Canal Towpath Trail, making it easily accessible to riders. If it has recently rained and the trail is muddy, riding is forbidden.

MAP 7: E. 49th St. near Grant Ave., Cleveland, www.clevelandmetroparks.com; dawn-dusk daily May-Dec.

✪ Ray's MTB Indoor Park

Ray's is the only attraction of its kind on the globe. Now approaching 100,000 square feet of indoor mountain bike and BMX nirvana, this remarkable place just keeps growing and growing. Set inside a cavernous warehouse complex about five miles west of downtown, Ray's features separate courses geared to beginner, intermediate, and expert riders. Race down narrow paths, around steeped embankments, through obstacle courses, over bumpity bridges, and into the air courtesy of vertical jumps. Riders come from all over the country to check out the rad madness. Ray's is a seasonal business that runs from early October to late April. The exact opening and closing dates vary from year to year. Ride your own

Lake Link Trail

Since adoption of the Cleveland Bikeway Master Plan in 2007, the City of Cleveland has made a serious commitment to becoming a bicycle-friendly community. Since then, more than 100 miles of bikeway have been added to city streets, consisting of dedicated bike lanes, shared lanes (sharrows), trails, and signage. Some of the most exciting additions have been small but mighty.

The Ohio & Erie Canal Towpath Trail, better known as just the **Towpath Trail,** is an 87-mile pathway that closely follows the route of the old Ohio and Erie Canal, where mule-powered canal boats ferried goods and passengers between the Ohio River to the south and Lake Erie to the north during the early to mid-1800s. While some of the most beautiful stretches of this bike- and pedestrian-friendly trail wind through the majestic Cuyahoga Valley National Park, some of the most challenging-to-complete stretches are at the very end, where the trail seeks to connect clear to Lake Erie and Wendy Park.

Thanks to a multifaceted partnership, that final push has never been closer to completion. The new **Lake Link Trail** is a 1.3-mile leg that follows an abandoned railroad right-of-way through Cleveland's industrial Flats neighborhood. The trail connects with the Towpath Trail at the southern end of Scranton Peninsula and moves walkers, joggers, and cyclists through an ever-changing landscape of nature, industry, and architecture. Views of the city skyline, a variety of turn-of-the-20th-century bridges, and the Cuyahoga River open up a rarely seen section of the city to a whole new population. The final leg of the trail, which will make the very short hop from the West Bank of the Flats to Wendy Park on Lake Erie, might be completed as early as 2019 if current plans to design and build a pedestrian bridge over the Cuyahoga River hold steady.

bike or rent one on-site. Riders under 16 must be accompanied by an adult, while those 16-18 must have a waiver signed by a parent.

MAP 7: 9801 Walford Ave., Cleveland, 216/631-7433, www.raysmtb.com; noon-10pm Mon.-Fri., 9am-10pm Sat.-Sun.; $23 Mon.-Fri., $30 Sat.-Sun.

ROCK CLIMBING
Cleveland Rock Gym

For nimble-fingered folks itching to scamper up a wall, this indoor climbing gym will more than satisfy the urge. What once was a light-industrial warehouse in Euclid has been converted into a more-than-acceptable winter substitute for rock climbing.

The facility comprises 30-foot top-rope walls and numerous bouldering areas, some featuring near-horizontal overhangs. Climbers who have no prior experience must make reservations for an introductory class. Those with enough knowledge to pass a basic belay test, however, are free to plan their routes up the tall walls. Passes do not include gear rental.

MAP 7: 21200 St. Clair Ave., Bldg. B3, Euclid, 216/692-3300, www. clevelandrockgym.com; 3pm-10pm Mon.-Fri., noon-7pm Sat.-Sun.; day pass adults $16, teens, military, and students $13, children 6-12 $11; five-visit or one-month pass $70

GOLF

Shawnee Hills Golf Course

Shawnee Hills offers golf for players of all skill levels, making it one of the most versatile of the Cleveland Metroparks' seven public courses. Beginners and pros alike can sharpen their short game on the zippy little 9-hole, par-3 course. More advanced players, meanwhile, will likely gravitate to the 18-hole 6,200-yard course, which features rolling terrain and unforgiving water hazards. Perhaps the most difficult hole of all the Metroparks courses, hole 4 is a tree-lined uphill 469-yard par-4 dogleg left that was converted from a par 5. The course also has a pro shop, snack bar, cart and club rental services, practice putting green, and driving range. It's located in the Bedford Reservation.

MAP 7: 18753 Egbert Rd., Bedford, 440/232-7184, www.clevelandmetroparks. com; dawn-dusk daily; greens fees $15-40

Sleepy Hollow Golf Course

This great Stanley Thompson-designed course opened in 1925 as a private country club. Today it is a part of the Cleveland Metroparks system, which runs seven public courses in and around Cuyahoga County. Considered brutally challenging yet also surprisingly beautiful, this 18-hole 6,700-yard course plays downhill and uphill, with and against the prevailing winds. Some holes play easier than others for that reason. Hole 2 is a long 240-yard par 3. The longest, hole 4, is a 590-yard par 5. In 2012, Sleepy Hollow was ranked *Golfweek Magazine*'s No. 1 municipal course in Ohio and No. 23 in the country. Golfers will find a pro shop, snack bar, cart and club rental services, practice putting green, and driving range. It's located in the Brecksville Reservation.

MAP 7: 9445 Brecksville Rd., Brecksville, 440/526-4285, www.clevelandmetroparks. com; dawn-dusk daily; greens fees $15-40

CROSS-COUNTRY SKIING, ICE-SKATING, AND SNOWSHOEING

Kendall Lake Winter Sports Center

Tucked deep within Cuyahoga Valley National Park, a cozy stone-and-chestnut shelter serves as the nucleus of winter activities in the park. In addition to the breathtaking scenery, the lodge offers cross-country ski instruction, equipment rental, and priceless information. Sign up for a weekend cross-country ski lesson on your skis or theirs, followed by a vigorous miles-long expedition down the Towpath Trail. For a slower, simpler pace, don a pair of rented snowshoes and head into the majestic backcountry. When nearby Kendall Lake is adequately frozen, take your ice-skating to the great outdoors. Don't have your own skates? No problem, the shelter rents them. Even if you prefer to pull on nothing more than a pair of hiking boots, come to this lodge for maps, hot

CLEVELAND VELODROME

In August of 2012, the **Cleveland Velodrome** (5033 Broadway Ave., http://clevelandvelodrome.org) opened in the Slavic Village neighborhood just south of the city. The 166-meter Olympic-style bicycle racing track is the only one of its kind between the East Coast and Chicago. The outdoor steel-and-wood track, which features 50-degree banked turns and 15-degree banked straightaways, is open to riders of all skill levels.

All first-timers must attend a Track 101 class to learn about track safety and track etiquette, and to acquire the necessary technical skills. The class is free and open to riders of all ages. The next level up is Track 201, which covers basic track-racing skills.

Riders can use their own bikes only if they fit the requirements; otherwise there are single-speed, fixed-gear track bikes for rental for both kids and adults ($10). Season passes ($200) and day passes ($15) are available. The track is open May through October, weather permitting.

chocolate, and like-minded companionship. Call for snow and ice reports before you visit.

MAP 7: Truxell Rd., Peninsula, 216/524-1497, www.nps.gov/cuva

SKIING, SNOWBOARDING, AND TUBING
Alpine Valley Ski Resort

Located smack-dab in the middle of the Snowbelt, Alpine Valley gets pounded by snowfall. With average yearly totals around 120 inches, the resort receives double that of Boston Mills and Brandywine. While compact, this charming resort has the look and feel of a quaint little ski village. But modern features like state-of-the-art snowmaking machines, a snow-tube park, and Ohio's longest half-pipe keep this place popular with winter enthusiasts. There are 11 trails covering 72 skiable acres, with a range of easy, moderate, and difficult runs. Lessons, equipment rental, and food service are available. Check the website for months, days, and hours of operation.

MAP 7: 10620 Mayfield Rd., Chesterland, 440/285-2211, www.alpinevalleyohio.com; adult lift passes $38-43, equipment rental package $30, tubing $25 for 3 hours

Boston Mills and Brandywine

The sister resorts of Boston Mills and Brandywine might not offer the best skiing in the country, but they do provide a surprisingly good downhill experience. And their location just 20 miles from town makes them all the more appealing. Combined, the two parks boast 18 trails covering 88 skiable acres. Both offer a nice mix of bunny runs, intermediate trails, and challenging black diamonds for skiers and snowboarders. When Mother Nature isn't cooperating, snow-making machines keep the slopes in business. Well-synchronized chairlifts can shuttle 20,000 skiers an hour while preventing overcrowding of the slopes. Boston Mills and Brandywine are two separate parks five minutes apart by car. Lift tickets and passes are valid at both, however, since they are owned by the same company. Lessons, equipment rental, and food service are available at both resorts, while inner tubing is offered only at Brandywine. Check the website for months, days, and hours of operation.

MAP 7: 7100 Riverview Rd., Peninsula, 330/657-2334, www.bmbw.com; lift passes $38-43, equipment rental package $30

TOBOGGANING
Mill Stream Run Reservation

Twin refrigerated chutes whisk adventurers 70 feet down and 1,000 feet out on toboggans built for four. This seasonal tradition kicks off the day after Thanksgiving and runs through the first weekend in March. Apart from really warm or really wet days, the chutes are open Thursday through Sunday and holidays. Be prepared to hike up 110 steps to the top to earn your exhilarating 15-second descent. Riders must be at least 42 inches tall and wear mittens or gloves. When you've had enough of the frosty free falls, head into the chalet to enjoy the warm glow of two fireplaces and a large-screen television.

MAP 7: 16200 Valley Parkway, Strongsville, 440/572-9990, www. clevelandmetroparks.com; one-ride ticket $6, multiple-run pass $10

AMUSEMENT PARKS
Memphis Kiddie Park

This is the amusement park where little ones get revenge on all those other parks—you know, the ones that say you have to be "this tall" to ride the rides. At Memphis, children must be *under* 50 inches tall to enjoy most rides. Not far from the zoo, this cherished Cleveland landmark has been putting smiles on kids' faces since 1952. Pint-size thrill seekers scramble for seats on trains, in boats, aboard spaceships, and high (well, not so high) atop the Ferris wheel. For something both young and old can get behind, consider an 18-hole round of championship minigolf. Good clean fun abounds at this tidy family-friendly park. Memphis runs on tickets, with each ride a pay-as-you-go affair.

MAP 7: 10340 Memphis Ave., Cleveland, 216/941-5995, www.memphiskiddiepark. com; hours vary May-Oct.; no admission fee, book of 25 ride tickets $35.50

Various Locations

PARTY BIKE TOURS
Cleveland Cycle Tours

If you have the itch to ride on a 15-person party bike, this tour company is for you. This fully pedal-powered vehicle can be rented by the group for neighborhood tours, pub crawls, or anything else you can think of. It's been spotted frequently in Ohio City, Tremont, and downtown, where it makes frequent stops for refreshments. Single seats can be had for as low as $35; rent the entire rig for $390.

Various locations: 440/532-9995, www. bikecct.com

BIKE TRAILS
Cleveland Metroparks All-Purpose Trails

Cleveland Metroparks maintains more than 100 miles of paved, all-purpose trails for bicycling, walking, jogging, and inline skating. They have more than a dozen different reservations scattered around town, so a trailhead is never too far away. A short drive from downtown is Rocky River Reservation, which features a scenic 13-mile stretch of all-purpose trail that sometimes follows the Rocky River. Though not directly connected, another nine miles of all-purpose trail through Mill Stream Run

Fortunately for the residents of Greater Cleveland, early city and county leaders had the foresight to set aside some ground for conservation, education, and recreation. Cobbling together patches of land, the park board ultimately assembled a remarkable chain of parks and connecting boulevards that encircled the whole of Cuyahoga County, called **Cleveland Metroparks** (216/635-3200, www.clevelandmetroparks.com). This ribbon of green space largely follows the waterways of the Rocky River, Chagrin River, Big Creek, Chippewa Creek, Tinkers Creek, and Euclid Creek. On a map, this patchwork of parks looks like a leafy necklace around the neck of Lady Cleveland—hence the Metroparks' nickname, the Emerald Necklace.

In 2013, the Metroparks entered into a long-term lease with the City of Cleveland to manage the city's six lakefront parks as well. Combined, the Metroparks' 18 reservations cover more than 23,000 acres of dense forest, wetland, prairie, ravines, lakes, and streams. The activities available within the park system are seemingly endless, including hiking, biking, swimming, fishing, golfing, cross-country skiing, birding, tobogganing, and geo-caching, not to mention visiting the Cleveland Metroparks Zoo and its RainForest exhibit.

In addition to all the standard recreational opportunities, the Metroparks presents a diverse calendar of programming that covers skills-based courses in photography, survival, fly-fishing, backpacking, canoeing, kayaking, and so much more. Throughout the entire year, captivating events are held at the reservations' various lodges, shelters, and nature centers. Folks assemble for moonlit owl walks, fall foliage strolls, and marshy reptile hunts. It would not be hyperbole to claim that you could spend the rest of your life taking advantage of the park's gifts without ever tapping them out.

Reservation can easily be accessed by a short ride along Valley Parkway, adding up to a very enjoyable 22-mile route. Other particularly picturesque rides can be found at the North and South Chagrin Reservations.

Various locations: www.clemetparks. com

SWIMMING POOLS
City of Cleveland

The City of Cleveland operates about 19 indoor and 21 outdoor swimming pools throughout the city. All of the outdoor pools are open noon-7pm Wednesday-Saturday from the second weekend in June through the second weekend in August. Many neighborhood pools offer learn-to-swim programs in addition to general open swim time. Check the city website for locations around town and hours of operation for indoor pools.

Various locations: 216/664-3018, www. city.cleveland.oh.us

ULTIMATE FRISBEE
Cleveland Disc Association

Cleveland-based devotees of the fast-moving sport of Ultimate Frisbee are blessed to have the organizing talent of the CDA. Literally hundreds of players and dozens of teams play in pickup games, competitive leagues, and tournaments at parks and school ballfields all over town. There's even a winter league, played indoors at a domed sports complex, for those who never want the fun to stop. The summer action culminates with the annual No Surf in Cleveland Tournament, a monster two-day event that draws players and teams from all across the region. For those who have always wondered what Disc is all about, simply check the website to find out where the next matches will be held.

Various locations: www.cleveland-disc. org

SHOPS

Like all major cities, Cleveland has more than its fair share of malls, shopping centers, and, uh, "lifestyle centers." But the big story in retail these days is the small-business renaissance taking place all over town. The maker movement is alive and thriving in neighborhoods like Ohio City, Detroit Shoreway, Tremont, Old Brooklyn, and others, where boot-strapped startups have graduated from pop-up to full-fledge brick-and-mortar business. From furniture makers to fashion designers, the indie retail scene has never been more vibrant and diverse.

5th Street Arcades

A person can lose track of time in countless bin-filled used vinyl shops, cozy bookstores, and eclectic vintage and resale shops sprinkled throughout town. Lorain Avenue in Detroit Shoreway is an antiques hunter's dream; Coventry Road in Cleveland Heights is nothing short of window-shopping nirvana; and even downtown is seeing a resurgence in retail, with a pair of historic arcades filling up with new shops run by fearless small operators with big ideas.

Clevelanders love to eat, as evidenced by a fresh wave of specialty foods ventures that peddle everything from chewy bagels to fine chocolates. Craft butcher shops, well-stocked wine stores, and gourmet popcorn providers are making the city more delicious than it has ever been.

HIGHLIGHTS

✪ **BEST PLACE TO CATCH CLEVE FEVE:** With the motto "Spreading Cleveland pride one T-shirt at a time," **CLE Clothing Co.** is like a team shop for the entire city. This upbeat downtown retail store sells Cleveland-themed clothing, books, and gifts (page 151).

✪ **MOST BEAUTIFUL FOOD MARKET:** Set inside the historic Cleveland Trust Rotunda Building, a neoclassical building from the early 20th century, **Heinen's Grocery** is likely the only supermarket with marble floors, column-ringed rotunda, and Tiffany-style stained-glass dome (page 151).

✪ **BEST SOURCE FOR NEW-OLD THINGS:** Somehow, the design-minded pickers at **All Things for You** manage to keep a 6,000-square-foot space filled with drool-worthy midcentury modern furniture, rustic antiques, vintage clothing, and eclectic home decor (page 154).

✪ **BEST PLACE TO DISCUSS KEROUAC: Visible Voice Books** owner Dave Ferrante can discuss boho lit with the best of them. And a sparkling new location gives him a better, bigger home in which to do so. As an added bonus, it now sits above a pizza parlor (page 155).

✪ **WHERE CRAFT MEETS MEAT: Ohio City Provisions** represents the very best of the local farm-to-table movement. Many of the chops, steaks, roasts, poultry, and cold cuts on display began life at Wholesome Valley, a 200-acre Amish-run farm about an hour south (page 157).

✪ **THAT BIKE SHOP IS HOW OLD? Fridrich Bicycle** began life as a feed store in the late-1800s, making it one of the oldest bike shops in the country. These days, the large showroom is filled with all manner of one-, two-, and three-wheeled bikes (page 159).

✪ **WHERE TO SHOP FOR THAT WEIRD UNCLE:** Oddities are big business, and **Cleveland Curiosities** has shoppers covered when it comes to antique medical equipment, taxidermied animals, articulated skeletons, and mounted and framed fruit bats (page 168).

✪ **BEST COMIC BOOK SHOP:** Thanks to frequent deliveries of big-name and small-run publications, great organization, and super-friendly customer service, **Carol & John's Comic Book Shop** has been in business since 1990 (page 169).

SHOPPING DISTRICTS

5th Street Arcades

Formerly the Colonial Arcade, one of two beautiful and historic downtown arcades built around the turn of the 20th century, 5th Street Arcades now houses an eclectic and evolving mix of shops, boutiques, and restaurants. Along with anchor tenants like Pour Coffee, Jack Flaps Luncheonette, and Barrio Gateway, new shops and galleries will cycle in and out in somewhat incubator fashion, with successful ones hopefully growing roots. Johnnyville Woods turns out colorful, custom-engraved baseball bats; Happy Hour Collection celebrates all things happy hour, carrying a line of vintage and modern barware; The Tea Lab stocks a large selection of quality teas and tea-making accessories; W Gallery is a high-end jewelry, art, and gift store and studio run by designers. In the summer, a farmers market occasionally pops up, as do events and after-work get-togethers, all catering to the growing downtown residential market.

MAP 1: 530 Euclid Ave., 216/583-0500, www.5thstreetarcades.com; hours vary by store

Lorain Avenue Antiques District

This ever-evolving collection of thrift, consignment, antiques, and restoration shops has long been a magnet for steely-eyed bargain hunters. Loosely centered around West 78th Street, the stores range from filthy dustbins to posh showrooms. There is never a dearth of architectural salvage, from stately wooden fireplace mantels and stained-glass windows to porcelain pedestal sinks and clawfoot tubs. Don't miss Suite Lorain for vintage collectibles, Antique Gallery at the Bijou for Arts and Crafts furnishings sold in an old theater, and Reincarnation Vintage Design for everything from farmhouse chic to midcentury modern. This urban landscape is better suited to the self-assured explorer than the high-maintenance mall-walker.

MAP 3: Lorain Ave. between W. 65th St. and West Blvd., www.discoverlorainave. com; hours vary but many shops open only noon-5pm Wed.-Sun.

Downtown   Map 1

ACCESSORIES AND SHOES

The Restock

This downtown shop is a bit of a passion project for former Cleveland Browns cornerback Joe Haden, a longtime buyer and collector of colorful (and pricey) sneakers. Working with collectors, Haden and company score rare, hard-to-find, and desirable new and vintage sneakers at prices well below those other popular spots. Yeezys, Jordans, and LeBrons all make their way through this hip, urban apparel shop, where it's not uncommon to see the pro himself.

MAP 1: 645 Prospect Ave., 216/862-4903, www.therestockcle.com; noon-8pm Tues.-Sat., noon-6pm Sun.

GIFT AND HOME
⭐ CLE Clothing Co.

With the motto "Spreading Cleveland pride one T-shirt at a time," this upbeat downtown retail store is like a team shop for the entire city. Adjacent to Destination Cleveland, the city's convention and visitors bureau, CLE Clothing sells Cleveland-themed clothing, books, and gifts. It doesn't take an urban sociologist to see that more and more locals are proud to call themselves Clevelanders, and they're expressing their civic pride with T-shirts emblazoned with "I liked Cleveland before it was cool" or "Cleveland is my Paris." Stop in for great gifts like stickers, coasters, beer koozies, key chains, hoodies, and more.

MAP 1: 342 Euclid Ave., 216/736-8879, www.cleclothingco.com; 11am-9pm Mon.-Sat., noon-6pm Sun.

CLE Clothing Co.

Rebuilders Xchange

This women-owned business buys and sells construction and architectural salvage, filling a 70,000-square-foot warehouse space just east of town. Working closely with individuals, builders, and contractors who have access to new or salvaged building material, the team amasses a unique and sought-after inventory of goods. On any given day, a homeowner or designer might find that perfect vintage farmhouse sink, enameled clawfoot tub, or industrial hanging light fixture. At one point, they had 100 stately wooden church pews and 1,000 antique doorknobs and fixtures.

MAP 1: 5401 Hamilton Ave., 216/551-8175, www.rbxhub.com; 9am-6pm Wed., 9am-3pm Thurs.-Fri., 9am-4pm Sat.

Surroundings Home Décor

Urban pioneers looking to furnish their modern downtown lofts know to come here for all manner of sleek home furnishings. Like many of the apartments and condos it outfits, Surroundings is housed in an open-plan Warehouse District showroom with support columns and exposed HVAC systems. A favorite of designers, architects, and consumers alike, the gallery stocks high-end European lines for both home and office, with numerous pieces for every room, need, style, and budget. This is also the place to come for the latest in lighting technology and design. For those who lack a sharp eye, Surroundings offers interior design consultation.

MAP 1: 850 W. St. Clair Ave., 216/623-4070, www.surroundingshomedecor.com; 11am-6pm Tues.-Fri., noon-6pm Sat.

SPECIALTY FOODS
⭐ Heinen's Grocery

Described by many as "the most beautiful grocery store in the nation," Heinen's is a must-visit for architecture fans. This flagship store for a local grocery chain is set inside the historic Cleveland Trust Rotunda Building, an early-20th-century neoclassical building designed by George Post, architect of the New York Stock Exchange. This top-flight example of adaptive reuse means that food shoppers can admire an inlaid marble

Heinen's Grocery

floor, column-ringed rotunda, and Tiffany-style stained-glass dome that rises high above one's head. Whether you're in the market for a bottle of wine, six-pack of beer, prepared-foods lunch, or side of fresh salmon, this urban amenity is at the ready.

MAP 1: 900 Euclid Ave., 216/302-3020, www.heinens.com; 8am-9pm Mon.-Fri., 9am-9pm Sat.-Sun.

Tink Holl

This granddaddy of Asian groceries carries a dizzying array of imported products, frozen foods, fresh produce, and live seafood. Home cooks come here for hard-to-find greens like pea shoots, baby bok choy, and Chinese mustard greens. Unsweetened soy milk is ground fresh on-site, and the copper-colored roast ducks that hang behind glass are sold by the half or whole. Asian snacks like freshly fried shrimp chips are sold by the bag, and the on-site restaurant Szechuan Gourmet is one of the best in town. There are other Asian markets in town, but this one manages to combine the best of all of them under one roof.

MAP 1: 1735 E. 36th St., 216/881-6996; 9:30am-8pm daily

HEALTH AND BEAUTY
Manifest

Manifest is a unique beauty salon in a number of ways. For starters, it services both men and women. Secondly, and perhaps more importantly, it prepares and serves craft cocktails. Men can get their beards trimmed, hairs cut, and fingernails manicured, while ladies have the full suite of treatments available. Making every service better is the fact that it can be paired with a well-crafted libation and enjoyed in an attractive and sophisticated setting. Guys who are just tagging along—or done before their companion—can sip and watch TV at the bar.

MAP 1: 668 Prospect Ave., 216/ 465-4006, www.manifestcle.com; noon-8pm Tues.-Fri., 10am-8pm Sat.

Marengo Luxury Spa

Within the Hyatt Regency at the Arcade, Marengo is one of the few full-service luxury day spas in the downtown area. The plush digs strike the right tone for a half or full day of premium pampering. While a tad pricey, the services offered are top-notch and professionally administered. Massage services include those geared specifically to pregnant women and sore-muscled athletes. Men's and women's facials, manicures, and waxing are available, as are traditional hair cutting, coloring, and styling services. This dreamy spa is popular with wedding parties getting their makeup and up-dos before the big event.

MAP 1: 401 Euclid Ave., 216/621-4600, www.marengospa.com; 10am-7pm Tues.-Fri., 9am-6pm Sat.

PETS
Cleveland MetroBark

MetroBark's location and hours make it popular with East Side commuters, who drop off their fur babies on the way to work and pick them up on the way home. Pets who spend the day romping in the 6,000-square-foot indoor and 14,000-square-foot outdoor pens have access to pools,

sprinklers, and fans. Grooming services range from a quick bath on up to full spa treatment. Both on-site and off-site boarding are offered. Campers must be at least three months old, nonaggressive, and current with their vaccinations.

MAP 1: 3939 Payne Ave., 216/881-3644, www.metrobark.com; 6:30am-7pm Mon.-Fri.; approx. $13 half day, $20 full day

OUTDOOR AND SPORTING GOODS
Geiger's

As more and more residents began calling downtown home, new retail soon followed. Geiger's, a clothing and sporting goods store that has existed for more than 80 years in Lakewood, is part of that movement. The prominent 4,200-square-foot shop in a 100-year-old building stocks an amazing selection of men's and women's apparel, footwear, outerwear, and travel accessories. You'll find the latest goods from brands like Patagonia, The North Face, Under Armour, Teva, and Yeti displayed in a spacious and attractive department store setting.

MAP 1: 1020 Euclid Ave., 216/755-4500, www.shopgeigers.com; 10am-6pm Mon.-Sat.

Ohio City and Tremont   Map 2

CLOTHING
Evie Lou

After years spent writing about fashion for the Cleveland *Plain Dealer,* former style editor Kim Crow opened this chic women's clothing shop in the hip Tremont neighborhood. While style is first and foremost on her mind, it's really the comfort of her customers that

drives her and her store. The shop sets out to prove that style and comfort are not mutually exclusive, dishing up the latest trends in eminently wearable fabrics. Though the shop carries a wide range of brands and designers, Crow keeps the ever-rotating stock down to a manageable size so as to not overwhelm her clients.

MAP 2: 2509 Professor Ave., 216/696-6675, www.evielou.com; 11am-7pm Mon.-Wed., 11am-8pm Thurs.-Sat., noon-4pm Sun.

VINTAGE AND ANTIQUES

✪ All Things for You

Vintage fans have followed owners Tim Yanko and Dwight Kaczmarek from flea market to cramped storefront and, ultimately, to here, a spacious 6,000-square-foot showroom in the heart of Ohio City. Years in the estate sale business have given them a keen eye and likely first dibs on great inventory. This sun-filled warehouse space is artfully arranged with midcentury modern furniture, rustic antiques, vintage clothing, eclectic home decor, and so much more. Shopping here feels like going garage sale shopping in the "good neighborhood" with great friends.

MAP 2: 3910 Lorain Ave., 216/273-7761, www.allthingsforu.com; 10am-4pm Wed., 9am-3pm Sat.-Sun.

Rook Modern

Owners John and Adam buy, collect, and curate high-quality vintage furnishings, decor, and art for sale online and at this cheery Tremont shop. Lucky shoppers who happened to visit recently might have called "dibs" on a set of Ludwig Mies van der Rohe chairs, a matching set of 1960s-era walnut chests from American of Martinsville, or a smashing teak sideboard by Poul Cadovius. This choice stuff moves fast thanks to a brisk presence on Facebook and Instagram, so visit early and often.

MAP 2: 2415 Tremont Ave., 216/543-2394; 5pm-9pm Fri., 2pm-9pm Sat., or by appointment

BOOKS AND MUSIC

Horizontal Books

Don't let the bland facade fool you; Horizontal is a bookworm's paradise. While a bit haphazard in layout and inventory, the massive and ever-changing selection of books is compelling. Buying overstock titles from publishers allows the owner to offer steep discounts on perfect-condition new books. Customers get 50 percent off the jacket price when buying one book, 60 percent off on two, and 70 percent off when buying three. Located on the main drag in Ohio City, this shop is a dying breed.

MAP 2: 1921 W. 25th St., 216/298-4411; 10am-6pm Mon.-Sat., 11am-4pm Sun.

Loop

If you're in the market for both a delicious cappuccino and the latest release from the Shins, Loop is the place for you. This sharp café inside a converted Tremont home has an upstairs record shop that carries a good selection of vinyl and CD indie releases. The main floor is largely devoted to the business of brewing high-quality coffee and tea. Loop is a great place to start the day, meet up for a midday interview, or kill an hour or two doing absolutely nothing important.

MAP 2: 2180 W. 11th St., 216/298-5096; 7am-9pm Mon.-Thurs., 7am-10pm Fri., 8am-10pm Sat., 8am-6pm Sun.

A Separate Reality Records

At last count, this modest record shop had 200,000 used titles in stock—and the selection is growing by the day. It would be impossible to tick off all the genres of vinyl that flow through here on any given day, but suffice it to say that if it spins, it's here. Rare and collectible jazz records share bin space with surf rock and soul platters. Of course, if you're in the market to unload Uncle Jim's obscure prog rock collection, this is the place to bring it.

MAP 2: 3932 Lorain Ave., 216/644-7934, www.aseparaterealityrecords.com; 11am-7pm Tues.-Thurs., 11am-8pm Fri.-Sat., noon-5pm Sun.

✪ Visible Voice Books

In 2017, this beloved indie bookstore was given fresh life in a new location after being shuttered for a handful of years. The store is run by the same proprietor and is situated in the same neighborhood, but there's now double the space, convenient parking, and a pizza parlor right downstairs. The eclectic catalog is hand selected by owner Dave Ferrante, and it strongly reflects his personal tastes, which lean toward the bohemian and erudite. Bonuses include frequent author readings and book signings, live acoustic music, and a café that dispenses coffee, seasonal wines, craft beer, and pastries.

MAP 2: 1023 Kenilworth Ave., 216/961-0084, www.visiblevoicebooks.com; noon-8pm Wed.-Thurs., noon-10pm Fri., 11am-10pm Sat., 11am-5pm Sun.

Visible Voice Books

GIFT AND HOME
Banyan Tree

In a neighborhood littered with boutiques, Banyan Tree rises to the top of the pack thanks to its well-edited and ever-evolving catalog of inventory. Blessed with a keen eye for fashion, home decor, and accessories trends, the owner has created one of the best go-to places for appreciated gifts. Once purchased, those gifts are lovingly and fashionably wrapped at no charge. Sleek and modern, this urban shop carries handmade textiles, season-appropriate designer garments, vintage jewelry, and funky home furnishings. Sorry, no tacky postcards or T-shirts here.

MAP 2: 2242 Professor Ave., 216/241-1209, www.shopbanyantree.com; 10am-7pm Mon.-Wed., 10am-9pm Thurs.-Sat., 11am-5pm Sun.

Everarbor

This homegrown business is a patchwork of disciplines. What began life as a landscaping business run by a forestry tech has evolved into an outdoor lifestyle company rooted in a passion for Mother Earth. There is a line of outdoor apparel that is designed and constructed in Cleveland, with T-shirts, hoodies, ball caps, and rain gear. The shop also sells Everbrew, an organic soil supplement made from coffee grounds rescued from local cafés. Also, if you happen across an ill or injured wild animal, the owner happens to offer rescue services as well.

MAP 2: 2617 Scranton Rd., 440/823-7945, www.everarborco.com; 4pm-8pm Fri., 11am-8pm Sat., 11am-5pm Sun.

Room Service

This popular Ohio City shop has a little bit of everything, but all of it is selected for its modern and quality design. Shoppers will find an ever-changing variety of goods that range from men's and women's apparel to home decor items to gifts and stationery. The design-minded owners have a knack for keeping abreast of the hippest, most up-to-date trends and finding the products that best represent those trends. They also go out of their way to stock locally made clothing, crafts, and art. Cleveland-themed T-shirts can be purchased, along with humorous cards and gift items.

MAP 2: 2078 W. 25th St., 216/696-6220, www.rscleveland.com; 11am-6pm Mon. and Wed.-Sat., 11am-5pm Sun.

Something Different

When tooling around the West 25th Street area of Ohio City, make a quick detour into this wildly eclectic shop. Slightly chaotic and cramped, Something Different carries gifts, souvenirs, fashions, jewelry, even toiletries, some admittedly more "different" than others. Knickknacks abound, like colorful glassware, greeting cards, and wine carriers. But fine art and sculpture can be found, too, and the gallery is a great outlet for local artists. Reasonable price points and complimentary designer gift wrapping add to the allure of this fun diversion.

MAP 2: 1899 W. 25th St., 216/696-5226, www.somethingdifferentgallery.com; 10:30am-6pm Mon. and Wed.-Sat.

Wine & Design

Stepping inside this renovated Tremont storefront feels a bit like being welcomed into the living room of a friend with great design sense. That's because the owner is indeed an interior designer, who decided to couple that business with a boutique that offers a unique and trendy selection of gifts, art, home decor, and affordable wines by the bottle. Pop in for a weekend wine tasting and you'll likely leave with a new favorite or two along with that perfect hostess gift.

MAP 2: 751 Starkweather Ave., 216/781-8000, www.wineanddesign. net; noon-7pm Tues.-Fri., 11am-6pm Sat., 11am-3pm Sun.

ARTS AND CRAFTS
Cleveland Blacksmithing

Thanks to a renewed interest in the skilled trades and ancient crafts, shops like Cleveland Blacksmithing are popping up all over. Sure, the forge is a hot, hellish place punctuated by the ever-present sound of hammer hitting steel. But folks swear by the satisfaction of transforming a scrap of metal into a practical or beautiful implement. This smith shop offers single and group classes and lessons, from a general one-day beginner's course on up to a three-week intensive program. Fun workshops will have newbies forging their very own bottle opener in as little as three hours.

MAP 2: 4009 Fulton Ct., 216/532-5351, www.clevelandblacksmithing.com; class times vary

Glass Bubble Project

Chances are you've never experienced a gallery like this one. It's an absolute blast—with a blast furnace, to boot. Tucked into a cramped garage, which itself is secreted behind a block of buildings, Glass Bubble Project is a glassblowing studio run by remarkable—and remarkably peculiar—artists. An open-studio policy means that visitors can stroll in anytime and catch the artists dipping blowpipes into glory holes. (That's glassblowing lingo, by the way.) Impromptu demonstrations are fine for most, but the Bubble also offers private lessons, easily scheduled with a phone call. Gift ideas abound, from one-of-a-kind blown-glass bowls and glassware to Christmas ornaments and found-art sculpture.

MAP 2: 2421 Bridge Ave., 216/696-7043, www.glassbubbleproject.com; 10am-6pm daily

SPECIALTY FOOD AND DRINK

Campbell's Sweets Factory

For years, Campbell's operated a popular stand down the street at the West Side Market. That was then, as they say, as the company has grown to include new locations and this busy central kitchen and retail outlet. Old and new fans of Campbell's gourmet popcorn—available in dozens of flavors, including the cheese-caramel Dichotomy—chocolate-covered pretzels and Oreos, and fluffy and flavorful cupcakes make regular pilgrimages here to satisfy their cravings. An open kitchen and front display window offer behind-the-scenes views of the action. If that's not enough, tours of the entire operation are also offered.
MAP 2: 1979 W. 25th St., 216/574-2899, www.campbellssweets.com; 10am-7pm Mon.-Thurs., 9am-7pm Fri.-Sat.

Cleveland Brew Shop

This truly is a one-stop shop for all your beer and winemaking needs, and it caters to an ever-growing and passionate base of skilled hobbyists. In addition to stocking quality equipment, fresh ingredients, and helpful literature, this friendly Tremont shop holds regularly scheduled classes for beginners and others. Complete beer kits bundle up everything a brewer will require to whip up a batch of American pale ale or a Belgian *tripel*.
MAP 2: 4142 Lorain Ave., 216/574-2271, www.clevelandbrewshop.com; 11am-7pm Tues.-Fri., 10am-5pm Sat., noon-4pm Sun.

Hansa Import Haus

Inside a kitschy faux-Swiss chalet, Hansa Import Haus provides a culinary lifeline for Cleveland's sizable German immigrant population. This quirky gingerbread shop has survived for more than half a century thanks to its deep selection of German, Swiss, and Austrian imports, ranging from hard-to-find spreads, meats, and cheeses to harder-to-find beers, including Bavarian *rauchbiers*. Rows of store shelving sag beneath the weight of enough cookies, cakes, and chocolates to make even the most stoic émigré weep with longing. An on-site brewpub is definitely worth a visit.
MAP 2: 2717 Lorain Ave., 216/281-3177, www.hansabrewery.com; 9am-5:30pm Mon.-Sat.

Market at the Fig

Chef Karen Small, who runs the wonderful Flying Fig bistro next door, transformed a seldom-used private dining room into a sleek gourmet retail marketplace. The European-style shop offers a deft mix of prepared foods, made-to-order sandwiches, specialty retail products, and beer and wine. Come here for a light breakfast, amazing chef-designed sandwiches, and heartier dinner-friendly fare. Also on hand are charcuterie, artisanal cheeses, house-made pastries, breads, pickles, and jams. Come here after a visit to the West Side Market to grab a nice bottle of wine and some snacks for the room.
MAP 2: 2523 Market Ave., 216/241-4243, www.theflyingfig.com; 11am-8pm Tues.-Fri., 10am-8pm Sat., noon-7pm Sun.

✪ Ohio City Provisions

Launched by a chef and a farmer, this craft butcher shop in the Ohio City neighborhood represents the very

Ohio City Provisions

best of the local farm-to-table movement. Many of the chops, steaks, roasts, and poultry on display began life at Wholesome Valley, a 200-acre Amish-run farm about an hour south. The heritage breed hogs, cattle, lamb, chicken, ducks, and turkeys are brought in whole and butchered onsite in the glass-walled cold room. Each day, the shimmering coolers are filled with cold cuts, charcuterie, fresh sausages, and a slew of other ready-to-cook meats. Those offerings are joined by freshly baked breads, seasonal vegetables, dry goods, prepared foods, and frozen soups.

MAP 2: 3208 Lorain Ave., Cleveland, 216/465-2762, www.ohiocityprovisions. com; 10am-7pm daily

Tremont General Store

Cleveland is blessed with a broad pool of indie food startups, from sauerkraut and bagels to pickles and hot sauce. Tremont General, which is a modern-day general store, is one of the best places to track them all down. Since opening the shop in 2016, owner Kevin Kubovcik has worked to amass as many local food products as he can, displaying them in bins, on shelves, and in reach-in coolers and freezers. This quirky shop also is a garden center, feed store, and neighborhood snack source.

MAP 2: 2418 Professor Ave., 216/288-7167; 10:30am-7pm Mon.-Fri., 10am-5pm Sat., 11am-3pm Sun.

Tremont General Store

HEALTH AND BEAUTY
Zen Metro Spa

This stylish urban salon is adored by some of this city's trendiest residents, who come for world-class talent, services, and products. Spread across three long and narrow floors is a full-service salon and spa offering everything from color and cuts to manicures and waxings. Spa services such as facials, massages, and salt glows are provided on the lower level. Owner Rob Torma has been in the salon business for decades, and he has assembled a professional team that seems obsessed with making people look and feel their absolute best.

MAP 2: 1870 W. 25th St., 216/939-1760, www.zenmetrospa.com; 10am-8pm Tues.-Thurs., 10am-6pm Fri., 10am-5pm Sat.

FURNITURE
Furniture Makers

The owners of this Tremont storefront are self-taught furniture makers who craft graceful, high-quality pieces made from hardwoods harvested from urban areas. For customers who know precisely what they want, the shop will build custom, one-of-a-kind pieces from pictures or even sketches. For those who would rather browse, the showroom stocks a selection of handsome desks, dressers, sideboards, cupboards, and consoles.

MAP 2: 767 Starkweather Ave., 440/724-5439, www. furnituremakercleveland.com; 10am-5pm Mon.-Fri.

OUTDOOR AND SPORTING GOODS
✪ Fridrich Bicycle

Fridrich Bicycle has been doing its thing in Ohio City since the late-1800s, making it one of the oldest bike shops in the country. What began as a feed store has evolved into a local institution that repairs, sells, and delivers bikes to riders of all ages and abilities. With more than 10,000 square feet of showroom, the shop stocks a bewildering inventory of mountain bikes, hybrids, cruisers, BMX, road bikes, fixies, tandems, tricycles, unicycles, and recumbents. These guys will even rent you a bike for the weekend if you're looking for wheels.

MAP 2: 3800 Lorain Ave., 216/651-3800, www.fridrichs.com; 11am-6:30pm Mon.-Thurs., 11am-7pm Fri., 10am-5pm Sat., noon-4pm Sun.

Joy Machines Bike Shop

In a bike-savvy community like Ohio City, where even the neighborhood bars offer bike maintenance stations, a shop like Joy Machines is a true asset. From a basic tune-up or flat tire repair to a complete overhaul, these guys have your bike needs covered. If you don't yet own a bicycle—or it's time to upgrade—the shop carries top lines like Surly, Jamis, Linus, and All-City, along with parts, accessories, and apparel.

MAP 2: 1836 W. 25th St., 216/394-0230, www.joymachines.net; 11am-7pm Mon.-Fri., 11am-5pm Sat., noon-4pm Sun.

Detroit Shoreway and Edgewater

Map 3

CLOTHING AND ACCESSORIES

Christophier Custom Clothier

When the time comes to man up in terms of fashion—you know, swap the snarky tees for a big-boy suit—shoppers would do well to visit Maurice Christophier. For decades, this well-dressed haberdasher has outfitted clients in timelessly classic apparel, much of it custom made, all of it flawlessly tailored. Bespoke shirts and suits are this shop's bread and butter, but a guy can also pick up a smart off-the-rack blazer and a pair of the world's most comfortable khakis. To finish the polished look, this West Side boutique maintains an unmatched collection of socks, belts, and cuff links.

MAP 3: 9308 Clifton Blvd., 216/961-5555, www.christophier.com; 10am-5:45pm Tues.-Fri., 10am-4pm Sat.

Fount

What started as a home-based business selling at local flea markets has exploded into a well-known luxury leather goods brand with an obsessive following. Attractive women's and men's totes, handbags, bags, duffels, backpacks, and wallets are all designed, cut, and sewn in a Cleveland warehouse and displayed for sale at this chic retail storefront. Made from durable Italian hides, the bags and straps come with a lifetime warranty.

MAP 3: 6706 Detroit Ave., 216/855-8751, www.fountleather.com; 11am-7pm Tues.-Thurs., 11am-8pm Fri.-Sat., 11am-5pm Sun.

VINTAGE AND ANTIQUES

Flower Child

Shoppers keen on a particular vintage era have it easy at Flower Child thanks to period-specific displays, which are arranged precisely as they might have been at department stores decades ago. This popular multi-room shop moves through inventory quickly, meaning that frequent visits net frequent scores. Expect furniture, clothing, jewelry, lighting, and accessories from the 1930s through the 1970s, all artfully displayed. It's a great source for midcentury furniture, vintage jewelry (including Bakelite and men's cuff links), and all manner of floor, wall, and ceiling lighting.

MAP 3: 11508 Clifton Blvd., 216/939-9933, www.flowerchildvintage.com; noon-7pm Mon. and Wed.-Thurs., noon-8pm Fri.-Sat., noon-5pm Sun.

Heck's Revival

Annoyed by the quality of modern furniture, Caley Coleff would scout out older pieces to customize and sell to a few friends and family. Business picked up, and she upgraded to this colorful neighborhood shop. While the location has changed, the system has not: The owner still unearths interesting used furniture (much of it plucked from the proverbial trash heap) before applying her own bold designs to it. In addition to bar stools, dressers, and armoires, there are smaller items like lamps, signs, and tableware. Brisk business means that items are constantly being replaced with new (old) stuff.

MAP 3: 11102 Detroit Ave., 216/221-8221; noon-7pm Tues.-Wed., noon-5pm Thurs.-Sat.

Reincarnation Vintage Design

Owner Ron Nicolson doesn't just re-sell old furniture, he repurposes it into hip home furnishings and accessories. By staying abreast of the latest home decor trends, Nicolson and wife Cyndy know what to look for when making the rounds of estate sales, auctions, antiques swaps, and demo sites. An old wooden door is transformed into a funky dinette table; a long-forgotten industrial workbench becomes a stainless-steel kitchen island; galvanized wire conveyor belting is segmented into durable and distinctive doormats. This two-level warehouse-style showroom is a must-visit when hitting the antiques and resale shops of Lorain Avenue. Being open only on weekends allows the team time to find new cool stuff.

MAP 3: 7810 Lorain Ave., 216/651-9806, www.rvdcleveland.com; noon-5pm Sat., noon-4pm Sun.

Suite Lorain

Easily one of the best vintage shops in Cleveland, Suite Lorain is 8,000 square feet of retro fun. The former bowling alley digs are an appropriate setting for the well-tended collection of clothing, home furnishings, small appliances, and accessories from the 1920s through the mid-20th century. Numerous vendors keep the place uber-stocked with cool kitsch and collectibles, including old records, magazines, and posters. A favorite among designers, touring musicians, and fashion-savvy ladies, this West Side shop knows the difference between trash and treasure.

MAP 3: 7105 Lorain Rd., 216/281-1959, www.sweetlorain.com; noon-5pm Sun.-Mon., noon-6pm Wed.-Sat.

BOOKS AND MUSIC

Bent Crayon Records

You won't find Top 40 music at this focused West Side shop. You will find bins full of "important music" like experimental, techno, house, electronic, drone, noise, post-punk, African dub, bass, and forward-thinking rock music. Obscure labels and imports draw a select demographic to be sure, but for these fans, Bent Crayon is a lifesaver. Don't know your emo from your trance? No problemo—the enthusiastic staffers will not only point you in the right direction, they'll likely pop some on the sound system for an auditory explanation.

MAP 3: 1305 W. 80th St., Ste. 216, 216/221-9200, www.bentcrayonrecords.com; 11am-6pm Tues.-Sat., noon-5pm Sun.

Guide to Kulchur

Guide to Kulchur is an indie-minded book, magazine, and periodicals shop run by husband-and-wife team Lyz Bly and R. A. Washington. A large emphasis is placed on fanzines (zines), and the operators hope to amass thousands of local, national, and international zines. More important, they hope to usher in the next generation of those writers with their co-op workshop for zines, handmade books, small pubs, chapbooks, and other printed ephemera. Look to this spot, too, to host writers, artists, and intellectuals to discuss the weighty topics of the day.

MAP 3: 5222 Lorain Ave., 216/647-8012; 10am-8pm Tues.-Thurs., 10am-10pm Fri.-Sat., 11am-6pm Sun.

Hausfrau Record Shop

At just around 400 square feet, Hausfrau Records can hardly be classified as a mega record store—or mega anything for that matter. But what this all-vinyl shop lacks in size it more than makes up for in spunk. Owner Steven Peffer manages to unearth and display vintage and not-so-vintage LPs and 45s in the genres of rock, punk, jazz, soul, and synth. Thanks to fair pricing and a keen eye, the owner moves through inventory (much of it obscure) at a steady clip. This spare, almost utilitarian store is immediately adjacent to Capitol Theatre, making it a natural pre- or post-show stop.

MAP 3: 1388 W. 65th St., 216/394-5171; noon-7pm Tues.-Sat.

OUTDOOR AND SPORTING GOODS

Blazing Saddle Cycle

Serving the bike-commuter-heavy community of Detroit Shoreway, this indie shop keeps its neighbors rolling. Set inside a former 100-year-old hardware store, the industrial space features antique bikes hanging from the rafters, while a beefy selection of commuter, racing, and even custom-built bikes line the room. In addition to sales, service, and rentals, Blazing Saddle will happily restore your vintage lugged-steel Pinarello from the 1980s. The shop also sells gear like messenger bags, cell phone mounts, and racks.

MAP 3: 7427 Detroit Ave., 216/218-1811, www.blazingsaddlecleveland.com; 10am-7pm Mon.-Fri., 10am-5pm Sat.

Cleveland CycleWerks

Cleveland has always been a manufacturing town, so it makes perfect sense that the city would give birth to an original line of motorcycles. Industrial designer Scott Colosimo had a dream to produce a stripped-down 1960s-inspired motorcycle that looked like a million bucks but cost less than $5,000. At Cleveland CycleWerks, that's precisely what he's accomplished. Models such as the Ace come in standard, café, and scrambler styles, while the Heist is a classic bobber. The bikes turn heads and run like heck, and they start at around $3,400. Check out the showroom and custom fabrication shop in Gordon Square Arts District.

MAP 3: 1265 W. 65th St., 216/651-0657, www.clevelandcyclewerks.com; hours vary

CLOTHING AND ACCESSORIES
Avalon Exchange
This local shop is part of a small multi-city group of buy-sell-trade resale clothing boutiques. Shops buy contemporary, vintage, and designer clothing, shoes, and accessories daily from individuals, ensuring a solid and steady inventory of desirable goods. Not only are the items more fashion-forward than what's found at the mainstream mall, they are less expensive. Swap your used (but nice) apparel for cash or store credit on the spot.
MAP 5: 1798 Coventry Rd., 216/320-9775, www.avalonexchange.com; 11am-8pm Mon.-Sat., noon-6pm Sun.

Cleveland Running Co.
Cleveland Heights is lucky to have a great roster of independently owned businesses, and Cleveland Running Co. is one of those shops. Owner Jeff Fisher ran track and cross country competitively in both high school and college, and he's more than happy to "walk" newbies through the basics of buying a pair of shoes for running, walking, or even hiking. The well-selected inventory is supplemented by outdoor apparel, nutritional products, and accessories.
MAP 5: 2248 Lee Rd., 216/991-2000, www.clevelandrunning.com; 10am-6pm Mon., 10am-7pm Tues.-Thurs., 10am-6pm Fri.-Sat., noon-5pm Sun.

Gentleman's Quarters/ Frog's Legs
Style-conscious men and women have been coming to this upscale clothier for roughly 50 years. Stocking mostly high-end European fashions, the Larchmere store caters less to hipsters than to upwardly mobile hautesters. An in-house tailor will make sure that those new threads from Italy, France, Sweden, and Germany fit like a glove and for no extra charge. Frog's Legs, the women's accessories shop within GQ, carries custom jewelry, purses, and scarves.
MAP 5: 12807 Larchmere Blvd., 216/229-7083; noon-7pm Tues.-Thurs., noon-6pm Fri., 10am-4:30pm Sat.

VINTAGE AND ANTIQUES
Attenson's Antiques & Books
In this spot since 1987, and established way back in 1965, this great family-run business keeps antiques hunters coming back for more. With the motto, "a thousand and one objects of beauty, history and mystery," Attenson's is a kaleidoscope of oddities both fine and kitschy. The double-storefront shop is filled to the brim with old books, local art, outmoded electronics, midcentury modern furniture, and real and costume jewelry. A person could lose track of time just thumbing through the stacks of old postcards.
MAP 5: 1771 Coventry Rd., 216/321-2515, www.attensonsantiques.com; 11:30am-5:30pm Mon.-Sat.

Heide Rivchun Conservation Studios

This Larchmere shop has a dual identity. It is the site of owner Heide Rivchun's renowned furniture conservation and restoration business, and it is the storefront where she displays her wonderful collection of antiques for sale. Stocking fine furniture largely from the 18th and 19th centuries, as well as striking architectural items, the store is popular with designers, decorators, and informed homeowners. Old globes, full fireplace mantels, stained-glass windows, portly earthenware casks—these are just some of the unique items on hand.

MAP 5: 12702 Larchmere Blvd., 216/231-1003, www.conservationstudios. org; 9am-5pm Mon.-Fri., 10am-4pm Sat.

BOOKS AND MUSIC
Appletree Books

Open since 1975, this Cedar-Fairmount District bookshop is beloved for its tight selection of new titles. The opposite of a dusty old book repository, this colorful storefront is an absolute joy to visit, with multiple genres geared to both children and adults. That inventory is supplemented with gifts, greeting cards, puzzles, bookends, and other accessories. Programs like weekly story time for young readers and live music performances only further endear this spot to the community at large.

MAP 5: 12419 Cedar Rd., 216/791-2665, www.appletree-books.com; 10am-6pm Tues.-Wed. and Sat., 10am-8pm Thurs.-Fri.

Loganberry Books

Established in 1994, this cozy book nook specializes in children's and illustrated books, women's history titles, and art and architecture tomes. Along with these genres, plus popular fiction, shoppers can find used rare books, including leather-bound first editions. Fans of traditional bookstores will adore Loganberry, which sports warm oriental rugs, wood floors, and row upon row of open shelving. Loganberry's popular "Stump the Bookseller," a web service where readers post often-sketchy details in hopes of identifying an old favorite book, has been featured in *The New York Times* and on NPR. Strong Bindery, an outfit that restores and repairs old books, is housed on-site.

MAP 5: 13015 Larchmere Blvd., 216/795-9800, www.loganberrybooks. com; 10am-6pm Mon.-Tues. and Fri.-Sat., 10am-8:30pm Wed.-Thurs., noon-4pm Sun.

Mac's Backs Books

It makes sense that Mac's carries works by adult-comic artists like Harvey Pekar and Robert Crumb: Both authors spent formative years tooling around this bohemian neighborhood. This delightfully cramped trilevel shop has an unrivaled selection of literary journals, hard-to-find magazines, classics, and nonfiction. Those looking for a lighter read can pore over thousands of new and used fiction, mystery, and science fiction titles. Equal parts town hall and bookseller, Mac's is the site of frequent neighborhood meetings, readings, discussions, and workshops.

MAP 5: 1820 Coventry Rd., 216/321-2665, www.macsbacks.com; 10am-9pm Mon.-Thurs., 10am-10pm Fri.-Sat., 11am-8pm Sun.

Record Revolution

Established in 1967, "Record Rev" is one of the oldest independent record stores in the country. This Coventry Road institution boasts a basement filled with new and used vinyl and

COMICS IN CLEVELAND

From Mr. Natural to Superman, Cleveland has had a hand in creating some of the most lasting comic characters. More recently, Cleveland has served as ground zero for the latest comics-themed Hollywood blockbusters, with both *The Avengers* and *Captain America: The Winter Soldier* being filmed in the 216. And judging by the comic book and novelty shops in town, people around here prefer to never grow up.

Jerry Siegel and **Joe Shuster** were just kids when they met at Glenville High in Cleveland. But these whiz kids soon found themselves writing and illustrating comics, including those of the popular Doctor Occult, for big-time mags like *New Fun*. Despite a few earlier failed attempts, Siegel and Shuster finally sold a story they had been working on for years about a mild-mannered reporter with superhuman abilities. In 1938, Superman debuted on the cover of Issue #1 of *Action Comics*. The Man of Steel soon found his way into newspapers, radio programs, television shows, motion pictures, and, if you can believe it, a Broadway musical. Fans can pay homage at the "birthplace of Superman," the childhood home of Siegel, where the 18-year-old first dreamed up the Man of Steel. The home (10622 Kimberly Ave.) in Cleveland's Glenville neighborhood is a private residence—you'll spot the red "S" logo on the fence—but the owners occasionally invite guests inside.

In the 1960s, Coventry Road in Cleveland Heights was a counterculturist's dream. The bohemian strip with a tie-dye vibe was home to **Harvey Pekar.** With the neighborhood as his backdrop, he began writing his curmudgeonly autobiographical comic *American Splendor*. The long-running strip was adapted into a successful film of the same name starring Paul Giamatti.

One of Pekar's earliest illustrators was **R. Crumb,** a friend who would go on to create such infamous characters as Fritz the Cat and Mr. Natural. Crumb's sexually and politically charged comics made him the darling of the antiestablishment crowd. And who can forget the lovable *Calvin and Hobbes,* penned by the famously shy native Bill Watterson.

To browse thousands of new and used comic books, locals hit **Carol & John's Comic Book Shop.** This mom-and-son operation has been chugging along since 1990 thanks to superhuman customer service and personal attention.

CDs. The underground setting suits the shop to a T considering the place was ground zero for the cultural revolutions that erupted some five decades ago. Vestiges of that counterculture remain today, largely in the form of smoking paraphernalia, incense, and hippie clothing. Young alternative types visit the main-floor boutique to stock their wardrobes with funky vintage clothing, jewelry, and accessories. Rounding out the inventory are obscure rock videos, posters, and DVDs.
MAP 5: 1832 Coventry Rd., 216/321-7661; 11am-9pm Mon.-Sat., noon-7pm Sun.

GIFT AND HOME
City Buddha

Follow the Buddha's teachings and you may buy nothing here but a carved wooden Buddha. But where's the fun in that? Like a street bazaar airlifted from Indonesia, this fragrant shop deals in imported exotica, mostly from Southeast Asia. Jammed with handmade furniture, hand-carved figurines, hand-painted pottery, and hypnotically beautiful textiles, City Buddha makes home design easy, cheap, and fun. What began as an open-air stand over a decade ago is now a bustling Coventry Road shop frequented by hippies, yuppies, and well-heeled travelers. As the Buddha might say, "Fill your mind with compassion, but fill your home with really cool stuff."
MAP 5: 1807 Coventry Rd., 216/397-5862, www.citybuddha.com; noon-8pm Mon.-Thurs., noon-9pm Fri., 11am-9pm Sat., noon-6pm Sun.

City Buddha

In the 216

When you've decided to take a little taste of Cleveland home for you or a friend, pop into this festive gift shop, named for the Cleveland area code. The owners do a remarkable job of sourcing Cleveland-themed art and memorabilia from a vast array of artists and producers. In one fell swoop a shopper can land a Cavs tank top, a script Cleveland ball cap, a skyline-emblazoned beer glass, and a jar of Bertman Original Ballpark Mustard. **MAP 5:** 1854 Coventry Rd., 216/862-4830, www.inthe216.com; 11am-8pm Mon.-Thurs., 11am-9pm Fri.-Sat., 10am-6pm Sun.

ARTS AND CRAFTS
Fine Points

Knitters and crocheters make journeys short and long to come to this distinctive shop. Inside this charming Victorian house on artsy Larchmere Boulevard is a kaleidoscope of today's hottest fibers, yarns, and textiles. Shoppers can purchase yarn to go, commission a one-of-a-kind garment, or snag one of the owner's handcrafted knit fashions. The boutique also stocks a full panoply of knitting supplies, including books, patterns, needles, and accessories. Newbies can sign up for an informal class to learn the ropes, so to speak. **MAP 5:** 12620 Larchmere Blvd., 216/229-6644, www.finepoints.com; 11am-6pm Tues.-Sat., noon-5pm Sun.

Larchmere Fire Works

If you've ever had the urge to dabble in the centuries-old crafts of blacksmithing, glassblowing, or glass fusing, give Larchmere Fire Works a call. This East Side studio offers both demos and hands-on classes in all of the above, with the assurance that every client regardless of talent will leave with at least one useable item. If shopping is more your speed, the studio doubles as a gallery for local artwork, such as jewelry, ceramics, glass, and more.

LOOK INTO LARCHMERE

A block north of Shaker Square sits Larchmere Boulevard, the spine and heart of an eclectic and eminently walkable community. This vibrant district has developed organically over the decades thanks to an easy mix of residential, indie-driven retail and access to Cleveland's light rail system.

While the district earned a reputation as an arts and antiques destination, with numerous high-end collectors and resellers, recent years have ushered in a broader mix of offerings. There are still amazing places to hunt for those midcentury modern lounge chairs, but now they are joined by shops like **Methany Weir** (13001 Larchmere Blvd., 216/707-0301, www.methenyweir.com), which carries unique hand-painted furniture and collectibles in addition to offering paint-finishing workshops to DIYers. **Two Crows for Joy** (13005 Larchmere Blvd., 216/920-7570, www.twocrowsforjoy.com) stocks organic, American-made children's clothing and gifts, while its neighbor **Eclectic Eccentric** (13005 Larchmere Blvd., 216/798-3002) carries a funky mix of modern and vintage home accessories and resale vintage clothing. A bibliophile could easily lose track of time at **Loganberry Books,** one of the city's largest indie bookstores.

If it's antiques ye seek, **Marc Goodman's Antique Mall** (12721 Larchmere Blvd., 216/229-8919) combines multiple vendors in one spot; **Bingham's Antiques** (12801 Larchmere Blvd., 216/721-1711) flies through vintage furniture, decorative arts, and even bikes; and **Wolfs Gallery** is a spacious multi-gallery building showcasing a wide selection of fine art.

The annual **Larchmere PorchFest** attracts thousands to the neighborhood thanks to its fun formula of 30 bands on 30 porches.

MAP 5: 12406 Larchmere Blvd., 216/246-4716, www.larchmerefireworks. com; noon-6pm Tues.-Thurs., noon-5pm Fri.-Sat.

Passport to Peru

Coventry was hippie central in the 1960s, and this store is a lasting legacy of those heady times. Incense fills the air and permeates all manner of imported merchandise, from downy alpaca sweaters and hats to trippy-dippy tie-dyes. Long the go-to source for Birkenstocks and Naot sandals, Passport is also a gift-hunter's best friend. Fine cultural jewelry, embroidered handbags, wooden wind chimes, and natural skin drums are just a sliver of the hippie-chic swag on tap. Grab an incense burner and satchel of sticks for the road. It'll keep fresh the memory of Coventry's rich past.

MAP 5: 1806 Coventry Rd., 216/932-9783; 11am-8pm Mon.-Sat., noon-5pm Sun.

SPECIALTY FOODS
Mitchell's Fine Chocolates

This confectionary, which opened in 1939, was on the brink of closing when a lifelong fan stepped up and saved the day—and the shop. Given the increased demand for artisanal, hand-crafted, local food products, the timing seemed right. Customers can still walk in and purchase an assortment of dark chocolate-covered apricots and orange peels, soft-centered chocolate nougats, silken butter creams, and various truffles, but Mitchell's also offers new creations like burnt-sugar marshmallows coated in milk chocolate and topped with crunchy caramelized sugar.

MAP 5: 2285 Lee Rd., 216/932-3200, www.mitchellschocolates.com; 10am-7pm Mon.-Thurs., 10am-9pm Fri.-Sat.

HEALTH AND BEAUTY
Quintana's Barber and Dream Spa

Owner Alex Quintana takes the art and practice of barbering seriously.

His domain is a charming renovated colonial in Cleveland Heights, divided downstairs and up by his barbershop and the sparkling Quintana's Speakeasy. Next door is the day spa, run by his wife and partner Dawn. Together, they keep neighbors looking and feeling great thanks to a long roster of professional services. Guys looking for a great cut or close shave would do well to book a chair here. Ladies and gents can book manis, pedis, massages, facials, and waxes. Look for the spinning barber pole, then head inside for a cup of hot coffee, a stack of great mags, and a pleasant environment.

MAP 5: 2200 S. Taylor Rd., 216/321-7889, www.qbds.net; noon-8pm Mon., 8am-8pm Tues.-Thurs., 8am-6pm Fri., 8am-4pm Sat., 10am-3pm Sun.

Lakewood

Map 6

CLOTHING AND ACCESSORIES

GV Art + Design

The owner of this bustling design and apparel shop is a Cleveland Institute of Art grad, and that shows in the creativity and quality of the inventory. The bulk of the biz comes from sports-themed clothing and gear rooted in steadfast support of the Browns, Cavs, and Indians. But this is more than just a team shop thanks to a colorful display of artwork and design pieces fueled by civic pride.

MAP 6: 17128 Detroit Ave., 216/273-7188, www.gvartwork.com; 11am-6pm Mon.-Wed. and Fri.-Sat., 11am-8pm Thurs.

Paisley Monkey

This homegrown Lakewood children's boutique started as an online business before graduating to a small retail shop and then graduating once again to a larger shop. They've done so by offering unique products from more than 120 manufacturers. There are literally are thousands of fun and colorful gift items, like toys, books, clothing, music, baby gear, and cloth diapers. The owners go out of their way to stock high-quality products that are sustainably made and often made in the United States.

MAP 6: 14417 Detroit Ave., 216/221-1091, www.paisleymonkey.com; 11am-8pm Tues.-Fri., 10am-5pm Sat.

VINTAGE AND ANTIQUES

✪ Cleveland Curiosities

Believe it or not, oddities are big business. Those peculiar, exotic, and macabre artifacts even spawned a hit television show of the same name. With Cleveland Curiosities, this city scored a destination-worthy antiques and oddities shop filled with museum-quality pieces that run the gamut of the genre. Ominous antique medical equipment, taxidermied animals, mounted and framed fauna, animal skeletons, the odd assortment of teeth, and postmortem photography are displayed for your viewing pleasure. Definitely not for the squeamish.

MAP 6: 13375 Madison Ave., 440/334-0455, www.clevelandcuriosities. com; 11am-8pm Wed.-Sat., 11am-6pm Sun.

Play It Again, Sam

Few shops have been as well positioned to take advantage of the rise

Cleveland Curiosities

in demand for old-school vinyl than Play It Again, Sam. This West Side institution doesn't sell records, but rather a bewildering selection of vintage two-channel stereo equipment. Audiophiles come here for both new and used tuners, preamps, receivers, turntables, cassette recorders, CD players—even reel-to-reel tape recorders. If you have a vinyl collection in need of a little TLC, bring it here for a trip through Sam's deep-cleaning machine. Those old platters will come out looking and sounding as good as new.

MAP 6: 14311 Madison Ave., 216/228-7330, www.playitagainsam.com; 10am-6pm Mon.-Tues. and Thurs.-Sat.

BOOKS AND MUSIC
The Bookshop in Lakewood

Indie-minded Lakewood residents eschew the big box bookstore in favor of this cozy shop. While not massive, it is well organized, with thousands of titles spanning genres like history, philosophy, cooking, art, political science, law, and religion. There are sections devoted to local authors and local interest. Root through the clearance bin

and you might walk away with a well-thumbed copy of Pynchon's *Gravity's Rainbow* that you'll never finish. On your way in or out, say hello to Hobbes, the store cat.

MAP 6: 15014 Madison Ave., 216/221-5222; noon-8pm Tues.-Sat.

✪ Carol & John's Comic Book Shop

This mom-and-son operation has been in business since 1990 thanks to its super-friendly, customer-oriented approach to sales. The owners pledge to read everything they stock so as to provide an honest, informed opinion when asked to do so. Anybody interested in new and used comics will have a field day at this tidy, well-organized shop, with weekly deliveries of both big-name and small-run publications. While at its heart a hard-core comic depot, Carol & John's also stocks a nice selection of graphic novels, action figures, posters, and apparel.

MAP 6: 17462 Lorain Ave., 216/252-0606, www.cnjcomics.com; noon-8pm Mon.-Fri., 10am-7pm Sat., noon-5pm Sun.

The Exchange

For more than four decades, this homegrown chain of resale shops has been supplying music and video game lovers with a steady supply of used vinyl, CDs, video game systems, and titles. Those used games, by the way, come with a money-back guarantee if they prove defective in any way. While you might have to dig deeply, there are plenty of great scores and bargains to be had. Over the years, this particular shop seems to have greatly improved its inventory, layout, and customer service.

MAP 6: 15100 Detroit Ave., 216/521-0045, www.theexchange.com; 10am-9pm Mon.-Sat., noon-6pm Sun.

My Mind's Eye Records

Vinyl junkies rejoice at the sight of this jam-packed Lakewood shop. Two rooms house an ever-changing catalog of new and used LPs, CDs, and DVDs. Hard-core music fans know to stop by regularly for the best chance to snag a rare gem, especially in the early-heavy metal and garage-rock genres. Dusty collections from the recently departed seem to arrive daily. If you didn't know better, you might assume store owner Charles Abou-Chebl had a hand in the process. But no, he merely dispenses an encyclopedic knowledge of music trivia while possessing an almost stereotypical indie-record-store persona. Heck, it's a joy to shoot the breeze with the dude, whether shopping or not.

MAP 6: 16010 Detroit Ave., 216/521-6660, www.mymindseyerecords.com; noon-9pm Mon.-Sat., noon-7pm Sun.

GIFT AND HOME
Plantation Home

There's a reason why home (and apartment, and condo, and mansion) owners go out of their way to visit this trendy home furnishings studio in Lakewood. The owner is an interior designer with more than three decades in the business of making the world more beautiful, comfortable, and functional. This stunning showroom is updated often with new furnishings, gifts, and entertaining accessories.

MAP 6: 14401 Detroit Ave., 216/227-4663, www.plantationhomelakewood.com; 10am-5pm Tues.-Wed. and Fri.-Sat., 10am-7pm Thurs.

OUTDOOR AND SPORTING GOODS
Beat Cycles

As the bike community in Cleveland continues to grow, more shops like the excellent Beat Cycles take root. In the bike-friendly community of Lakewood, a former Army and Navy recruiting office is now filled with inventory from Cannondale, Brooklyn Bicycle, Rocky Mountain, Norco, and others. Of course, there's plenty of sweet gear and accessories, plus a service-minded crew that can and will fix just about anything.

MAP 6: 15608 Detroit Ave., 440/799-8788, www.beatcycles.com; 10am-7pm Tues.-Fri., 9am-5pm Sat., 10am-4pm Sun.

Westside Skates

Since opening the doors in 1995, this Lakewood skateboard shop has continued to make a name for itself locally, regionally, and beyond thanks to its matchless selection, prices, and customer service. Owned and operated by passionate skateboarders, this colorful shop is the place to go for information, advice, and gear. Every wall is plastered with a bewildering amount of decks, trucks, wheels, streetwear, and shoes. All styles of deck are covered, including short boards, cruisers, old-school, and longboard. In the rear of the roomy shop is a half-pipe.

MAP 6: 14047 Madison Ave., 216/226-2470, www.westsideskates.net; noon-8pm Mon.-Fri., 11am-8pm Sat., noon-6pm Sun.

CIGARS
Robusto & Briar

The old-world luxury that is a fine cigar is on full display at this handsome Lakewood smoke shop. Gorgeous old cabinets, rescued from an old cigar and candy store, are topped with jars of pipe tobacco blends from Dunhill, Ashton, Drew Estate, and others. A walk-in humidor is a little slice of heaven thanks to 400 types of cigars held in optimal conditions. All the best from

UP-AND-COMING NEIGHBORHOOD: COLLINWOOD

The artsy, easy-going **Collinwood** neighborhood, nine miles east of downtown Cleveland, is emerging as one of Cleveland's latest comeback stories. On the shores of Lake Erie, this is one of the few communities with affordable access to one of the region's best assets. Accessible housing, a grassroots arts movement, and an increasing number of restaurant and retail options are combining to turn Collinwood into one the city's hottest neighborhoods.

Guided by one of the city's most fervent arts organizations, Waterloo Arts, this close-knit community has taken bold steps to attract artists, who increasingly are being priced out of bigger (and prohibitively expensive) markets. Grant programs help artists buy or rehab homes in the area, build out their dream gallery or studio, support their work, and promote the efforts in a national marketing campaign.

The primary gallery in the area is **Waterloo Arts Gallery** (15605 Waterloo Rd., 216/692-9500, www.artscollinwood.org), run by the local arts organization. Others in the area include **Waterloo 7 Studio** (15315 Waterloo Rd., 239/293-9548, www.schmidtsculpture.com), **ArtiCle Gallery** (15316 Waterloo Rd., 440/655-6954), **Waterloo Studios** (15316 Waterloo Rd., 216/383-8002), **Miller Schneider Gallery** (16008 Waterloo Rd., 440/715-0603), **Brick Ceramic + Design Studio** (420 E. 161st St., www.brickceramics.com), and **Praxis Fiber Workshop** (15301 Waterloo Rd., 216/644-8661, www.praxisfiberworkshop.com).

On the first Friday of every month, **Walk All Over Waterloo** invites people to explore the area's art galleries, restaurants, and shops, which keep their doors open a little later. Each year in June, the **Waterloo Arts Fest** (www.waterlooarts.org) attracts approximately 5,000 attendees, who come for art and stay for the live music, food, and fun. More than 60 art vendors share the half-mile strip with 10 live music stages, dozens of arts activists and organizations, and plenty of surprises.

One of the country's top live-music venues, the **Beachland Ballroom,** has been hosting the best touring talent in an old Croatian social hall in this neighborhood since 2000. Show or no show, **This Way Out** (15711 Waterloo Rd., 216/458-1156), below the ballroom, is a quirky place to shop for vintage clothing, used vinyl, and other old oddities. **Blue Arrow Records** (16001 Waterloo Rd., 216/486-2415, www.bluearrowrecords.com) offers an extensive collection of LPs and 45s from the 1950s to today. **Star Pop** (15813 Waterloo Rd., 216/965-2368, www.starpopcleveland.com) buys and sells old toys, vintage clothing, classic video games, used vinyl, and other pop culture collectibles.

Following years of construction grief, a sleek new streetscape has emerged, improving flow and parking, while introducing splashy new murals, public art, and seating.

Avo, Macanudo, Padron, Arturo Fuente, C.L.E., Montecristo, Romeo y Julieta, and so many more are here. Lounges equipped with high-efficiency ventilation systems provide a cozy nest in which to linger with that fresh stogie. This tidy shop also has smokers covered with respect to gear and accessories.
MAP 6: 1388 Riverside Dr., 216/767-5338, www.robustobriar.com; 10am-10pm Tues.-Sat., 11am-6pm Sun.

SPECIALTY FOODS

B. A. Sweetie Candy Company

With some 300,000 pounds of candy on stock at all times, it's safe to assume that this confection warehouse can satisfy any sweet tooth. Around since the 1950s, Sweetie has grown into a major player in the candy wholesale business, buying and selling ridiculous amounts of the stuff. Luckily for sugar lovers, they also run a retail shop, well stocked with the same dizzying array of treats, including a pretty awesome Pez display. With rows and rows of bulk, retro, and hard-to-find gems like Moon Pies and Mary Janes, this place is like the Sam's Club of sourballs.

MAP 7: 7480 Brookpark Rd., Cleveland, 216/739-2244, www.sweetiescandy.com; 10am-8pm Mon.-Sat., 11am-5pm Sun.

Bialy's Bagels

If you're the sort of foodie who seeks out the very best of certain delicacies wherever you land, and bagels happen to be one of those foods, make the pilgrimage to this institution. In 1966, a New York transplant opened this iconic East Side bagel store in University Heights, a neighborhood chosen for its proximity to Jewish customers. The shop is now under the ownership of twin sisters Rachel and Sarah Gross, who grew up down the street. The New York-style water bagels are every bit as fresh, malty, and delicious as ever, with approximately 20 different varieties, including the classic and quickly vanishing onion-topped bialy. But the best seller by a wide margin is the mish-mosh, the orthodox name for what is often labeled an "everything" bagel.

MAP 7: 2267 Warrensville Center Rd., University Heights, 216/371-1088, www.bialysbagels.com; 5:30am-3pm daily

Bialy's Bagels

Gallucci's Italian Foods

When Gust Gallucci came to Cleveland in the early 1900s, he joined an already large and growing Italian population who longed for authentic products from the Old World. So, in 1912, he opened the first imported foods store, which later moved to this location. Still family owned and operated, this jam-packed store boasts a meat and cheese counter, a pastry counter, a prepared foods section, and shelves and shelves of imported ingredients, wines, and packaged items. This is where people come for sliced prosciutto, real Parmigiano-Reggiano cheese, pizza dough, tomato sauce, pasta, and cannoli shells. During lunch, nearby workers stream in for hearty, homemade meatball sandwiches, lasagna, and deep-dish pizza by the slice.

MAP 7: 6610 Euclid Ave., Cleveland, 216/881-0045, www.tasteitaly.com; 8am-6pm Mon.-Fri., 8am-5pm Sat.

SHOPPING CENTERS AND MALLS

Beachwood Place

It may be a mall, and it may be loaded with mostly chain stores, but Beachwood Place still ranks as one of the premier shopping destinations in the region. Where else will shoppers find under one glorious roof H&M, Kate Spade, Lucky Brand, and BCBG? Origins and Sephora are here, as are L'Occitane and Lush Cosmetics. Gap, Pottery Barn, and Banana Republic are anchored by Saks Fifth Avenue, Nordstrom, and Dillard's. Far from just another depressing indoor mall, Beachwood Place is bright, airy, and somewhat cheerful.

MAP 7: 26300 Cedar Rd., Beachwood, 216/464-9460, www.beachwoodplace.com; 10am-9pm Mon.-Sat., noon-6pm Sun.

Crocker Park

This development 15 miles west of downtown seems to grow by the day. Encompassing wide swaths of the planet, Crocker Park is much more than just a shrine to capitalism; it is becoming a bona fide village. People actually elect to live at this lifestyle center, snatching up apartments and condos so as to be close to shops like Urban Outfitters, Orvis, MAC, Lush, Lululemon, Evereve, and the Apple Store. There are tons of dining options, from the fast-casual Liquid Planet, Five Guys, and Aladdin's Eatery to full-service spots like Hyde Park Steakhouse and Yard House. On warm days, the cafés along Main and Market streets throw open their doors and offer alfresco seating on the generously proportioned sidewalks.

MAP 7: 177 Market St., Westlake, 440/871-6880, www.crockerpark.com; hours vary by store

Eton Chagrin Boulevard

Rarely does a mall get a second chance. But when developers added on to this fading mall, essentially giving it more of a street-side feel, they infused it with fresh life. Today, the mall has grown into an attractive indoor/outdoor multiplex boasting numerous independent clothing shops, most not found elsewhere. This is where you'll find Kilgore Trout, Audrey's Sweet Threads, and Amy's Shoes. Restaurants like Fleming's, Michael Symon's B Spot, and the homegrown *nuevo* Latino spot Paladar make this a destination for foodies. This center is also home to an Apple Store, Anthropologie, The North Face, Tiffany & Co., and Sur La Table.

MAP 7: 28601 Chagrin Blvd., Woodmere, 216/591-0544, www.etonchagrinblvd.com; hours vary by store

Legacy Village

Euphemistically billed as a "lifestyle center," Legacy Village is essentially an outdoor mall. But built at a cost of $150 million, at least it is an attractive outdoor mall. Constructed to resemble a faux "town square" setting, complete with centrally located village green, the 80-acre complex boasts retail attractions like Crate & Barrel, L.L. Bean, Nordstrom Rack, and the excellent furniture, art, and home decor store Z Gallerie. Popular chain restaurants like The Cheesecake Factory, The Capital Grille, and California Pizza Kitchen are joined by a few locals like Wild Mango and Black Box Fix.

MAP 7: 25001 Cedar Rd., Lyndhurst, 216/382-3871, www.legacy-village.com; 10am-8pm Mon.-Thurs., 10am-8pm Fri.-Sat., noon-6pm Sun.

CHAGRIN FALLS: WORTH THE TRIP

It might take a good 35 minutes to reach Chagrin Falls from downtown Cleveland, but the destination makes the journey worthwhile. Reminiscent of a quaint New England town, this charming burg boasts a village square (triangle, actually), bustling Main Street, and the namesake waterfall, which runs right under the main road. Make the trip in mid-October and you might mistake it for a fall foliage trip to Vermont.

Wear comfortable shoes and you can easily hit all the popular spots on foot. Park your car near the centrally located square and you'll be able to drop off shopping bags as they accumulate. A wise place to start is the **Chagrin Falls Village Visitor Center** (83 N. Main St., 440/247-0900, 11am-3pm Wed.-Sun. Apr.-Oct.).

Every small town needs an independent bookstore, and in Chagrin Falls it's **Fireside Book Shop** (29 N. Franklin St., 440/247-4050, www.firesidebookshop.com). Since 1963, this cozy bookshop has kept locals well informed thanks to its new and used titles. Fireside also carries an uncharacteristically large selection of children's toys, puzzles, and games. Music buffs make the short trek to **Warren Henry Music** (49 W. Orange St., 440/247-0300, www.warrenhenrymusic.com) for high-quality musical instruments (especially guitars), sheet music, books, and accessories.

Chagrin Falls residents take pride in their lovely Western Reserve-style homes, and they have no shortage of shops to keep them well furnished. **Chestnut Hill Home** (27 N. Franklin St., 440/247-6858, www.chestnuthillhomechagrin.com) deals in high-style home furnishings, lighting, decor, and tableware. **White Magnolia** (46 N. Main St., 440/247-5800) is an airy shop loaded with trend-conscious treasures such as antique crystal chandeliers, Parisian textiles, and architectural-salvage items. For those with more traditional tastes, **Chagrin Antiques** (516 E. Washington St., 440/247-1080) stocks high-end collectibles like 19th-century English furniture, rare jewelry, and porcelain. **Chagrin Hardware** (82 N. Main St., 440/247-7514) is a living relic that has been dispensing home, kitchen, and garden supplies and expert advice to the close-knit community since 1857.

Clothes-obsessed ladies can lose track of entire afternoons in Chagrin Falls. **Juicy Lucy** (31 W. Orange St., 440/247-5748, www.juicylucyaclothingstore.com) attracts women from all over the region thanks to its high-end collection of New York and European fashions and jewelry. **Blush Boutique** (7 N. Franklin St., 440/394-8600) is an award-winning clothing boutique, while the more sophisticated gal hits **Find Me!** (24 N. Main St., 440/247-3131, www.findmechagrinfalls.com) to shop for clothing, shoes, and accessories in an elegant antique setting. Men are well taken care of at **Cuffs** (18 E. Orange St., 440/247-2828, www.cuffsclothing.com), an old-fashioned gentlemen's outfitter housed in a brick 19th-century home. When Cuffs customers tire of shopping for timeless Italian, French, and American designs, they can enjoy a glass of wine at the in-store wine bar. If you prefer to purchase an entire bottle, stop by **Chuck's Fine Wines** (23 Bell St., 440/247-7534, www.chucksfinewines.com) for matchless selection and service. **Chagrin River Outfitters** (100 N. Main St., 440/247-7110, www.chagrinriveroutfitters.com) is the region's premier fly-fishing outfitter and guide service.

You can't travel to Chagrin Falls and not stop for an ice cream cone at **Jeni's Splendid Ice Creams** (67 North Main St., 440/247-2064, www.jenis.com) or bag of popcorn at the old-timey **Popcorn Shop** (53 Main St., 440/247-6577, www.chagrinfallspopcorn.com), both perched above the rushing falls. For a great burger and a beer hit up **Flip Side** (44 N. Main St., 440/600-7274, www.flipsideburger.com); for a light lunch to go from a sunny café pop into **Lemon Falls** (95 N. Main St., 440/247-8000, www.lemonfalls.com); and for a full meal, make reservations at **Umami Asian Kitchen** (42 N. Main St., 440/247-8600, www.umamichagrinfalls.com) for seafood-heavy Pacific Rim cuisine.

To turn your day trip into an overnight stay, book a room with a fireplace at the charming **Inn of Chagrin Falls** (87 West St., 440/247-1200, www.innofchagrinfalls.com).

WHERE TO STAY

Since 2012, Cleveland has added more than 1,200 hotel rooms in the downtown core alone, a 25 percent jump that reflects the real and steady increase in business and pleasure visitors to the region. Chief among them is the gleaming glass-and-steel Hilton Cleveland Downtown, which rises 32 stories above the Lake Erie shoreline. That 600-room tower joins one of the state's hippest and most attractive new accommodations, the Kimpton Schofield Hotel, in the heart of downtown. Not to be left out, the new Drury Plaza Hotel is a clever adaptive reuse project that has travelers sleeping in a former Board of Education building from the early 20th century.

As for the icing on the cake, The Ritz-Carlton Cleveland has wrapped up an 18-month-long, multimillion-dollar, top-to-bottom renovation of its downtown asset; the Westin Cleveland Downtown underwent a $74 million renovation; and the former Wyndham Cleveland at Playhouse Square undertook a $6 million transformation and emerged as a Crowne Plaza.

Hilton Cleveland Downtown

Apart from those downtown, new hotels have popped up in and around University Circle, near Hopkins International Airport, and close to popular suburban shopping destinations in Beachwood and Westlake, ensuring that there are enough brand-name hotels, independent inns, charming bed-and-breakfasts, and budget-minded hostels so every budget, style preference, and location requirement can be met with relative ease.

HIGHLIGHTS

✪ **BEST HOTEL BAR WITH A VIEW:** Step onto the terrace of Bar 32 in the new **Hilton Cleveland Downtown** and you'll be perched 32 floors above Lake Erie. Enjoy cocktails with views of the Rock Hall, FirstEnergy Stadium, and the setting sun over the lake (page 178).

✪ **SCHMANCIEST LOBBY:** Carved of marble pulled from the same quarry as Michelangelo's *David*, the central fountain in the lobby of the **Renaissance Cleveland Hotel** is truly a work of art. The rest of this grand entrance hall is nothing to sneeze at either (page 178).

✪ **BEST HOTEL MAKEOVER: The Ritz-Carlton** on Public Square just underwent a massive transformation that touched every aspect of the hotel, restoring its standing as one of the city's top lodging spots (page 178).

✪ **FINEST REUSE OF A REALLY OLD MALL:** The Arcade is likely the most magical interior space in Cleveland, and now you can sleep there. One hundred years after it was built, the attractive Victorian atrium was converted into the sharp-dressed **Hyatt Regency Cleveland at the Arcade.** At least now those gargoyles have something to guard come nightfall (page 180).

✪ **MOST MODERN HOSTEL:** Banish notions of dank hostels with rentable sheets. The **Cleveland Hostel** is a contemporary if spare 60-bed inn in the middle of bustling Ohio City. Bike storage, a communal kitchen, in-house café, and rooftop patio make this the perfect urban perch (page 182).

✪ **BEST JAZZ CLUB TURNED HOTEL:** One would be hard pressed to find a more interesting backstory than that of **The Tudor Arms Hotel Cleveland.** Built in 1933, the 12-story Gothic Revival building originally was the fashionable Cleveland Club. Later, it was the Tudor Arms, a popular jazz club (page 183).

✪ **BEST BED FOR BICYCLISTS:** The **Inn at Brandywine Falls** is tucked into Cuyahoga Valley National Park, literally steps from its namesake falls. Better yet, the lengthy and scenic Ohio & Erie Canal Towpath Trail is only a mile and a half from the front door (page 187).

PRICE KEY

$	Less than $150 per night
$ $	$150-300 per night
$ $ $	More than $300 per night

CHOOSING A HOTEL

For most business and pleasure visits, a downtown address is the most practical option. And downtown is manageable enough in size that lodging decisions need not be based solely on proximity to a sight, event, or organization. Options range from very basic budget inns on the fringes of town to ritzy four-star gems right on Public Square. How you ultimately decide will likely be a combination of availability, location, budget, and occasion. Two buddies cycling across the United States might not require the same level of comfort and service as, say, that honeymooning couple from Albuquerque. When staying downtown and traveling by car, it almost always makes financial sense to find overnight parking outside the hotel.

Despite the fact that 2.5 million people visit University Circle each year, it used to be a chore to track down a decent room there. That's no longer the case thanks to a trio of new hotels, which join the two large InterContinental hotels near the Cleveland Clinic campus and a few smaller inns. RTA's speedy HealthLine Rapid Transit buses connect downtown and University Circle like never before.

Due to its bounty of charming century homes, Ohio City has developed a happy little cluster of bed-and-breakfasts. A handful of well-run inns can be found within blocks of one another, and each offers the sort of personality and personal attention that fans of the genre seek. A contemporary hostel (not a youth hostel) in the heart of Ohio City has become an instant hit with budget-minded travelers or just those who appreciate "experiencing" rather than just visiting a new city.

There are options for those who prefer to stay close to the airport, Cleveland Metroparks, Cuyahoga Valley National Park, or Chagrin Falls.

ALTERNATIVE LODGING OPTIONS

As the number of travelers to Cleveland rises, so too does the number of folks eager and willing to rent those visitors a shared room, private room, or entire house on virtual marketplaces like Airbnb, VRBO, and others. A recent search turned up hundreds of options that range from a $50-a-night room on up to a contemporary penthouse in the heart of downtown. Not only do many of these accommodations cost less than an average night's stay at a traditional hotel, they place travelers smack dab in the middle of neighborhoods that lack a supply of conventional options, like Ohio City, Tremont, and Detroit Shoreway.

If you love hitting the open road in an RV, or prefer to pitch a tent in a quiet woodland setting, you're not going to find Cleveland super amenable, as most RV parks and campsites are miles from town.

Despite reliable and speedy public transportation between Hopkins International Airport and downtown, most travelers tend to utilize the hotels near the airport for those occasions when they have a particularly early flight, late landing, or business in the immediate area.

✪ Hilton Cleveland Downtown $$$

Built in 2016 to accommodate the crowds from the nearby Huntington Convention Center, the 600-room Hilton Cleveland Downtown is a jewel in the Cleveland skyline. The shimmering glass-and-steel tower rises 32 stories above Lake Erie, and the glassy shell floods the modern hotel with light. Multiple bars, restaurants, and gathering places make this building a draw to more than just overnight guests, while the aptly named Bar 32, perched inside and out on the 32nd floor, is one of the most dramatic places in the city to enjoy a cocktail.

MAP 1: 100 Lakeside Ave. E., 216/413-5000, www.clevelanddowntown.hilton.com

Kimpton Schofield Hotel $$$

Following a $50 million renovation of a gorgeous circa-1900 building that unearthed a stunning terra cotta facade, Ohio's first Kimpton hotel debuted in the heart of downtown in 2016. The boutique brand is beloved for its high-end design, crisp, comfortable guest rooms, and quirky amenities like loaner bikes and in-room accessories for pets. The hotel restaurant, Parker's Downtown, is helmed by a Culinary Institute of America-trained chef.

MAP 1: 2000 E. 9th St., 216/357-3250, www.theschofieldhotel.com

✪ Renaissance Cleveland Hotel $$$

Originally opened in 1918 as the Cleveland Hotel, this beaux arts gem exudes opulence, grace, and beauty. More reminiscent of a museum than a hotel lobby, its entrance hall features a soaring barrel-vaulted ceiling, massive marble fountains, and high arched windows that perfectly frame the city outside. The upmarket address right on Public Square comes with a price, of course, but the setting, service, and surroundings more than make up for it. After a long day touring the city, settle into the classy Lobby Court Bar for a classic cocktail. This 500-room property also offers a wonderful French bistro, an indoor pool, and a well-stocked fitness center. With the RTA just steps away, transportation to and from the airport, University Circle, and Shaker Square could not be simpler.

MAP 1: 24 Public Sq., 216/696-5600, www.marriott.com

✪ The Ritz-Carlton $$$

Cleveland's Ritz-Carlton was in desperate need of an update, and boy did it ever get one. In 2017, following a multimillion-dollar renovation, Cleveland's ritziest hotel now lives up to its pedigree. Gone are the dowdy fixtures and furnishings, replaced by a crisp, casual sophistication that matches the times. A major reworking of the reception floor now boasts an open-plan interior that merges reception with a multifaceted restaurant, Turn Bar + Kitchen. Guest rooms feature new marble bathrooms and smart TVs, and a new fitness center is equipped with Peloton.

MAP 1: 1515 W. 3rd St., 216/623-1300, www.ritzcarlton.com

The Ritz-Carlton

Aloft Cleveland Downtown $$

Aloft, a boutique brand from Starwood Hotels, opened this contemporary 150-room hotel in the summer of 2013. It is part of the Flats East Bank development, which overlooks the Cuyahoga River and includes hotel, office, and restaurant properties. The hotel is about a 15-minute walk from the Public Square and is directly accessible from Hopkins International Airport via RTA's light-rail service. Aloft hotels are consistently ranked among the best in terms of design, technology, and service. A second-floor bar and common space features a 24-hour pantry and patio boasting great downtown views. Free hotel-wide high-speed internet access (wired and wireless) and electronics charging stations in all rooms are ideal for tech-focused travelers.

MAP 1: 1111 W. 10th St., 216/400-6469, www.starwoodhotels.com

Crowne Plaza Cleveland at Playhouse Square $$

Formerly the Wyndham, this hotel, updated in 2017, boasts a stellar location in the heart of Playhouse Square, Cleveland's world-class theater district. Guest rooms offer a blend of comfort, connectivity, and flexibility, while a dozen new suites overlook the streetscape below. The lobby area has been completely redone, as has the property's signature restaurant and bar. The hotel's perch on Euclid Avenue makes trips to University Circle via the RTA HealthLine an absolute breeze.

MAP 1: 1260 Euclid Ave., 216/615-7500, www.crowneplaza.com

Drury Plaza Hotel $$

Since 1931, when it was designed and built by the architecture firm behind Severance Hall and other grand public structures, this building had been home to the Cleveland Board of Education. The building reopened its doors in 2016 as the Drury Plaza

Hotel. In addition to its prime location steps from Public Square and the Cleveland Convention Center, this architecturally compelling 190-room hotel combines historic original fixtures with modern amenities such as Wi-Fi, a fitness center, and a swimming pool.

MAP 1: 1380 E. 6th St., 216/357-3100, www.druryhotels.com

Hilton Garden Inn $$

If you're in town to catch a Cavs or Indians game, it's tough to book a room much closer to the action. In fact, you can see Progressive Field from many of Hilton Garden Inn's 240 guest rooms. Prices tend to fluctuate alongside the activity at the nearby stadiums and arenas, but tend to stay in the middle of the pack. To save some cash, check the website for packages built around sporting events, museum passes, and musical performances that include breakfast, parking, and admission. Like most modern hotels, this one offers complimentary high-speed internet and a microwave, refrigerator, and coffeemaker in every room. It has a casual restaurant, fitness center, and small pool on-site. Located adjacent to highway on-ramps, this hotel provides easy access into and out of the city.

MAP 1: 1100 Carnegie Ave., 216/658-6400, www.hiltongardeninn.com

✪ Hyatt Regency Cleveland at the Arcade $$

Hyatt spent approximately $60 million to retrofit the upper floors and adjoining towers of the stunning 1890 Arcade into a comfortable, modern hotel. Most rooms are generously proportioned and feature vaulted ceilings, original artwork, and stellar views of either the Arcade or the city. Guests enjoy wireless internet access, a fitness center, and easy access to the Arcade's shops, services, and restaurants. This hotel is conveniently located near Public Square and the East 4th Street entertainment district.

MAP 1: 420 Superior Ave., 216/575-1234, www.cleveland.hyatt.com

Westin Cleveland Downtown $$

In 2014, a dated Crowne Plaza hotel transformed into a swanky new Westin Cleveland, a 500-room gem in the heart of the city, following a $74 million renovation. Inside and out, the once-dated building has emerged anew, with a crisp new facade, state-of-the-art guest rooms and suites, a spacious fitness center, and more than 1,000 pieces of local contemporary artwork throughout. Urban Farmer, a farm-to-table steakhouse and bar, now commands attention at street level.

MAP 1: 777 St. Clair Ave. NE, 216/771-7700, www.westincleveland.com

Comfort Inn Downtown $

If you're searching for a basic hotel at a great rate, the Comfort Inn Downtown may be the best option. Situated just blocks from Public Square, this hotel is far cheaper than its location would have you believe. Granted, the bargain-basement rates tend to attract a more boisterous crowd, including those visiting for rock concerts and sporting events. Invest in a good pair of earplugs, however, and your stay may indeed be comfortable. Continental breakfast, wireless internet, and local phone calls are included in the rate.

MAP 1: 1800 Euclid Ave., 216/861-0001, www.choicehotels.com

Holiday Inn Express Hotel and Suites $

Perhaps the best union of location, price, and good looks, this Holiday Inn Express often pleasantly surprises first-time guests who are expecting a plain-vanilla property. In a retrofitted 19th-century bank, the hotel may be one of the most architecturally striking Holiday Inns around. From the gorgeous former bank lobby to the spacious, high-ceilinged rooms, nothing is standard-issue budget hotel. Guests can choose between single rooms or suites, but all have free high-speed internet, a mini fridge, and a coffeemaker, while some even boast hardwood floors and whirlpool tubs. Stays also include free hot breakfast, access to the fitness center, and use of a game room with pool tables and pinball machines. For killer views, request rooms on the upper floors of this 15-story building. The hotel is conveniently located six blocks from Public Square.

MAP 1: 629 Euclid Ave., 216/443-1000, www.ihg.com

Ohio City and Tremont   Map 2

Clifford House Bed and Breakfast $$

Innkeeper Jim Miner describes his house as eclectic—and that may be an understatement. Built in 1868, added onto in 1890, and renovated in the 1970s, the structure features architectural elements as varied as Tuscan, Queen Anne Victorian, Georgian colonial, and Louis XIV. Despite the mishmash, the result is a cozy home with space enough for privacy. Accommodations range from a single room that shares a bath to a self-contained mother-in-law suite ideal for longer stays and families. A private third-floor suite includes a queen bed, private bath, and fridge. Stays at the inn include a full hot breakfast and wireless internet. Miner, who lives on-site, has a dog and a cat, so those with relevant allergies should take note.

MAP 2: 1810 W. 28th St., 216/589-0121, www.cliffordhouse.com

J. Palen House $$

Ohio City's newest bed-and-breakfast, J. Palen House seems to try a little bit harder to please its guests. Once a 14-room flophouse, the main 1872 Victorian structure has been gently converted into a comfortable three-suite urban inn. Thankfully, architectural highlights like original parquet wood floors, pocket doors, and a two-story stained-glass window have withstood multiple remodels. While historical touches remain, including the quirky skeleton-style room keys, modern amenities like guest-controlled thermostats, wireless internet, and a fully outfitted business center make this inn a best-of-both-worlds proposition. In the morning, chat with houseguests over freshly squeezed orange juice, stuffed French toast, and Belgian waffles. Additional nearby properties have provided even more options for B&B-loving travelers. Free off-street parking is included.

MAP 2: 2708 Bridge Ave., 216/664-0813, www.jpalenhouse.com

Stone Gables Inn $$

Innkeepers Jeff and Connie Homes first fell in love with Stone Gables as guests. They took over ownership of the popular, long-running bed-and-breakfast in 2017. Originally built in 1883, the lovingly restored Queen Anne Victorian boasts 6,000 square feet of living space graced with 12-foot ceilings, handsome fireplaces, original wood work, and fine antiques. The property offers five rooms, each with king- or queen-size beds, private baths, and wireless internet. A full breakfast is included on weekends and holidays, while continental breakfasts are served on weekdays. Private on-site parking is available.

MAP 2: 3806 Franklin Blvd., 216/961-4654, www.stonegablesinn.com

✪ Cleveland Hostel $

In 2012, the same year that the West Side Market celebrated its 100th birthday, a brand-new hostel opened up down the block in a 100-year-old building. No neighborhood has evolved as swiftly and significantly as Ohio City has done in the past 10 years, and the opening of this contemporary hostel is proof of that. Owner Mark Raymond has created a haven for budget-minded travelers who want to immerse themselves in their surroundings. A common area with fridge and kitchen means that guests can shop at the market and prepare their own meal. A rooftop patio offers stunning views of the city skyline while an on-site café prepares world-class coffee. There are 60 beds in rooms that range from fully private with a bathroom to shared accommodations. Prices per night start as low as $30. On-site bike storage and proximity to RTA's light-rail make this a great home base from which to explore the city.

MAP 2: 2090 W. 25th St., 216/394-0616, www.theclevelandhostel.com

Cleveland Hostel

University Circle and Little Italy

Map 4

Courtyard by Marriott Cleveland University Circle $$

This Courtyard by Marriott, which opened in 2013, is situated in the heart of University Circle, making it convenient for travelers planning to hit the museums, explore Little Italy, visit local universities, or tend to those requiring care at University Hospitals or the Cleveland Clinic. This contemporary 155-room hotel features a crisp wood-trimmed lobby with computer-friendly stations, 24-hour convenience market, and quick-service bistro. It has an on-site pool and fitness center, business center, and an outdoor terrace with gas fire pit. Complimentary high-speed internet access is available throughout the property.

MAP 4: 2021 Cornell Rd., 216/791-5678, www.marriott.com

✪ The Tudor Arms Hotel Cleveland, A DoubleTree by Hilton $$

One would be hard pressed to find a more elegant, attractive hotel in Cleveland than the DoubleTree by Hilton, also referred to as the Tudor Arms Hotel. Built in 1933, the 12-story Gothic Revival building originally was the fashionable Cleveland Club. Later, it was the Tudor Arms, a popular jazz club. After years of neglect, the property was restored at a cost of $22 million and reopened as this hotel. It's about halfway between downtown and the East Side neighborhoods of Shaker and Cleveland Heights. Drop-dead beautiful ballrooms here attract countless weddings and celebrations. An on-site Mediterranean restaurant, plush rooms, and complimentary high-speed internet access make this a fine choice for long and short stays.

MAP 4: 10660 Carnegie Ave., 216/455-1260, www.doubletree3.hilton.com

Glidden House $$

For forays into the cultural playground that is University Circle, there may be no better jumping-off point than the Glidden House. Once you park your car at this 1910 French Gothic mansion, you can rely solely on foot power to get to the orchestra, museums, and institutions that dot the circle. Located on the campus of Case Western Reserve University, the inn also is convenient for appointments at the school. If there is a consistent complaint about the Glidden House, it is that some rooms do not live up to the grandeur of the building's exterior and common areas. In fact, some rooms have little more appeal than a standard chain experience. As at many off-brand hotels, rooms, suites, and experiences can vary widely. A continental-style breakfast buffet is served each morning in a lovely interior chamber. Check the hotel's website for various packages that combine a room with theater tickets and museum passes.

MAP 4: 1901 Ford Dr., 866/812-4537, www.gliddenhouse.com

THE BED-AND-BREAKFASTS OF OHIO CITY

The singular arrangement of restored Civil War-era homes, a walkable neighborhood with a wealth of attractions, and proximity to downtown and public transportation has made Ohio City fertile ground for bed-and-breakfasts.

Despite its petite size, this picturesque neighborhood boasts at least four privately operated urban inns, each with its own charms, quirks, and stories to tell. Less than a mile from Public Square, Ohio City is close to downtown's major offerings. But the area's narrow lanes, leafy canopies, and distinctive architecture can make it feel a million miles—and years—away from big-city life. The neighborhood's main drag of West 25th Street is loaded with enough bars, breweries, restaurants, and shops to keep one pleasantly occupied for days (and nights). A nearby light-rail stop makes for a breezy trip to the airport, downtown, or points east.

The largest of the bed-and-breakfasts is **Stone Gables Inn,** a roomy Queen Anne Victorian with a welcoming double-stair front porch and festive color scheme. Bridge Avenue is one of the most aesthetically pleasing stretches of Ohio City, and it is home to two of the area's four inns. **J. Palen House,** the relative newcomer, gracefully straddles the line between antiquity and modernity. Long a flophouse, the 1872 Victorian features original floors, doors, and stained-glass windows. Yet, it also boasts wireless internet, a fully outfitted business center, and an eager-to-please innkeeper. Additional nearby properties now provide even more overnight options, and there's even talk of the innkeepers opening a nearby bistro. Just around the corner, **Clifford House Bed and Breakfast** might be the homiest inn of them all. Innkeeper Jim Miner lives here with his pets, and there is nothing like a warm slobber from a happy puppy to remind you why you sidestepped that big, anonymous hotel in the first place. Rounding out the list is **Wallace Manor** (4724 Franklin Blvd., 216/961-6298, www.wallacemanor.com), four separate accommodations, each with private bath, set in a Romanesque Revival from the 1880s.

Holiday Inn Cleveland Clinic $$

Located on the campus of the prestigious Cleveland Clinic, the 2016 glass-wrapped Holiday Inn Cleveland Clinic is a 276-room property in the heart of the University Circle neighborhood. Given its proximity to the world-class health-care provider, the hotel is ideally situated for patients and their families, with special rates for both. Amenities include a welcoming lobby, café and bar, fitness room, small pool, and outdoor patio.

MAP 4: 8650 Euclid Ave., 216/707-4200, www.hiclevelandclinic.com

InterContinental Hotel and Conference Center $$

It's understandable that travelers have difficulty making sense of the InterContinental hotels situation in Cleveland, since there are two separate properties located five blocks apart on the Cleveland Clinic campus. The far grander sibling in this hotel family is unquestionably the InterContinental Hotel and Conference Center. Completed in 2003 at a cost of around $100 million, this luxury 330-room hotel wows visitors from the get-go thanks to a 3,000-piece granite mosaic world map that serves as the lobby floor. Modern, well-appointed rooms feature high-speed internet connections, 27-inch flat-screen televisions, minibars, coffeemakers, and CD players. The on-site fitness center is equipped with state-of-the-art cardiovascular and strength-training machines, plus locker rooms, showers, and sauna. Hungry guests can dine at the world-class Table 45 or the more casual North Coast Café. Of course, as the style, service, and amenities rise, so too does the price. Rooms at this hotel are consistently more expensive than those at the InterContinental Suites Hotel Cleveland, with rates ranging $200-300 and up per night. Both InterCons are less than two

Glidden House

miles from University Circle, Case Western Reserve University, and Little Italy. Downtown is about a 10-minute drive away.

MAP 4: 9801 Carnegie Ave., 216/707-4100, www.ihg.com

University Circle Bed and Breakfast $

"This is not the romantic-getaway-type bed-and-breakfast," admits innkeeper William Bowman. "You won't find hot tubs in all the rooms." What you will find at University Circle Bed and Breakfast is a clean, professional, and well-placed inn less than a mile from University Circle's major cultural attractions. As a short-term corporate-stay facility, the renovated century home is popular with professionals visiting the nearby universities, hospitals, and institutions. Typical guests stay about a week, and some even come from overseas. Rates include breakfast, wireless internet, and free off-street parking. Additional accommodations are available at Bowman's sister operation, Larchmere House (12404 Larchmere Blvd., 216/721-8968, www.larchmerehouse.com), near Shaker Square.

MAP 4: 1575 E. 108th St., 216/721-8968, www.ucbnb.com

COUCH-SURF YOUR WAY TO A GOOD (AND FREE) NIGHT'S REST

Maybe it's just our Midwestern sensibilities, but Clevelanders have always been a generous lot. So it's no surprise that so many locals participate in the **CouchSurfing Project** (www.couchsurfing.com).

The couch-surfing craze helps to remove financial barriers from domestic and international travel, but that's not all. Participants open up their homes to travelers, asking for nothing in return apart from a thank-you. Many go well beyond simply providing a roof, offering to pick folks up from public transport, preparing a home-cooked meal, and showing guests around the city. The benefits, in addition to the cash savings, are a more personal experience, heightened cultural exchange, and quite possibly a new friend.

A recent search of Cleveland members offering a free stay resulted in thousands of hits. The list includes people with such occupations as paramedic, chef, student, teacher, journalist, photographer, and musician. They are young and old, male and female, attached and single. The only universal quality among them seems to be a spirit of adventure, philanthropy, and camaraderie.

Lakewood   Map 6

Days Inn $

Lakewood is a beautiful tree-lined community about five miles west of downtown. When it comes to commercial lodging, however, options are few. For the price, this Days Inn offers a clean, comfortable, and efficient place to rest your head. No, it's not the Ritz, and yes, it can get noisy, but this locale provides a decent home base for exploring Cleveland and its western suburbs. The cut-rate price includes complimentary continental breakfast, free wireless internet, free off-street parking, and cable, making it a sensible, albeit nondescript, temporary address.

MAP 6: 12019 Lake Ave., 216/226-4800, www.daysinn.com

Emerald Necklace Inn $

If plans call for hitting the bike paths of Cleveland Metroparks' Rocky River Reservation, consider this inn your cozy home base. Literally steps from the park, this charming Victorian bed-and-breakfast is close to golf, tennis, fishing, and cross-country skiing. Or simply enjoy the inn's impeccable gardens and surrounding green space. The bed-and-breakfast offers guests a choice of three rooms, all with private baths, some with views of the lush woodlands. Stays include complimentary full breakfast, free wireless internet, and off-street parking. Have the staff pack a picnic lunch for your travels through the park. Better yet, arrange to have an in-room massage waiting when you return. Reminiscent of days gone by, the snug little country inn also runs a tea parlor that is open to the public.

MAP 6: 18840 Lorain Rd., Fairview Park, 440/333-9100, www.emeraldnecklaceinn.com

The Club at Hillbrook $$$

Mention Hillbrook Club to most East Siders and you're bound to receive some oohs and ahhs. The tony private club is in the densely forested Chagrin River Valley, and it is the preferred wedding site of the area's wealthiest socialites. But you needn't be a Rockefeller to experience this 40-room English Tudor mansion. The Hillbrook Inn allows guests to live like a member for a fraction of the cost. A night's stay includes access to the private dining room, swimming pool, fitness center, and tennis courts. Approximately seven different suites are available, each with a private bathroom and wireless internet. Most feature original architectural accents like leaded-glass windows, black-walnut moldings, and stately fireplaces. A continental breakfast is included.

MAP 7: 14800 Hillbrook Dr., Chagrin Falls, 440/247-4940, www.clubhillbrook.com

AC Hotel Cleveland Beachwood $$

Located in the freshly minted Pinecrest Development on Cleveland's East Side, the boutique-style AC Hotel offers contemporary Euro-styling, superior service, and exceptional amenities. The 145-room hotel, which opened in 2018, features sleek guest rooms with comfortable beds, an on-site fitness center, free high-speed internet and complimentary on-site parking. The property resides within a ritzy live/work/play lifestyle center with numerous high-end shops, restaurants, and entertainment options, including sought-after names like Shake Shack, REI, and West Elm.

MAP 7: 300 Park Ave., Orange Village, 216/831-1108, www.marriott.com

Aloft Cleveland Airport $$

Aloft, a boutique brand from Starwood Hotels, opened this contemporary 150-room hotel in the summer of 2017. It's five miles from Cleveland Hopkins International Airport and offers free parking along with complimentary shuttle service that runs from morning until midnight. Guest rooms feature high ceilings, platform beds, and SPG Keyless entry, which unlocks doors with a smartphone. Like most Aloft hotels, this one has a WXYZ Bar, 24-hour Re:fuel snack shop, a fitness center, and free Wi-Fi.

MAP 7: 5550 Great Northern Blvd., North Olmsted, 440/772-4300, www.starwoodhotels.com

✪ Inn at Brandywine Falls $$

This 165-year-old farmhouse estate is tucked into the Cuyahoga Valley National Park, literally steps from scenic Brandywine Falls, a 65-foot gem. Guests who book a room or suite at this charming inn likely do so because they plan on taking advantage of the wealth of recreational pursuits in the area. The Ohio & Erie Canal Towpath Trail and Cuyahoga Valley Scenic Railroad are both about 1.5 miles from the front door. Ohio's best ski resorts are around the corner. And Blossom Music Center, the summer home of the

Cleveland Orchestra, is just down the road. Rooms range from cozy second-floor nooks to spacious suites with wood-burning Franklin stoves. Vertically gifted guests are advised to avoid the low-ceilinged Anna Hale's Garret. Despite the historical nature of the house and property, all rooms feature private baths and free wireless internet.

MAP 7: 8230 Brandywine Rd., Sagamore Hills, 888/306-3381, www. innatbrandywinefalls.com

Inn of Chagrin Falls $$

Though only 35 minutes from downtown Cleveland, Chagrin Falls has enough charms to warrant an overnight stay. Situated around the town's village square are scores of independent boutiques, galleries, shops, and restaurants, not to mention the namesake waterfall. Granted, as the town's only hotel, the Inn of Chagrin Falls has a bit of a lock on the local lodging. But this graceful Western Reserve building has charms all its own. Many of the 15 rooms boast gas fireplaces, and some of those also have a whirlpool tub. Guests can expect a certain country-style decor, and the finishes may not be the most up-to-date. But calm, comfort, and service seem to make up for the inn's lack of panache.

MAP 7: 87 West St., Chagrin Falls, 440/247-1200, www.innofchagrinfalls.com

Cleveland Airport Marriott $

When an early flight out of town awaits, it might be wise to stay near the airport. This nicely appointed Marriott is five minutes from Hopkins International, and the hotel offers a free round-the-clock shuttle

service. While nothing to write home about on the outside, this 370-room property is actually quite attractive inside. It offers an elegant terrazzo lobby, a restaurant featuring local, handcrafted cuisine, a lounge, indoor pool, and 24-hour fitness center. The comfortable guest rooms all offer wireless internet service, crisp new linens, and a workstation outfitted with an ergonomic chair. Not only is this location situated by the airport, it is close to the I-X Center and a highway that offers a straight shot to downtown.

MAP 7: 4277 W. 150th St., Cleveland, 216/252-5333, www.marriott.com/cleap

Embassy Suites Cleveland Rockside

Embassy Suites Cleveland Rockside $

Independence is a popular stop for business travelers; the city includes a thriving economic corridor home to numerous Northeast Ohio companies. Situated at the crossroads of I-77 and I-480, the location also puts travelers about 15 minutes from downtown and 10 minutes from the airport. Like other Embassy Suites, this one features a roomy central atrium around which are the balconied hotel floors. Rooms in the all-suites hotel include separate spaces for sleeping and living, with an additional sleeper sofa, armchair, and TV. Rooms offer wired high-speed internet access, while wireless access is available for a nominal fee. All stays include a full breakfast, nightly manager's receptions with free snacks and beverages, and complimentary transportation to the airport. Other amenities include an indoor pool, fitness center, business office, and free parking. MAP 7: 5800 Rockside Woods Blvd., Independence, 216/986-9900, www. embassysuites.com

DAY TRIPS

Ohio is a state of remarkable contrasts. Tucked alongside metropolitan areas like Cleveland, Akron, and Columbus is the world's largest Amish community. A day or two spent exploring these scenic back roads is like a trip back in time. Jimmy Buffett may have Key West, but North Coasters have Put-in-Bay, an island town

with similar hedonistic sensibilities that attracts a million revelers each summer. And thanks to peculiar microclimates, scores of modern winemakers continue to set up shop along the southeastern shores of Lake Erie, where they produce intensely flavored fruit and high-quality wines—and operate cozy tasting rooms in which to sample them.

Lake Erie Canopy Tours in Ashtabula County

PLANNING YOUR TIME

While visits to Akron, Ashtabula County, and Amish Country can conceivably be accomplished as part of a day trip, spending the night at any of these destinations will allow you to more thoroughly delve into the local color. Along these same lines, it's more than doable to enjoy Cedar Point Amusement Park in a there-and-back trip, but visits to the Lake Erie islands, which require a round-trip ferry ride from the mainland, are best coupled with an overnight stay.

As for which trip is best for you, let the destination be your guide. Thrill ride fanatics travel great distances to spend the day at Cedar Point, where the tallest, fastest, longest, and scariest roller coasters consistently garner national acclaim. Families with children should consider spending the night in the area, where kid-friendly attractions like Kalahari Waterpark and African Safari Wildlife Park will keep the little ones entertained for hours on end.

While Put-in-Bay and South Bass Island get most of the attention, Kelleys Island is equally adored for different reasons. About 300 residents call this

HIGHLIGHTS

✪ **BEST PLACE TO SEE CHUCK CLOSE UP CLOSE:** The renovated **Akron Art Museum** has one of the most impressive collections of 20th-century art. Fans of Chuck Close's large-scale photorealistic paintings can ogle at his mesmerizing *Linda* here, as well as works by Andy Warhol and Frank Stella (page 193).

✪ **MOST COMPLETE COLLECTION OF SUPER BOWL RINGS:** Gridiron fans make the pilgrimage to Canton from points afar to wallow in the memorabilia at the **Pro Football Hall of Fame.** The museum's Super Bowl Room contains collectibles from every championship game played to date (page 197).

✪ **LONGEST COVERED BRIDGE IN AMERICA:** Ashtabula County is home to 19 covered bridges, including **Smolen-Gulf Bridge,** the longest in the United States. Bridge buffs come here to admire the craftsmanship and charm of these handsome overpasses (page 202).

✪ **MOST INTERESTING SOUVENIR FROM THE ICE AGE:** When a massive glacier rubbed its way across the northern tip of Kelleys Island about 18,000 years ago, it etched striking **Glacial Grooves** into solid bedrock. Measuring 10 feet deep, 35 feet wide, and 400 feet long, the furrows are remnants of the Pleistocene Ice Age (page 211).

✪ **MOST APPROPRIATE PLACE TO SCREAM:** Thanks to its matchless collection of the world's tallest, fastest, and steepest roller coasters, **Cedar Point Amusement Park** is consistently heralded as the world's best amusement park. Hop on Top Thrill Dragster to zip to a speed of 120 miles per hour before climbing to a height of 420 feet (page 213).

✪ **BEST PLACE TO BUY A GOAT:** When farmers need to buy livestock, they head to the **Kidron Auction.** This lively Amish Country auction is open to the public, making the weekly event a popular, albeit unconventional, tourist attraction (page 218).

four-square-mile island home year-round. The rest of the population comprises weekend and summertime visitors from the mainland. Popular activities include sunbathing, swimming, fishing, boating, and hiking ecologically diverse nature preserves. Of course, there also are bars, restaurants, and breweries at which to enjoy a nice dinner or nightcap. The Lake Erie islands shut down after Labor Day, so make sure to schedule your visit between Memorial Day and early September to enjoy the festive atmosphere.

Lovers of fine wine and picturesque scenery should head east to Ashtabula County, the official capital of the Ohio wine industry. Two dozen wineries and tasting rooms dot the scenic landscape, and most drives include passages through postcard-worthy covered bridges. This excursion is likely best for adult couples looking to slow down, get off the grid, and savor Ohio's finest wines and, in autumn, stunning fall foliage.

Amish Country is at its peak in the fall, when the leafy rural landscape changes color from verdant green to crimson and gold. It is also the busiest time here, when shops, restaurants, and hotels all get crowded. Children will get a kick out of seeing horse-drawn buggies share the road with "English" automobiles, while the massive Lehman's Hardware is a veritable treasure trove of old-timey products, gifts, and toys.

Art and/or sports fans should plan the short trip south to the Akron/Canton region. To gridiron fanatics, the Pro Football Hall of Fame in Canton is a bucket list topper, where the whole of professional football history is on display for die-hard fanatics to peruse and absorb. Not far from the hall of fame is the Akron Art Museum, one of the best repositories for 20th-century art in the region, with particularly close attention paid to postmodern painting, photorealism, surrealism, and pop art.

Akron and Vicinity

Akron, a short drive south of Cleveland, presents travelers with enticing attractions. Smaller and more manageable than Cleveland, the city can certainly be the site of a wonderful day trip. But an overnight stay will accommodate a more vigorous exploration of the city's attractions. Art fans will doubtless plan a visit to the Akron Art Museum, while minor league baseball buffs will want to take in an Akron RubberDucks game at Canal Park. Garden and architecture aficionados absolutely must discover

the grandeur of Stan Hywet Hall. If there are football fans in the group, a stop in Canton to explore the Pro Football Hall of Fame on the way to or from Akron is required. Outdoor enthusiasts will love the Ohio & Erie Canal Towpath Trail (an 87-mile all-purpose path) and Cuyahoga Valley National Park.

SIGHTS
AKRON RUBBERDUCKS
Many fans of America's favorite pastime hold minor league ball in higher

regard than the big leagues. Citing cheaper outings, a more manageable setting, elevated player passion, and better in-park promotions, true baseball fans are wild about the minors. As the Cleveland Indians' AA affiliate, the **Akron RubberDucks** (300 S. Main St., 330/253-5153, www.akronaeros.com, $25 reserved, $11 bleachers, $5 general admission) are a proving ground for the big-brother team to the north. And the RubberDucks' home, **Canal Park**, is an absolute gem of a ballpark. Designed by the same firm behind Progressive Field and Camden Yards, the park is modern, intimate, and integrated within its downtown environment. The park seats 7,500 and treats fans to the largest freestanding scoreboard in the minor leagues. The 70-game home season runs from early April through August. Single-game tickets can be purchased over the phone, online, or in person at the box office.

⊙ AKRON ART MUSEUM

Akron Art Museum (1 S. High St., 330/376-9185, www.akronartmuseum. org, 11am-5pm Tues.-Sun., 11am-9pm Thurs., adults $10, seniors and students $8), which opened in 1924, unveiled the John S. and James L. Knight Building in 2007 to much fanfare. Combined with an original 1899 structure, the addition more than tripled the size of the gallery. Upon its debut the ultramodern glass-and-steel edifice was the talk of the art and architecture world. With "floating" gallery spaces and exaggerated cantilevered overhangs, the contemporary building rivals its contents for attention.

While smaller than many major museum holdings, Akron's 5,000-work collection is a tightly curated sampling of important 20th-century art, with particularly close attention to postmodern painting, photorealism, surrealism, and pop art.

Akron Art Museum

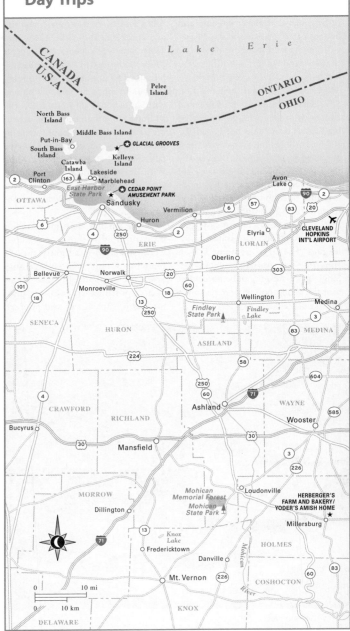

Day Trips

Lake Erie

CANADA
U.S.A.

ONTARIO
OHIO

Pelee Island

North Bass Island

Middle Bass Island

Put-in-Bay
South Bass Island

★ ✿ GLACIAL GROOVES

Catawba Island
Lakeside
Kelleys Island

Port Clinton
163
East Harbor State Park
Marblehead

2

OTTAWA

★ ✿ CEDAR POINT AMUSEMENT PARK

Sandusky

Vermilion

Avon Lake

90 2

6

57

83

20

CLEVELAND HOPKINS INT'L AIRPORT

6

4

250

90

ERIE

Huron

2

Elyria

LORAIN

Oberlin

Bellevue

Norwalk

20

60

Wellington

Medina

101

Monroeville

18

13

18

303

3

250

Findley State Park

Findley Lake

SENECA

HURON

224

58

ASHLAND

604

4

250

60

71

WAYNE

585

CRAWFORD

RICHLAND

Ashland

30

Wooster

Bucyrus

30

3

Mansfield

226

MORROW

Mohican Memorial Forest
Mohican State Park

Loudonville

HERBERGER'S FARM AND BAKERY/ YODER'S AMISH HOME ★

Dillington

71

13

Knox Lake

Fredericktown

Danville

Millersburg

HOLMES

226

60

83

Mt. Vernon

KNOX

COSHOCTON

Mohican River

DELAWARE

0   10 mi

0   10 km

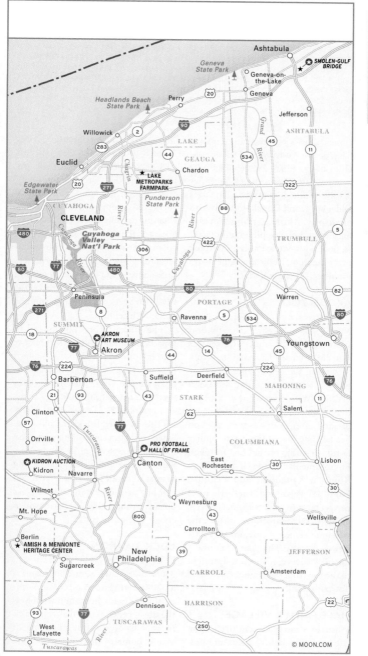

Ashtabula
★ SMOLEN-GULF BRIDGE
Geneva State Park
Geneva-on-the-Lake
Geneva
Jefferson
Headlands Beach State Park
Perry
20
45
11
ASHTABULA
Willowick
283
2
LAKE
44
GEAUGA
534
Grand River
Euclid
20
271
★ LAKE METROPARKS FARMPARK
Chardon
322
Edgewater State Park
Chagrin River
Punderson State Park
88
5
CUYAHOGA
CLEVELAND
Cuyahoga Valley Nat'l Park
306
422
Cuyahoga River
TRUMBULL
480
80
77
Cuyahoga River
480
Peninsula
80
PORTAGE
Warren
82
271
8
Ravenna
5
534
80
SUMMIT
18
★ AKRON ART MUSEUM
Akron
44
14
76
45
Youngstown
76
224
224
Barberton
21
93
43
STARK
Suffield
Deerfield
MAHONING
11
Salem
Clinton
62
57
Orrville
77
COLUMBIANA
★ KIDRON AUCTION
Kidron
★ PRO FOOTBALL HALL OF FAME
Canton
East Rochester
30
Lisbon
Navarre
Tuscarawas River
30
Wilmot
Waynesburg
Wellsville
Mt. Hope
800
43
Berlin
★ AMISH & MENNONITE HERITAGE CENTER
Carrollton
JEFFERSON
Sugarcreek
New Philadelphia
39
Amsterdam
CARROLL
HARRISON
22
Dennison
250
93
West Lafayette
77
TUSCARAWAS
Tuscarawas River

© MOON.COM

195

WHY CANTON IS HOME TO THE FOOTBALL HALL OF FAME

By the 1900s, organized football had become a popular American pastime. Many cities fielded teams, but they largely remained individual entities. Ohio was a particular hotbed of football activity, with numerous teams spread throughout the state. In 1920, the American Professional Football Association (now the NFL) was founded in Canton with 11 teams in the league. Football legend Jim Thorpe was selected as president. Five of the league's teams were from Ohio, including the Canton Bulldogs, Cleveland Tigers, and Akron Professionals. In 1961, the City of Canton made an official bid to the NFL to be the site of the hall. Acceptance soon followed, and the Hall of Fame opened to the public two years later.

Chuck Close's mesmerizing *Linda* is here, as are Andy Warhol's *Elvis* and Ohio-native Elijah Pierce's *The Wise and Foolish Virgins and Four Other Scenes*. Works by Frank Stella, Claes Oldenburg, and Donald Judd are also on display. Akron Art Museum also maintains a choice photography collection, with whole galleries devoted to the medium. Ironically, cameras are prohibited in the galleries.

AKRON ZOO

The Akron Zoo (505 Euclid Ave., 330/375-2550, www.akronzoo.org, 10am-5pm daily, adults $12, seniors $10, children $9) has been on a roll, attracting its largest audience ever in 2017, with close to half a million visitors. With tons of new exhibits, major physical upgrades, and expanded after-hours events, the zoo has become one of the most popular family-friendly attractions in town. Environments include Grizzly Ridge, Komodo Kingdom, and Penguin Point. At Farmland, the little ones can get nose-to-nose with goats, sheep, and pigs. Other amenities include the welcome center, a café, and a solar-powered train. Thanks to a connector, bike riders can now travel straight to the zoo from the Ohio & Erie Canal Towpath Trail.

HALE FARM & VILLAGE

Want to show your children what life was like before smartphones, computers, and refrigerators? Hale Farm & Village (2686 Oak Hill Rd., Bath, 800/589-9703, www.wrhs.org, 10am-5pm Wed.-Sat. summer, 10am-5pm Sat.-Sun. fall, adults $10, children $5) is a town trapped in the mid-1800s, when things like electricity, automobiles, and iPhones were still a few years down the road. This living history museum employs historical interpreters dressed in period costume to recount the story of the Western Reserve, the Civil War years, and life in the middle of the 19th century.

The land originally belonged to Jonathan Hale, a Connecticut farmer who relocated in 1810 to the Western Reserve. Today, skilled artisans demonstrate the very same techniques used to construct the buildings, tools, and crafts of Hale's day. Brick makers fire air-dried bricks the old-fashioned way; blacksmiths forge farm and household implements by hand; glassblowers keep Ohio's rich glassmaking history alive. In fact, at the farm you can buy primitive hand-blown glass objects in their characteristic amber, cobalt, and green tints.

LOCK 3 AKRON

Lock 3 Akron (200 S. Main St., 330/375-2877, www.lock3live.com) is a 5,000-seat general admission amphitheater in the heart of town that is the site of concerts, festivals, and family-friendly events all summer long. It also is home to the City of Akron's official Fourth of July fireworks display. In fall and winter, seasonal events like Oktoberfest and the Downtown Holiday Lighting Ceremony join attractions such as outdoor ice skating, a sledding hill, and Polar Putt-Putt to keep the site activated. Guests can bring their own lawn chairs and blankets to summer concerts or rent them for a small fee. For concerts that have an admission charge, tickets are available at the gate the night of the show. Children 48 inches and under are admitted free.

Pro Football Hall of Fame

✪ PRO FOOTBALL HALL OF FAME

Since opening in 1963, the Canton-based Pro Football Hall of Fame (2121 George Halas Dr. NW, 330/456-8207, www.profootballhof.com, 9am-8pm daily Memorial Day-Labor Day, 9am-5pm daily Labor Day-Memorial Day, adults $25, seniors $21, children $18) has been attracting gridiron fans with its shrine to the legends of the game. This museum of football history has expanded four times to accommodate its growing collection and its burgeoning attendance figures. In fact, the hall of fame completed the largest expansion and renovation project in its history in time to celebrate the museum's 50th anniversary in

2013. The property grew from 85,000 square feet to 118,000 square feet, with an additional 37,000 square feet renovated.

Nearly half a million visitors per year travel to sleepy Canton, Ohio, to pay tribute to football's past and present superstars. Most popular on the must-see list likely is the Hall of Fame Gallery, where bronze busts of all enshrinees are on permanent display. Cleveland Browns fans might want to bypass the Super Bowl Room, which exhibits memories and memorabilia from every championship played to date.

Real football fans strive to attend the annual Pro Football Hall of Fame Enshrinement Festival, a days-long event held each summer that includes the Enshrinement Ceremony, dinner, parties, and the NFL Hall of Fame Game. Tickets are hard to come by, so phone early (888/310-4255).

STAN HYWET HALL

Akron's Stan Hywet Hall (714 N. Portage Path, 330/836-5533, www.stanhywet.org, 10am-4:30pm Tues.-Sun. Apr.-Dec., adults $15, students $6, tours extra) is considered one of the finest examples of Tudor Revival architecture in the region. The moniker is Old English for "stone quarry," a fitting name for this stunning American country estate built in 1912 by F. A. Seiberling, cofounder of Goodyear Tire & Rubber. Akron's only National Historic Landmark, the magnificent manor house, along with its outbuildings and gardens, is open to the public for self-guided and guided tours.

The manor house alone boasts 21,000 panes of glass, 23 fireplaces, and 65 rooms. Guided one-hour tours take visitors throughout the house, paying special attention to the Great Hall, Music Room, and Billiards Room. Well preserved and brimming with original fixtures, furnishings, and priceless antiques, the house was a model of modernity when it was completed. Tours begin on the hour most days.

While considerably smaller than its original 1,000 acres, the lush estate surrounding the home is filled with botanical treasures. Perched on the precipice of the Cuyahoga Valley, the 70 acres feature English and Japanese gardens, an apple orchard, and a stately birch tree allée. Throughout the year, the grounds are the site of outdoor theater and musical performances, as well as food and wine festivals. Check the website for special events.

RESTAURANTS

In the heart of downtown Akron, Crave (59 E. Market St., 330/253-1234, www.eatdrinkcrave.com, 11am-10pm Mon.-Thurs., 11am-11pm Fri., 5pm-11pm Sat., $20-30) is a contemporary bistro that specializes in eclectic, affordable comfort food. The menu features a raft of creative small plates, sandwiches, and entrées. Wildly unconventional-sounding combinations invariably work to create unforgettable tastes. Cumin-scented fried pickles, Guinness-glazed steak skewers, and sour cherry-infused duck breast are just some of the 50 or so dishes available on the all-day menu. Wine and beer fans will dig Crave's lengthy and equally affordable roster of great finds. When booking a table, it might be helpful to know Crave has an airy dining room, a long communal table, and a lively barroom, so choose accordingly.

From the curb, the Diamond Grille (77 W. Market St., 330/253-0041, www.diamondgrille.com, 11am-10pm Mon.-Thurs., 11am-11pm Fri., 5pm-11pm Sat., $26-40) looks more like a shuttered shot-and-a-beer saloon than a popular steakhouse. In fact, if it weren't for the dimly illuminated neon sign, you'd swear the place was toast. But this clubby Akron landmark is beloved precisely for that understated elegance. This is where professional golfers like Tiger Woods and Vijay Singh come to protein-load before hitting the links at nearby Firestone Country Club. Nationally recognized as the place to be for stiff martinis, thick slabs of prime beef, and, perhaps, a heaping serving of nostalgia, the grill can be tough to get into on a busy night, so call in advance. And don't expect cushy leather banquettes when you do score a table—the interior matches the exterior. As one might expect, the food's not cheap, with steaks priced well north of $30. To sample this anachronistic steak sensation, you can leave the charge cards at home: Diamond Grille accepts only cash and checks.

Any way you slice it, Luigi's (105 N. Main St., 330/253-2999, www.luigisrestaurant.com, 11am-midnight Mon.-Thurs., 11am-2am Fri., 3pm-2am Sat., 3pm-midnight Sun., $9-11) is an Akron institution. Since 1949, folks have been coming here for what many argue is the city's best pizza, lasagna, and Italian comfort food. The setting is casual, lively, and fun, with walls of old black-and-white photos to keep you occupied during the (sometimes lengthy) wait for a table. Readers of the comic Funky Winkerbean will recognize Luigi's as the inspiration behind Montoni's, a recurring location owing to the cartoonist's fondness for the place. Perhaps unique to this family-run eatery are the late-night hours, which on Friday and Saturday stretch well into the next morning. Bring cash; Luigi's doesn't accept credit cards (but there is an ATM on-site).

Since 1934, Swenson's Drive-In (658 E. Cuyahoga Falls Ave., 330/928-8515, www.swensonsdriveins.com, 11am-1am daily, $2-5) has been filling the hearts and bellies of burger fans, who make pilgrimages here for soul-satisfying food. Now with multiple locations, these old-school drive-ins feature curbside ordering and delivery of wonderful diner-style burgers, fries, and milk shakes. The Galley Boy—a double cheeseburger with two special sauces—is a house favorite, as are the onion rings and thick and creamy milkshakes.

When the craving for ice cream strikes, head over to the Historic Arts District, where Chill Ice Cream (21 Maiden Lane, 330/649-2834, www.chill-icecream.com, noon-9pm Tues.-Thurs., noon-10pm Fri.-Sat., 1pm-7pm Sun., $3-4) dishes up artisanal, small-batch creations. This adored local creamery has a knack for creating intoxicating flavors like Blackout Double Dark Chocolate, Lavender Queen Bee, and Sea Salt Caramel Truffle.

NIGHTLIFE

Blu Jazz+ (47 E. Market St., 330/252-1190, www.blujazzakron.com, times and prices vary based on show) is one of the best live music clubs around. In fact, the club was named one of the "Best Jazz Venues in the World" by Downbeat Magazine. Top-quality live jazz shows featuring renowned talent are dished up in a cool, relaxed, and intimate setting. There's a full-service bar serving cocktails, wine, and beer, plus a restaurant offering small plates and Southern-style favorites. Purchase a pair of tickets to any show and take 15 percent off your dinner tab.

Hoppin' Frog (680 E. Waterloo Rd., 330/352-4578, www.hoppinfrog.com, 5pm-10pm Mon., 11am-10pm Tues.-Wed., 11am-11pm Thurs.-Sat.) is one of the most popular breweries in Ohio and has been on the receiving end of scores of beer-fest medals. This fun taproom is a great place to sample a variety of fresh brews, like the famous B.O.R.I.S. the Crusher Oatmeal Imperial Stout, Turbo Shandy Citrus Ale, and Frosted Frog Christmas Ale Winter Ale. Snacks like Bavarian pretzels, chips and dip, and meat and cheese boards make perfect partners for the suds.

Often billed as the "next hot neighborhood" of Akron, Kenmore has an eclectic mix of businesses that include a recording studio, comic book store, and the Old 97 (1503 Kenmore Blvd., 330/745-5493, www.theold97.com, 4:30pm-1am Wed.-Sat), which is named after the last stop on the old streetcar line. These days that number conjures images of a hip neighborhood tavern that serves cocktails, food, and fun in the form of darts, Ping-Pong, corn hole, and alfresco bocce.

Wine lovers adore 750ml (2287 W. Market St., 330/794-5754, www.750mlwines.com, noon-10pm Mon.-Thurs., 11am-11pm Fri.-Sat.), a cozy wine bar with a laid-back vibe. Numerous high-quality wine selections can be had, with approximately 10 reds and 10 whites by the glass and 800 by the bottle. A limited food menu offers up salads, small plates, flatbreads, and desserts.

SHOPS
DON DRUMM STUDIOS AND GALLERY

Artist Don Drumm has made a name for himself by pioneering the use of cast aluminum as an artistic medium. His distinctive sculptures have been commissioned by fans worldwide, but Ohio natives appear to be most smitten. Art lovers flock to Don Drumm Studios and Gallery (437 Crouse St., 330/253-6268, www.dondrummstudios.com, 10am-6pm Mon.-Wed. and Fri., 10am-8pm Thurs., 10am-5pm Sat.), home to two wonderful galleries that showcase works not just by Drumm but also some 500 other North American craftspeople, artists, and designers. To wipe out your holiday gift lists in one fell swoop, come here to shop the huge inventory of handcrafted jewelry, glass, crafts, and sculptures. Large alfresco courtyards are stocked with unique outdoor home accessories like wind chimes, water fountains, and sculptural wall hangings.

HARTVILLE MARKETPLACE AND FLEA MARKET

Roughly halfway between Akron and Canton, the Hartville Marketplace and Flea Market (1289 Edison St., Hartville, 330/877-9860, www.hartvillemarketplace.com, 9am-5pm Mon. and Thurs.-Sat.) is a 100,000-square-foot building stuffed to the rafters with more than 100 independently owned and operated 10-foot-by-10-foot shops. The variety is staggering. While live animals are no longer traded here, shoppers still can walk away with pet-related items like treats and collars. Vendors come and go, but you can always count on finding books, clothing, antiques, cheese, fudge, nuts, coins, jewelry, sports memorabilia, and hardware. There is an equally large outdoor flea market, arranged on more than 20 acres of blacktop, that bursts with additional vendors during the summer months (though it is open year-round). When you're hungry for some biscuits and gravy, sidle on over to Sarah's Grille, the on-site restaurant.

THE PEANUT SHOPPE

It's almost impossible to walk past The Peanut Shoppe (203 S. Main St., 330/376-7020, www.akronpeanuts.com, 9am-5pm Mon.-Thurs., 9am-10pm Fri., 9am-5pm Sat.), an old-school nut roaster in downtown Akron. The smells alone will draw you inside, and when you get there you'll be surrounded by nuts, candies, and memorabilia dating back to the store's genesis in the 1930s. Friendly service, plenty of samples, and enough nostalgia to tide you over until the next visit are the order of the day.

WHERE TO STAY

Set inside a magnificent 1923 Tudor Revival mansion, the O'Neil House (1290 W. Exchange St., 330/867-2650, www.oneilhouse.com, $75-200) is not your run-of-the-mill bed-and-breakfast. Once the home of William O'Neil, founder of Akron's General Tire Company, the museum-quality residence now offers discerning travelers a choice of four glorious suites, each with private bath. The 19-room property boasts oak-paneled walls, leaded-glass windows, and oriental rug-clad wood floors. Gourmet breakfast, served in a lovely sunroom, is included in the room price. Innkeeper Gayle Johnson maintains pets of her own, so none are welcome.

For a clean, comfortable, convenient, and affordable night's stay just outside Akron, the Courtyard by Marriott Akron Fairlawn (100 Springside Dr., 330/668-9090, www.marriott.com, $140-300) is a good bet. The 75 guest rooms include all the usual amenities, including wireless Internet, coffeemakers, and large TVs. Food and beverages, including a breakfast buffet, are served in the lobby Bistro. Amenities include an indoor pool, whirlpool, and fitness center.

The Hampton Inn & Suites (5256 Broadmoor Cir. NW, 330/491-4335, www.hamptoninn3.hilton.com, $120-170) in Canton is conveniently located to both the Akron-Canton Regional Airport and the Pro Football Hall of Fame, with either less than 10 minutes away by car. A free hot breakfast is included with every stay, and a daily shuttle zips travelers to the airport.

TRANSPORTATION AND SERVICES
TOURIST INFORMATION
The Akron/Summit Convention & Visitors Bureau (77 E. Mill St., 330/374-7560, www.visitakron-summit.org, 8am-5pm Mon.-Fri.) is inside the John S. Knight Center, Akron's convention center. By phone, online, or in person, the CVB helps potential visitors with all aspects of their trip, including finding accommodations, planning excursions, suggesting attractions, and locating discounts.

You'll find the Stark County Convention & Visitors Bureau (222 Market Ave. N., 800/552-6051, www.

visitcanton.com, 8:30am-5pm Mon.-Fri.) inside the Millennium Centre office building in downtown Canton. Or simply visit the website, which has all the information a visitor to Stark County might need when planning a short or extended stay in the area.

For information on a host of Ohio sights, attractions, and activities, contact the Ohio Division of Travel and Tourism (800/282-5393, www.ohio.org).

GETTING THERE
From Cleveland, getting to Akron and Canton is a relatively straight shot south on I-77. Akron is approximately 45 minutes by car, while Canton is closer to 70 minutes. Many frugal travelers to Akron, Canton, and Cleveland choose the Akron-Canton Airport (888/434-2359, www.akroncantonairport.com) over Cleveland Hopkins International Airport because of cheaper fares and fewer hassles. American Airlines, Delta, Spirit, and United Airlines operate flights from here. For less than $25, travelers can hop a Greyhound (www.greyhound.com) in Cleveland and travel south to either city.

GETTING AROUND
A traveler abandoned in Akron or Canton without wheels could manage thanks to ride-hail services such as Lyft (www.lyft.com) and Uber (www.uber.com). For a cab, call City Yellow Cab (234/542-3941) or Anytime Taxi (330/252-7400).

Ashtabula County

A short ride east from Cleveland lands travelers in one of the most scenic patches of the state. Out here, there is a closer connection to the landscape, with much of the tourist industry hinging on proximity to Lake Erie. Geneva-on-the-Lake is a century-old lakeside resort, complete with old-time strip, cozy rental cottages, and family-friendly activities. The Grand River Valley, Ohio's largest and most successful wine-growing region, is loaded with two dozen wineries, many boasting lovely tasting rooms and picturesque patios. There are 19 covered bridges in the county, including the shortest and longest ones in the nation. In recent years, the largely agricultural area has added more outdoor recreational activities, like ziplines and canopy tours, as well as kayak, canoe, and paddleboard outfitters.

SIGHTS

LAKE ERIE CANOPY TOURS

Lake Erie Canopy Tours (4888 N. Broadway, 866/601-1973, www. lakeeriecanopytours.com, 9am-6pm daily late May-Oct., $19-79), which opened in 2017 at the Lodge at Geneva-on-the-Lake, sends bold visitors on a network of ziplines that slice through the treetops at speeds of up to 30 mph. For those who prefer to climb rather than fly, a pair of challenge courses, also elevated above the forest floor, offer a series of wood and rope obstacles that test one's endurance, balance, and agility.

✪ SMOLEN-GULF BRIDGE

They are still building covered bridges in Ashtabula County, if you can believe that. The Smolen-Gulf Bridge, built in 2008, is the longest covered bridge in the United States at 613 feet. For those keeping track, that makes 19 covered bridges in the county, more than any other in Ohio. Most are far older than the Smolen-Gulf, with some dating all the way back to 1867. Bridge fans come to admire the craftsmanship of the various construction methods, which include Pratt truss, Howe truss, and Town lattice designs. Self-guided auto tours of the bridges are very popular, especially in the picturesque autumn months. The routes are well marked and maps can be downloaded from the Ashtabula County Visitors Bureau website (www. visitashtabulacounty.com).

GENEVA-ON-THE-LAKE

Ohio's oldest summer resort district, Geneva-on-the-Lake (800/862-9948, www.visitgenevaonthelake. com) has been enticing vacationers from nearby cities since the turn of the 20th century with its beaches, burgers, and big bands. While "progress" has tarnished some of this historical town's old-timey charm, there is still plenty to do, see, and enjoy in and around this lakefront village. Charming cottages and bed-and-breakfasts still dot the shoreline, along with new hotels and condos. Like a Jersey Shore midway, the famous strip is lined up and down with fast-food snack bars, ice-cream parlors, arcades, bars, and nightclubs. Cars, motorcycles, and golf carts prowl the road in search of adventure, camaraderie, and entertainment.

covered bridge in Ashtabula County

GENEVA STATE PARK

This 700-acre lakefront park (4499 Padanarum Rd., 440/466-8400, www.parks.ohiodnr.gov/geneva) offers a wealth of recreational pursuits. Options include a 100-yard sandy beachhead, boat marina, ramps for launching watercraft into Lake Erie, and numerous all-purpose trails that snake through the terrain. The park is popular with hunters, cross-country skiers, and anglers who fish for walleye, yellow perch, and even salmon. Stop by the park's Geneva Marina (440/466-7565, www.genevamarina. com) to get your fishing license, bait and tackle supplies, and boating accessories. When you've reached your daily limit, come back and take advantage of the marina's fish-cleaning services.

DOWNTOWN ASHTABULA

At one point in time, Ashtabula Harbor was one of the busiest shipping ports on Lake Erie. These days, it's a charming small town with a Main Street lined with handsome brick buildings filled with shops, cafés, wine bars, and restaurants. Walk to the namesake harbor, where a mesmerizing bascule bridge rises to let marine traffic flow through.

Dining options in the area range from the uber-casual Hil-Mak Seafood (449 Lake Ave., 440/964-3222), a fish market that prepares heavenly fried perch sandwiches, to Bascule Bridge Grill (1006 Bridge St., 440/964-0301, www. basculebridgegrille.com), a seasonal, chef-owned bistro with an amazing wine list featuring many local names. Rennick Meat Market (1104 Bridge St., 440/964-6328, www.rennickmeatmarket.com), and Briquettes Smokehouse (405 Morton Dr., 440/964-2273, www. briquettessmokehouse.com) are also worth checking out.

GRAND RIVER VALLEY AVA

It often surprises folks to learn that Ohio winemakers produce great wine. And not just the sickly sweet stuff, either. Currently, there are more than 280 licensed wineries in the state, making the Buckeye State the sixth-largest wine producer in the nation. In 1860, Ohio led the entire country in wine production.

The two-mile-wide strip of land that hugs the Grand River in Ashtabula County is known as the Grand River Valley AVA, an American Viticultural Area. Along Lake Erie's southeastern shore, wineries enjoy a unique microclimate that delivers long, dry autumns that provide grapes plenty of time to ripen and mature. That's why wine made here from local fruit often is regarded as some of the best in the state and even beyond.

Ohio has earned a reputation for producing sweet wine, and many wineries do still concentrate on those styles. But for decades, sophisticated winemakers have been planting classic European varietals such as cabernet franc, chardonnay, and pinot noir, which thrive in the relatively cool climate. The so-called "pinot belt" that slices through Oregon's Willamette Valley and France's Burgundy also bisects this very region.

While visiting all the wineries in the area would be admirable, most people choose to arrange more reasonable expeditions. The Ohio Wine Producers Association (www. ohiowines.org) has downloadable maps for various wine trails. Stretching from Cleveland to the Pennsylvania border is the **Lake Erie Vines and Wines Trail,** a strip of 40 some wineries, most of which have tasting rooms. To sample some great juice, visit M Cellars, Laurentia, Laurello, Ferrante, Debonné, Harpersfield, Kosicek, or South River Vineyards, to name a few.

If you are in the area over the first weekend in August, consider hitting **Vintage Ohio** (www.visitvintageohio.com), a two-day wine and food festival held at Lake Metroparks Farmpark.

LAKE METROPARKS FARMPARK

Agrarian-minded parents may wish to make a stopover at Lake Metroparks Farmpark (8800 Chardon Rd., Kirtland, 800/366-3276, www.lakemetroparks. com, 9am-5pm Tues.-Sun., closed major holidays, adults $8, seniors $7, children $6) on their way to or from Ashtabula County. At this 235-acre working farm, city folk can experience all manner of country life, from milking a cow to enjoying a wagon ride or corn maze. Demonstrations cover such agricultural activities as sheepherding, cheese making, maple syrup tapping, and crop harvesting. More than 50 breeds of livestock, including a dozen endangered breeds, are on hand to inspire future PETA members. Solar- and wind-power exhibits show off the future of sustainable energy production. A farmers market selling locally grown produce runs here June through October. Many other interesting seasonal events take place throughout the year.

WINERIES

Hugging the southeastern shore of Lake Erie is a microclimate ideally suited to growing wine grapes. The lake's accumulated heat from summer provides warm autumn breezes that extend the grape-growing season well into fall, giving the fruit time to fully ripen. Ohio is one of the top wine-producing states in the nation, and the lush Grand River Valley is home to more than half of the state's vineyard acres. Like other wine-producing regions, this one is filled with wineries offering tastings, bottle sales, and winery tours. A day or two exploring the numerous wineries that populate the landscape is time very well spent.

Debonne Vineyards (7743 Doty Rd., Madison, 440/466-3485, www. debonne.com) is one of the oldest, largest, and most commercially successful wine producers in the state. The 110-acre vineyard produces riesling, chardonnay, pinot gris, and cabernet franc. Debonne also produces ice wine, which is unique to very few regions in the world. Vidal blanc grapes are left on the vine to freeze, then they are immediately picked and pressed, and the highly concentrated nectar transforms into a deliciously sweet dessert wine. The large, modern facility offers tours and tastings year-round, and an outdoor grill serves food in the summertime.

At 18 acres, Harpersfield Vineyard (6387 Rte. 307W, Geneva, 440/466-4739, www.harpersfield.com) is a moderately sized estate winery, but it boasts charm in spades. Come during winter and you'll sample the vineyard's fine wines by the fireside in the rustic tasting room. Imagine sipping gewürztraminer, pinot noir, and late-harvest pinot gris as freshly baked baguettes are plucked from the wood-fired brick oven. Gourmet cheeses and specialty foods are also served in the tasting room, and there is live entertainment during summer weekends.

When owner and winemaker Matt Meineke of M Cellars (6193 S. River Rd., 440/361-4104, www.mcellars.com) first got hold of his 12.6-acre plot, he ripped out every last vine of native Niagara and replaced them with vinifera grapes like riesling, pinot noir, cabernet sauvignon, merlot, and chardonnay. The small but stylish tasting room is a great place to

sample some of the best wines from the Grand River Valley. A patio in the rear overlooks the vineyards.

Anything but quaint, Laurentia Vineyard & Winery (4599 S. Madison Rd., 440/296-9175, www.laurentiawinery.com) is a majestic mansion set amid 117 gorgeous acres, 43 of which are dedicated to growing wine grapes like pinot noir and cabernet sauvignon. Inside, reclaimed hickory wood floors, a massive stone hearth, and forged iron railings convey the feel of a lavish hunting lodge. A tasting room, lower-level wine cellar, and expansive outdoor space combine to create one of the most sought-after destinations in the region. It just so happens that the winemakers also produce world-class wine.

RESTAURANTS

Eddie's Grill (5377 Lake Rd., Geneva-on-the-Lake, 440/466-8720, www.eddiesgrill.com, 11am-11pm daily Memorial Day-Labor Day, $4-6) is rightly famous for its killer cheeseburgers, foot-long chili dogs, and freshly cut fries. The popular 1950s-style diner features open-air counter service, indoor booths with personal jukeboxes, and youthful servers. This place gets super crowded on warm summer nights, but things move quickly. Bring cash or a bank card for the nearby ATM. No credit cards are accepted.

Just down the road from the scenic Harpersfield covered bridge is Ferrante Winery & Ristorante (5585 Rte. 307, Harpersfield, 440/466-8466, www.ferrantewinery.com, hours vary by month, $11-20), a family-friendly winery and restaurant. Complementing the house-made wines are hearty Italian-style specialties. Pizza, pasta, and chicken and veal dishes rule the menu, and many are

Laurentia Vineyard & Winery

made with the winery's award-winning vintages. During summer, a sprawling outdoor patio overlooking the vineyards is host to live music, wine-tastings, and light meals. A large gift shop stocks wine and wine accessories.

Folks trek to the Ashtabula Harbor for swimmingly fresh fried perch dinners at Hil-Mak Seafood (449 Lake Ave., Ashtabula, 440/964-3222, 11:30am-2:30pm and 5pm-10pm Tues.-Sat., $10-18). Because Hil-Mak also operates a fish market, the restaurant has access to a full roster of local and regional seafood. They don't do fancy here; they specialize in great clam chowder, perch sandwiches, fried clams, crab cakes, and onion rings. Seafood aficionados will swear they were dining on the East Coast instead of the North Coast.

Rennick Meat Market (1104 Bridge St., 440/964-6328, www.rennickmeatmarket.com, 11am-close Mon. and Wed.-Fri., 10am-close Sat.-Sun., $17-30) wasn't designed to look like an old butcher shop; it *is* an old butcher shop, one that served downtown Ashtabula from 1889 until the 1960s. These days, it's a chic farm-to-table bistro serving cocktails, local wines, Italian entrées, and great steaks. Located just steps from the harbor, the restaurant is lovely year-round.

WHERE TO STAY

Vineyard Woods (740 State Rte. 534, 440/624-3054, www.vineyardwoods.com, $220-280) is a collection of well-appointed private cottages tucked deep into the woods, which back up to 10 acres of scenic vineyards. Each attractive unit is equipped with a kitchen, spa-like bath, veranda, and fire pit. These modern and secluded cabins make ideal home bases from which to explore wine country and the surrounding areas.

The Lakehouse Inn (5653 Lake Rd., 440/466-8668, www.thelakehouseinn.com, $140-400) is a picturesque bed-and-breakfast perched along the shores of Lake Erie. Located in Geneva-on-the-Lake, the lovely property has a variety of accommodations, from charming guest rooms to a private beach house. Enjoy wine tastings on the patio overlooking the lake, as well as farm-to-table breakfasts and dinners in the exceptional Crosswinds Grille.

The Lodge at Geneva-on-the-Lake (4888 Rte. 534, 866/806-8066, www.thelodgeatgeneva.com, $100-250) is the natural choice for travelers who prefer modern amenities over country charm. The 100-room complex offers guests numerous lodging choices, ranging from comfortable standard rooms to premium lake-view rooms with balconies. Multiroom suites are ideal for families. An outdoor pool and kid zone are open during summer, while a glass-enclosed pool and hot tub are available year-round. Other amenities include a great game room, a fitness center overlooking Lake Erie, and massage services. Rent a bike from the lodge and hit the trails that hug the Lake Erie shoreline. Folks traveling with pets will be happy to know that the lodge offers pet-friendly rooms with direct access to a grassy expanse.

Romantic getaways are the order of the day (and night) at Peggy's Bed and Breakfast (8721 Munson Hill Rd., Ashtabula, 440/969-1996, www.peggysbedandbreakfast.com, $135-170). Tucked into a leafy landscape, Peggy's one and only cottage is nothing if it isn't private. The snug environment features a full kitchen, loft bedroom, two fireplaces, patio, and screened porch. Breakfast is delivered in the

The Lakehouse Inn

morning right to your residence. Peggy offers her guests a full menu of gourmet options, including cream caramel French toast, corned-beef hash, and corn muffins with pecans and maple syrup. The location is ideal for hitting the trails, wineries, covered bridges, or Lake Erie shore, and you can even borrow one of Peggy's bikes.

TRANSPORTATION AND SERVICES
TOURIST INFORMATION

Information and maps of Ashtabula County covered bridges can be obtained by contacting the Ashtabula County Covered Bridge Festival (25 W. Jefferson St., 440/576-3769, www.coveredbridgefestival.org). The Ashtabula County Visitors Bureau can be reached by calling 800/337-6746 or going to www.visitashtabulacounty.com.

For information on Geneva-on-the-Lake, contact Visit Geneva-on-the-Lake (800/862-9948, www.visitgenevaonthelake.com). For information on Ohio's wine industry, wine-related events, and wine-trail maps, contact the Ohio Wine Producers Association (800/227-6972, www.ohiowines.org).

GETTING THERE

Expect a nonstop drive from downtown Cleveland to Geneva-on-the-Lake to take just over an hour. The trip is easily accomplished by taking I-90 to OH 2 to US 20. Greyhound (www.greyhound.com) has a station in Ashtabula at 1520 Bunker Hill Road (440/992-7550).

GETTING AROUND

Serious cyclists can get along just fine on a good bike (depending on the weather, of course), but others will likely need a car to move about since major sights and attractions are miles apart. Ride-hail services such as Lyft (www.lyft.com) and Uber (www.uber.com) are here but in small numbers. For a cab, call Premier Taxi (440/466-1515).

Lake Erie Islands and Vicinity

Just an hour west of Cleveland is an entirely different landscape. From Memorial Day until Labor Day, typically sleepy lakeside communities transform into seasonal hot spots, teeming with pleasure boaters, nature-loving day-trippers, and hard-partying overnighters. Comprising mainland towns like Sandusky, Lakeside, Marblehead, and Port Clinton, and islands such as South Bass and Kelleys, the Lake Erie Islands region is a magnet for summer fun. The epicenter of this party is assuredly Put-in-Bay, but Cedar Point in Sandusky is no slouch either. To reach South Bass and Kelleys Islands you'll need to ride a ferry from the mainland, making a day trip impractical. Many businesses in the area are seasonal, so check before planning a stop.

SOUTH BASS ISLAND

Home to rowdy Put-in-Bay, South Bass Island often is described as the Key West of the North Coast. While downtown is indeed party central, the island can be extremely accommodating to families, especially during the week and away from downtown. But many come to South Bass precisely for the no-holds-barred party atmosphere, and they are rarely disappointed.

SIGHTS

If you enjoy the cold comfort of caves, consider a visit to Crystal Cave (978 Catawba Ave., 419/285-2811, www. heinemanswinery.com, tours daily early May-late Sept., adults $8, children $4), thought to be the world's largest geode. The 55°F chamber is lined with sky-blue celestite crystals, some sticking out a full foot and a half, and it feels like you're walking through the inside of a paperweight. Non-gemstone fans may not see what all the fuss is about, but crystal collectors might just call this place mecca. When the tour is through, visit the attached Heineman Winery, which has been making wine for over a century. Tours of the winery are offered, and wine and grape juice tastings are held in a picturesque garden.

Rising 352 feet above Lake Erie, Perry's Victory and International Peace Memorial (93 Delaware Ave., Put-in-Bay, 419/285-2184, www.nps.gov/pevi, 10am-6pm daily late Apr.-mid-Oct., limited or no hours the rest of the year, adults $7, children free) is a conspicuous landmark on the shoreline. Established in honor of those who fought in the Battle of Lake Erie during the War of 1812, from the top the monument offers visitors views of the islands, Michigan, and Ontario. The memorial is now a national park, and on weekends uniformed rangers do history demonstrations capped off by the firing of flintlock muskets.

Parents in search of a surefire way to occupy the kids should plan a visit to Perry's Cave Family Fun Center (979 Catawba Ave., 419/285-2283, www.perryscave.com, daily May-Sept., Sat.-Sun. Apr. and Oct.). This family entertainment center is jam-packed with enjoyable time-killers. Best among them is the War of 18 Holes miniature golf course ($5-8), which peppers kids with historical facts about the War of 1812 and

Commodore Perry along the way. The rather challenging course is surrounded by mature trees and winding (faux) streams. If you can differentiate between a swallowtail and a lacewing you might really enjoy the Butterfly House ($5-8). This 4,000-square-foot butterfly aviary houses more than 500 different varieties of exotic butterflies. For help identifying the species, tap the knowledge of the helpful staff. Kids can strap into a harness and tie onto a safety rope at the 25-foot climbing wall ($10). Varying degrees of difficulty ensure that even the most novice climber should be able to have some degree of success. Pan for gemstones at the Gemstone Mining Sluice (from $7), stop by the Antique Car Museum (free), or spelunk in Perry's Cave ($5-8): There is no shortage of low-impact fun at this place. Because each attraction is separately priced, the fees can quickly add up.

RESTAURANTS

Praised equally for its waterfront views and lobster bisque, the Boardwalk (341 Bayview Ave., 419/285-3695, www.the-boardwalk.com, noon-8pm daily Memorial Day-Labor Day, Sat.-Sun. Apr. and Oct., $6-25) is one of the most popular dining and entertainment spots on the island. Enjoy views of the harbor boat traffic from elevated decks. Meals are casual, affordable, and delicious, and include live Maine lobster, shrimp, and that island-famous bisque. Live music and dancing keep this joint jumping well into the night.

Frosty's Bar (252 Delaware Ave., 419/285-3278, www.frostys.com, 7am-1am daily Memorial Day-Labor Day, Sat.-Sun. Apr. and Oct., $8-19) is busy morning, noon, night, and late-night

thanks to a full slate of tasty offerings. Many island-hoppers start their day with eggs Benedict or a big plate of blueberry pancakes made with fresh fruit. Others start with a Bloody Mary to clear away the cobwebs. Frosty's pizza has been a Put-in-Bay staple for over 60 years.

Put-in-Bay is more famous for the drinks and depravity than good grub, but that doesn't mean you can't score a decent platter of fish. Goat Soup and Whiskey (820 Catawba Ave., 419/285-4628, www.soupandwhiskey.com, daily Memorial Day-Labor Day, $15-35) seems to validate the maxim that states the farther from the main strip you go, the better the food and service. A half mile from the harbor, the Goat is laid-back, family-friendly, and committed to putting out quality fare. Get the perch tacos—flour tortillas stuffed with fresh fried fish, cabbage slaw, and house-made taco sauce. Cocktails benefit from freshly squeezed fruit juices, a rarity in these parts.

NIGHTLIFE

Depending on what sort of crowds you can handle, the Beer Barrel Saloon (441 Catawba Ave., 419/285-7281, www.beerbarrelpib.com, mid-Apr.-Oct.) and the Roundhouse Bar (60 Delaware Ave., 419/285-2323, www.theroundhousebar.com, 11am-1am daily mid-Apr.-Oct.) are notorious nightspots. As such, they can be insufferably loud, crowded, and crass. But given the right time of day and proper frame of mind, they also can be riotously fun. Typically, weekend nights are the craziest times. Beer Barrel claims rights to the world's longest permanent bar, a commendable 400-footer that if placed on its end would best Perry's Memorial. Both bars play host to some of the finest island musicians, so check the schedules to see if Mike "Mad Dog" Adams or Pat Daily is on tap to play.

FESTIVALS AND EVENTS

Plan well ahead if you intend to visit South Bass Island for its popular Christmas in July weekend. Hotels, bed-and-breakfasts, and campgrounds fill up early and fast, and some ferry companies require proof of lodging before you can come aboard. But book in advance and you'll enjoy a wild weekend filled with Christmas-themed entertainment, anachronistic holiday decorations, and bachelorettes in Santa caps. Look for it in late July.

South Bass Island takes on a whole new charm come October, and many people elect to delay their visit until then so as to enjoy Put-in-Bay sans the crowds. Hence the popularity of mid-October's Island Oktoberfest, an annual smorgasbord of German food, drink, and entertainment, complete with beer halls and bratwurst.

RECREATION

There is little sense visiting the walleye capital of the world only to leave the fishing to everybody else. Get a group of five or six together and contact Put in Bay Charter Fishing Service (419/341-2805, www.putinbaycharterfishingservice.com) for a half or full day of chartered boat fishing. All you need to bring is cash, an Ohio fishing license, and a cooler full of snacks: Captain Bruce will handle the rest. Packages range $450-650 and include all bait, tackle, and equipment. Fish cleaning is extra. If you prefer to travel the waterways without a guide, call the folks at Put-in-Bay Watercraft (419/285-2628,

www.pibjetski.com) to rent fishing and powerboats, personal watercraft, and kayaks. They are located within South Bass Island State Park.

WHERE TO STAY

Host to one million visitors per year, South Bass Island has as many lodging options as there are tastes. From pitching a tent to renting a multi-room luxury cottage, the sleep of one's dreams is easy to land given a little advance planning.

Folks looking for a slower pace and quainter setting should book a night's stay at the Anchor Inn (500 Catawba Ave., 419/285-5055, www.anchorinnpib.com, $185-300). This 1917 bungalow-turned-boutique hotel boasts classic front-porch charm and gracious hospitality. Close to the action but far enough away to be peaceful, this romantic getaway is popular with couples, honeymooners, and mature travelers. Lovely gardens attract a multitude of migratory birds and provide a delightful spot for the day's included breakfast. This bed-and-breakfast has grown to include a dozen different accommodations, which range from simple guest rooms to suites with private baths. One has its own balcony overlooking the gardens.

Stay at the Grand Islander Hotel (432 Catawba Ave., 419/285-5555, www.putinbaygrandislander.com, $120-290) if you want a lively pool scene: Splash! is billed as the world's largest swim-up bar. The hotel also promises a pirate ship (with a bar) and an on-site Vegas-style nightclub (without gambling). Comfortable if not glamorous lodging is the order of the day, but most guests could care less where they pass out after a long night of fun. This festive complex is not exactly what one might call kid-friendly, though during the week things tend to be on the mild side.

Got a crowd? Book a suite at the Put-in-Bay Resort (439 Loraine Ave., 888/742-7829, www.putinbayresort. com, $125-950) and you and seven friends can sleep comfortably. This hotel's three-bed grand suite features a living room, kitchenette with refrigerator, wet bar, and private bath with bathtub. Rates range from $125 for a standard room up to $950 for a multiroom suite.

KELLEYS ISLAND

If South Bass Island is the Key West of the North Coast, then Kelleys Island is Sanibel. A slower pace and more nature-centric pursuits attract families looking for a true island getaway. Bird-watchers flock here in spring and fall to catch the migratory bird scene. Anglers and water-sports enthusiasts spend hours in and around the lake. Honeymooners and amorous couples hole up in romantic Victorian inns. The above is not meant to imply that Kelleys Island is a snooze; a party is always happening somewhere.

SIGHTS
Caddy Shack Square
In downtown Kelleys Island is Caddy Shack Square (115 Division St., www. caddyshacksquare.com), a complex with family entertainment, shopping, and food and drink. This is where folks can rent bikes and golf carts, play 18 holes of miniature golf, hit the arcade, or relax with a massage. If you're searching for a souvenir or gift, try the Booga Shack, which sells original island wear. No need to divulge what the Flip Flop Shop sells. Dessert fans swear by the hand-dipped cones

at Dipper Dan's Ice Cream Stand, while caffeine junkies line up for a fix at Taste by the Lake.

✪ Glacial Grooves
Trek to the northern tip of the island to see what effects a little ice can have on solid bedrock. Sometime near the tail end of the Pleistocene Ice Age, a massive glacial sheet rubbed its way across this stretch of North America, leaving behind an otherworldly landscape. These deeply etched Glacial Grooves (419/797-4530, dawn-dusk daily, free), some 10 feet deep, 35 feet wide, and 400 feet long, are striking illustrations of nature's potent force. The immediate area is fenced off, but a walkway takes visitors close to the action, which likely took place 18,000 years ago.

Kelleys Island State Park
While partiers flock to nearby South Bass Island, nature lovers gravitate to Kelleys. One of the major draws is Kelleys Island State Park (920 Division St., 419/797-4530, dawn-dusk daily, free), a 677-acre park in the north-central portion of the island. Six miles of hiking trails wind sightseers past scenic lake views and through beautiful nature preserves. Take the one-mile North Shore Loop trail to enjoy shoreline vistas, blooming wildflowers, and, in spring and fall, an anthology of migratory birds that use the island as a stopover point in their travels. Bring a towel and plop down at the sandy beach or drop a fishing line into the lake from a pier. Looking for something higher impact than pier fishing or birding? Contact Kelley's Island Kayak Rental (419/285-2628, www. kelleysisland.info) within the park to rent your own craft.

RESTAURANTS AND NIGHTLIFE

Enjoying a handcrafted microbrew on the shores of Lake Erie is hard to beat. Kelleys Island Brewery (504 W. Lakeshore Dr., 419/746-2314, www.kelleysislandbrewpub.com, daily in season, $10-19) brews great small-batch beer just yards from the water, and a pet-friendly patio means you don't have to enjoy a pint in solitude. Come here for a satisfying lunch of burgers, brats, and beer. For dessert, there are fantastic root beer floats and milk shakes. If you have an action-packed morning planned, call ahead to order the Wake and Bake, a pot of hot coffee and a half dozen muffins packed up to go with all the fixings.

More than just a restaurant, Kelley's Island Wine Co. (418 Woodford Rd., 419/746-2678, www.kelleysislandwineco.com, daily in season, $8-12) is a family-friendly entertainment destination. Set apart from downtown, the spacious location has room enough for volleyball courts, horseshoe pits, and plenty of alfresco dining. The wine, like most produced in the area, leans toward the sweet and rosy variety. But the straightforward food seems to be liked by all. Great pizzas, pastas, fish skewers, and steak are served by a gracious staff.

For some odd reason, the Brandy Alexander is the official drink of Kelleys Island, and the Village Pump (103 Lakeshore Dr., 419/746-2281, www.villagepumpkioh.com, daily Mar.-Dec., $9-26) is the official supplier. This historic building once housed a post office and then the town gas station (hence the name). On a prime summer weekend, this homey tavern might serve 3,000 hungry guests, an eclectic mix of locals, island-hoppers, and families.

Favorites here include textbook fried lake perch, home-style specials, and those addictive ice cream-infused Brandy Alexanders.

FESTIVALS AND EVENTS

South Bass has its wild Christmas in July, while Kelleys throws the more family-friendly Island Fest. The event kicks off with dancing, parades, and craft fairs and culminates with a rousing fireworks display. If you plan on visiting the island in mid-July when this popular weekend-long party takes place, you'll want to plan well ahead. In late July, the annual Kelleys Island Film Fest is a series of indoor and outdoor screenings. Information for both events can be found at the website for the Kelleys Island Chamber of Commerce (www.kelleysislandchamber.com).

WHERE TO STAY

Scenic Lakeshore Drive is sprinkled with attractive Victorian homes. Few are as graceful as A Water's Edge Retreat (827 E. Lakeshore Dr., 800/884-5143, www.watersedgeretreat.com, $200-280), a three-story beauty that houses a luxury bed-and-breakfast. The impeccable inn offers six suites with private baths and views of Lake Erie, Cedar Point, and Marblehead Lighthouse. Book a sailing trip on the owner's 35-foot yacht or just kick back with a glass of wine on the sweeping front porch. Prices include a gourmet hot breakfast, use of a bicycle, and a discount on golf-cart rentals.

Campers have it made on Kelleys Island. Kelleys Island State Park (920 Division St., 419/746-2546, $25-100) offers numerous shaded campsites, many with electric hookups. For something a little more out of the

Cedar Point Amusement Park

ordinary, put in a reservation for one of the park's yurts. These large circular canvas tents provide a nice middle ground between roughing it and luxury. Each has a kitchen, living area, and private bath.

MAINLAND

You don't have to hop a ferry to enjoy the mainland communities of Lakeside, Port Clinton, Marblehead, and Sandusky. Home to major tourist attractions and out-of-the-way finds, these seaside locales buzz all summer long with activity.

SIGHTS

African Safari Wildlife Park

We assume camels don't drive, but judging by the way these beasts of burden inspect automobiles at African Safari Wildlife Park (267 Lightner Rd., Port Clinton, 800/521-2660, www.africansafariwildlifepark. com, daily late May-early Nov., hours and admission vary), you'd swear they were in the market for a new

ride. This 100-acre wildlife preserve is a must-do adventure for families with children. During the drive-through portion of the park, animals literally poke their heads inside the car to snack on grain and carrots. Gentle zebras, alpacas, camels, and elands all approach the cars, absolutely thrilling the youngsters within. A walk-through portion has other animal-related activities, including pony and camel rides. Pig races are a popular daily diversion. Come to the park early, bring your own carrots (much cheaper than at the park), and leave the Ferrari at home—cars routinely endure bumps, occasional bruises, and plenty of slobber. Check the website for "carload" discounts.

✪ Cedar Point Amusement Park

Thanks in no small part to its collection of the tallest, fastest, steepest roller coasters, Cedar Point Amusement Park (1 Cedar Point Dr., Sandusky, 419/627-2350, www.cedarpoint.com, daily mid-May-Aug., Sat.-Sun. Sept.-Oct., $72 at gate, discounts available online, parking $15) is widely recognized as the world's best thrill park. Top Thrill Dragster zips to a speed of 120 miles per hour before climbing to a height of 420 feet. Steel Vengeance, introduced in 2018, is billed as the world's first steel-on-wood hybrid roller coaster to stand over 200 feet tall. GateKeeper is the tallest, fastest, and longest wing roller coaster in the world. Maverick is a mile-long ride through canyons, dark tunnels, and around embankments. Tamer children's rides, live entertainment, and food options abound at this massive 370-acre amusement park. To avoid the longest lines, try scheduling your visit between Sunday and Wednesday. It is helpful to know that rides do shut down due to rain, high winds, or lightning, and no, rain checks and refunds are not awarded. Next to Cedar Point is Cedar Point Shores Waterpark (daily late May-Aug., $39 adults, $26 children under 48 inches and seniors), an 18-acre water park with dozens of waterslides, a sizable wave pool, inner tube river rides, and sun-soaked spots for kicking back. Season passes, Ride & Slide tickets good for both Cedar Point and the waterpark, and AAA passes all can save considerable money on admission.

Kalahari Waterpark

One of three in the nation, the 880-room African-themed Kalahari Waterpark (7000 Kalahari Dr., Sandusky, 877/525-2427, www.kalahariresort.com, 10am-9pm Sun.-Thurs., 10am-10pm Fri.-Sat., $55-69) is Ohio's largest indoor/outdoor water and adventure park. Regardless of the weather outside, families can hit the beach all year long at this ginormous all-in-one entertainment complex. A FlowRider offers surfable waves every day; the Zip Coaster is a wet-and-wild roller coaster; and a 12,000-square-foot wave pool keeps the swells steady despite the tide. An equally enjoyable outdoor water park, open Memorial Day through Labor Day, adds a whole new dimension of fun come summertime. Hotel stays include admission to the parks.

Marblehead Lighthouse

The view from the top of Marblehead Lighthouse (110 Lighthouse Dr., Marblehead, 419/734-4424, www.marbleheadlighthouseohio.org, tours late May-mid-Oct., $3 to climb the tower, grounds free) includes Kelleys Island, South Bass Island, and the beautiful Sandusky Bay. This landmark lighthouse has guided sailors since 1822, making it the oldest continuously operated lighthouse on the Great Lakes. Selected for inclusion on a U.S. postage stamp, the classic form rises to a height of 65 feet and is one of the most photographed structures on the lake. The picturesque grounds also make a great location for a family picnic, as they are filled with scenic vistas, room to relax, and massive stones that kids can scramble up and over. An old lighthouse keeper's house now serves as a museum operated by the Marblehead Lighthouse Historical Society. It is open whenever the tower is open.

Thomas Edison's Birthplace

In 1841, Nancy Elliott Edison and Samuel Edison began building a house in Milan, Ohio, a small town on the Huron River. On February 11, 1847, Thomas Alva Edison was born in that very house. Today, the building is home to the **Edison Birthplace Museum** (9 N. Edison Dr., Milan, 419/499-2135, www.tomedison.org; tours 1pm-5pm Tues.-Sun. Apr.-May and Sept.-Oct., 10am-5pm Tues.-Sat., 1pm-5pm Sun. Jun.-Aug., 1pm-5pm Fri.-Sun. Nov.-Dec. and Feb.-Mar.; tours Feb.-Dec.; adults $9, seniors $8, children $5), a worthwhile destination for fans of the famous American inventor. As the only Edison site that has family involved, the museum holds a collection of rare Edisonia, including examples of early inventions, documents, and family mementos. Knowledgeable and passionate guides make the experience all the richer.

Thomas Edison's Birthplace

RESTAURANTS

Since 1987, **Chez Francois** (555 Main St., Vermillion, 440/967-0630, www.chezfrancois.com, 5pm-9pm Tues.-Thurs., 5pm-10pm Fri.-Sat., 4pm-9pm Sun. mid-Mar.-Dec., $40-50) has offered matchless French cuisine in a romantic post-and-beam structure. Classics like escargot, veal sweetbreads, and beef Wellington are freshened up by seasonal ingredients and matchless execution. The restaurant maintains a dress code (jackets for men, no flip-flops, etc.), but the more casual riverfront café serves the same food without the fuss. Pleasure boaters can tie up at the nearby **Vermilion**

Public Guest Docks (dockmaster 440/204-2474).

In an area festooned with fried-fish shacks, **Jolly Roger Seafood House** (1737 E. Perry St., Port Clinton, 419/732-3382, 11am-9pm Sun.-Thurs., 11am-10pm Fri.-Sat. mid-Feb.-late Nov., $8-15) stands out for its quality, consistency, and value. Baskets overflowing with fresh fried perch, walleye, onion rings, and hush puppies stream out of this busy little kitchen. As it should be, Jolly Roger is a no-frills operation, with disposable plates, plastic cutlery, and paper napkins.

Know going in that **Mon Ami** (3845 E. Wine Cellar Rd., Port Clinton, 800/777-4266, www.monamiwinery.com, daily, hours vary by season, $15-33) has changed considerably since its days as a quaint winery restaurant. This operation seems to grow each year, making it one of the busiest attractions in the region. Depending on the season, visitors can expect crowds of hungry day-trippers lining up for the popular all-you-can-eat buffet. Folks in search of peace, quiet, and romance would do well to pick out a spot in the dining room, while those looking for a party should make a beeline to the Chalet, a massive bar area with live entertainment. Mon Ami shines on warm summer nights as the food and party spill outdoors.

FESTIVALS AND EVENTS

Times Square has its fancy-schmancy LED-powered crystal ball. Port Clinton has a 20-foot-long, 600-pound fiberglass walleye named Wylie. Each New Year's Eve, the tiny town of Port Clinton doubles in size from 6,000 to 12,000 when enthusiastic crowds brave frigid temps to experience the **Walleye Drop** (Madison St. in downtown Port Clinton, www.walleyemadness.com).

Festivities begin at 3pm and climax at the stroke of midnight, when Wylie makes the plunge from his comically large rod and reel. Like a viral video clip, this event has been featured on David Letterman and NPR.

WHERE TO STAY

With the rugged good looks of a northwestern lumberjack, Great Wolf Lodge (4600 Milan Rd., Sandusky, 888/779-2327, www.greatwolflodge. com, $150-350) is a wilderness-themed resort and indoor water park. The 271-suite hotel is loaded with family-friendly attractions and activities. There are two casual restaurants, game arcades, a rock climbing wall, and a fitness center, not to mention one of the largest indoor water parks in the nation. In the summer, an outdoor pool joins the list.

If you want a short two-minute walk to Cedar Point and its neighboring water park, stay at the historic Hotel Breakers (1 Cedar Point Dr., Sandusky, 419/627-2350, www. cedarpoint.com, $150-350), Cedar Point's signature hotel. It was completely renovated in 2015. Following construction of a new tower, Hotel Breakers has a total of 669 rooms, making it one of the largest hotels on the Great Lakes. This beachside hotel is on Cedar Point Peninsula and features two outdoor pools, an indoor pool, and beach access. Prices can vary widely based on room size and location within the complex, so do your research before booking. Guests get to enter the amusement park an hour before the general public, making rollercoaster lines short and sweet.

Adults traveling without children might prefer to book a room at Hotel Kilbourne (223 W. Water St., Sandusky, 844/373-2223, www. hotelkilbourne.com, $220-280), a nine-room boutique hotel in downtown Sandusky. Each well-appointed urban suite has a king bed, comfy mattress, fine linens, spa-like bath, desk, mini-fridge, and free high-speed Wi-Fi. This hip hotel is home to a main floor pub and rooftop bar, both of which attract locals and travelers alike.

TRANSPORTATION AND SERVICES
TOURIST INFORMATION

For more information on Lake Erie's shores and islands, contact the Lake Erie Shores & Islands Welcome Center (419/625-2984, www. shoresandislands.com), which has two locations, one in Port Clinton (770 SE Catawba Rd., 419/734-4386, 8am-5pm Mon.-Fri. year-round, plus weekends Apr.-Aug.) and another in Sandusky (216 E. Water St., 419/625-2984 or 800/255-3743, 8am-5pm Mon.-Fri. Nov.-Apr., 8am-5pm Mon.-Fri., 9am-3pm Sat. May and Sept.-Aug., 8am-6pm Mon.-Fri. 9am-4pm Sat., 9am-2pm Sun. Jun.-Aug.).

GETTING THERE
Islands

If you've got your own boat, just punch 41° 39' 15" N, 82° 49' 15" W into your GPS to find Put-in-Bay; otherwise you'll need to hop a ferry. The Jet Express (800/245-1538, www. jet-express.com, $5-23 one-way) is the fastest way to the islands, but it is also the most expensive. The Jet Express hits ports in Port Clinton, Kelleys Island, Sandusky, Put-in-Bay, and Cedar Point. The Kelleys Island Ferry (510 W. Main St., 419/798-9763, www.kelleysislandferry.com, people $10, cars $16 one-way) shuttles people and cars back and forth between Marblehead and Kelleys Island. Miller

Boat Line (800/500-2421, www.millerferry.com, $7.50-10 one-way) operates a ferry between Catawba and South Bass Island and Middle Bass Island. Free overnight parking makes this option a great choice.

Regardless of which option you choose, make sure you are familiar with the ferry's return schedule before booking passage; some operate later than others.

Mainland

To get to Sandusky, Marblehead, and Port Clinton from Cleveland, simply take I-90 west to OH 2 west. Greyhound (www.greyhound.com) will drive you from Cleveland to Sandusky for about $25 with advance purchase.

GETTING AROUND

The preferred modes of transportation on Kelleys and South Bass Islands include golf carts, mopeds, bicycles, and feet. Wise visitors know to leave their cars on the mainland. To rent a golf cart on South Bass Island contact Delaware Carts (266 Delaware Ave., 419/285-2724, www.putinbayrentals.com), which rents four-, six-, and eight-person gas-powered carts by the hour, day, or week. Prices range $60-100 per day based on cart model and day of the week. For bicycles stop by Boathouse Cart and Bike Rental (194 Hartford Ave., 419/285-2113, www.boathousecartrental.com, $16 per day), which is conveniently located near the *Jet Express* or Miller Boat Line. They stock cruiser-style bicycles in three sizes as well as tandems.

On Kelleys Island, contact Caddy Shack Rentals (Caddy Shack Sq., 419/746-2518, www.caddyshacksquare.com, $15 for an all-day bike rental, $96 for an all-day cart rental) for a full range of bike and golf-cart rentals.

To move from South Bass Island to Kelleys Island and vice versa, contact *Jet Express* (800/245-1538, www.jet-express.com).

Amish Country

The world's largest Amish and Mennonite community resides in a five-county area of rural Ohio, and Holmes County is home to about half of them. A day or two spent exploring the scenic back roads of this lush and fertile landscape can be pure magic. Filled with blazing red barns, productive farms, and horse-drawn buggies, the scene is one visitors often cherish for a lifetime. Despite what you may have read or heard about the Amish, they are a warm, gentle community that welcomes visitors into their villages, shops, and even homes. They support themselves largely by crafting furniture, foodstuffs, and handicrafts that they sell to "English" folk like you and me. You can pick out the Amish and Mennonite homes by the presence of clotheslines and the absence of power lines connecting them to the main distribution lines. Make sure to explore the historic Main Streets of Millersburg, Berlin, and Charm. Autumn, when visitors are treated to the tail end of the harvest, colorful fall foliage, and cooler temps, is the busiest time in Amish Country. Most Amish businesses are also closed on Good

Friday, Thanksgiving, and Christmas. In Amish Country, Sunday is a day of rest and worship. Some stores, attractions, and restaurants are closed, but you can always find a place to eat or shop in Millersburg or Berlin.

It's wise to bring cash and a large cooler loaded with ice to stow spontaneous purchases from roadside stands. Dotting the landscape are makeshift markets that sell everything from fresh eggs and just-picked fruit to jars of golden honey. Often, the prices will be listed alongside a receptacle for cash; the honor system is alive and well in Amish Country.

SIGHTS
AMISH & MENNONITE HERITAGE CENTER

Your first stop in Amish Country should be the Amish & Mennonite Heritage Center (5798 County Rd. 77, Berlin, 877/858-4634, www.behalt. com, 9am-5pm Mon.-Sat. Mar.-Nov., 9:30am-4:30pm Mon.-Sat. Dec.-Feb.). Start with an informative tour or video on the local Amish and Mennonite community, then immerse yourself in *Behalt*, a 265-foot cyclorama, or cylindrical panoramic painting. Observers standing in the middle have a 360-degree view of the painting, which depicts the heritage of the Amish people from 1525 Zurich to the present day. This is a good place to stock up on area maps, brochures, and books about the Amish written by the Amish.

HERSHBERGER'S FARM AND BAKERY

If you're traveling with children (or simply love freshly baked goods) stop by Hershberger's Farm and Bakery (5452 OH 557, Millersburg, 330/674-6096, 10am-5pm Mon.-Sat. mid-Apr.-Oct.). This large, popular destination

features a market that sells local produce, freshly baked goods, and loads of pantry items. This is the place to load up on loaves of bread, cinnamon rolls, grape pie, maple syrup, honey, apple cider, canned pickled vegetables, dried egg noodles, and every conceivable flavor of jam and jelly. Outside, a stall sells hot kettle corn, a window dispenses ice cream treats, and a shop sells local hardware items. But the biggest attraction for the little ones is the barn, where a 3,000-pound Belgian draft horse resides alongside dozens and dozens of farm animals. Feed carrot chips to the horses, pigs, sheep, and goats, which climb to the roof to retrieve cones filled with grain that travel up a mechanical conveyor belt.

✪ KIDRON AUCTION

When farmers need to buy or sell farm animals, they visit their local livestock auction. Luckily for you, the experience is open to the public. The oldest and largest livestock auction in the state, the Kidron Auction (4885 Kidron Rd., Kidron, 330/857-2641, www.kidronauction.com, Thurs.) has been in operation since 1924, with weekly events since 1932. Farmers or the just plain curious are welcome to sit in and observe the lively action. The event opens with a hay and straw sale at 10:15am before moving on to dairy cattle, feed pigs, sheep, and goats. Get here early to grab a good seat in the selling ring; it fills up fast.

SCENIC DRIVES

One of the most enjoyable things to do in Amish Country is to take a leisurely drive on the many scenic back roads and byways that crisscross the area. It is here that you'll get the best glimpses of everyday life in one of the most beautiful and peaceful places on Earth.

NEGOTIATING AMISH BUGGIES

Holmes County is Amish Country, and this picturesque rural region looks, sounds, and smells different from any other place on Earth. The Amish believe in simplicity, hard work, and religion, and their old-fashioned customs are designed to foster strong family bonds. Because they eschew modern technologies like automobiles, the Amish travel by horse and buggy.

Almost every road in Holmes County is a designated National Scenic Byway, and motoring along these gorgeous country lanes is a true delight. But beauty quickly can turn to tragedy when a fast-moving car collides with a slow-moving buggy. Buggies travel at speeds of just five miles per hour and seemingly can appear out of nowhere. Drive slowly and cautiously at all times, but especially at night and when approaching a hill. And if you do approach a buggy, do not tailgate or honk, which can spook the horse. Simply pass by slowly, making sure to leave plenty of room between car and buggy. Keep in mind that it is considered disrespectful to stare, take photographs, or enter someone's private property.

OH 39 runs east and west through the heart of Amish Country. You can pick it up in Dover, which is exit 83 off of I-77 coming south from Cleveland. Working west you'll pass through the towns of Sugarcreek, Walnut Creek, Berlin, and Millersburg. Smaller side trips can include a short venture south on OH 557 to the aptly named village of Charm, north on OH 241 to Mt. Hope, and south on County Road 68 (also known as Port Washington Road) to Baltic.

BIKE TRAILS

Labeled as the first trail in the nation to accommodate both cyclists and Amish buggies, the scenic Holmes County Trail (www.holmestrail.org) runs for miles and miles, with a few gaps here and there. When completed, the Holmes County Trail will run the 29 miles between Fredericksburg and Killbuck, passing right through Millersburg. When it's combined with the nearby Mohican Valley Trail and Kokosing Gap Trail (complete with 370-foot-long covered bridge), a biker can cover some 50 miles of scenic trailway through America's heartland. You can download maps from the website.

TREE FROG CANOPY TOURS

Ohio's longest, fastest, and highest zipline tour is about nine miles south of Amish Country. More accurately, Tree Frog (21899 Wally Rd., 740/599-2662, www.treefrogcanopytours. com, 8am-5pm daily, $75) is a "canopy tour" because in addition to ziplines, the adventure includes suspension bridges and a few short rappels through the treetops.

YODER'S AMISH HOME

Eli and Gloria Yoder have made a living by sharing with outsiders the unique culture of their Amish past. They open their 116-acre Yoder's Amish Home (6050 OH 515, Millersburg, 330/893-2541, www.yodersamishhome.com, 10am-5pm Mon.-Sat. mid-Apr.-Oct., adults $13, children $9) to visitors and along the way convey interesting facts about the history and lifestyle of the Amish people. Tour a 130-year-old barn constructed in the old-fashioned peg-and-beam design. The barn is filled with bunnies, lambs, horses, and puppies. Prices include a ride around the farm in a horse-drawn buggy. Before you leave, load up on sweets from the bakery.

Amish buggy

RESTAURANTS

The granddaddy of Amish restaurants, **Amish Door** (1210 Winesburg St., Wilmot, 888/264-7436, www.amishdoor.com, 7am-8pm Mon.-Sat., $8-16), has been serving stick-to-your-ribs comfort food for more than 40 years. What began as a small eatery has ballooned into an entire complex, complete with dining, shopping, and lodging. Dinners are filling, fabulous, and wallet-friendly. The menu is loaded with Amish kitchen classics like meat loaf, roast turkey, and chopped steak. Folks travel miles out of their way to tuck into plates of "broasted" fried chicken. Dinners include salad bar, vegetable, real mashed potatoes with gravy, and stuffing. If that doesn't push you over the edge, stop by the amazing bakery on your way out this Amish door.

For traditional Swiss, Austrian, and Amish cuisine, hit **Chalet in the Valley** (5060 OH 557, Millersburg, 330/893-2550, www.chaletinthevalley.

com, 11am-8pm Tues.-Sat. mid-Mar.-Dec., $11-18). Run by the Guggisberg Cheese family, this cute and only moderately kitschy restaurant dishes up crispy veal and pork schnitzel, bratwurst and sauerkraut platters, and gently bubbling pots of fondue, all warmly served by dirndl-clad servers. Made with baby Swiss, Gruyère, and a hint of sherry, the fondue is rich, silky, and delicious. Across the street is the Guggisberg Cheese facility, where you can purchase cheese from the source.

For something a touch lighter and fresher, stop into **Olde World Bakery and Bistro** (4363 OH 39, Berlin, 330/893-1077, www.oldeworldbakeryandbistro.com, 8am-8pm Mon.-Sat., $6-8) for breakfast, lunch, dinner, or carry-out. In the morning, this quiet café dishes up egg platters, pancakes, French toast, and freshly baked pastries. At lunch and dinner, hot soups and crisp salads are joined by grilled chicken club sandwiches and burgers made from locally raised beef.

SHOPS

Calling themselves "the Grandma of bulk foods," the Ashery Country Store (8922 OH 241, Fredericksburg, 330/359-5615, www. asherycountrystore.com, 8am-5pm Mon.-Sat.) specializes in bulk sales of spices, nuts, candy, dried fruit, pasta, and baking supplies. This old-fashioned general store stocks more than 1,200 items, with a matchless inventory of spices, cheese, meats, and freshly baked goods. Home cooks and bakers used to high grocery-store prices will be in happy disbelief when they shop at the Ashery. You'll often see horse-drawn buggies tied up in the parking lot while their owners are inside shopping.

About two miles from downtown Berlin, in the picturesque Doughty Valley, Guggisberg Cheese (5060 OH 557, Millersburg, 800/262-2505, 8am-6pm Mon.-Sat., 11am-4pm Sun. Apr.-Oct., 8am-5pm Mon.-Sat. Nov.-Mar.) is home to the original baby Swiss. Founded by a cheese maker of Swiss origin, the factory and retail store stocks a vast array of dairy and meat products, plus imported Swiss cuckoo clocks. Buy a four-pound wheel of the cheese that made Guggisberg famous, or select others from the amazing variety of distinctive cheeses. On weekday mornings

Lehman's Hardware

visitors can peek through a window to watch cheese being made.

Concerned that the Amish community would begin to have trouble finding the nonelectric tools they needed to survive, in 1955 Jay Lehman founded Lehman's Hardware (1 Lehman Cir., Kidron, 330/857-5757, www.lehmans.com, 8am-5:30pm Mon.-Sat.). Of course, it isn't just the Amish who crave old-fashioned, high-quality nonelectric merchandise. Survivalists, environmentalists, victims of natural disasters, and nostalgia buffs all have needs that are satisfied by this amazing store. The rambling 32,000-square-foot facility is nirvana for tinkerers, gardeners, home cooks, and those who enjoy doing things the old-fashioned way. From oil lamps and soap-making supplies to wood stoves and beekeeping equipment, Lehman's has antiquated covered. Ironically, it is now the Amish themselves who are stocking the store with their high-quality handmade products.

WHERE TO STAY

Folks who relish the homey atmosphere of a bed-and-breakfast while enjoying the amenities of a contemporary hotel will appreciate the Barn Inn Bed & Breakfast (6838 County Rd., Millersburg, 877/674-7600, www. thebarninn.com, $150-250). Clean, comfortable, and gracious, the inn offers 11 well-appointed rooms, all with private entrances, private baths, and wireless Internet. Rooms also include a full country breakfast. The location is ideal for exploring Amish Country, and the innkeepers will be glad to provide guests with recommendations.

The modern 81-room Berlin Encore Hotel (4365 OH 39, Berlin, 888/988-2414, www.berlinencorehotel. com, $99-159) offers exceptional value, comfort, and amenities in the heart of Amish Country. A rustic, atrium-style lobby with comfortable seating, exposed beams, and fireplace welcomes visitors. Guest rooms and suites all are equipped with refrigerators, microwaves, coffeemakers, flat-screen TVs, and Wi-Fi. The hotel has an indoor swimming pool.

Set on a 70-acre farm overlooking scenic Holmes County, The Charm Countryview Inn (3334 OH 557, 330/893-3003, www.charmcountryviewinn.com, $109-149) is an ideal bed-and-breakfast option just a few miles from the aptly named village of Charm. All 15 guest rooms have private baths, queen-size beds, solid oak furniture, and handmade quilts. Home-cooked breakfasts, prepared by Amish and Mennonite cooks, are served family style.

Perched on a hilltop overlooking the beautiful Holmes County countryside, Holmes with a View (3672 Township Rd. 154, Millersburg, 877/831-2736, www.holmeswithaview.com, $128-260) truly does offer stellar vistas. Stacked into a trio of unique round buildings, six circular suites come fully equipped with kitchen, living, and dining areas, gas fireplace, whirlpool tub, and entertainment center. The location is close to many Amish Country sites, yet the inn is sheltered away in a quiet corner of the county.

The serene and stunning Inn and Spa at Honey Run (6920 County Rd. 203, Millersburg, 800/468-6639, www.innathoneyrun.com, $190-370) fits well into its attractive landscape. Surrounded by 70 natural acres, this private retreat offers wonderful accommodations. The Main Lodge has rooms with views of nearby bird feeders that attract a wealth of avian activity. In the unique earth-sheltered Honeycomb, guests stay in rooms carved into a hillside. Small families or couples looking for solitude will appreciate the cabins, which are tucked into the woods and feature a kitchen, living area with stone fireplace, and whirlpool tub.

TRANSPORTATION AND SERVICES
GUIDED TOURS AND MAPS

Why don't Amish wear mustaches? How can you tell if the Amish are married? Do they pay taxes, serve in the military, vote, or go to college? These are just a few of the questions answered by Amish Heartland Tours (330/893-3248, www.amishheartlandtours.com), a locally run company that dates back to 1993. They offer a wide range of informative and captivating excursions, from half-day trips to overnight adventures. Participants are granted entry into private Amish homes for dinner, taken for a ride in a horse-drawn buggy, or whisked away on a narrated drive through the back roads of Amish Country. This outfit will even custom design a multiday voyage, with all arrangements for lodging, meals, and attractions mapped out in advance.

The next best thing to a well-versed insider is a good map. When in Amish County, pick up a copy of the Amish Highways and Byways Map, which is available at most shops for around $4. (Or visit www.amishcountrymap.com to purchase and ship one in advance) This invaluable resource contains detailed maps of Holmes County, Millersburg, Berlin, Walnut Creek, and Sugarcreek, allowing tourists to get lost on out-of-the-way back roads without ever really getting lost.

TOURIST INFORMATION

There are some particularly helpful organizations and websites to give you a hand in planning your visit to Amish Country. Perhaps the best resource is the Holmes County Chamber of Commerce (877/643-8824, www. visitamishcountry.com). Their website is jammed with all sorts of wonderful info on area sights, shops, restaurants, hotels, and maps. While not an official tourism site, Experience Ohio Amish Country (www.experience-ohio-amish-country.com) is one of the best out there, especially when it comes to detailing the Amish way of life. It is written by passionate fans of the area.

GETTING THERE

Holmes County is about 80 miles south of Cleveland. There are any number of ways to get here, but the best combination of direct and scenic is to go south on I-77 until you hit Dover. From there you can travel west along scenic OH 39, which passes through the most visited villages and towns of Sugarcreek, Berlin, and Millersburg.

GETTING AROUND

While rural Holmes County has plenty of scenic country roads, it has zero interstate highways. Getting around requires a car or bike and a very good map. (GPS wouldn't hurt either.) Towns, attractions, and sights are spread apart by miles of farmland, making an automobile or motorcycle one's best bet for experiencing as much as possible.

BACKGROUND

The Landscape

GEOGRAPHY AND CLIMATE

City Hall

The dominant natural feature of Cleveland isn't land but water. Lake Erie, the southernmost of the Great Lakes, occupies a none-too-subtle position due north of the city. The lake's freshwater supports local industry, sustains sport fish populations, irrigates regional crops, flows through kitchen faucets, and falls as winter precipitation. Despite the importance and proximity of this sizable body of water, many Clevelanders largely ignore it. It isn't their fault: A shoreline freeway thwarts easy access, a municipal airport gobbles up prime real estate, and exclusive marinas snub the masses. But recent changes to infrastructure, like traffic easing on the West Shoreway, new pedestrian and bike tunnels under the roadway, and improved beach management at the hands of the Cleveland Metroparks, have provided a much more meaningful connection with the lake.

The city's second most defining physical feature is likely the Cuyahoga River, which slices through town, dividing Cleveland into two distinct and distinctive sides. To locals, east and west are not merely points on a compass, but rather lifelong labels affixed at birth. Here, you are either an East Sider or West Sider, and as such possess a certain set of stereotypical characteristics, accurate or otherwise. In the old days, it was rare for folks to venture from one side to the other, as odd as that sounds. These days, those traditions are as outdated as the aforementioned stereotypes.

LAKE ERIE MIRAGE EFFECT

Imagine standing on the banks of Lake Erie in Cleveland and suddenly the Canadian shore comes into perfect view, as though the 50-mile divide had been whittled down to one mile. A rare optical phenomenon known as the Lake Erie Mirage Effect can do just that, making buildings, cars, and even people seem like they are close enough to reach out and touch.

Mirages occur all the time. Whether it's the proverbial oasis in a desert or a shimmering highway on a sun-soaked day, the optical trickery is the result of light refracting as it passes through layers of variously heated air. But while highway mirages are an everyday occurrence, the Lake Erie Mirage is not. Still, there are numerous reports by people on both sides of the lake who have experienced this remarkable spectacle.

During an atmospheric inversion, cold dense air hovers near the lake's surface and warm air floats in layers above. As light travels through these layers, it refracts, or bends, acting like a magnifying lens that brings distant objects into clear view. So if you find yourself by the water's edge on a calm day, glance across the lake; you might just spot a Canadian flag.

Much fuss has been made of Cleveland's weather, but apart from the six months of winter (kidding), the region possesses a fairly typical continental climate. Spring can provide a loathsome late-season snowfall before warming up to a seasonable 70 degrees by June. Summers are hot, occasionally humid, and punctuated by spectacular thunderstorms. Don't worry—they pass through briskly, leaving cooler, clearer, and drier weather in their wake. Fall is Cleveland's most cherished season, boasting warm, dry days, crisp, cool evenings, and a backdrop of luminous fall foliage. In Northeast Ohio, smart brides skip the June wedding in favor of early October. Winters start slower around here than in other parts of the Midwest thanks to the lake, with its accumulated warmth acting as a sort of down blanket. Cleveland's impressive snow totals can be blamed—or credited, depending on one's point of view—on a phenomenon known as the lake effect. As cold arctic air passes over the relatively warm lake water, it picks up evaporated moisture and dumps it as shovelfuls of snow on area driveways. The largest snow accumulations occur well south and east of downtown in an area appropriately dubbed the Snow Belt, but rare are the occasions when road crews don't immediately clear it from the streets.

ENVIRONMENTAL ISSUES

In many ways, the environmental challenges faced by Cleveland and Cuyahoga County mirror those found elsewhere in the nation. Unchecked urban sprawl has seen the creation of numerous exurban communities, along with the requisite big-box shopping centers, all at the expense of once-fertile farmland. What do we have to show for all that progress? How about lengthy commutes, increased air pollution, and deteriorating inner-ring neighborhoods and infrastructure. Add to that Cleveland's proximity to coal-fired power plants, soot and sulfur dioxide-spewing steel mills, and other heavy industry and you get a city with elevated levels of ozone and particle pollution.

But the news is not all bad. Ambitious downtown development projects and a renewed interest in urban living show promise in stemming the outward migration and already are bringing thousands of new residents into the city center. Better still, many of these new structures are taking advantage of ecoconscious green-building techniques. The recently completed $200 million HealthLine links Public Square and University Circle, Cleveland's two most dynamic employment centers, with a shiny fleet of environmentally friendly hybrid-electric buses. Bike lanes allow nearby commuters to pedal to work. And a recent national study recognized Cleveland as one of the country's most walkable cities, with special nods to the neighborhoods of downtown, Ohio City, Tremont, and Detroit Shoreway.

Cleveland was the butt of innumerable jokes when, in 1969, the Cuyahoga River burst into flames thanks to layers of oily industrial runoff. That shameful fire brought national attention to environmental issues everywhere, eventually leading to the passage of the Clean Water Act. While nobody

dips their canteen into the Cuyahoga, wastewater treatment improvements have brought the river within accepted water-quality standards, and it's not uncommon to spot snapping turtles, great blue herons, and red-tailed hawks along the banks. Lake Erie, once a pea-green cesspool of runoff and decay, is far cleaner, clearer, and teeming with sport fish. There are still water-quality issues, and swimmers are cautioned to keep apprised of no-swim advisories at area beaches (check www.ohionowcast.info), but even those appear to be decreasing from year to year.

Best of all, perhaps, is a 2008 study that recorded wind speeds off Lake Erie's shoreline as well above those necessary to support energy-producing turbines. Such promising reports could very well translate into jobs, clean energy, and a progressive new image for Cleveland.

History

Long before there were the Cleveland Indians there were Indians in Cleveland. The area's first settlers, members of various Native American tribes, gave the twisty-turny Cuyahoga River its name: *Cuyahoga* is the Indian word for "crooked river." In 1796, Moses Cleaveland departed his vessel at the mouth of that very river to begin surveying the Western Reserve, a three-million-acre tract of land governed by Connecticut. In the process, he established the city that would become the territory's capital. Cleaveland became Cleveland, anecdotal lore will have one believe, when the village newspaper dropped the "a"

in order to squeeze the name onto the paper's masthead.

The swampy flats on either side of the Cuyahoga River, which served as a trading post and pioneer hangout, soon became the epicenter of commerce and industry. It was on the banks of this river that Cleveland generated its fortunes, with steel mills, shipyards, oil refineries, breweries, and assembly plants springing up like shiitakes. The Ohio & Erie Canal opened up Cleveland and the interior of Ohio to the Ohio River and points east and south, providing a massive new market for its goods. The rapidly developing city was the first to employ electric streetlights, streetcars, and traffic signals. Cleveland was the site of the first automobile sale and offered free home mail delivery before any other U.S. city.

John D. Rockefeller, "the richest man in America," transformed the Flats into the nation's oil capital. By the late 1800s, Standard Oil controlled most of the nation's refining capacity. Rockefeller's unlawful monopoly was broken up soon after the turn of the 20th century, but his largesse lives on in named buildings and parks, and through generous donations and endowments.

By 1920, Cleveland was the nation's fifth-largest city. That same year the Cleveland Indians defeated the Brooklyn Dodgers to win the World Series, no doubt helped along by the first unassisted triple play in a world championship game. Despite the nationwide Depression, Cleveland, for two summers in 1936 and 1937, hosted the elaborate Great Lakes Exposition. Similar in size and scope to a World's Fair, the event saw the construction of 200 art deco-style buildings stretching from Public Square to the lakefront. Literally millions of people traveled from far and wide to experience exotic cultures, theatrical performances, and spectacular attractions. Billy Rose's Aquacade was a floating extravaganza filled with singers, dancers, and swimmers, including Olympic gold medalist Johnny Weissmuller. General Electric debuted the nation's first 50,000-watt light bulb, a glowing achievement to be sure.

Following its peak in 1950, Cleveland's population began a slow and steady decline. Industrial production waned, white residents fled the city for neighboring suburbs, and the once-mighty Flats conflagrated into a national disgrace. Racial unrest visited many U.S. cities in the 1960s, and Cleveland was not immune. For six days in 1966, the 20-block neighborhood of Hough was the scene of fires, gunplay, and looting. When all was said and done, four were dead and another two dozen severely injured. Just one year later, however, Carl Stokes was elected as the first black mayor of a major U.S. city. His victory made the cover of *Time* magazine.

Cleveland's darkest days, perhaps, were in the late 1970s, when it became the first major U.S. city since the Depression to default on its financial obligations. Yet, by the bicentennial celebrations of 1996, the "Mistake on the Lake" had begun its transformation into "The New American City." Ambitious new downtown projects saw the construction of three new professional sports venues, a state-of-the-art science center, and the Rock and Roll Hall of Fame. The Flats were reborn, this time as a nationally recognized adult playground with nightclubs, restaurants, and brewpubs. Offering more than just something to do on a weekend, this compilation of civic triumphs buoyed the spirit of an entire city, signaling brighter days ahead. Some were even calling it a renaissance.

Present-day Cleveland is enjoying some of its brightest days yet. More people are living downtown than at any time in recent history. By the end of 2018, that number is estimated to approach 18,000, an increase of nearly 80 percent from 2000. A steady 98 percent occupancy rate for an apartment or condo has translated into $4.5 billion in new residential and commercial development. Buildings long home to commercial tenants are being bought, emptied, transformed, and reintroduced as residential. Snatching up all those shiny-new spots, often at the tail end of a months-long waiting list, are millennials and baby boomers.

THE MAD BUTCHER OF KINGSBURY RUN

When two boys playing in the Kingsbury Run area of Cleveland stumbled across a decapitated body, it was the beginning of a citywide reign of terror that would last for years. What police discovered when they arrived on the scene was not one but two decapitated bodies.

It was September of 1935, and over the next three years a dozen other victims would turn up, all decapitated and most dismembered. The Mad Butcher of Kingsbury Run, as he would soon be called, was one of the most depraved serial killers in our nation's history. Officially, the case has never been solved, despite having Eliot Ness in charge of the investigation.

When Ness accepted the job of Cleveland Safety Director, he intended to focus on greed, corruption, and fraud. But soon, the lawman found himself in charge of quelling one of the most heinous killing sprees in history. He personally interviewed witnesses, placed 20 of his best officers on the case, and rounded up every bum in Kingsbury Run for questioning.

Because the heads and hands were removed from the bodies, identifying the victims was nearly impossible. Many remain nameless to this day. In an attempt to identify one of the last victims, Ness ordered a plaster cast to be made of the severed head. This "death mask" was then displayed during the 1936 Great Lakes Exposition, a Cleveland-based World's Fair that attracted four million visitors in a single summer. Nobody recognized the face. This mask and three others are on display at the Cleveland Police Museum.

As a profile emerged, it was believed police were looking for a killer with a firm grasp of anatomy and a private place to perform the messy business. Butchers, hunters, and even doctors were considered likely suspects. But an almost complete lack of clues made finding the suspect extremely challenging.

Attention soon turned to Dr. Frank Sweeney, a big, strapping man who grew up in the Kingsbury Run area and had an alcohol problem. Despite overwhelming confidence that Sweeney was the killer, a lack of direct evidence prevented a conviction. Two days after he was interrogated, Sweeney voluntarily admitted himself to a hospital. The murder spree stopped at the same time.

Government and Economy

GOVERNMENT

Cleveland is the county seat of Cuyahoga County, Ohio's most populous county as of the last census, with almost 1.3 million residents. The historically progressive district has voted Democrat in all but one presidential election since the 1960s. Despite a record 227,000-vote advantage over President George W. Bush in the 2004 election, John Kerry went on to lose the state of Ohio and thus his bid for the White House. Much to the dismay of many local residents, Cleveland hosted the Republican National Convention in 2016. In that year's presidential election, Hillary Clinton carried 65.8 percent of the vote in the county to Trump's 30.8 percent, but, of course, Ohio as a whole went in another direction.

For decades, Cuyahoga County had been governed by a three-member board of county commissioners. But after a years-long FBI probe uncovered massive county corruption and landed numerous politicians and business leaders in jail, county residents voted in 2009 to abolish the commissioner system in favor of a charter government with an elected county executive and an 11-member county council. Because of the council's greater transparency and accountability, people once again have confidence in their elected officials.

When it comes to city government, Cleveland has been under the administration of Mayor Frank Jackson since 2006. The city operates under the strong-mayor form of government, with Jackson sharing power with a 17-person city council.

ECONOMY

Despite its Rust Belt roots, the region is fast becoming a hotbed of high-tech activity in the areas of health care, bioscience, information and health-care technology, and alternative energy solutions. While overall employment in manufacturing has naturally taken a hit, the industry still accounts for about a fifth of the jobs in the region. But these days, in addition to rolling out steel, rubber, and automobile parts, area factories are beginning to focus on next-gen polymers, innovative medical devices, and tomorrow's fuel cell components. In the latest reports, the unemployment rate in metro Cleveland is falling and the city is on its way to returning to pre-Recession employment levels.

Spurred on by initiatives like the Third Frontier project, a 10-year $1.6 billion cash infusion; grants from the Cleveland Foundation, one of the country's most generous philanthropic organizations; and JumpStart, a business accelerator, area institutions continue to expand and spin off new start-ups. Greater Cleveland companies collectively attracted more than $2 billion in health-care venture capital alone over the past decade. Technology leaders like NASA Glenn Research Center, Case Western Reserve University, Cleveland State University, and Parker Hannifin are helping to cultivate a "green-collar" workforce centered on the field of renewable energy. The state is poised to become a leader in fuel cells, biofuels, and wind-turbine-component manufacturing.

HEALTH CARE AND EDUCATION

Cleveland is home to top hospitals, medical schools, and universities, such as the Cleveland Clinic, Case Western Reserve University, and University Hospitals, and it appears that health care is becoming the economic engine of this ship. The epicenter of this activity is University Circle, which is often called the city's "second downtown." In approximately one square mile are numerous cultural, educational, and medical institutions. The district is the second-largest employment center in Cleveland. Each day, approximately 42,000 people go to work at 50 or so organizations, pulling down a collective $850 million per year. An estimated $1.3 billion worth of development projects are on the way or in the planning phase.

In addition to being among the most respected health-care facilities in the world, the Cleveland Clinic is an economic powerhouse, with revenues topping $4 billion annually. The immense hospital system employs 52,000 people, making it Ohio's second-largest private employer. It even maintains its own police force. The clinic continues to expand its Midtown footprint, steadily replacing deserted brownfields and neglected warehouses with new medical buildings and parking garages. Built at a cost of over $600 million, the Miller Family Pavilion and the adjacent Glickman Tower are just a few of the latest additions to the sprawling campus. In 2017, the seven-story, glass-clad Taussig Cancer

Center came online at a cost of $275 million. Meanwhile, on the main campus of nearby University Hospitals, the 375,000-square-foot Seidman Cancer Center opened in spring 2011.

Thanks in no small part to the presence of these educational and medical powerhouses, the nearby Cleveland Health-Tech Corridor and surrounding region is attracting more bioscience deals than almost any city in the Midwest. This robust grouping of biomedical, health-care and technology companies is helping to propel the entire region's economy in ways city founders never could have imagined.

LEGAL
Home to the founding offices of Jones Day, Squire, Sanders & Dempsey, Baker Hostetler, and Thompson Hine, among other firms, Cleveland has long been a legal powerhouse. There are over 10,000 registered attorneys in Greater Cleveland, giving the region a lawyer density on par with Chicago, Atlanta, and New York. The legal profession is one of the city's largest employment sectors, following closely behind health care and education.

BANKING AND FINANCE
Up until the recent economic meltdown, Cleveland was home to two of this nation's biggest banks, National City and KeyCorp. Early advances in steel, oil, and auto industries, coupled with favorable banking laws, turned Cleveland into a major financial center. Banking and finance still play a major role in the local economy, with one of the country's 12 Federal Reserve Banks, plus sizable offices for money giants JPMorgan Chase and Fifth Third, calling Cleveland home.

FORTUNE 500
Northeast Ohio is home to a number of Fortune 500 companies, including Progressive Insurance, Goodyear Tire, Eaton Corporation, Sherwin-Williams, KeyCorp, Parker-Hannifin, TravelCenters of America, and American Greetings.

TRAVEL AND TOURISM
In 2016, Cuyahoga County welcomed a record 18 million visitors to its region, a figure that continues to creep up year after year. High-profile events such as the MLB World Series, NBA Finals, and Republican National Convention have introduced this great city to an ever-broader audience. Locally, the travel and tourism sector accounts for 61,000 jobs.

EUCLID CORRIDOR PROJECT
Greater Cleveland Regional Transit Authority's $200 million bus-rapid-transit project saw the rehabilitation of seven miles of Euclid Avenue, paving the way for speedy transport service along dedicated bus lanes between Public Square and University Circle. According to some estimates, close to $6 billion is being invested along the refurbished HealthLine route. Piggybacking off those sporty new buses, streetscapes, and transit stations are renovated apartment buildings, fashionable restaurants, and fresh tech start-ups. Ever-expanding Cleveland State University, which is bisected by Euclid Avenue, is spending $300 million alone on new academic buildings and student housing.

LOOKING AHEAD

Water helped make Cleveland an industrial powerhouse decades ago, and it may play an even more important role in the city's economic future. While Southern and Southwestern U.S. cities are battling over access to freshwater, Ohio, along with seven other U.S. states and two Canadian provinces, signed the Great Lakes Compact in 2008. The Great Lakes-St. Lawrence River Basin Water Resources Compact was then signed into federal law, preventing thirsty outsiders from diverting water from the Great Lakes, the largest source of freshwater outside the polar ice caps. As freshwater becomes an increasingly sought-after resource, one necessary for business and development, not to mention that thing called life, some foretell a reverse migration back to Midwestern cities with access to that water.

Local Culture

Roughly equidistant from Chicago and New York City, Cleveland is described as the point where the East Coast meets the Midwest. The city is close enough to the heartland to reap the hospitable sensibilities of that region—hence the saying: "Winters here may be harsh, but never the people." Quick jaunts to the Big Apple are easy as pie, creating locally a demand for the same products, fashions, restaurants, and nightlife enjoyed out of town. Cleveland's best-of-both-worlds situation translates to hurried commuters, dressed to the nines, stopping to point a misguided soul in the right direction.

If any word accurately describes the people of Greater Cleveland, it is diverse. After the initial settling of transplanted British colonists, Cleveland enjoyed numerous waves of ethnic-specific immigration. By the late 1800s, a full 10 percent of the population was Irish. Most lived in Ohio City and worked at the docks unloading cargo. A comparatively larger contingent of German immigrants followed, some coming from as near as Pennsylvania, others straight from the motherland. Other significant migrations included large contingents of Italians, Russians, Jews, Slovenians, Slovakians, Poles, Hungarians, and Ukrainians. Much later, the city welcomed Asian immigrants, specifically Chinese, Korean, and Vietnamese, but also Thai, Laotian, and Indian. Hispanics came in equally impressive numbers too. Walk into the West Side Market on a busy Saturday morning and you might be able to pick out a dozen different languages.

Cleveland's present-day population is just under a half million, down about 8 percent from the late 1990s. The city suffered its biggest losses in the 1970s, when almost 25 percent of its residents fled town, many simply relocating to suburban environs. Today, the five-county Greater Cleveland area contains well over two million people, making it one of the most densely populated regions in the country.

There are signs that this outward migration may slow, even reverse, in the coming years. Massive new investment in University Circle-area hospitals, spurred by a surging knowledge economy and coupled with a boom of downtown residential projects, shows promise in stemming the tide.

THE ARTS

Cleveland has always been a leader in the cultural arts. Its impressive collection of world-class institutions would be a boon for a city of any size, let alone one of only a half million. Supported by a long-standing tradition of generous arts philanthropy, the city's theaters, museums, music ensembles, dance companies, and independent galleries enjoy a relatively strong footing despite rocky economic times.

For more than 100 years, the Cleveland Museum of Art has been regarded as one of the finest repositories of visual art in the world. Generous donations and a sizable endowment made possible an eight-year, $350 million expansion and renovation completed in 2013. For just as long, the Cleveland Orchestra—"the Best Band in the Land," according to *Time* in 1994—has regaled listeners from its majestic perch in Severance Hall. Established in the same era, the Cleveland Play House was the nation's first professional theater company. Playhouse Square is the second-largest arts district in the country, bested only by New York's Lincoln Center. All five of the district's 1920s-era theaters have been carefully restored.

University Circle, just one square mile, contains the country's greatest concentration of cultural and educational institutions. In addition to Severance Hall and the Cleveland Museum of Art, the dense enclave is home to the Cleveland Botanical Garden, Western Reserve Historical Society, Cleveland Museum of Natural History, Cleveland Institute of Music, Cleveland Institute of Art, and the Children's Museum of Cleveland. The Museum of Contemporary Art opened its multimillion-dollar showcase for cutting-edge art there in 2013. Many of these institutions are enjoying financial support thanks to a voter-backed cigarette tax, with 1.5 cents per cigarette going to numerous arts and cultural organizations.

The Cleveland International Film Fest is a 12-day event featuring more than 200 films and 165 shorts from 60 countries. As many as 100,000 viewers attend screenings at Tower City Cinemas. The IngenuityFest returns annually with a weekend-long celebration of art and technology, filling the lakeshore with live and interactive exhibits in visual art, music, dance, and video.

Art has and continues to be a driving force in the resurrection of urban neighborhoods. Tremont is buoyed by a vast array of independent galleries, studios, and boutiques, and its monthly art walks keep the area's shops, restaurants, and bars hopping year-round. Little Italy has carved a sort of double-sided niche for itself, with art and food sharing equal billing. Detroit Shoreway can credit theater as one the main drivers of its present-day success.

Cleveland has music in its blood, plain and simple. The "Rock and Roll Capital of the World" loves its live music, and countless clubs around town regularly attract yesterday's, today's, and tomorrow's

CLEVELAND SPORTS: HOPE AND HEARTACHE

Year after year, die-hard Cleveland sports fans pin their hopes and dreams on a championship run only to have their hearts torn asunder by a last-minute calamity. And those are the good years; most leave no hope for a championship run whatsoever. For what seemed like an eternity, this sports-loving town had endured one of the longest championship droughts when it came to its three professional sports teams, stretching back to 1964, when the Browns won a pre-Super Bowl ring.

Ask locals about "The Drive," "The Fumble," "The Shot," or "The Decision" and watch as their faces sag into a familiar contortion of woe. These phrases might sound like simple game plays, but in truth they represent the heartbreaking moments that forever scarred generations of Clevelanders.

All the 1987 Browns had to do to reach the Super Bowl was prevent John Elway and the Denver Broncos from scoring all the way from their own two-yard line with a little over five minutes left to play in the game. Instead, Elway managed to march his team in a 15-play drive all the way to the end zone to send the game into overtime. We know what happened then.

Against all odds, the Browns managed to make it back to the AFC Championship Game the following season, only to face off against the Denver Broncos. With less than two minutes to play in the game, Cleveland needed a touchdown to tie the game. No problem, since they drove the ball all the way down to the eight-yard line. Bernie Kosar's handoff to Ernest Byner was clean, and it looked like the running back would take the ball in for a game-tying touchdown. Instead, he fumbled the ball on the goal line; Denver recovered it and went on to win the game.

Starring in "The Shot" was basketball superstar Michael Jordan. In Game 5 of the NBA Playoffs, Cleveland led the Chicago Bulls by one point. The series was tied 2-2, so whichever team won the game moved on to the semifinals. With just 3.2 seconds left in the game, the ball was inbounded to Jordan for one quick shot. He made it, clinching both the game and the series.

On July 8, 2010, during a live public broadcast dubbed *The Decision*, LeBron James famously told the breathless world that he was "taking my talents to South Beach," dashing all hopes for a Cavs championship anytime soon.

While lacking a catchy tagline, the Indians' 1997 loss to the Florida Marlins in the 11th inning of the seventh game of the World Series ranks up there with the saddest moments in Cleveland sports. Others include blowing a 3-1 lead over the Boston Red Sox in the 2007 ALCS, losing to the Oakland Raiders in the 1981 AFC Playoff Game, and the Cavs getting swept by the San Antonio Spurs in their first-ever NBA Finals appearance in 2007.

But then fortunes began to shift. In 2014, LeBron James announced to the world that he would be "coming home" after four seasons with the Miami Heat. Under his lead, the team advanced to three consecutive Finals appearances and, in 2016, became the first team to overcome a 3-1 deficit to win the championship.

As for the Indians, the team clinched the Central Division, claimed their sixth American League pennant, and advanced to the 2016 World Series, thanks in large part to skipper Terry Francona. In what will forever be regarded as one of the greatest Series ever played, the Chicago Cubs edged out the Indians in a 10-inning Game 7 to win the Commissioner's Trophy.

You'd think the recent successes of the Cavs and Indians would be a salve for long-suffering sports fans, but all residents seem to focus on is LeBron James's decision to call it quits again, this time taking his talents to Los Angeles. And then there are the Cleveland Browns, who provide a bottomless well of despair. After decades of heartache, you'd expect Cleveland sports fans simply to abandon hope. But that's not the case. After a few weeks of inconsolable crying, fans here stand up, brush it off, and say, "Wait till next year."

hottest acts. Meanwhile, the Rock and Roll Hall of Fame attracts everybody else, with millions flocking to the museum to take a stroll down musical memory lane.

All of these quality-of-life amenities combine to create a city that is vibrant, relevant, intelligent, and fun, which is one of the reasons Cleveland regularly finds itself near the top of lists ranking livability, literacy, and places to raise a family.

ESSENTIALS

Transportation

GETTING THERE

Cleveland is serviced by a major international airport, a Greyhound bus terminal, an Amtrak station, numerous interstate highways, and a turnpike, making travel to and from the city a relative breeze.

AIR

Superior Bridge at night

Cleveland Hopkins International Airport (CLE, 216/781-6411, www.clevelandairport.com) is the largest commercial airport in Ohio, serving around nine million passengers annually. Most major airlines and regional jets operate into and out of the airport. CLE is a major hub for United Airlines (800/864-8331, www.united.com), often making that airline the best and most afford-able option. Other major carriers include Delta (800/221-1212, www.delta.com) and Southwest (800/435-9792, www.southwest.com).

CLE offers more than 160 daily nonstop flights to more than 50 destinations, with direct international service to cities in Canada, Jamaica, Mexico, Iceland, and the Dominican Republic. The busiest times at the airport are 6am-7:30am and 4:30-6:30pm. Parking is available 24 hours a day, 365 days a year in short- and long-term garages.

Ground transportation to downtown Cleveland is cheap, easy, and efficient thanks to a light-rail service that transports passengers from an airport train station directly to Public Square. The Greater Cleveland Regional Transit

Authority (216/566-5100, www. riderta.com) Red Line operates daily roughly every 15 or 20 minutes from 4am until 1am. The train costs $2.50 for the one-way trip and takes approximately 25 minutes to travel from the airport to downtown.

To hail a cab, travelers need to make their way to the taxi stand located at the southern end of the lower-level baggage claim area. The journey to town takes between 20 and 30 minutes and costs approximately $40. Most area hotels offer complimentary shuttle service to and from the airport, and like the taxicabs, the shuttles are accessed on the lower-level baggage claim area. Call your hotel from the lower-level courtesy phones to verify service times.

A dedicated ride share pickup is located in the Ground Transportation Center, which is midway between the terminal and Smart Parking Garage. Follow the signs for ride share from the baggage-claim-level welcome center. All Uber and Lyft drivers will meet you there.

CAR

Those traveling by car from the south will enter Cleveland via either I-71 or I-77. Those traveling from the east or west will approach the city via I-90. The trip from Columbus clocks in at around 2.5 hours; the trip from Chicago can be completed in just over five; those traveling from Pittsburgh should expect to land in C-Town in just over two hours; while Detroiters can look forward to a 2.5-hour journey.

TRAIN

Cleveland is serviced by Amtrak (200 Cleveland Memorial Shoreway, 216/696-5115, www.amtrak.com),

but arrival and departure times are anything but convenient. The *Capitol Limited* runs daily between Washington DC and Chicago, stopping in Cleveland around 3am. The *Lake Shore Limited* travels daily between Chicago and New York City, stopping in Cleveland around 6am.

BUS

Travelers can leave the driving to Greyhound by visiting what once was a flagship hub for the bus line. Built in 1948, the Greyhound terminal (1465 Chester Ave., 216/781-0520, www.greyhound.com) is one of the finest examples of Streamline Moderne design in the nation. The terminal is conveniently located downtown and is accessible by foot, car, and cab from most area hotels. Megabus (www.megabus.com), the low-cost express bus service, now shuttles travelers between Cleveland and cities such as Columbus, Cincinnati, Chicago, Detroit, Buffalo, and Erie, Pennsylvania.

GETTING AROUND
PUBLIC TRANSPORTATION

The Greater Cleveland Regional Transit Authority (216/566-5100, www.riderta.com), known locally as the RTA, operates buses, light-rail, community circulators, and downtown trolleys throughout Greater Cleveland. Fares are $2.50 for buses and trains, with one-day and seven-day passes available for $5.50 and $25 respectively. Free downtown trolleys run every 10 or 15 minutes seven days a week until 7pm or 11pm, depending on the line. Four rail lines make up the Rapid Transit System. With Tower City as the hub, lines take riders as far west as Cleveland Hopkins International Airport, north to the lakefront and North Coast Harbor, and east to East Cleveland and Shaker Heights. Fares on trains are typically paid when entering or exiting at Tower City station.

All of RTA's buses are equipped with external bike racks. To use the service, riders should visually signal the bus driver before loading his or her bike onto the rack. Additionally, bikes are permitted on all RTA trains at all times. Just cautiously roll your bike onto the train and stand with it. In 2007, RTA was named by the American Public Transportation Association as North America's Best Public Transportation System.

Completed in the fall of 2008, RTA's HealthLine, a bus-rapid-transit system, offers quick and efficient service between Public Square and University Circle, with stops in between, on electric-hybrid buses.

DRIVING

To take advantage of most of the attractions and activities in this book, a comfortable pair of shoes and access to the RTA are all that is required. The trains quickly and safely move people between the airport, downtown, and University Circle, and the city center isn't so large that walking between destinations is a marathon. Toss in some inclement weather, however, and those leisurely strolls can become rather unpleasant. When weather or distance prevents walking or riding, a car might come in handy. If renting one, make your life easy and spring for GPS; Cleveland's East Side contains a healthy number of roundabouts that often confuse drivers. For those drivers with AAA memberships, emergency roadside assistance is available 24 hours a day, seven days a week by calling 800/222-4357.

CAR RENTAL

Naturally, Cleveland Hopkins International Airport hosts a full lineup of national car-rental agencies. While agents are located in the airport, the rental-car agencies are off the airport grounds. Nonstop shuttle service transports rental-car customers from the baggage claim level of the main terminal to the rental-car facilities. As for downtown rental agencies, consider contacting Budget (1717 E. 9th St., 216/696-7133, www.budget. com), Avis (1717 E. 9th St., 216/696-1568, www.avis.com), Hertz (1701 E. 12th St., 216/685-1790, www.hertz. com), or Enterprise (1802 Superior Ave. E., 216/696-7500, www.enterprise.com).

PARKING

There is no shortage of parking lots and garages to take your money in return for a small patch of concrete. For a good interactive map of downtown lots, visit Downtown Cleveland Alliance (www.parking.downtowncleveland.com). Websites and apps like ParkingPanda (www.parkingpanda. com), BestParking (www.bestparking.com), and ParkMe (www.parkme. com) also can be helpful tools to locate the best option.

TAXIS AND RIDE-HAILING SERVICES

To put it bluntly, hailing a cab in Cleveland can be like waiting for Godot: Hope quickly fades to frustration. If you want a cab and you are not at the airport or a hotel, call one on the phone. A few popular companies are Ace Taxi (216/361-4700), Americab (216/881-1111), and Yellow Cab (216/623-1550).

Both Uber (www.uber.com) and Lyft (www.lyft.com) have a robust

This massive infrastructure project took two years to complete and cost $200 million. But supporters say it has already spurred more than $6 billion in new investment along the seven-mile route.

What some deride as simply a fancy new bus system is being billed by others as the rebirth of Euclid Avenue. Once called "Millionaire's Row," Euclid was known the world over for its unparalleled beauty and unrivaled concentration of wealth. Prosperous industrialists like John D. Rockefeller, Charles Brush, and Marcus Hanna all had stately mansions along the tree-lined avenue. Famous department stores like Higbee's, May Co., Halle Bros., and Sterling-Linder-Davis attracted well-heeled shoppers from all over the region and beyond. But thanks in large part to suburban sprawl, once-great Euclid Avenue crumbled like a sandcastle at high tide.

These days, Euclid is making a comeback. This major artery connects Cleveland's two most dynamic employment zones, Public Square and University Circle. It bisects Cleveland State University, Playhouse Square, the Cleveland Clinic, and the region's burgeoning Midtown tech sector. And the Euclid Corridor Project, now called the RTA HealthLine (www.rtahealthline.com), is making life a whole lot better for everybody along the way.

In addition to new roadways, bike lanes, sidewalks, transit stations, and streetscaping, the most noticeable newcomers are the buses themselves. Called rapid transit vehicles (RTVs), these extra-long hybrid-electric buses produce 90 percent less emissions than a traditional bus and zip passengers from downtown to University Circle in 20 minutes flat. To accomplish that feat, the RTVs travel in dedicated bus lanes down the middle of the street, and GPS systems communicate with traffic signals. Also, riders pay fares before boarding, resulting in faster pickups.

Because of the unconventional traffic arrangement caused by the dedicated bus lanes, drivers need to be hyper-aware when traveling along Euclid Avenue. To avoid traffic tickets and collisions with large moving objects, drive only in the marked car-only lanes. There are close to 60 new stations, also located in the middle of the street, and crosswalks are everywhere, so keep a vigilant eye out for pedestrians. To make a left turn, look for the marked left-turn lanes. When you see the green left arrow, it is safe to turn, even in front of a bus.

To ride the HealthLine, use the crosswalk to reach the station. Some dual-purpose stations service both east and west routes, while others are dedicated for only east or west travel; they are marked. Vending machines at all stations dispense single-trip, all-day, seven-day, and monthly passes. They are good for use throughout the RTA public transportation system. When boarding, there is no need to show your ticket to the driver—just enter through either door and sit down.

The HealthLine runs 24 hours a day, seven days a week. During peak times, buses come every five minutes. Between 11pm and 5am they slow to one every half hour. Fares are $2.50 for a single trip.

presence in and around Cleveland for those who prefer to use those popular ride-hailing services.

BICYCLING

While far from two-wheeled nirvana, Cleveland is beginning to see the light when it comes to providing access for riders. New bike lanes, bike paths, bike racks, and bike-awareness programs are converging to make the city much more conducive to pedal power. After much debate, bike lanes were added to the final design for the Euclid Corridor Project. A new city law requires all downtown parking lot operators to install bike racks. And the RTA installed bike racks on all of its buses, making bike-and-ride commuting a reality.

MOTORCYCLING

Ohio requires only riders under the age of 18 or riders in their first year of motorcycle licensure to wear a protective helmet. Passengers riding with such young or novice drivers must also wear helmets.

INNERBELT BRIDGE

From 1959 to 2013, the Innerbelt Bridge was the main link into and out of downtown Cleveland, handling at last count more than 138,000 vehicles every day. In 2009, the Ohio Department of Transportation revealed plans for a new two-bridge highway that would replace the original aging Innerbelt Bridge over the Cuyahoga River. The first new bridge was completed in 2013, at which point all eastbound and westbound traffic from the original bridge was diverted to the new span. Upon completion of the first bridge, the old bridge was demolished and the second new bridge was built. Now complete, each of the **George V. Voinovich Bridges** features five lanes of either westbound or eastbound traffic. In addition to sturdy bridges with free-flowing traffic, the project has made some much-needed improvements to the street infrastructure near the "touch down" points. The intersection of Ontario Street and Carnegie Avenue, for one, features a new pedestrian plaza with granite block pavers and curbs, great news for those approaching Progressive Field on foot or bike.

ACCESSIBLE TRANSPORTATION

RTA is one of the first transit authorities in the country to operate a bus fleet that is 100 percent wheelchair accessible. Buses have a low-floor design that makes it easier for senior citizens, persons with disabilities, and everybody else to board and exit the vehicles. They also feature an easy-to-use ramp that works faster than traditional wheelchair lifts found on other buses. **Ace Taxi** (216/361-4700) operates wheelchair-accessible vans that can accommodate one wheelchair passenger and three other riders, or two wheelchair passengers and one additional rider. Those who are arriving at or departing from Cleveland Hopkins Airport should contact Standard Parking (216/265-7816) in advance of travel to ensure they are aware of your accessibility needs.

Travel Tips

WHAT TO PACK

Common sense and a good **umbrella** go a long way in Cleveland: This city fully experiences all four seasons (sometimes in the course of a single day). If attending a Browns game, for instance, it might be wise to dress as if one were leading an Antarctic expedition. Baseball games at Progressive Field, depending on the month, weather, and time of day, can be scorching hot, miserably wet, or, in early spring, even snowy. For much of the summer, the plan of attack is layers, a wide-brimmed hat, sunglasses, and sunscreen.

Appropriate footwear in C-Town can range from flip-flops to mukluks. **Lightweight rain gear** is always nice to have on hand, as is a sweatshirt. In the fall, temps can plummet from a balmy 75 degrees to a chilly 55 degrees just a minute after sundown.

Upscale-casual dress will work at almost any Cleveland restaurant. Most do get dolled up, however, when attending concerts at Severance Hall or the theater at Playhouse Square.

Golfers should really consider bringing their clubs when visiting between May and October. Northeast Ohio has some spectacular golf courses, with more than 120 public courses reachable in under an hour's drive.

TOURIST INFORMATION

Cleveland Visitors Center, which is operated by Destination Cleveland, is conveniently located downtown at the corner of Euclid Avenue and East 4th Street (334 Euclid Ave., 800/321-1001, www.thisiscleveland.com). Stop in every day but Sunday for maps and directions, customized itinerary planning, sightseeing tour information, event ticket sales, and restaurant, hotel, and car-rental reservations. Visitors can also download the Destination Cleveland app to their smartphone or device.

SMOKING

Despite the state's relatively high number of smokers, Ohio voters approved a comprehensive smoking ban that went into effect in late 2006. The sweeping ban covers most public spaces and places of employment, including bars, restaurants, and bowling alleys. What does this mean for smokers? It means they spend a lot more time standing around on sidewalks, for starters. Bars and restaurants with patios have become popular with smokers because they are some of the few remaining public places to puff. Some restaurants, especially those that offer more upscale dining, do not allow their patios to become smoker havens. It's always wise to seek permission before lighting up.

TIPPING

Considering that restaurant servers earn $4.15 an hour, it is reasonable to assume that most rely on tips as their major source of income. It is customary to tip 15-20 percent of the pretax total for competent service. And it is never fair to penalize a server for the faults of a kitchen. If the food is poor, send it back and get something else. Don't stiff the waiter because the cook is lousy. At bars, the going rate is about a buck per drink when ordering one or two, less when picking up a round. Cabbies expect a tip; no surprise there. A good rule of thumb is to round up to the nearest dollar and then add another dollar or two, depending on the distance. For long trips, 10 percent of the fare may be appropriate, assuming you ended up at the proper destination.

GAMBLING

In 2009, Ohio voters said yes to a ballot measure that allowed four full-scale, Vegas-style casinos to be built in the entire state. Cleveland's is the JACK Cleveland Casino downtown. Additionally, the state later allowed Ohio's seven horse-racing tracks to install slot machine-style video lottery terminals (or VLTs). Two, Hard Rock Rocksino Northfield Park and JACK Thistledown Racino, are close to Cleveland.

GAY AND LESBIAN TRAVELERS

Thanks to a thriving arts and culture scene, Cleveland enjoys a robust gay and lesbian population. In fact, in 2014, the Gay Games took place here. Lakewood likely contains the largest concentration of gay residents, and thus it boasts many gay-owned and gay-friendly businesses. Cleveland's annual Pride Parade and Festival, held in June, is well attended by both gay and straight revelers. Some bed-and-breakfasts, like Ohio City's Clifford House and Wallace Manor, are gay-friendly. For more information contact the Lesbian, Gay, Bisexual and Transgender Community Center of Greater Cleveland (216/651-5428, www.lgbt-cleveland.org).

HEALTH AND SAFETY
EMERGENCIES, HOSPITALS, AND PHARMACIES

Dial 911 for all fire, police, or medical emergencies. The U.S. Coast Guard can be reached by calling 216/937-0141. The Greater Cleveland Poison Control Center can be reached at 216/231-4455. The Cleveland Clinic (800/223-2273, www.clevelandclinic.org) operates dozens of regional hospitals, family health centers, emergency rooms, and surgery centers throughout Cuyahoga County and beyond. Likewise, University Hospitals (866/844-2273, www.uhhospitals.org) offers high-quality medical care at locations throughout Northeast Ohio.

CRIME

All cities of a certain size have crime, and Cleveland is certainly no exception. While the rates of homicides and other violent crimes are down overall across the city, there can be danger lurking around the bend. But by and large, the bulk of the hazardous activity is confined to a handful of impoverished neighborhoods well outside the scope of most visits. That doesn't mean that care should not be taken everywhere, especially at night. Whenever possible, travel in groups, stick to well-lighted and well-traveled lanes, and know your route. Need an escort? Call the Downtown Cleveland Alliance (216/621-6000), and they will send out one of their ambassadors to lend a hand.

Downtown is very safe, even at night. Most parts of Ohio City and Tremont are well-traveled and thus safe, but as one ventures toward the fringes, things can get a bit dicier. Same goes for Detroit Shoreway.

COMMUNICATIONS AND MEDIA
PHONES AND INTERNET ACCESS

For the most part, Cleveland telephone numbers fall within the 216 area code. As one travels west or east, 216 gives way to area code 440. Well south of town, 330 is the name of the game. When calling from one area code to another, it is necessary to dial a 1 before the 10-digit phone number. Time and weather reports can be accessed by calling 216/881-0880.

Cleveland is served by all major cellular carriers, including Verizon, Sprint, and AT&T.

Free wireless Internet service is available at most Cleveland Public Library branches, including the main branch downtown and those in Tremont and Ohio City (and all branches have public computers with Internet access). Free wireless Internet also blankets much of the University Circle area. Countless coffee shops, restaurants, and hotels offer free access as well, guaranteeing that a hotspot is never far away.

POSTAL SERVICES

Those who need to send mail or set up a post office box can do so throughout town at numerous United States Postal Service locations. Call 800/275-8777 or visit www.usps.com to find the closest one. For additional mail and shipping services, contact The UPS Store (800/789-4623, www.theupsstore.com) or FedEx (800/463-3339, www.fedex.com), both of which maintain numerous Cuyahoga County outposts.

NEWSPAPERS AND MAGAZINES

Cleveland's one major newspaper, the *Plain Dealer* (www.cleveland.com), is printed daily but stopped seven-day delivery in 2013, offering home delivery just four days a week, coupled with an online version. The *Sun News* (www.cleveland.com/sun) publishes approximately 20 different community-specific weekly newspapers that come out on Thursday. For some of the best arts, entertainment, and political coverage, grab a copy of *Cleveland Scene* (www.clevescene.com), a free alternative weekly that is available all over town.

For a more in-depth look into the goings on in and around Northeast Ohio, purchase the latest issue of *Cleveland Magazine* (www.clevelandmagazine.com), a glossy. For all the latest business news, Crain's *Cleveland Business* (www.crainscleveland.com), a weekly news magazine, is tough to beat. For comprehensive coverage of the local arts scene, including a breakdown of every worthwhile gallery and exhibit, grab a copy of the latest *Collective Arts Network Journal* (www.canjournal.org) from any coffee shop. Foodies should seek out *Edible Cleveland* (www.ediblecleveland.com) each quarter for in-depth coverage of the local food scene, from farm-to-table and beyond.

RADIO AND TV

All major television affiliates are present and accounted for in Cleveland, while public television fans are serviced by WVIZ/PBS (www.wviz.org). The Cleveland radio dial has a little bit of everything when it comes to sports, news, talk, and music. For classic rock tune into WMMS 100.7 FM and WLFM 87.7 FM; for Top 40 try WQAL 104.1 or WMVX 106.5; for hip-hop and R&B hit WENZ 107.9 FM; for country music tune into WGAR 99.5 FM; for news, talk, and sports visit WTAM 1100 AM and WKNR 850 AM; for talk and oldies hit WMJI 105.7 FM; for Christian go to WFHM 95.5 FM; for classical and public radio WKSU 89.7 FM or WCPN 90.3 FM.

RESOURCES

Suggested Reading

HISTORY AND GENERAL INFORMATION

Cayton, Andrew R. L. *Ohio: The History of a People*. Columbus, OH: Ohio State University Press, 2002. This contemporary text covers a lot of ground, from the attainment of statehood in 1803 all the way to the new millennium. Way more than a dusty history book, this entertaining read relies on letters, fiction, art, architecture, and sports to tell the story of this complicated state in the heartland.

Franklin, David. *Cleveland Museum of Art: Director's Choice*. New York: Scala Arts & Heritage Publishers, 2012. Part of the Director's Choice series, this book is penned by the museum's new director, David Franklin, who offers a personal tour of some of his favorite objects selected from holdings that span 6,000 years of artistic achievement. Each entry offers a reflection on the work of art, explaining why it is one of his highlights.

Glanville, Justin, and Julia Kuo. *New to Cleveland: A Guide to (Re)Discovering the City*. Cleveland: New to Cleveland, 2011. With more than 50 illustrations by local artist Julia Kuo and text by writer and urban planner Justin Glanville, this is no ordinary guidebook. Inside are sections on choosing the best neighborhoods for students, artists, and professionals; advice on where to send your kids to school; and insights on the Cleveland real estate market.

Grabowski, John J. *Cleveland, Then and Now*. Berkeley, CA: Thunder Bay Press, 2002. Serving as a sort of visual narrative, this book juxtaposes historical photographs with modern color images of the identical scene. In order to know who we are, we must know from whence we came, and this book offers a unique vehicle to get there.

Miller, Carol Poh. *Cleveland: A Concise History, 1796-1996*. Bloomington, IN: Indiana University Press, 1997. While indeed concise, this thorough book spans 200 years of Cleveland history, from the moment Moses Cleaveland stepped off his dinghy in the Flats to the city's bicentennial celebration. Augmented by wonderful illustrations and photographs, this methodical book brings people up to speed in record time.

Nickel, Steven. *Torso: The Story of Eliot Ness & the Search for a Psychopathic Killer*. Winston-Salem, NC: John F. Blair, 2001. Most know about Eliot Ness only through his dealings with Al Capone and his depiction in *The Untouchables* of TV and film. But as Cleveland's safety director, Ness was placed in charge of tracking down one of the most heinous serial killers of all time, the Mad Butcher of Kingsbury Run. This book tells the tale.

Van Tassel, David. *The Encyclopedia of Cleveland History.* Bloomington, IN: Indiana University Press, 1996. There may be no more comprehensive historical text of any city than this exhaustive tome. This 1,100-page hardback covers seemingly every aspect of Cleveland's first 200 years, with entries on industry, philanthropy, art, music, and flight. Add to that hundreds of photos, numerous maps, and the sharp writing of more than 200 journalists, and you get an encyclopedic digest that makes others in the genre look like tourist pamphlets.

Woods, Terry K. *Ohio's Grand Canal: A Brief History of the Ohio & Erie Canal.* Kent, OH: Kent State University Press, 2008. The Ohio & Erie Canal was so influential in the development of Cleveland and the entire state of Ohio, it is no wonder there are so many titles on the subject. Few, however, can match the level of detail captured in this thoroughly researched and well-penned account of the events surrounding Ohio's most ambitious infrastructure project.

RECREATION, ART, FOOD, MUSIC, AND SPORTS

Adams, Deanna R. *Rock 'N' Roll and the Cleveland Connection.* Kent, OH: Kent State University Press, 2002.

Weighing in at more than 600 pages, this comprehensive tome leaves no doubt as to why Cleveland landed the Rock and Roll Hall of Fame. The book tracks the history of rock as it applies to Cleveland, touching on early musicians, local DJs, trendsetting radio stations, and the lead up to acquiring the Rock Hall.

Gorman, John. *The Buzzard: Inside the Glory Days of WMMS and Cleveland Rock Radio.* Cleveland: Gray & Co., 2008. Gorman, who served as WMMS's program director in the 1970s, offers readers a salacious glimpse into life at one of the most influential rock radio stations in the country. No surprise: This one includes tales of sex, drugs, and rock and roll.

Hoskins, Patience Cameron. *Cleveland on Foot: 50 Walks & Hikes in Greater Cleveland.* Cleveland: Gray & Co., 2004. Walkers, hikers, and outdoors enthusiasts will have a field day with this guide, which points folks in the direction of some of the most picturesque walks around town. Northeast Ohio is blessed with great parks, and this handy book will help you explore them.

Latimer, Patricia. *Ohio Wine Country Excursions.* Cincinnati: Emmis Books, 2005. Few people outside Ohio realize just how much quality wine production goes on in the state. For those who are eager to learn more, this great guide offers detailed info on more than 60 Ohio wineries. In addition to some historical context, the indispensable book contains maps, photos, and tasting guides.

Macoska, Janet. *All Access Cleveland: The Rock and Roll Photography of Janet Macoska*. Cleveland Landmarks Press, 2015. Janet Macoska's rock photography has been displayed in the Smithsonian, the National Portrait Gallery in London, the Rock and Roll Hall of Fame and Museum, the Grammy Museum, and in Hard Rock properties around the world. This compendium, co-authored by Peter Chakerian, features iconic imagery and behind-the-scenes stories from the Cleveland native's 40 years on the beat.

Piiparinen, Richey, and Anne Trubek. *Rust Belt Chic: The Cleveland Anthology*. Cleveland: Rust Belt Chic Press, 2012. Answering a call for entries, dozens of established Cleveland writers, such as David Giffels, Connie Schultz, and Michael Ruhlman, offer "the longer view" of what it means to live in a recovering Rust Belt city. Within are narratives of failure, conflict, growth, and renewal—the same themes we find in Cleveland.

Pluto, Terry. *The Curse of Rocky Colavito: A Loving Look at a Thirty-Year Slump*. Cleveland: Gray & Co., 1995. Pluto, who covers sports for the Cleveland *Plain Dealer,* is one of the country's best sports reporters. He has penned a number of books on Cleveland sports, including those on the Browns and the Cavs. This one links the Cleveland Indians' lengthy championship drought to the fateful day in 1960 when the team traded away beloved slugger Rocky Colavito.

Raab, Scott. *The Whore of Akron: One Man's Search for the Soul of LeBron James*. New York: HarperCollins, 2011. Writer-at-large for *Esquire* and Cleveland-born expat, Scott Raab is a lifelong Cleveland sports fan who suffers right along with the rest of us. But when LeBron James announced his defection to South Beach on a nationally televised show, Raab snapped and penned this biting look at the man, myth, and meanie who broke the hearts of too many.

Suszko, Marilou, and Laura Taxel. *Cleveland's West Side Market: 100 Years and Still Cooking*. Akron, OH: University of Akron Press, 2012. Penned by two well-known Cleveland food writers, this book takes readers on a nostalgic tour of the West Side Market and into the lives of many vendors and market families, who are the true foundation of this historic public space. The volume is rich with many rare and previously unpublished vintage and contemporary photographs and images that provide a delightful armchair tour of this magnificent landmark, which is a must-see destination for food lovers.

FICTION, POETRY, AND CHILDREN

Holbrook, Sara. *What's So Big About Cleveland, Ohio?* Cleveland: Gray & Co., 1997. When a well-traveled 10-year-old is dragged by her parents to dull old Cleveland, she expects to be bored to tears. And she is—until she discovers a secret about the city that changes her outlook. What better way to get your kids excited about C-Town than with this illustrated children's book?

Lax, Scott. *The Year That Trembled.* Forest Dale, VT: Paul S. Eriksson, 1998. This coming-of-age novel by Cleveland writer Scott Lax is set in Northeast Ohio and tracks a close-knit group of friends in the days leading up to the Vietnam draft. In 2002, the book was adapted into an independent film.

Ng, Celeste. *Little Fires Everywhere.* Penguin Press, 2017. The best-selling author of *Everything I Never Told You* spent some of her childhood in Shaker Heights, Ohio. This very special book about two very different families in that wealthy Cleveland suburb is a page-turner.

Roberts, Les. *Pepper Pike.* Cleveland: Gray & Co. Roberts, the recipient of the prestigious Cleveland Arts Prize for Literature, is a mystery writer with dozens of novels under his belt. He is best known for his Milan Jacovich series, which revolve around a likable blue-collar private eye of the same name. *Pepper Pike* kicks off the series, and other books include *Full Cleveland, The Lake Effect,* and *Deep Shaker.* No surprise that the novels are set in and around Cleveland.

Swanberg, Ingrid (ed.). *D. A. Levy and the Mimeograph Revolution.* Huron, OH: Bottom Dog Press, 2007. Underground poet d. a. levy used his relationship with Cleveland as the fuel for his stirring poetry, prose, and art. Modern readers walk away with a unique and moving perspective of 1960s Cleveland. Levy used his own photocopier to self-publish his works, essentially kick-starting the local alternative press movement. This anthology of his work is supplemented with interviews, essays, and letters.

Winegardner, Mark. *Crooked River Burning.* Orlando: Harcourt, 2001. In this ambitious American novel, Winegardner weaves fictional and nonfictional events into a patchwork tale of a once-great city in decline. The stars of this drama hail from opposite sides of town—he from blue-collar Old Brooklyn, she from affluent Shaker Heights—but fate has a way of bridging divides. In spite of its negative circumstances, Cleveland somehow shines through it all.

Internet Resources

GENERAL INFORMATION

ArtHopper.org
www.arthopper.org

This Cleveland-based website keeps tabs on the Midwest's art scene with high-quality arts journalism that covers the Greater Lake Erie region, including Cleveland,

Columbus, Akron, Cincinnati, Dayton, Detroit, Pittsburgh, Toledo, and Youngstown.

City of Cleveland
www.city.cleveland.oh.us

The official City of Cleveland website is intended as a portal to government services, residential information, and city jobs listings. This is also where folks pay their parking tickets online.

Cleveland.com
www.cleveland.com
This online version of the Cleveland *Plain Dealer* and its sister outlet Cleveland.com tracks not only local, regional, national, and international news, but also sports, weather, entertainment, and seasonal events.

Cleveland Memory Project
www.clevelandmemory.org
Get lost in the Special Collections archives of the Cleveland State University Library at this beautiful website. Compiled here are more than 500,000 newspaper photographs covering decades of Cleveland history, architecture, and events. There are 6,000 images documenting the construction of the Terminal Tower alone. Bridge fans will go nuts over the vast catalog of historic bridge pics. This website also holds the full text of hundreds of rare books.

Cleveland Metroparks
www.clevelandmetroparks.com
The official website of the Cleveland Metroparks is full of information on the park system's reservations, golf courses, lakefront parks, and zoo.

Cleveland Plus Living
www.clevelandplusliving.com
Hosted by area chambers of commerce, regional business-growth associations, and travel and tourism professionals, Cleveland Plus Living is designed to attract skilled residents to Northeast Ohio. More stuff than fluff, the site contains hard info on the region's top employers, housing and cost of living, and education from kindergarten through postgrad.

There is also a comprehensive listing of visitor sites for nearby counties, cities, and attractions.

Cuyahoga County
www.cuyahogacounty.us
The official government website of Cuyahoga County, this portal publishes important news and safety information, links to county agencies and organizations, and a calendar of events.

Cuyahoga Valley National Park
www.nps.gov/cuva
This is the official U.S. National Park Service site for Cuyahoga Valley National Park, a 33,000-acre sanctuary 15 minutes south of Cleveland. The well-organized site includes information on the park's history, its diverse flora and fauna, and the numerous recreational activities that exist throughout the park. The downloadable PDF maps of the park, its trails and waterfalls, and the popular Ohio & Erie Canal Towpath Trail make this site an indispensable resource.

Destination Cleveland
www.thisiscleveland.com
The official website for the Convention and Visitors Bureau of Greater Cleveland, Destination Cleveland is extremely useful for tourists, potential new residents, travel professionals, and meeting planners. It is chock-full of info regarding attractions, accommodations, shopping, transportation, and excursions from town. Suggested itineraries take all the guesswork out of planning a short stay.

Encyclopedia of Cleveland History
www.case.edu/ech
This is the online version of *The Encyclopedia of Cleveland History*,

which is the authoritative text on historical information about Cleveland. In addition to all the articles from the print version of the book, this easy-to-search website includes revised text, tons of new content, and high-res photos and documents.

GreenCityBlueLake
www.gcbl.org
Promoting environmentally friendly redevelopment, stemming the tide of urban sprawl, and improving the quality of life for all residents are the breezes that propel this organization, which is the sustainability center of the Cleveland Museum of Natural History. Visit this site to read about living sans car in Cleveland, where to find green housing, and why moving to former cornfields is bad for everybody.

Ohio Division of Travel and Tourism
www.ohio.org
This official travel and tourism site covers the great state of Ohio from border to border. In addition to information on where to go, what to do, and when to do it, the well-designed site also features interactive maps, glossy publications, and special deals and discounts. Travelers will also find listings for every local tourism organization throughout the entire state.

University Circle Inc.
www.universitycircle.org
University Circle is the epicenter of arts, culture, education, and health care in Northeast Ohio, and this official website is a great place to begin your exploration. Geared to both visitors and job seekers, this thorough site has information on major cultural attractions, seasonal events and exhibits, dining and nightlife, accommodations, career listings, and real estate.

EVENT LISTINGS

Cleveland.com
www.cleveland.com/events
This helpful tool searches upcoming events by day, week, or month. Further sorting by event type, location, and entertainment genre makes it easy to pinpoint your way to fun.

Cleveland Magazine
http://clevelandmagazine.com/events
Rounds up a solid listing of art, food, and cultural events taking place around town.

Cleveland Scene
www.clevescene.coms
Cleveland's premier alternative weekly publishes comprehensive entertainment listings covering art, music, dance, theater, film, dining, and nightlife.

Cool Cleveland
www.coolcleveland.com
Tens of thousands of Clevelanders get a weekly email newsletter from this organization detailing all the cool stuff going on around town. One of the most complete listings of arts and culture events, it is worth checking out before stepping out.

Index

Restaurants Index

Nightlife Index

Shops Index

Hotels Index

Photo Credits

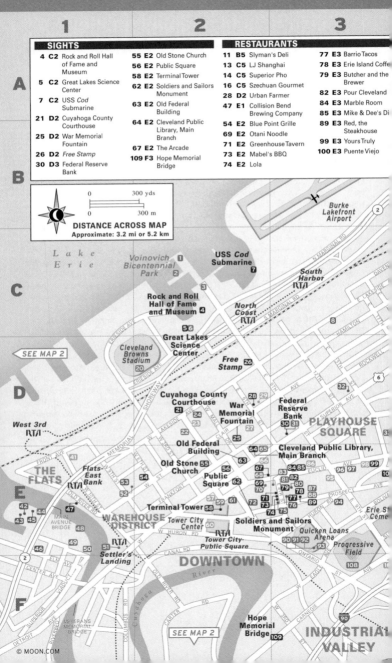

SIGHTS

4	C2	Rock and Roll Hall of Fame and Museum
5	C2	Great Lakes Science Center
7	C2	USS Cod Submarine
21	D2	Cuyahoga County Courthouse
25	D2	War Memorial Fountain
26	D2	Free Stamp
30	D3	Federal Reserve Bank
55	E2	Old Stone Church
56	E2	Public Square
58	E2	Terminal Tower
62	E2	Soldiers and Sailors Monument
63	E2	Old Federal Building
64	E2	Cleveland Public Library, Main Branch
67	E2	The Arcade
109	F3	Hope Memorial Bridge

RESTAURANTS

11	B5	Slyman's Deli
13	C5	LJ Shanghai
14	C5	Superior Pho
16	C5	Szechuan Gourmet
28	D2	Urban Farmer
47	E1	Collision Bend Brewing Company
54	E2	Blue Point Grille
69	E2	Otani Noodle
71	E2	Greenhouse Tavern
73	E2	Mabel's BBQ
74	E2	Lola
77	E3	Barrio Tacos
78	E3	Erie Island Coffe
79	E3	Butcher and the Brewer
82	E3	Pour Cleveland
84	E3	Marble Room
85	E3	Mike & Dee's Di
89	E3	Red, the Steakhouse
99	E3	Yours Truly
100	E3	Puente Viejo

© MOON.COM

4   5   6

NIGHTLIFE

- 8 **C3** Noble Beast Brewing Co.
- 15 **C5** Galaxy KTV
- 24 **D2** Bar 32
- 32 **D3** Masthead Brewing
- 36 **D4** Hofbräuhaus Cleveland
- 42 **E1** Music Box Supper Club
- 43 **E1** Shooter's
- 45 **E1** The Improv
- 46 **E1** Harbor Inn
- 53 **E1** Gillespie's Map Room
- 61 **E2** JACK Cleveland Casino
- 72 **E2** Ontario Street Café
- 75 **E3** Flannery's Pub
- 76 **E3** Society Lounge
- 80 **E3** Hilarities 4th Street Theater
- 94 **E3** Wilbert's Food & Music

ARTS AND CULTURE

- 6 **C2** Dome Theater
- 9 **C4** Cleveland Print Room
- 12 **C5** Zygote Press
- 19 **C6** Morgan Conservatory
- 22 **D2** Cleveland Police Museum
- 31 **D3** Money Museum at Federal Reserve Bank
- 33 **D3** Cleveland Play House
- 34 **D4** The Galleries at Cleveland State University
- 35 **D4** Playhouse Square
- 37 **D4** Wooltex Gallery
- 38 **D6** Cleveland Masonic Temple
- 39 **D6** Children's Museum of Cleveland
- 40 **D6** Agora Theatre & Ballroom
- 49 **E1** Greater Cleveland Aquarium
- 50 **E1** Jacobs Pavilion at Nautica
- 59 **E2** Tower City Cinemas
- 70 **E2** House of Blues
- 93 **E3** Quicken Loans Arena
- 101 **E4** Cleveland Ballet
- 103 **E4** Bonfoey Gallery
- 104 **E4** Great Lakes Theater
- 105 **E4** Wolstein Center
- 110 **F5** Rock and Roll Hall of Fame Library and Archives

RECREATION

- 1 **C2** *Goodtime III*
- 2 **C2** Voinovich Bicentennial Park
- 3 **C2** Rock & Dock at North Coast Harbor Marina
- 20 **D2** Cleveland Browns
- 44 **E1** Great Lakes Watersports
- 48 **E1** *Nautica Queen*
- 51 **E1** Downtown Dog Park
- 65 **E2** Cleveland Public Library Eastman Reading Garden
- 81 **E3** The Corner Alley
- 90 **E3** Cleveland Monsters
- 91 **E3** Cleveland Gladiators
- 92 **E3** Cleveland Cavaliers
- 106 **E4** Cleveland State University Vikings
- 108 **F3** Cleveland Indians

SHOPS

- 10 **B5** Rebuilders Xchange
- 17 **C6** Tink Holl
- 18 **C6** Cleveland MetroBark
- 52 **E1** Surroundings Home Décor
- 68 **E2** Marengo Luxury Spa
- 83 **E3** CLE Clothing Co.
- 87 **E3** Manifest
- 88 **E3** The Restock
- 96 **E3** Heinen's Grocery
- 97 **E3** Geiger's

HOTELS

- 23 **D2** Hilton Cleveland Downtown
- 27 **D2** Drury Plaza Hotel
- 29 **D2** Westin Cleveland Downtown
- 41 **E1** Aloft Cleveland Downtown
- 57 **E2** Renaissance Cleveland Hotel
- 60 **E2** The Ritz-Carlton
- 66 **E2** Hyatt Regency Cleveland at the Arcade
- 86 **E3** Holiday Inn Express Hotel and Suites
- 95 **E3** Kimpton Schofield Hotel
- 98 **E3** Crowne Plaza Cleveland at Playhouse Square
- 102 **E4** Comfort Inn Downtown
- 107 **F3** Hilton Garden Inn

To 10 Rebuilders Xchange

PAYNE/GOODRICH KIRTLAND PARK

SEE MAP 4

Cleveland State University

Cleveland State University

Cuyahoga Community College - Metro Campus

To 1 Wendy Park at Whiskey Island, 2 BrewBoat, and 3 SUP Cleveland

SEE MAP 1

VETERANS MEMORIAL BRIDGE

To Ho Memo Bridg

St. John's Episcopal Church

Cuyahoga River

To H Memo Bridg

SEE DETAIL

RTA West 25th-Ohio City

Franklin Castle

Fairview Park

St. Patrick's Church

John Heisman's Birthsite

St. Ignatius High School

Carnegie West Library

OHIO CITY

To 61 Forest City Shuffleboard

Jay Avenue Homes

West Side Market

SEE MAP 3

DISTANCE ACROSS MAP
Approximate: 2.6 mi or 4.2 km

0   300 yds
0   300 m

0   100 yds
0   100 m

© MOON.COM

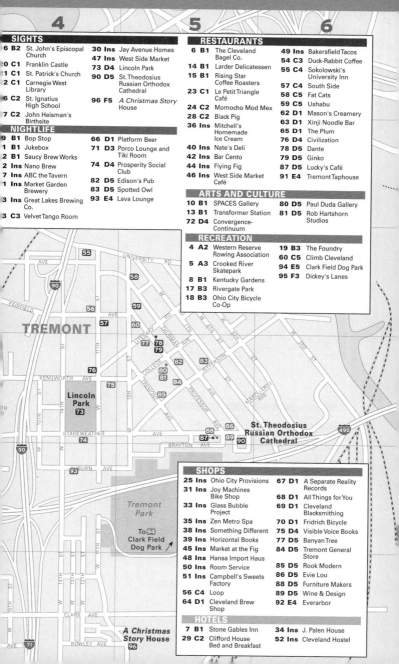

SIGHTS

- 6 **B2** St. John's Episcopal Church
- 0 **C1** Franklin Castle
- 1 **C1** St. Patrick's Church
- 2 **C1** Carnegie West Library
- 6 **C2** St. Ignatius High School
- 7 **C2** John Heisman's Birthsite

NIGHTLIFE

- 9 **B1** Bop Stop
- 1 **B1** Jukebox
- 2 **B1** Saucy Brew Works
- 2 **Ins** Nano Brew
- 7 **Ins** ABC the Tavern
- 1 **Ins** Market Garden Brewery
- 3 **Ins** Great Lakes Brewing Co.
- 3 **C3** Velvet Tango Room

- 30 **Ins** Jay Avenue Homes
- 47 **Ins** West Side Market
- 73 **D4** Lincoln Park
- 90 **D5** St. Theodosius Russian Orthodox Cathedral
- 96 **F5** *A Christmas Story* House

- 66 **D1** Platform Beer
- 71 **D3** Porco Lounge and Tiki Room
- 74 **D4** Prosperity Social Club
- 82 **D5** Edison's Pub
- 83 **D5** Spotted Owl
- 93 **E4** Lava Lounge

RESTAURANTS

- 6 **B1** The Cleveland Bagel Co.
- 14 **B1** Larder Delicatessen
- 15 **B1** Rising Star Coffee Roasters
- 23 **C1** Le Petit Triangle Café
- 24 **C2** Momocho Mod Mex
- 28 **C2** Black Pig
- 36 **Ins** Mitchell's Homemade Ice Cream
- 40 **Ins** Nate's Deli
- 42 **Ins** Bar Cento
- 44 **Ins** Flying Fig
- 46 **Ins** West Side Market Café

- 49 **Ins** Bakersfield Tacos
- 54 **C3** Duck-Rabbit Coffee
- 55 **C4** Sokolowski's University Inn
- 57 **C4** South Side
- 58 **C5** Fat Cats
- 59 **C5** Ushabu
- 62 **D1** Mason's Creamery
- 63 **D1** Xinji Noodle Bar
- 65 **D1** The Plum
- 76 **D4** Civilization
- 78 **D5** Dante
- 79 **D5** Ginko
- 87 **D5** Lucky's Café
- 91 **E4** Tremont Taphouse

ARTS AND CULTURE

- 10 **B1** SPACES Gallery
- 13 **B1** Transformer Station
- 72 **D4** Convergence-Continuum

- 80 **D5** Paul Duda Gallery
- 81 **D5** Rob Hartshorn Studios

RECREATION

- 4 **A2** Western Reserve Rowing Association
- 5 **A3** Crooked River Skatepark
- 8 **B1** Kentucky Gardens
- 17 **B3** Rivergate Park
- 18 **B3** Ohio City Bicycle Co-op

- 19 **B3** The Foundry
- 60 **C5** Climb Cleveland
- 94 **E5** Clark Field Dog Park
- 95 **F3** Dickey's Lanes

SHOPS

- 25 **Ins** Ohio City Provisions
- 31 **Ins** Joy Machines Bike Shop
- 33 **Ins** Glass Bubble Project
- 35 **Ins** Zen Metro Spa
- 38 **Ins** Something Different
- 39 **Ins** Horizontal Books
- 45 **Ins** Market at the Fig
- 48 **Ins** Hansa Import Haus
- 50 **Ins** Room Service
- 51 **Ins** Campbell's Sweets Factory
- 56 **C4** Loop
- 64 **D1** Cleveland Brew Shop

- 67 **D1** A Separate Reality Records
- 68 **D1** All Things for You
- 69 **D1** Cleveland Blacksmithing
- 70 **D1** Fridrich Bicycle
- 75 **D4** Visible Voice Books
- 77 **D5** Banyan Tree
- 84 **D5** Tremont General Store
- 85 **D5** Rook Modern
- 86 **D5** Evie Lou
- 88 **D5** Furniture Makers
- 89 **D5** Wine & Design
- 92 **E4** Everarbor

HOTELS

- 7 **B1** Stone Gables Inn
- 29 **C2** Clifford House Bed and Breakfast
- 52 **Ins** Cleveland Hostel

- 34 **Ins** J. Palen House
- 52 **Ins** Cleveland Hostel

DISTANCE ACROSS MAP
Approximate: 2.6 mi or 4.2 km

EDGEWATER

Lake Eri

West Blvd-Cudell

Cudell Commons Park

SEE MAP 6

CUDELL

WEST BOULEVARD

SIGHTS
- 1 **A5** Edgewater Park
- 20 **B5** Gordon Square Arts District
- 36 **C6** St. Stephen Catholic Church

RESTAURANTS
- 12 **B5** Il Rione Pizzeria
- 13 **B5** Sweet Moses Soda Fountain
- 14 **B5** Luxe Kitchen & Lounge
- 19 **B5** Brewnuts
- 21 **B6** Gypsy Beans & Bakery
- 24 **B6** Spice Kitchen & Bar
- 25 **B6** Happy Dog
- 28 **B6** Astoria Market and Café
- 33 **C5** Banter
- 35 **C6** Frank's Falafel

NIGHTLIFE
- 3 **A6** Parkview Nite Club
- 4 **B1** Twist Social Club
- 11 **B5** Stone Mad Irish Pub
- 26 **B6** Tina's Nite Club
- 27 **B6** Tributary
- 31 **C1** Brothers Lounge
- 37 **D2** Judd's City Tavern

ARTS AND CULTURE
- 8 **B4** 78th Street Studios
- 9 **B4** Blank Canvas Theatre
- 16 **B5** Near West Theatre
- 17 **B5** Capitol Theatre
- 22 **B6** 1point618 Gallery
- 23 **B6** Cleveland Public Theatre
- 29 **B6** Maelstrom Collaborative Arts
- 30 **B6** Talespinner Children's Theatre

© MOON.COM

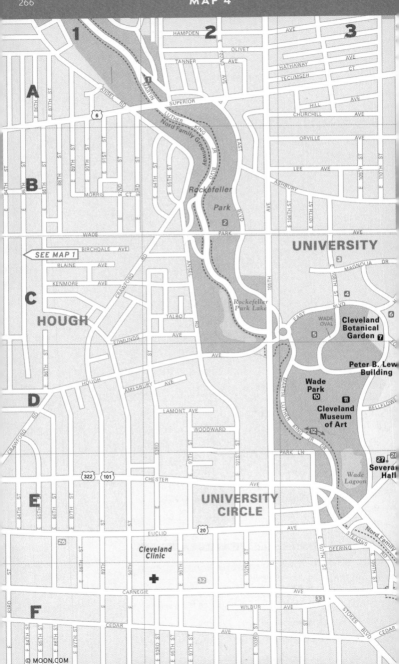

SEE MAP 1

UNIVERSITY

HOUGH

Rockefeller Park Lake

Cleveland Botanical Garden

Peter B. Lewis Building

Wade Park

Cleveland Museum of Art

Wade Oval

Severance Hall

Wade Lagoon

Nord Family

UNIVERSITY CIRCLE

Cleveland Clinic

© MOON.COM

0   300 yds
0   300 m

DISTANCE ACROSS MAP
Approximate: 3.2 mi or 5.2 km

SIGHTS

7 **C3** Cleveland Botanical Garden
9 **D3** Peter B. Lewis Building
10 **D3** Wade Park
11 **D3** Cleveland Museum of Art
14 **D4** Hessler Road and Hessler Court
27 **E3** Severance Hall

RESTAURANTS

13 **D4** L'Albatros
21 **D5** Presti's Bakery & Café
23 **D5** La Dolce Vita
24 **D5** Corbo's Bakery
29 **E4** Algebra Tea House
31 **E5** Nora

NIGHTLIFE

15 **D4** Happy Dog at the Euclid Tavern
18 **D4** ABC the Tavern
22 **D5** Tavern of Little Italy

ARTS AND CULTURE

4 **C3** Western Reserve Historical Society
5 **C3** Cleveland Museum of Natural History
6 **C3** Cleveland Institute of Music
16 **D4** Cleveland Institute of Art Cinematheque
17 **D4** Reinberger Gallery
19 **D4** Museum of Contemporary Art
25 **D5** Murray Hill Galleries
28 **E3** Cleveland Orchestra
30 **E4** Verne Collection

RECREATION

1 **A2** Cleveland Cultural Gardens
2 **B2** Rockefeller Park
12 **D3** Nord Family Greenway

HOTELS

3 **C3** University Circle Bed and Breakfast
8 **D3** Glidden House
20 **D4** Courtyard by Marriott Cleveland University Circle
26 **E1** Holiday Inn Cleveland Clinic
32 **F2** InterContinental Hotel and Conference Center
33 **F3** The Tudor Arms Hotel Cleveland, A DoubleTree by Hilton

SEE MAP 5

Finnigan Fields

Lake View Cemetery

SEE MAP 4

0   300 yds
0   300 m

DISTANCE ACROSS MAP
Approximate: 3.2 mi or 5.2 km

Euclid-
E 120th RTA

MAYFIELD RD

SEE MAP 4

(20)
(322)

LITTLE
ITALY

Case
Western
Reserve
University

EDWARDS RD

DERBYSHIRE RD

CEDAR RD

Fairmount
Boulevard
District

NOTTINGHILL LN

CLARKSON DR

FAIRMOUNT BLVD

JAMES PKWY

COLCHESTER RD

PARK

FAIRHILL RD

Shaker Lakes

Park

Lower Shaker La

LARCHMERE

BROWNING AVE

HAMLEN AVE

ROMWELL AVE

BUCKINGHAM AVE

SHAKER
HEIGHTS

ARDOON AVE

Shaker
Square

RTA

Shaker
Square

Coventry
RTA

WILLIAMS RD

(87)

SHAKER BLVD

(87)

Shaker Square
Shopping Center

SIGHTS

1	**A1**	Lake View Cemetery
14	**B5**	Cain Park
23	**C2**	Fairmount Boulevard District
46	**F2**	Shaker Square

RESTAURANTS

7	**A3**	Tommy's
9	**B3**	Inn on Coventry
18	**C2**	Vero Bistro
22	**C2**	Luna Bakery & Cafe
30	**C5**	Stone Oven
37	**E2**	Felice Urban Café
38	**E2**	Big Al's Diner
44	**F2**	Edwins
47	**F2**	Fire Food & Drink
49	**F6**	On the Rise

NIGHTLIFE

10	**B3**	B Side Liquor Lounge
11	**B3**	Grog Shop
16	**C2**	Nighttown
19	**C2**	Parnell's Pub
21	**C2**	The Fairmount
24	**C5**	Bottlehouse Brewery
26	**C5**	CLE Urban Winery
27	**C5**	Boss Dog Brewing
31	**C6**	Quintana's Speakeasy
33	**D5**	The Wine Spot

ARTS AND CULTURE

13	**B4**	Ensemble Theatre
15	**B5**	Evans Amphitheater
20	**C2**	Still Point Gallery
25	**C5**	Cedar Lee Theatre
28	**C5**	Heights Arts Gallery
35	**D5**	Dobama Theatre
43	**F2**	Wolfs Gallery
45	**F2**	Shaker Square Cinemas

RECREATION

48	**F4**	Nature Center at Shaker Lakes
50	**F6**	Horseshoe Lake Park

4 322 MAYFIELD

MIDDLEHURST RD

O'CONNOR RD

HAMPSHIRE

SUPERIOR

Cumberland

Park

COVENTRY VILLAGE

SOMERTON RD

HEIGHTS RD

EUCLID

LINCOLN BLVD

EDGEHILL

WOODWARD AVE

WASHINGTON

GROVE

PARKWAY DR

DR

OVERLOOK

BERKSHIRE

YORKSHIRE

BLVD

E DERBYSHIRE RD

LAMBERTON RD

RD

MEADOWBROOK

KENWOOD

MAPLEWOOD

BRIARWOOD

COTTAGE RD

LEXWOOD

OAKDALE

EDGEWOOD

BLVD

KENSINGTON RD

WESTMINSTER RD

ESSEX RD

CORYDON RD

LAMBERTON RD

COLERIDGE RD

SCARBOROUGH RD

FAIRFAX

RD

STRATFORD RD

FAIRMOUNT

MARLBORO RD

MONMOUTH RD

ARLINGTON

GUILFORD RD

WELLINGTON RD

N PARK

48 W PARK BLVD

Southington TA

Horseshoe

Southern Park

S PARK

5 OAK

CUMBERLAND RD

BLVD

EUCLID HEIGHTS BLVD

HYDE PARK AVE

Cain Park **14 15**

BLANCHE AVE

SUPERIOR DR

RD

RD

RD

24

CLEVELAND HEIGHTS

25 27

26

28

MARLINDALE

ROSSMOOR

HAMPSTEAD

KILDARE RD **31**

CEDARBROOK RD **32**

TULLAMORE RD

30

29

33 34

SILSBY RD

35

MEADOWBROOK BLVD

DELLWOOD RD

TAYLOR RD

S TAYLOR

BLVD

LEE

BLVD

49

SCOTTSDALE

BLVD

Lake

Horseshoe Lake 50

Horseshoe Park

6 Severence Town Center

SHOPS	
2 A3 Attenson's Antiques & Books	**34 D5** Mitchell's Fine Chocolates
3 A3 Avalon Exchange	**36 E2** Larchmere Fire Works
4 A3 City Buddha	**39 E2** Fine Points
5 A3 Passport to Peru	**40 E2** Heide Rivchun Conservation Studios
6 A3 Mac's Backs Books	
8 A3 Record Revolution	**41 E2** Gentleman's Quarters/Frog's Legs
12 B3 In the 216	
17 C2 Appletree Books	
29 C5 Cleveland Running Co.	**42 E2** Loganberry Books
32 C6 Quintana's Barber and Dream Spa	

© MOON.COM

SIGHTS

| 1 | **A4** | Oldest Stone House | 42 | **C6** | Museum of Divine Statues |
| 12 | **B2** | Beck Center for the Arts | | | |

RESTAURANTS

3	**A5**	Pier W	24	**B4**	Deagan's Kitchen & Bar
5	**B1**	Rosso Gelato	25	**B4**	Melt Bar & Grilled
7	**B1**	Blackbird Baking Company	31	**C3**	Buckeye Beer Engine
8	**B1**	Borderline Café	33	**C4**	Malley's Chocolates
15	**B2**	Salt	36	**C5**	Thai Thai
16	**B2**	Proper Pig Smokehouse	41	**C6**	Barroco Grill
21	**B4**	The Root Cafe			

NIGHTLIFE

10	**B1**	Around the Corner Saloon	30	**B6**	Five O'Clock Lounge
13	**B2**	Something Dada	38	**C5**	Mahall's 20 Lanes
20	**B3**	Humble Wine Bar	43	**C6**	LBM
23	**B4**	16-Bit Bar + Arcade	44	**C6**	Winchester Tavern and Concert Club
29	**B5**	Lizardville			

ARTS AND CULTURE

| 14 | **B2** | Beck Center for the Arts | 40 | **C5** | Screw Factory Artists |

RECREATION

2	**A4**	Lakewood Park	39	**C5**	Mahall's 20 Lanes
6	**B1**	41° North Kayak Adventures	45	**D4**	Serpentini Winterhurst Arena
11	**C2**	Lakewood Off-Leash Dog Park	48	**F6**	Halloran Ice Skating Rink
28	**B4**	Nosotros Rock Climbing Gym			

To **47** Carol & John's Comic Book Shop

SHOPS

9	B1	Robusto & Briar
17	B2	GV Art + Design
18	B3	My Mind's Eye Records
19	B3	Beat Cycles
22	B4	The Exchange
26	B4	Paisley Monkey
27	B4	Plantation Home
32	C4	The Bookshop in Lakewood
34	C4	Play It Again, Sam
35	C4	Westside Skates
37	C5	Cleveland Curiosities
47	F2	Carol & John's Comic Book Shop

HOTELS

4	A6	Days Inn
46	F1	Emerald Necklace Inn

0   500 yds
0   500 m

DISTANCE ACROSS MAP
Approximate: 4.3 mi or 7 km

© MOON.COM

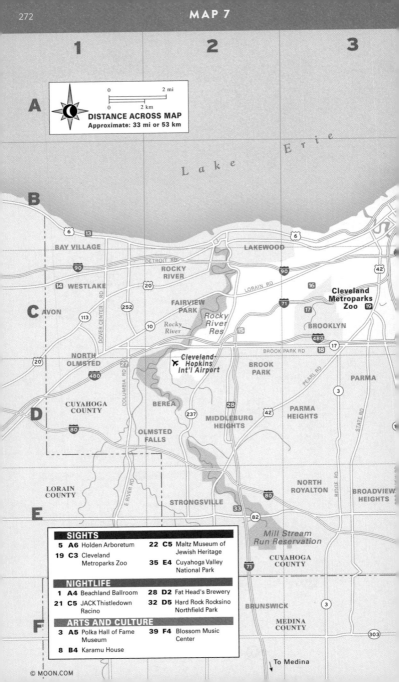

DISTANCE ACROSS MAP
Approximate: 33 mi or 53 km

SIGHTS

5	**A6**	Holden Arboretum
19	**C3**	Cleveland Metroparks Zoo
22	**C5**	Maltz Museum of Jewish Heritage
35	**E4**	Cuyahoga Valley National Park

NIGHTLIFE

1	**A4**	Beachland Ballroom
21	**C5**	JACK Thistledown Racino
28	**D2**	Fat Head's Brewery
32	**D5**	Hard Rock Rocksino Northfield Park

ARTS AND CULTURE

3	**A5**	Polka Hall of Fame Museum
8	**B4**	Karamu House
39	**F4**	Blossom Music Center

© MOON.COM

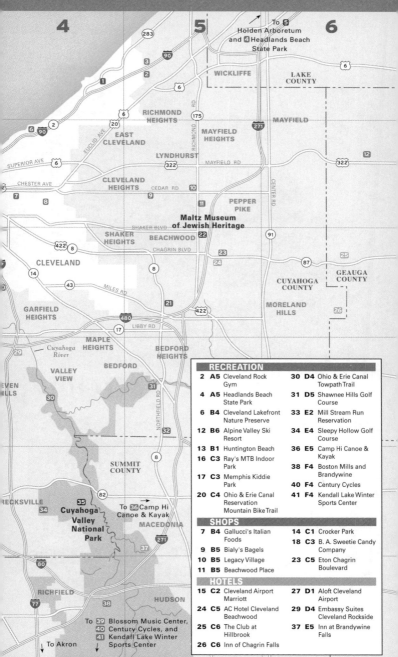

RECREATION

- **2** **A5** Cleveland Rock Gym
- **4** **A5** Headlands Beach State Park
- **6** **B4** Cleveland Lakefront Nature Preserve
- **12** **B6** Alpine Valley Ski Resort
- **13** **B1** Huntington Beach
- **16** **C3** Ray's MTB Indoor Park
- **17** **C3** Memphis Kiddie Park
- **20** **C4** Ohio & Erie Canal Reservation Mountain Bike Trail
- **30** **D4** Ohio & Erie Canal Towpath Trail
- **31** **D5** Shawnee Hills Golf Course
- **33** **E2** Mill Stream Run Reservation
- **34** **E4** Sleepy Hollow Golf Course
- **36** **E5** Camp Hi Canoe & Kayak
- **38** **F4** Boston Mills and Brandywine
- **40** **F4** Century Cycles
- **41** **F4** Kendall Lake Winter Sports Center

SHOPS

- **7** **B4** Gallucci's Italian Foods
- **9** **B5** Bialy's Bagels
- **10** **B5** Legacy Village
- **11** **B5** Beachwood Place
- **14** **C1** Crocker Park
- **18** **C3** B. A. Sweetie Candy Company
- **23** **C5** Eton Chagrin Boulevard

HOTELS

- **15** **C2** Cleveland Airport Marriott
- **24** **C5** AC Hotel Cleveland Beachwood
- **25** **C6** The Club at Hillbrook
- **26** **C6** Inn of Chagrin Falls
- **27** **D1** Aloft Cleveland Airport
- **29** **D4** Embassy Suites Cleveland Rockside
- **37** **E5** Inn at Brandywine Falls

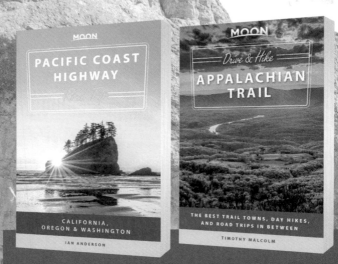

Advice on where to sleep, eat, and explore

Detailed driving directions including mileage and drive times

Itineraries for a range of timelines

MOON
NEW ENGLAND
Road Trip

BOSTON, ACADIA NATIONAL PARK, WHITE MOUNTAINS, BERKSHIRES, NEWPORT, AND CAPE COD

JEN ROSE SMITH

MOON
PACIFIC NORTHWEST
Road Trip

SEATTLE, VANCOUVER, VICTORIA, THE OLYMPIC PENINSULA, PORTLAND, THE OREGON COAST & MOUNT RAINIER

ALLISON WILLIAMS

MOON
ROUTE 66
Road Trip

JESSICA DUNHAM

MOON
SOUTH FLORIDA & THE KEYS
Road Trip

WITH MIAMI, WALT DISNEY WORLD, TAMPA & THE EVERGLADES

JASON FERGUSON

MOON
SOUTHWEST
Road Trip

LAS VEGAS, ZION & BRYCE, MONUMENT VALLEY, SANTA FE & TAOS, AND THE GRAND CANYON

TIM HULL

MOON
VANCOUVER & CANADIAN ROCKIES
Road Trip

VICTORIA, BANFF, JASPER, CALGARY, THE OKANAGAN, WHISTLER & THE SEA-TO-SKY HIGHWAY

CAROLYN B. HELLER

Gear up for a bucket list vacation

or plan your next beachy getaway!

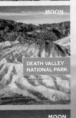

USA
NATIONAL PARKS
THE COMPLETE GUIDE TO ALL
59 PARKS
BECKY LOMAX

MOON USA NATIONAL PARKS
THE COMPLETE GUIDE TO ALL 59 PARKS

Full color • 700 pages
US $24.99 | CAN $32.49

Inside *Moon USA National Parks* find:

- Lists of the best parks for you: Find out where to hike, ski, camp, spot wildlife and more
- Handy resources: planning tips, detailed maps, and full-color photos
- Epic road trips linking multiple parks together
- Spaces to collect each national park's stamp and a fold-out map to chart your adventure

MAP SYMBOLS

■	Sights	⊛	National Capital	▲	Mountain	═══	Major Hwy
■	Restaurants	⊚	State Capital	✦	Natural Feature	═══	Road/Hwy
■	Nightlife	○	City/Town	🗲	Waterfall	═══	Pedestrian Friendly
■	Arts and Culture	★	Point of Interest	♠	Park	- - - - -	Trail
■	Sports and Activities	•	Accommodation	≜	Archaeological Site	▪▪▪▪▪	Stairs
■	Shops	▼	Restaurant/Bar	🛈	Trailhead	··········	Ferry
■	Hotels	▪	Other Location	🅿	Parking Area	⌐⌐⌐⌐	Railroad

CONVERSION TABLES

$°C = (°F - 32) / 1.8$
$°F = (°C \times 1.8) + 32$
1 inch = 2.54 centimeters (cm)
1 foot = 0.304 meters (m)
1 yard = 0.914 meters
1 mile = 1.6093 kilometers (km)
1 km = 0.6214 miles
1 fathom = 1.8288 m
1 chain = 20.1168 m
1 furlong = 201.168 m
1 acre = 0.4047 hectares
1 sq km = 100 hectares
1 sq mile = 2.59 square km
1 ounce = 28.35 grams
1 pound = 0.4536 kilograms
1 short ton = 0.90718 metric ton
1 short ton = 2,000 pounds
1 long ton = 1.016 metric tons
1 long ton = 2,240 pounds
1 metric ton = 1,000 kilograms
1 quart = 0.94635 liters
1 US gallon = 3.7854 liters
1 Imperial gallon = 4.5459 liters
1 nautical mile = 1.852 km

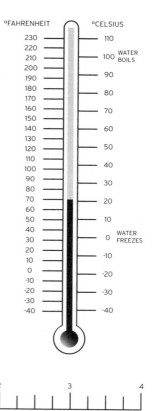

MOON CLEVELAND
Avalon Travel
Hachette Book Group
1700 Fourth Street
Berkeley, CA 94710, USA
www.moon.com

Editor and Series Manager: Leah Gordon
Copy Editor: Deana Shields
Graphics and Production Coordinator: Lucie Ericksen
Cover Design: Faceout Studios, Charles Brock
Interior Design: Megan Jones Design
Moon Logo: Tim McGrath
Map Editor: Kat Bennett
Cartographers: Karin Dahl, Kat Bennett
Indexer: Rachel Kuhn

ISBN-13: 9781640493575

Printing History
1st Edition — 2009
3rd Edition — May 2019
5 4 3 2 1

Front cover photo: Rock and Roll Hall of Fame © Johnny Stockshooter/Alamy Stock Photo;
Time Warp Stratocaster sculpture © Pat Downey / Pete Gonzales 2012

Printed in China by RR Donnelly